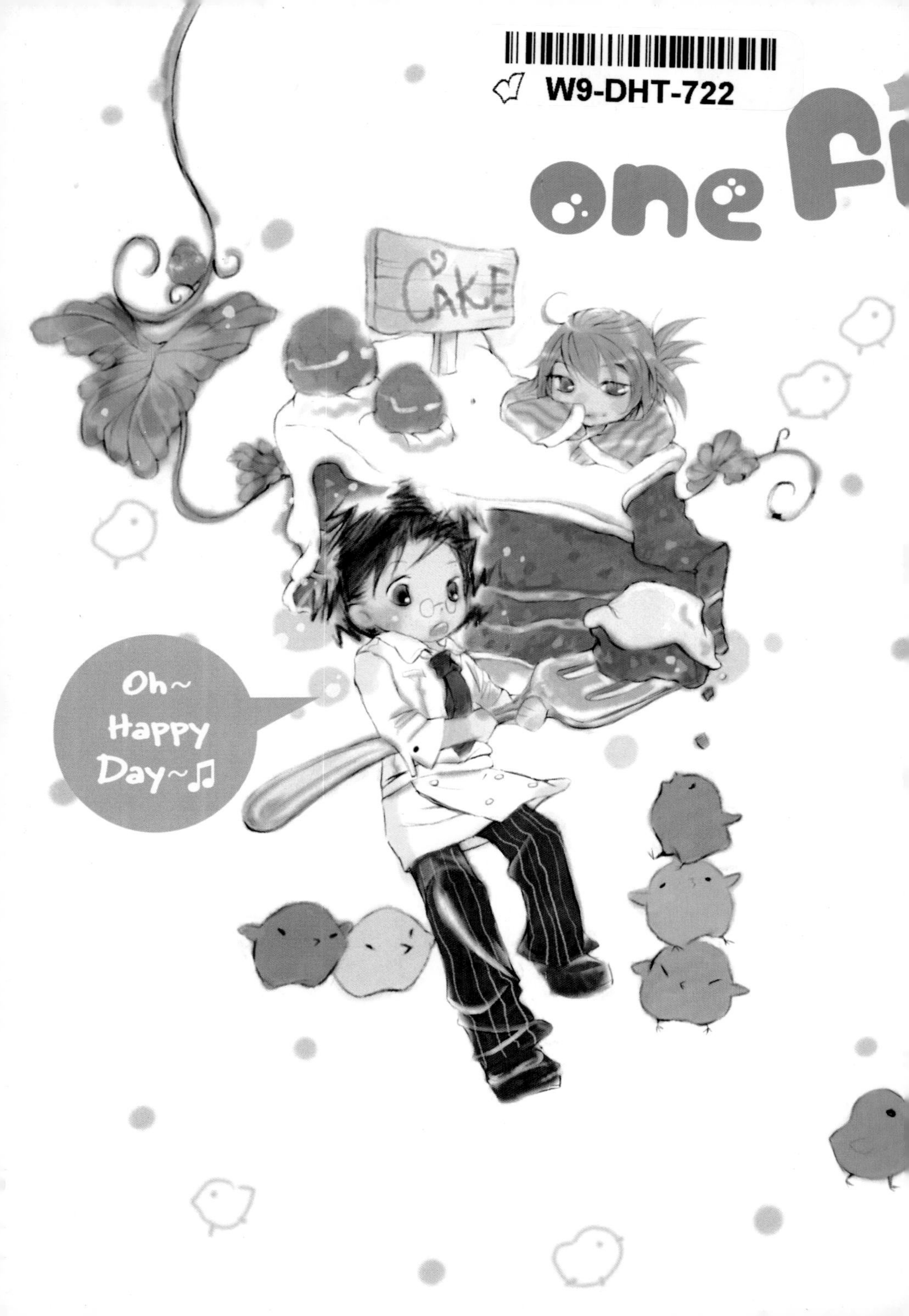
one
CAKE
Oh~ Happy Day~♫

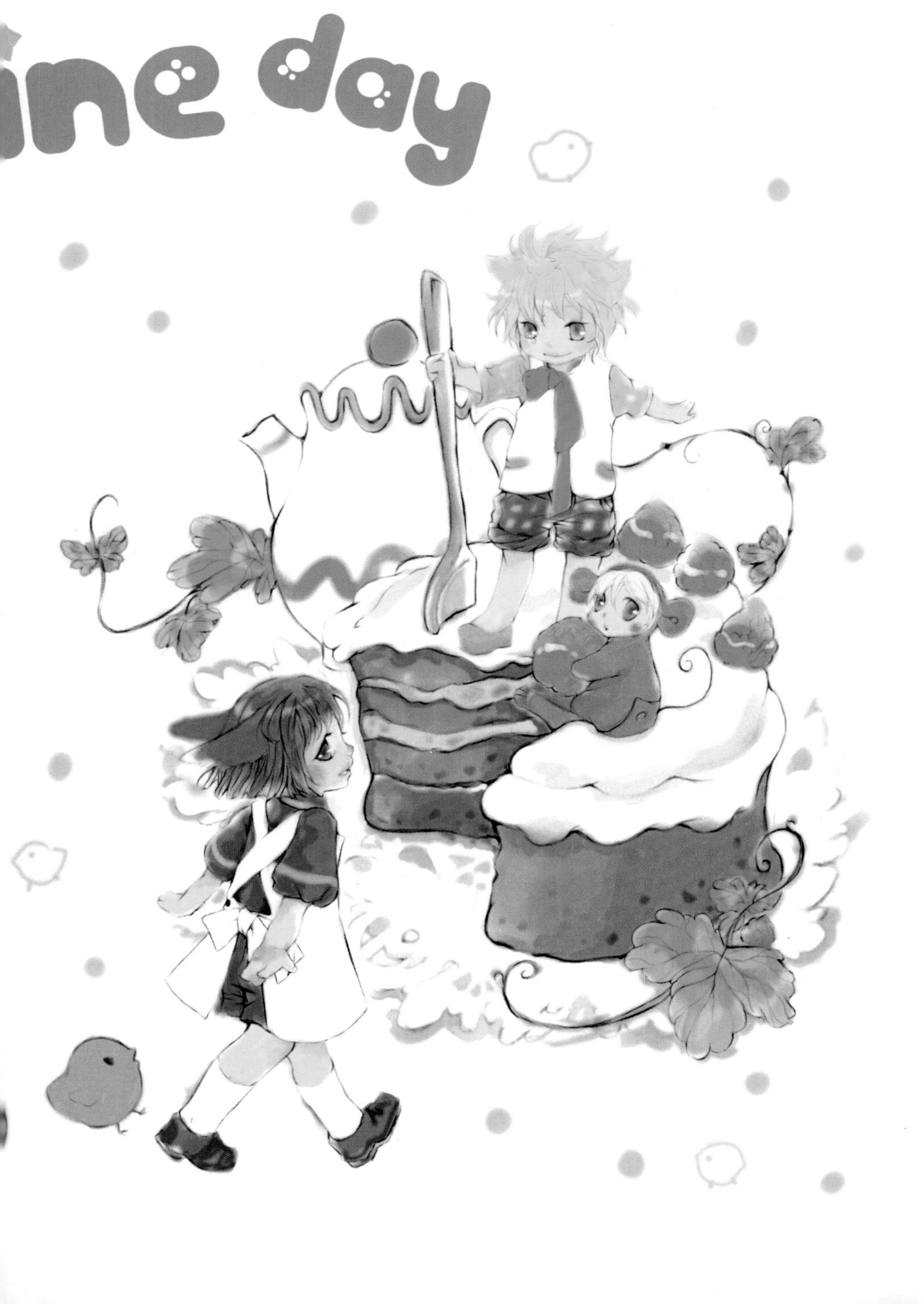
ine day

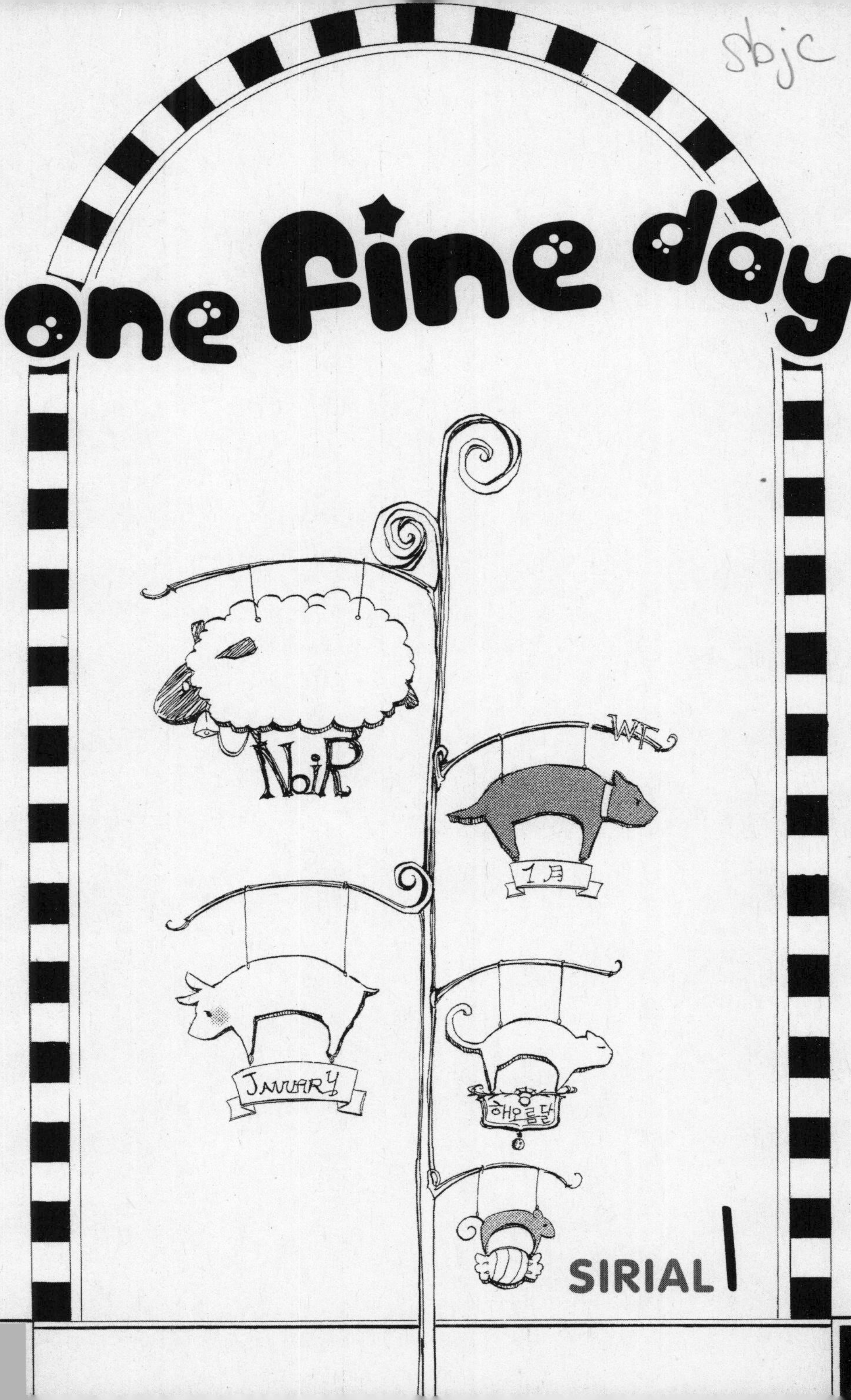
one fine day
NoiR
WF
1月
JANUARY
해오름달
SIRIAL 1

**CONTENTS**

DAY 1.
COOKIE-BAKING DAY          13

DAY 2.
OH, RAINY DAY ♫          23

DAY 3.
A NOVICE MAGICIAN...          35

DAY 4.
A LOVELY, CLEAR DAY          47

DAY 5.
FIND THE CULPRIT!          57

DAY 6.
BE MY GUEST!!          67

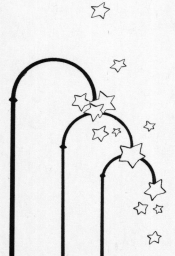

**DAY 7.**
**TYPHOON IN A TINY TEACUP**　　81
(PART 1 OF 2)


**DAY 8.**
**TYPHOON IN A TINY TEACUP**　　93
(PART 2 OF 2)


**DAY 9.**
**OUR MEMORIES**　　105


**DAY 10.**
**TYPHOON COMING!**　　119


**DAY 11.**
**SNOWY, SNOWY NIGHT**　　131


**DAY 12.**
**SUNNY LAUNDRY**　　143


**DAY 13.**
**ADULTS' WORLD**　　155

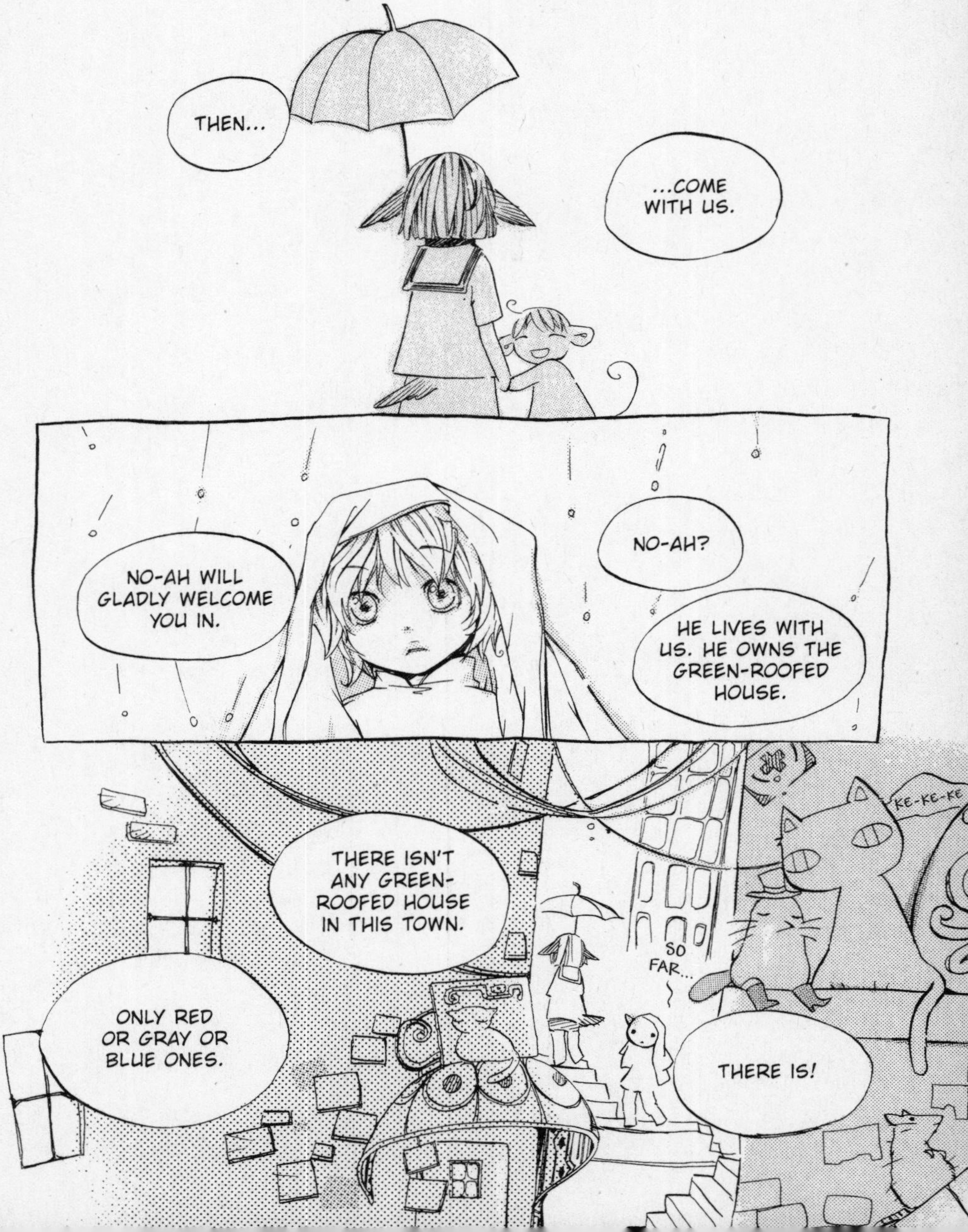
THEN...
...COME WITH US.
NO-AH WILL GLADLY WELCOME YOU IN.
NO-AH?
HE LIVES WITH US. HE OWNS THE GREEN-ROOFED HOUSE.
THERE ISN'T ANY GREEN-ROOFED HOUSE IN THIS TOWN.
KE-KE-KE
ONLY RED OR GRAY OR BLUE ONES.
SO FAR...
THERE IS!

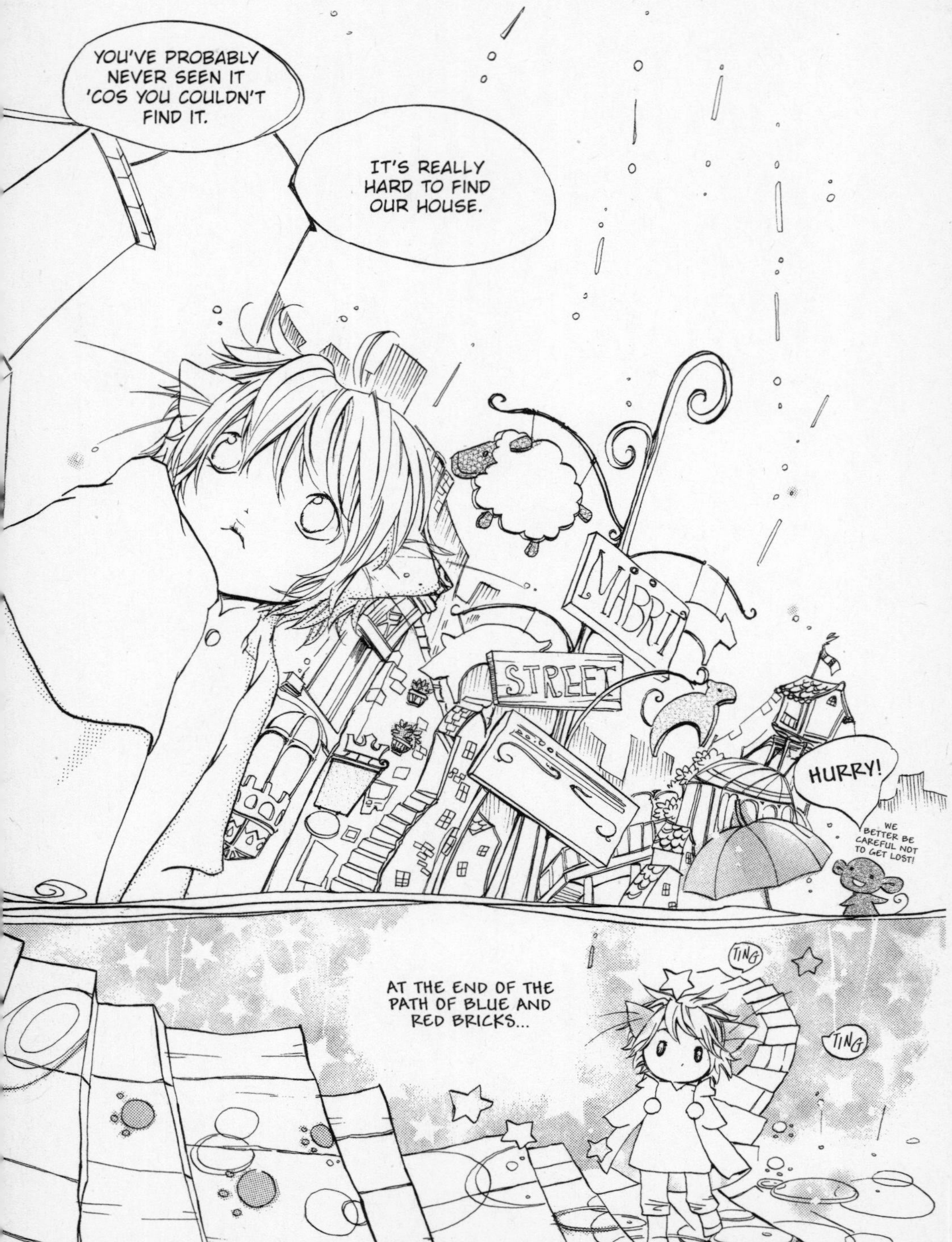
YOU'VE PROBABLY NEVER SEEN IT 'COS YOU COULDN'T FIND IT.
IT'S REALLY HARD TO FIND OUR HOUSE.
MABRI
STREET
HURRY!
WE BETTER BE CAREFUL NOT TO GET LOST!
AT THE END OF THE PATH OF BLUE AND RED BRICKS...
TING
TING

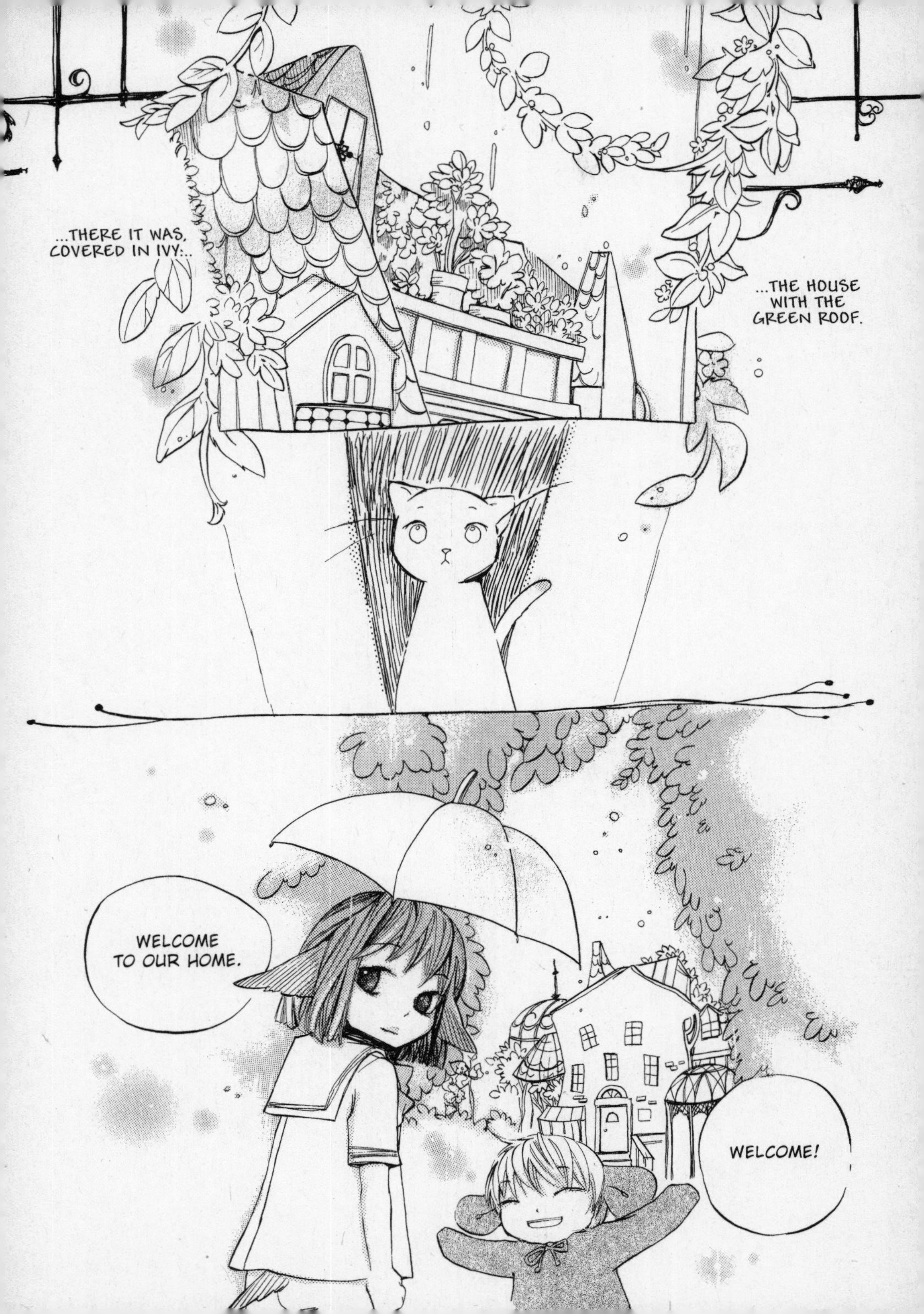
...THERE IT WAS, COVERED IN IVY:..
...THE HOUSE WITH THE GREEN ROOF.
WELCOME TO OUR HOME.
WELCOME!

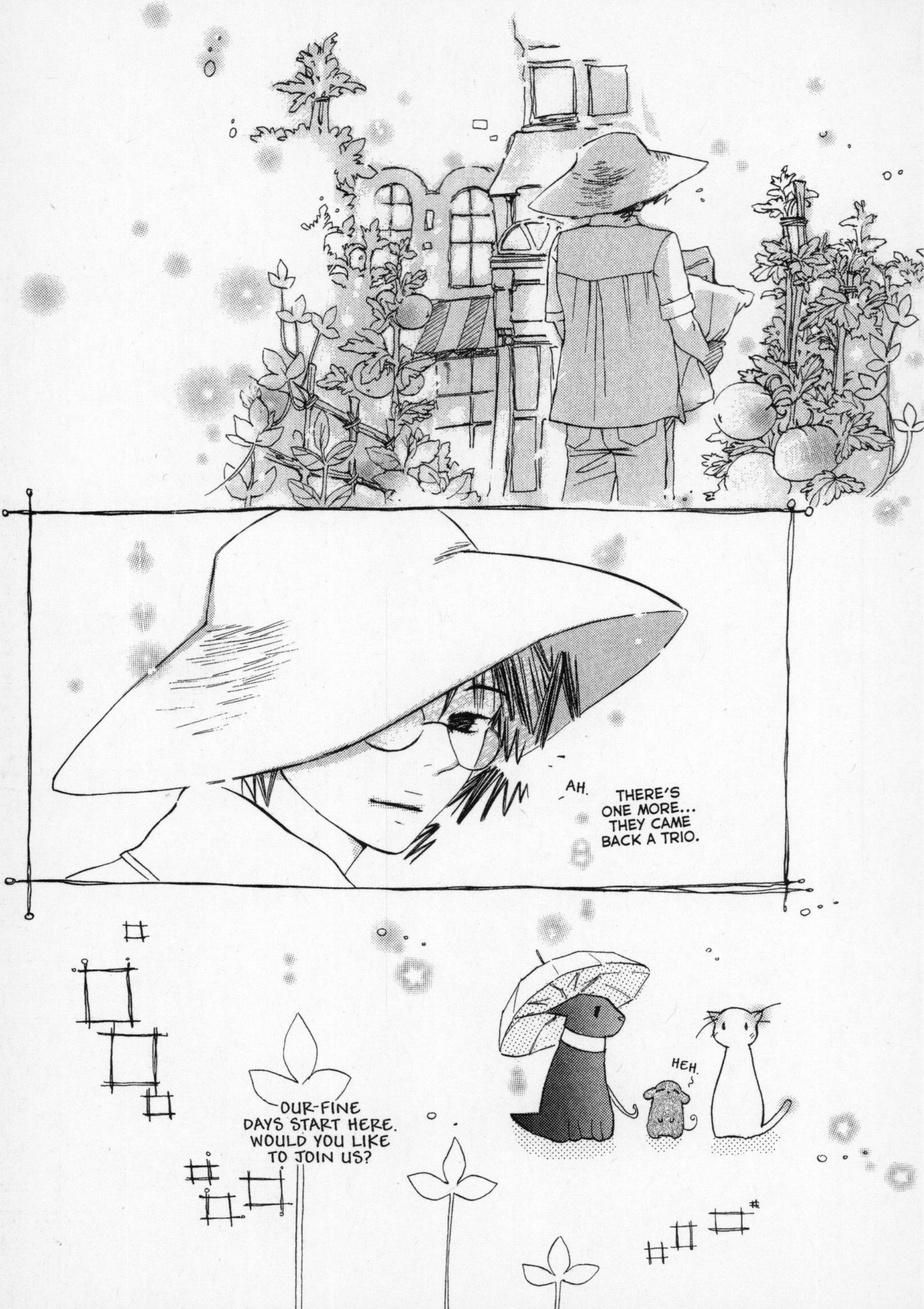
AH.
THERE'S ONE MORE... THEY CAME BACK A TRIO.
OUR-FINE DAYS START HERE. WOULD YOU LIKE TO JOIN US?
HEH.

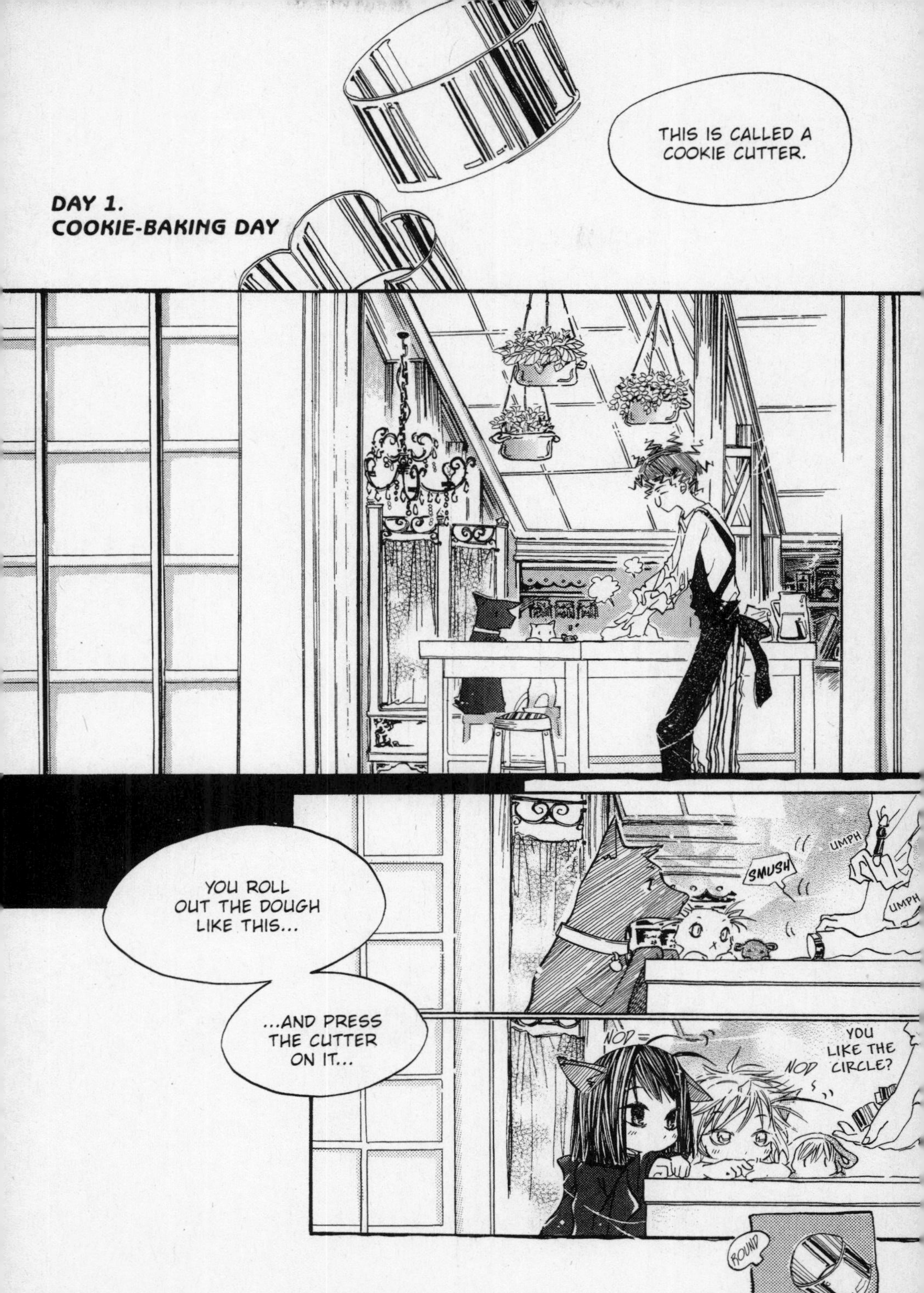
THIS IS CALLED A COOKIE CUTTER.
DAY 1.
COOKIE-BAKING DAY
YOU ROLL OUT THE DOUGH LIKE THIS...
SMUSH
UMPH
UMPH
...AND PRESS THE CUTTER ON IT...
NOD
NOD
YOU LIKE THE CIRCLE?
ROUND

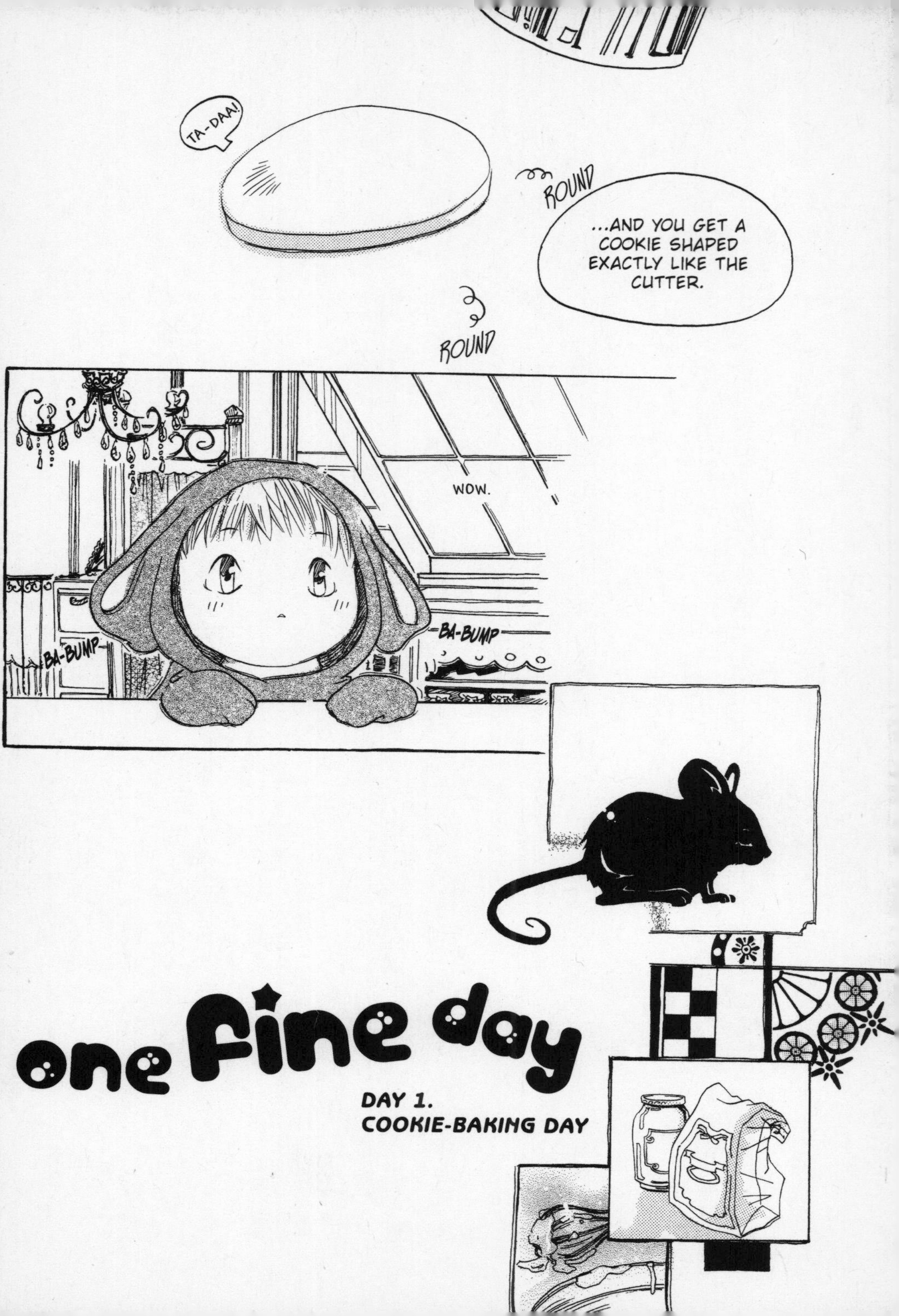
TA-DAA!
ROUND
...AND YOU GET A COOKIE SHAPED EXACTLY LIKE THE CUTTER.
ROUND
WOW.
BA-BUMP
BA-BUMP
one fine day
DAY 1.
COOKIE-BAKING DAY

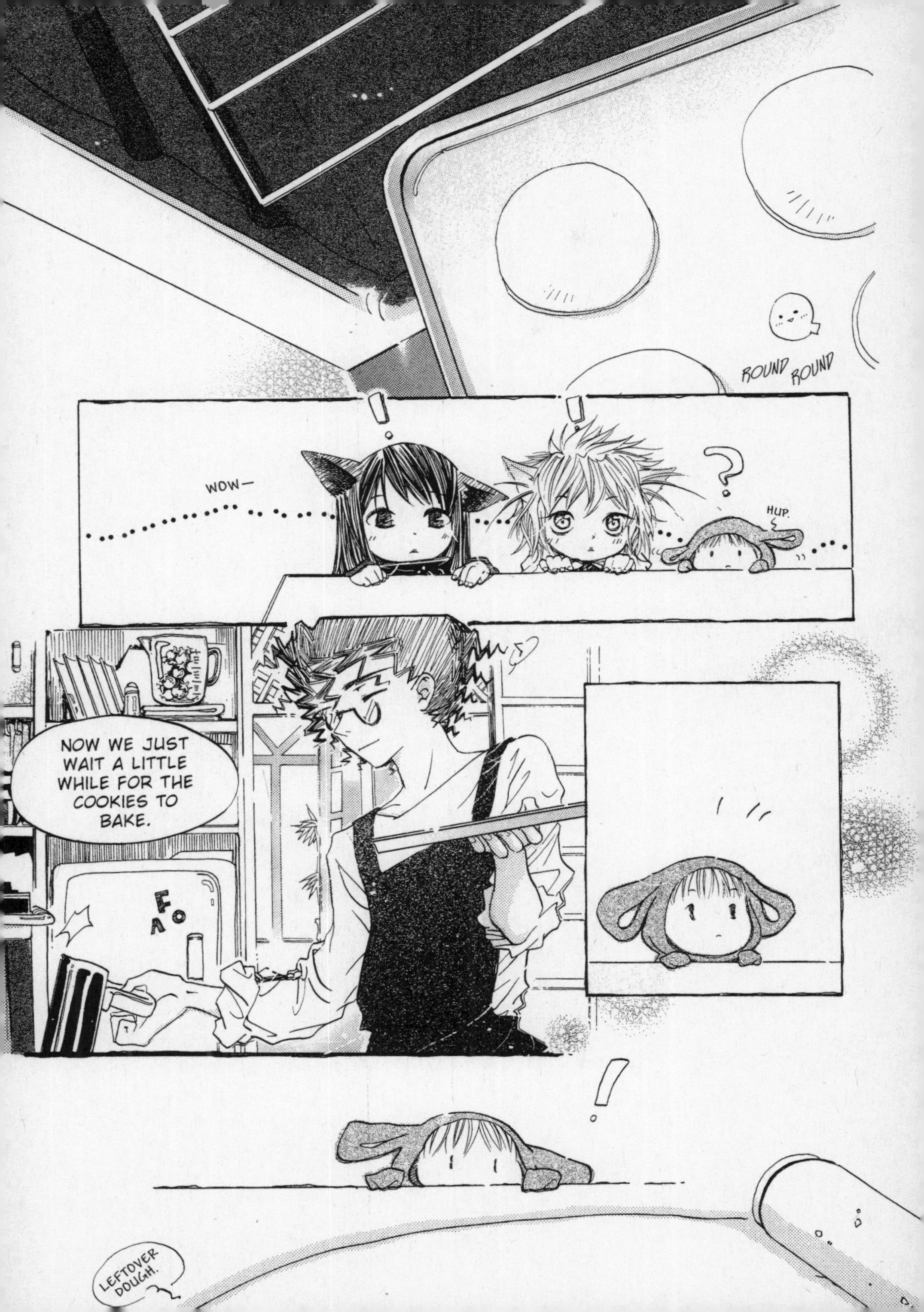
ROUND ROUND
WOW—
HUP.
NOW WE JUST WAIT A LITTLE WHILE FOR THE COOKIES TO BAKE.
LEFTOVER DOUGH.

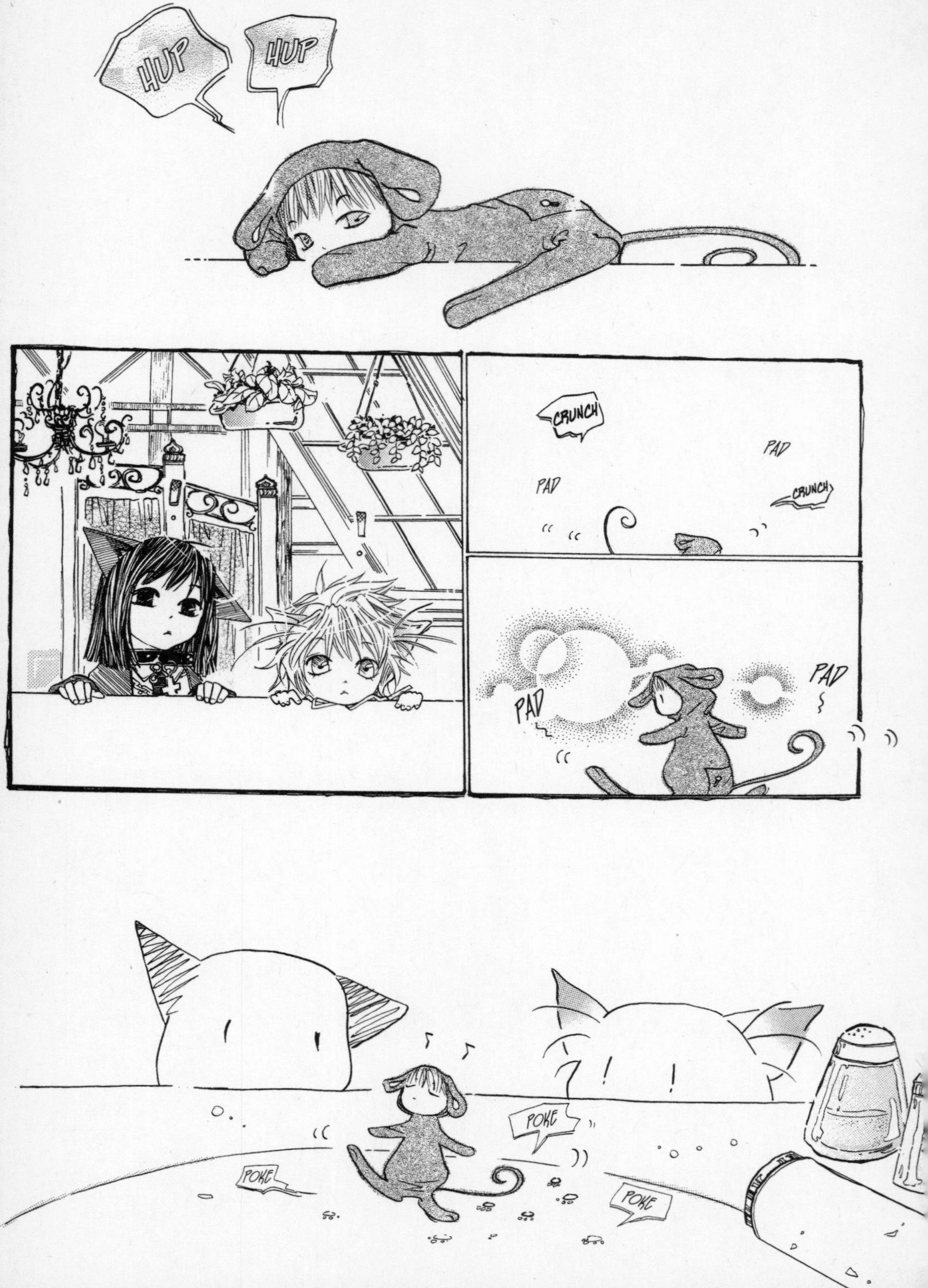
HUP
HUP
CRUNCH
PAD
PAD
CRUNCH
PAD
PAD
POKE
POKE
POKE

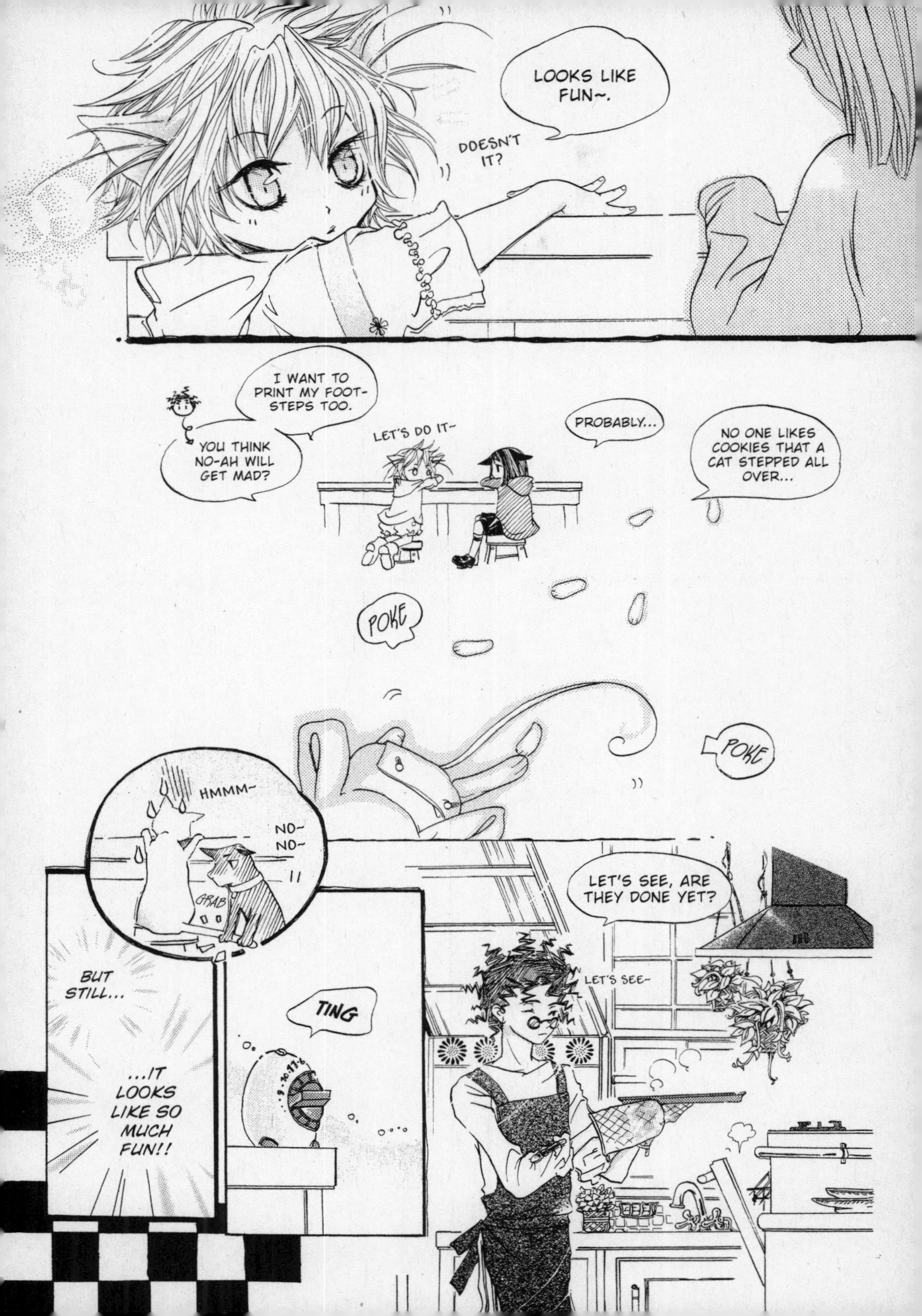
LOOKS LIKE FUN~.
DOESN'T IT?
I WANT TO PRINT MY FOOT-STEPS TOO.
YOU THINK NO-AH WILL GET MAD?
LET'S DO IT~
PROBABLY...
NO ONE LIKES COOKIES THAT A CAT STEPPED ALL OVER...
POKE
POKE
HMMM~
NO~ NO~
GRAB
BUT STILL...
...IT LOOKS LIKE SO MUCH FUN!!
TING
LET'S SEE, ARE THEY DONE YET?
LET'S SEE~

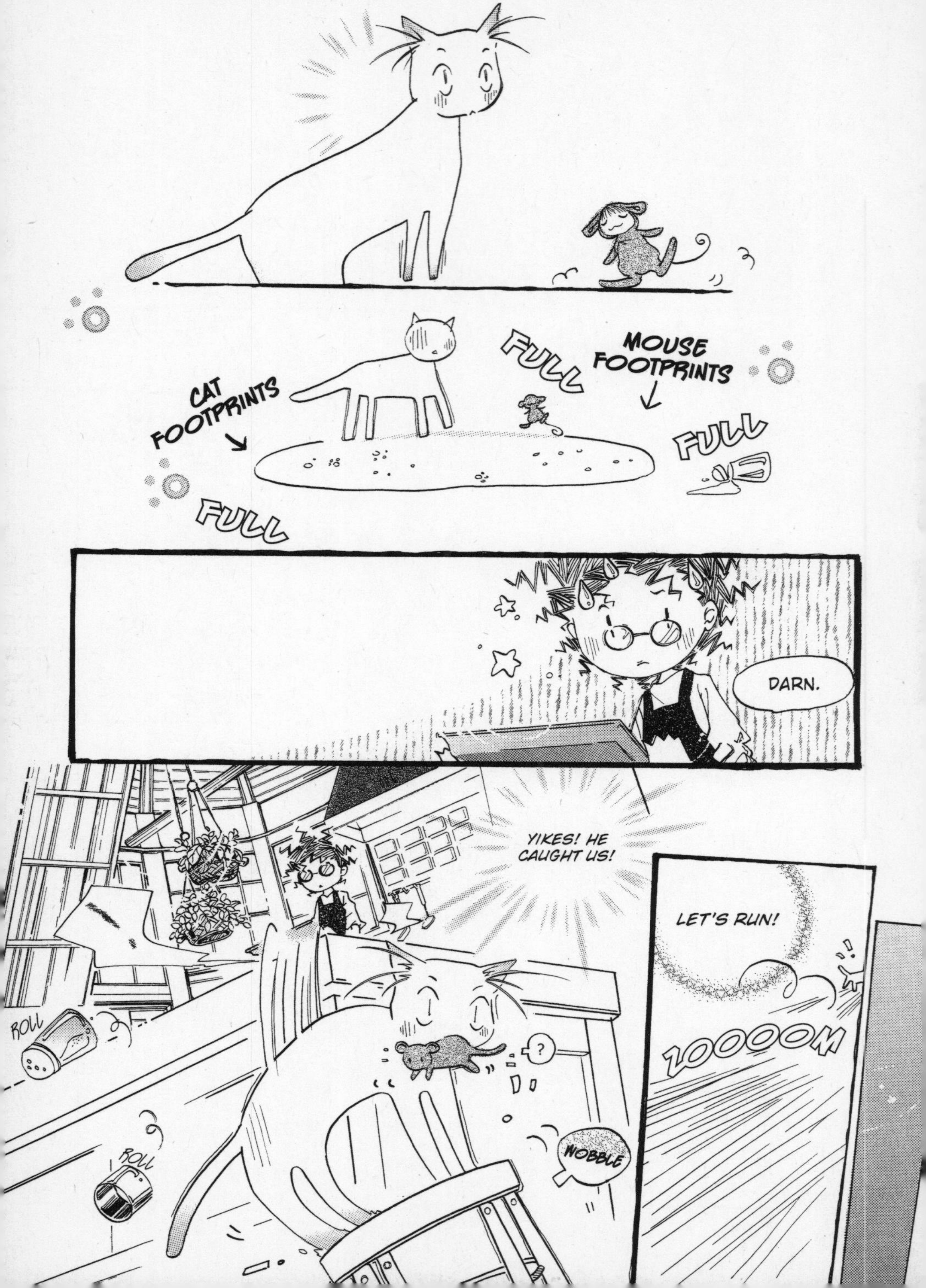
FULL
MOUSE FOOTPRINTS
CAT FOOTPRINTS
FULL
FULL
DARN.
YIKES! HE CAUGHT US!
ROLL
?
ROLL
WOBBLE
LET'S RUN!
!
ZOOOOOM

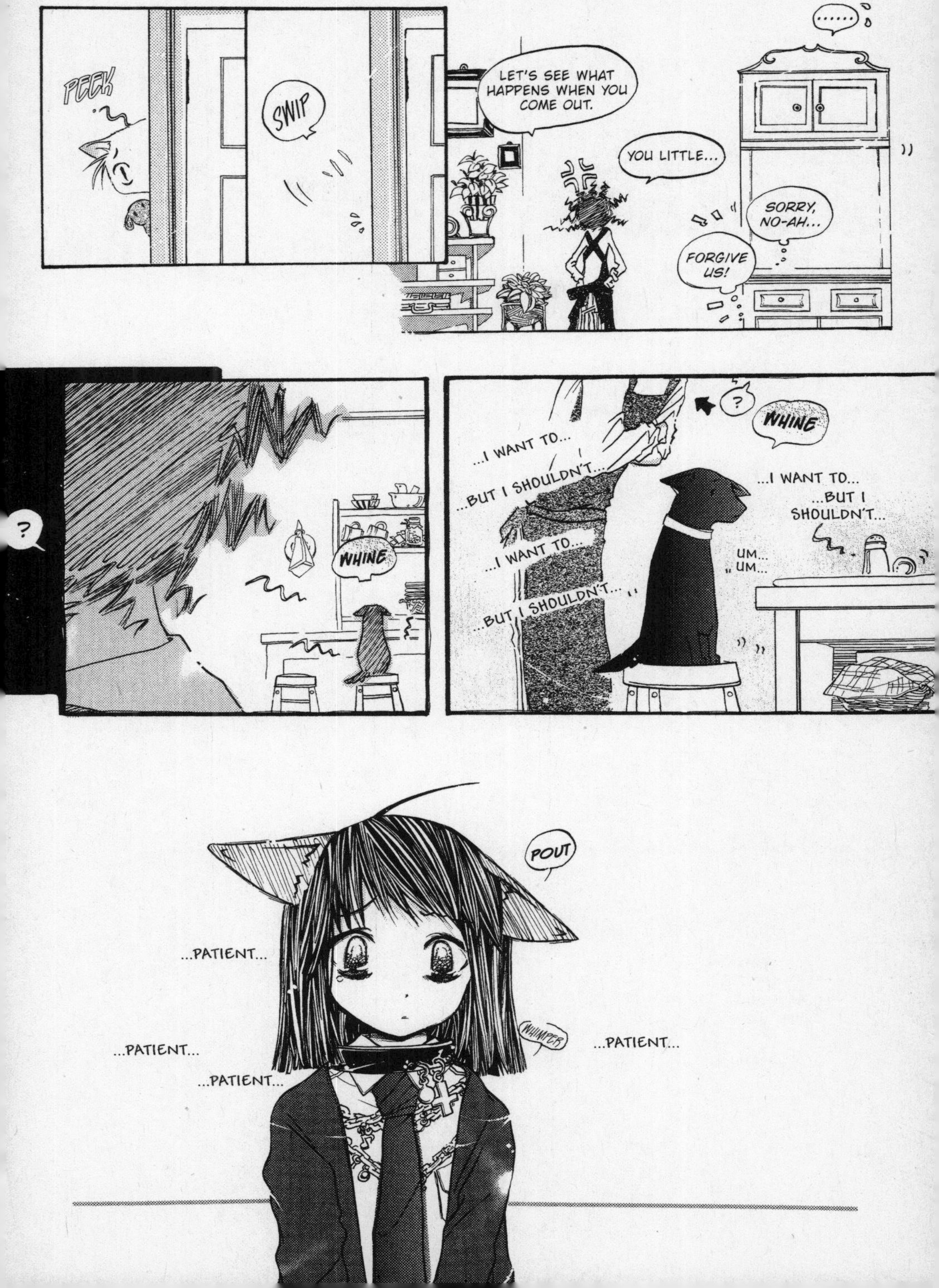

PEEK
SWIP
LET'S SEE WHAT HAPPENS WHEN YOU COME OUT.
YOU LITTLE...
......
SORRY, NO-AH...
FORGIVE US!
?
WHINE
...I WANT TO...
...BUT I SHOULDN'T...
...I WANT TO...
...BUT I SHOULDN'T...
?
WHINE
...I WANT TO...
...BUT I SHOULDN'T...
UM... UM...
POUT
...PATIENT...
...PATIENT...
...PATIENT...
WHIMPER
...PATIENT...

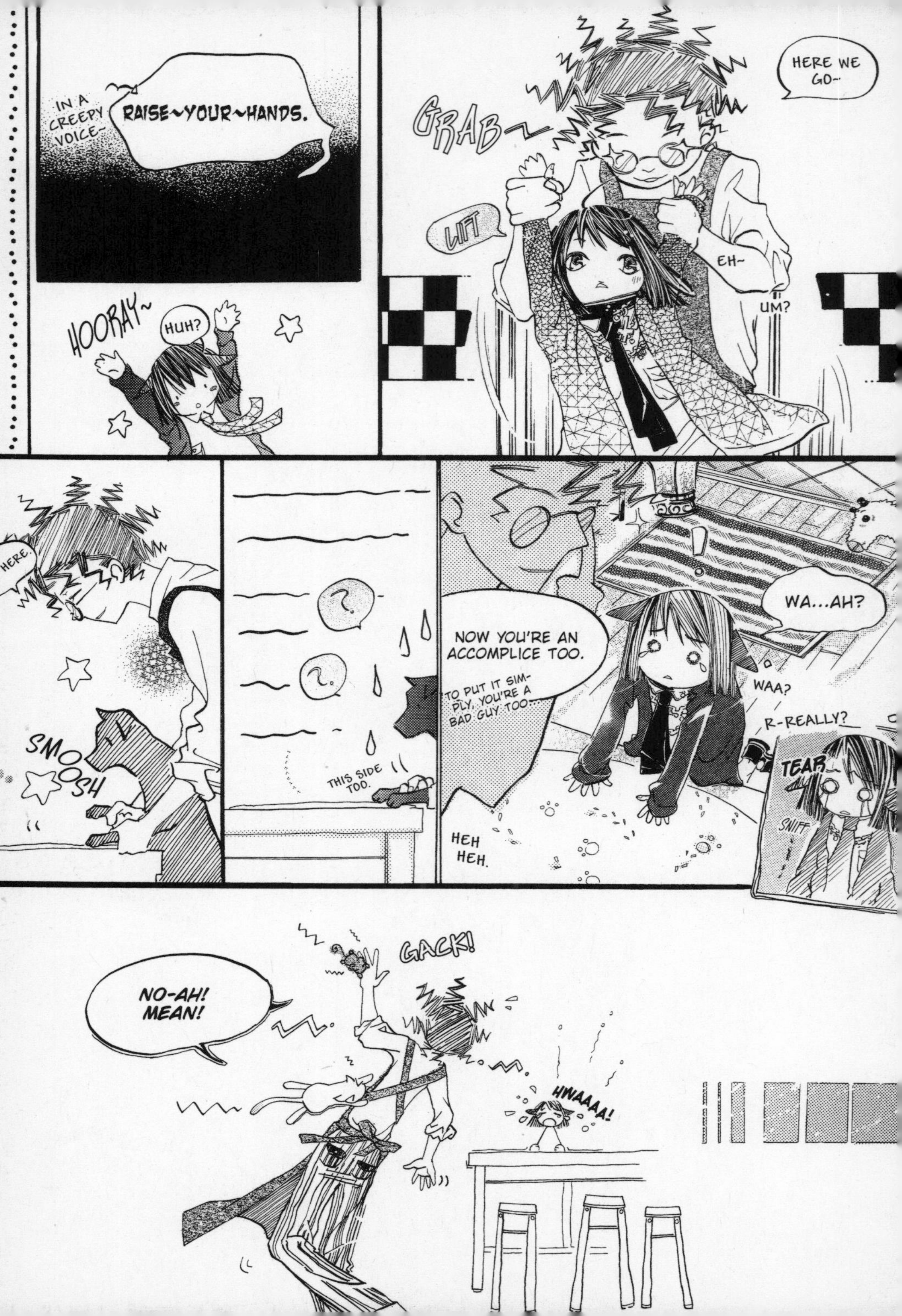
IN A CREEPY VOICE~
RAISE~YOUR~HANDS.
HOORAY~
HUH?
GRAB~
HERE WE GO~
LIFT
EH~
UM?
HERE.
SMOOSH
THIS SIDE TOO.
NOW YOU'RE AN ACCOMPLICE TOO.
TO PUT IT SIMPLY, YOU'RE A BAD GUY TOO...
HEH HEH.
WA...AH?
WAA?
R-REALLY?
TEAR
SNIFF
GACK!
NO-AH! MEAN!
HWAAAA!

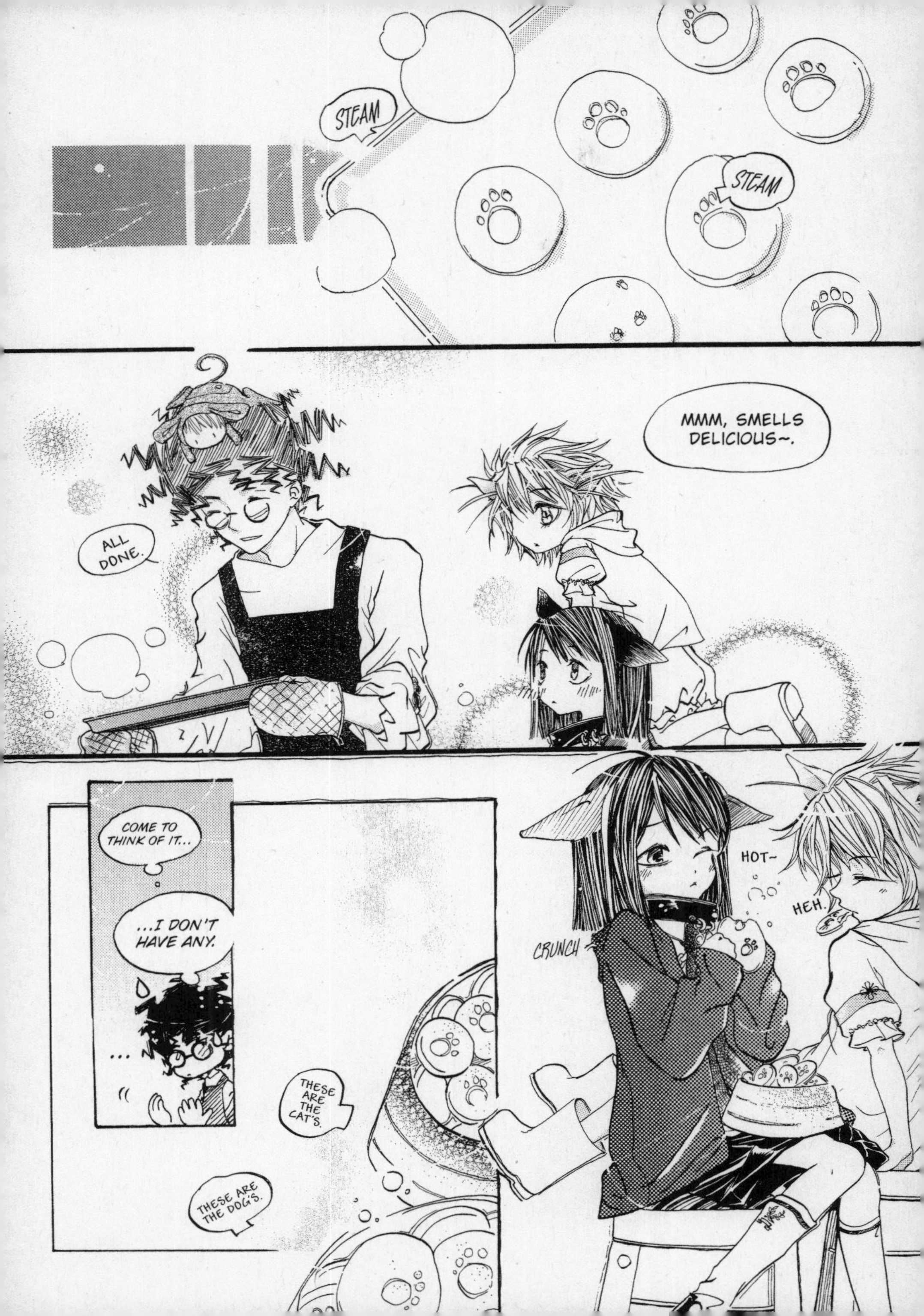
STEAM
STEAM
ALL DONE.
MMM, SMELLS DELICIOUS~.
COME TO THINK OF IT...
...I DON'T HAVE ANY.
...
THESE ARE THE CAT'S.
THESE ARE THE DOG'S.
HOT~
CRUNCH
HEH.

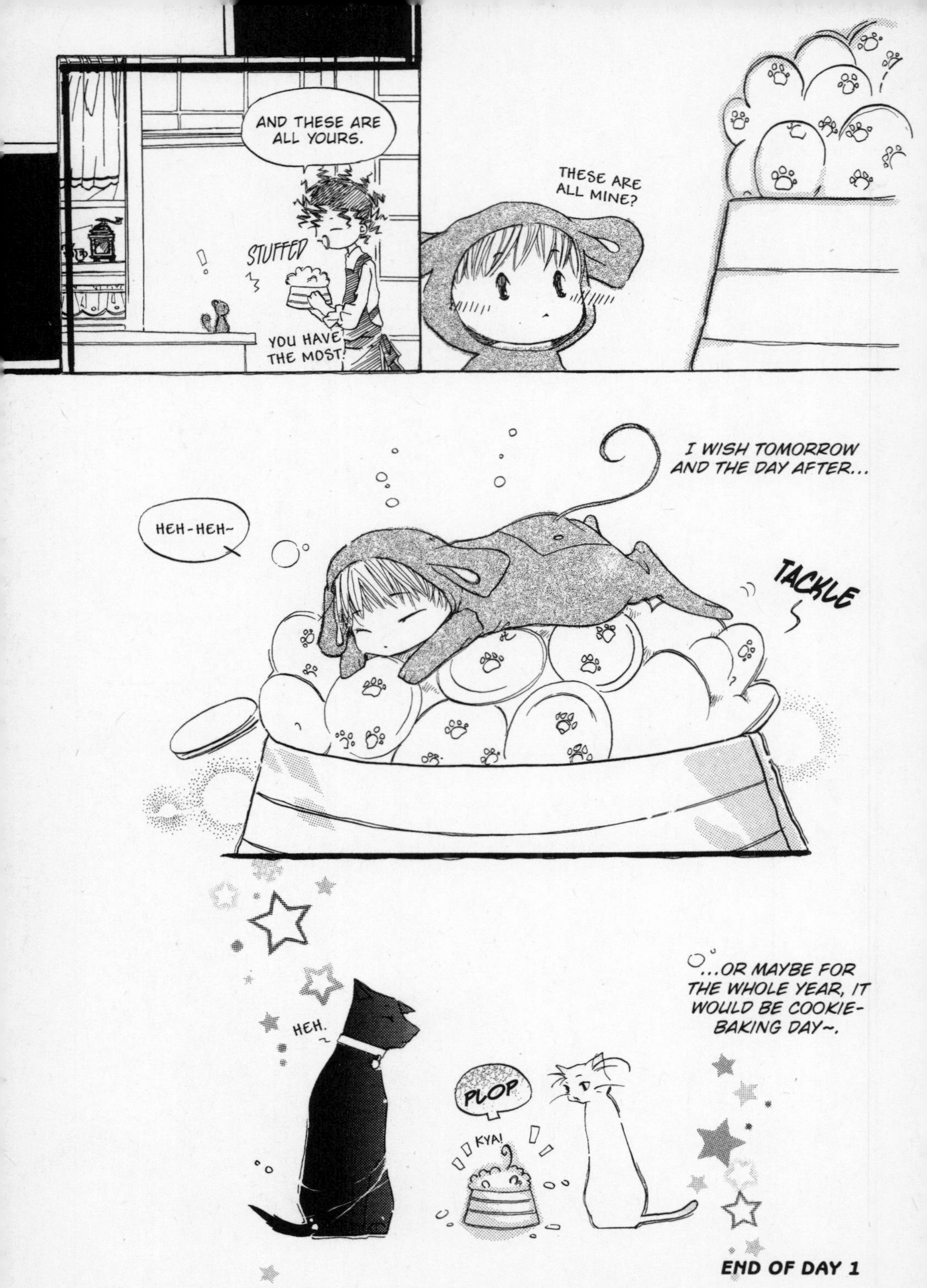
AND THESE ARE ALL YOURS.
STUFFED
YOU HAVE THE MOST!
THESE ARE ALL MINE?
HEH-HEH~
I WISH TOMORROW AND THE DAY AFTER...
TACKLE
HEH.
PLOP
KYA!
...OR MAYBE FOR THE WHOLE YEAR, IT WOULD BE COOKIE-BAKING DAY~.

END OF DAY 1

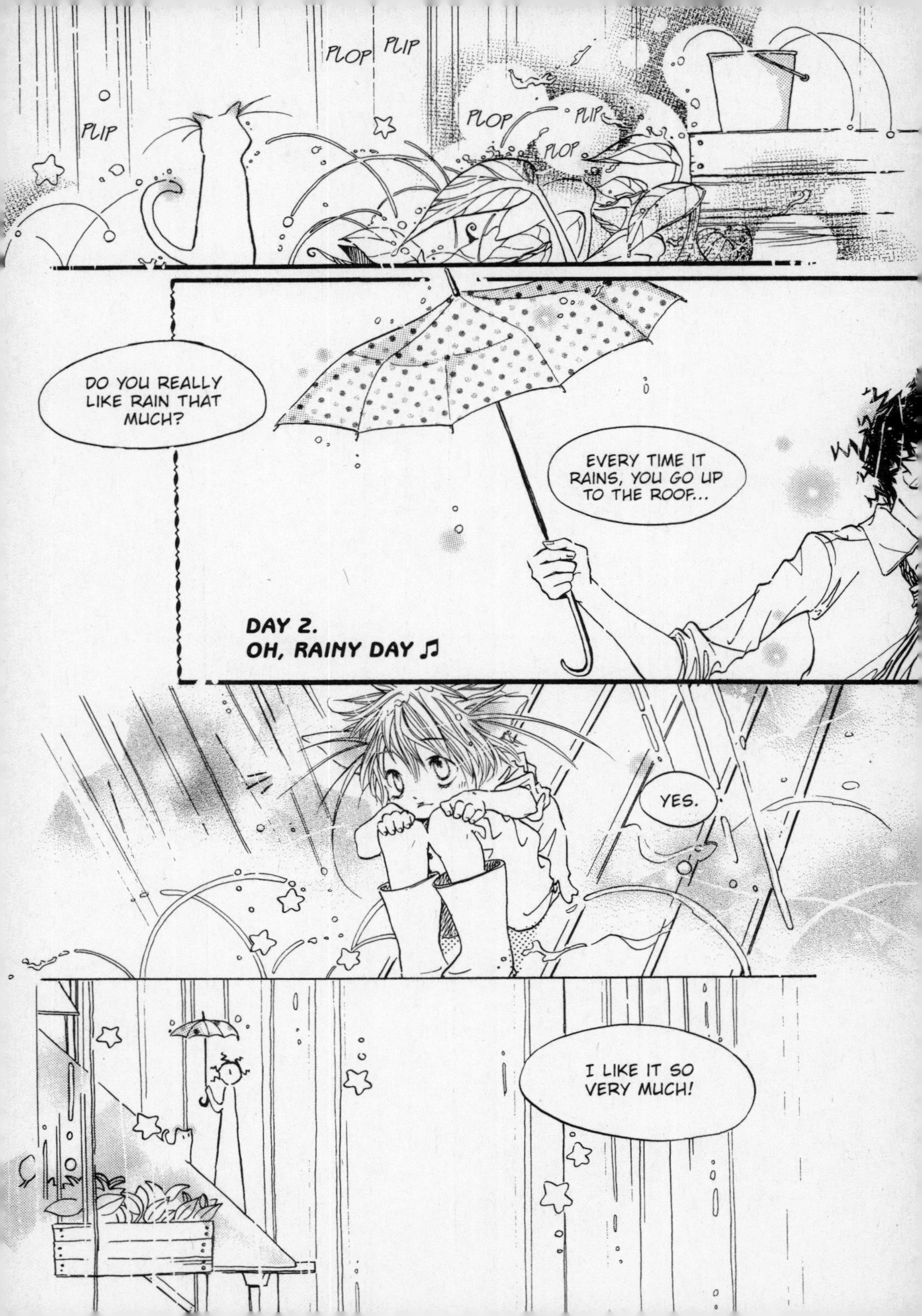
PLOP
PLIP
PLIP
PLOP
PLIP
PLOP
DO YOU REALLY LIKE RAIN THAT MUCH?
EVERY TIME IT RAINS, YOU GO UP TO THE ROOF...
DAY 2. OH, RAINY DAY ♫
YES.
I LIKE IT SO VERY MUCH!

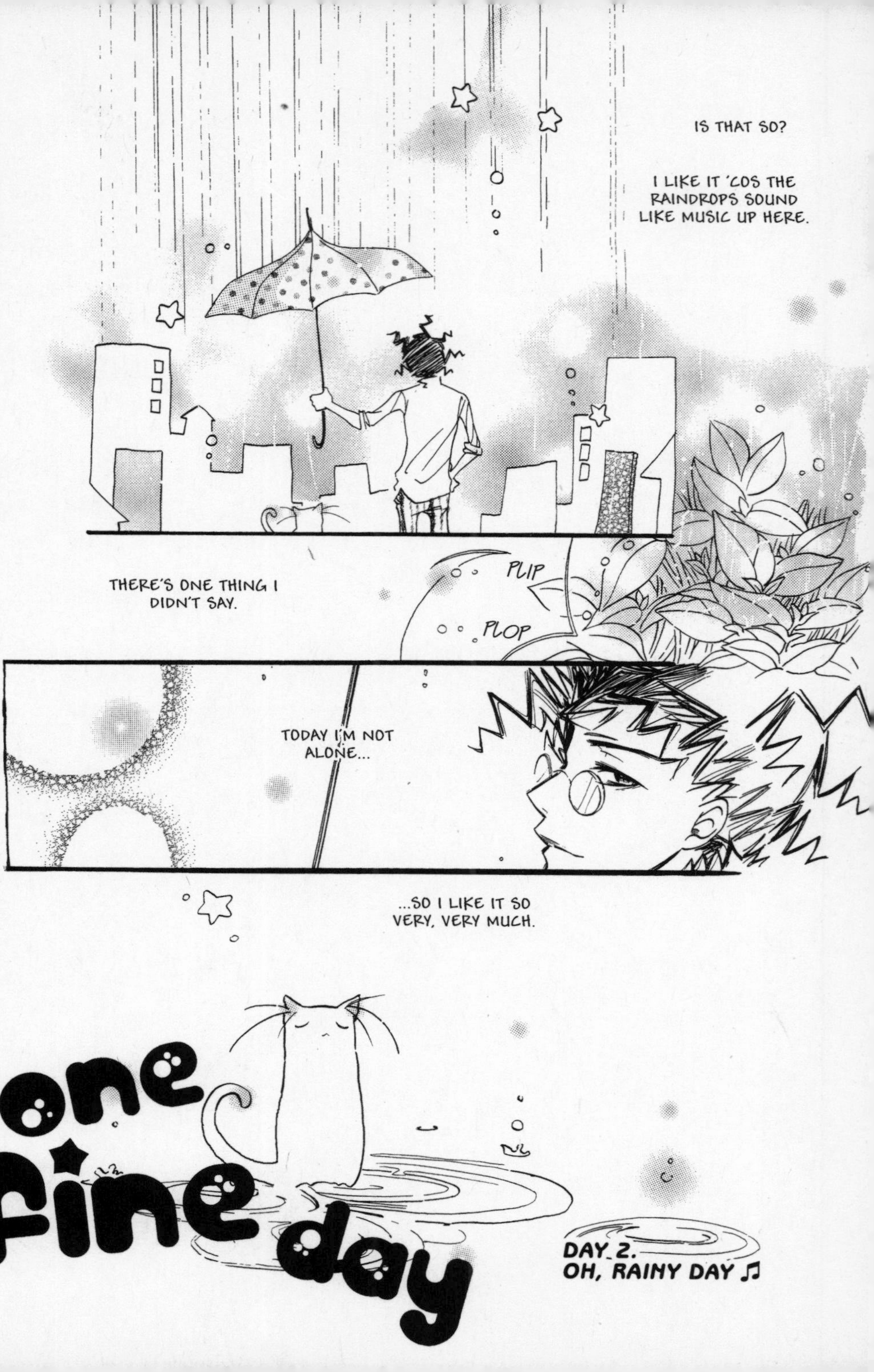
IS THAT SO?
I LIKE IT 'COS THE RAINDROPS SOUND LIKE MUSIC UP HERE.
THERE'S ONE THING I DIDN'T SAY.
PLIP
PLOP
TODAY I'M NOT ALONE...
...SO I LIKE IT SO VERY, VERY MUCH.
one Fine day
DAY 2.
OH, RAINY DAY ♫

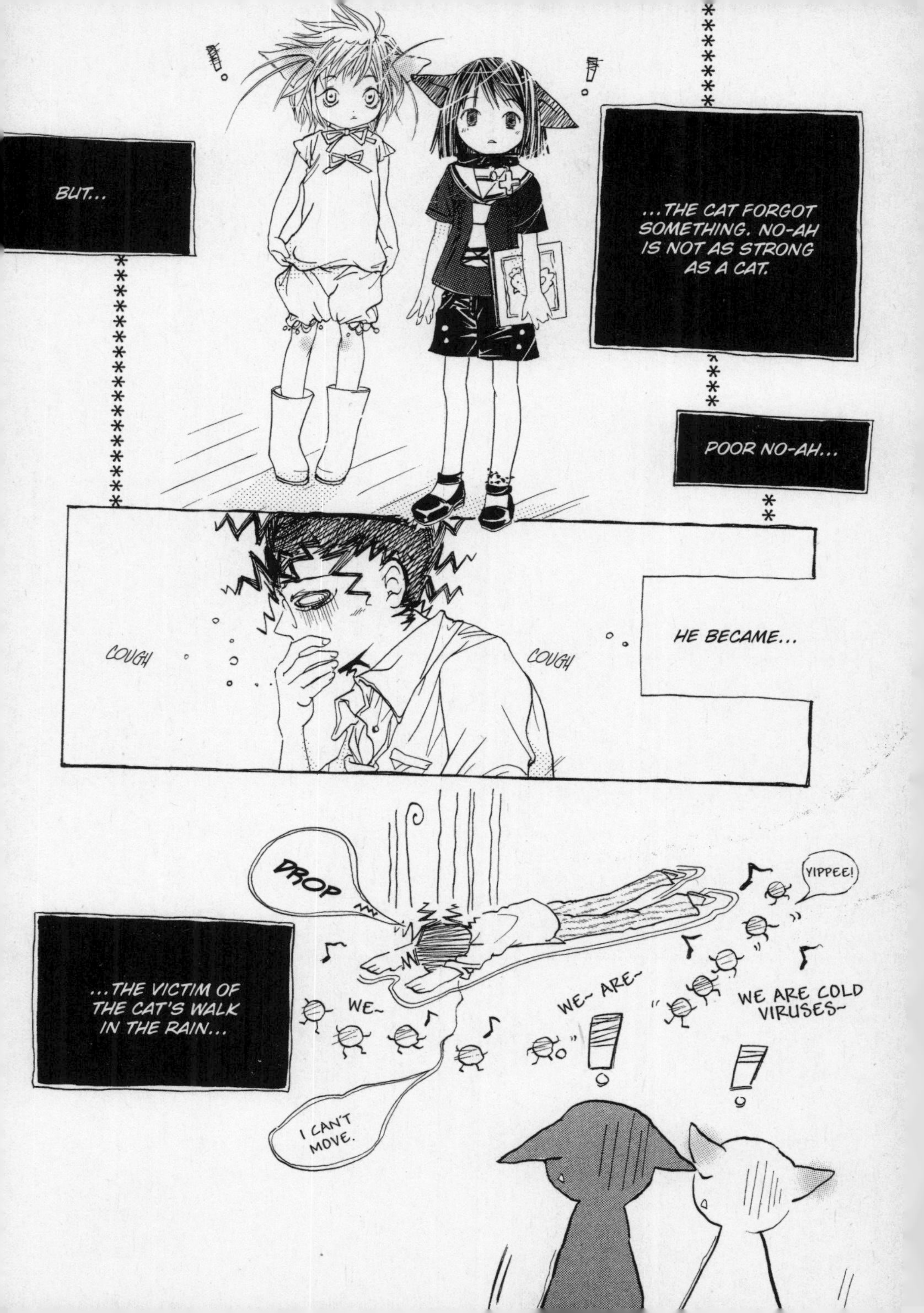
BUT...
!
!
...THE CAT FORGOT SOMETHING. NO-AH IS NOT AS STRONG AS A CAT.
POOR NO-AH...
COUGH
COUGH
HE BECAME...
DROP
YIPPEE!
...THE VICTIM OF THE CAT'S WALK IN THE RAIN...
WE~
WE~ ARE~
WE ARE COLD VIRUSES~
I CAN'T MOVE.
!
!

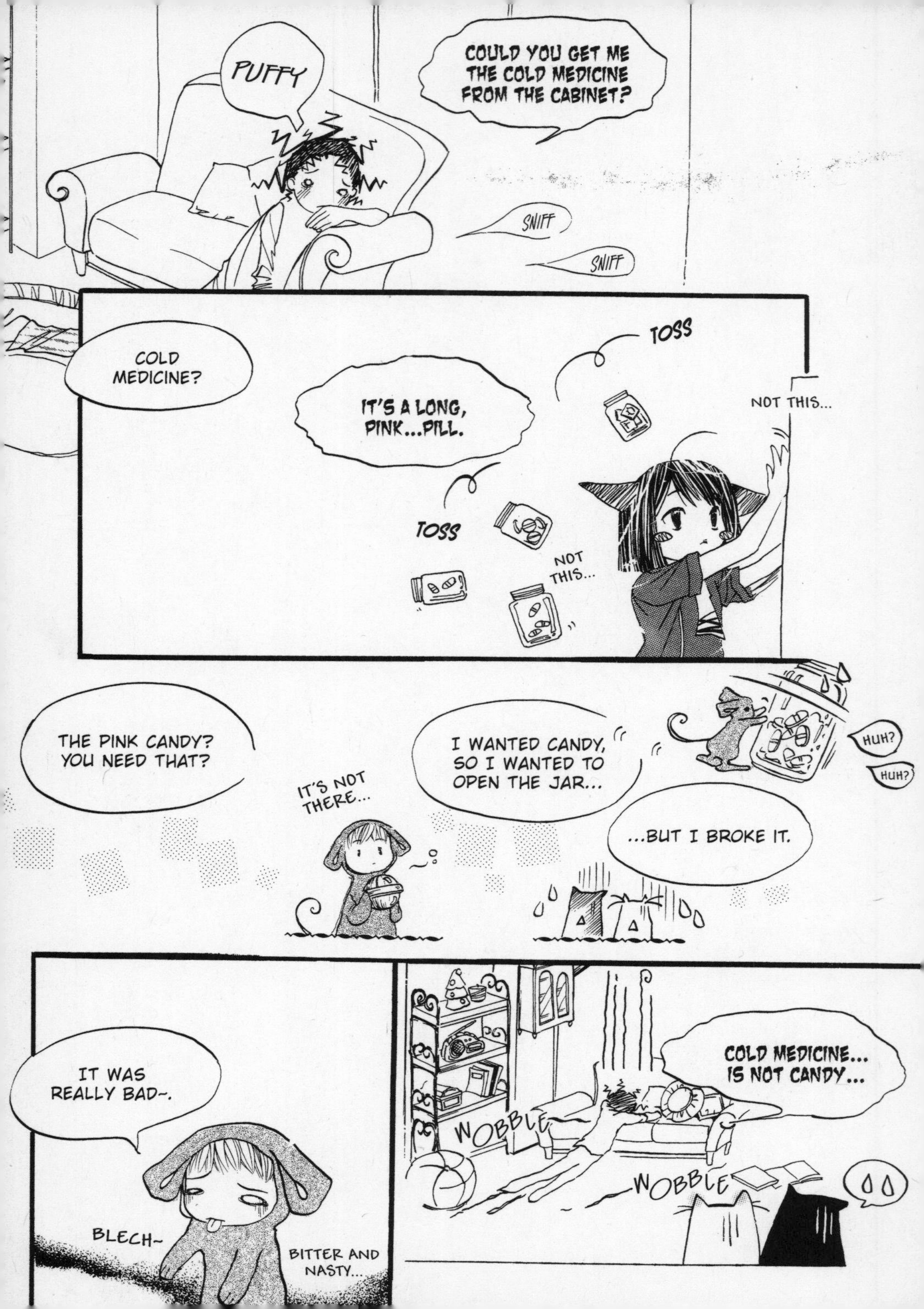
PUFFY
COULD YOU GET ME THE COLD MEDICINE FROM THE CABINET?
SNIFF
SNIFF
COLD MEDICINE?
IT'S A LONG, PINK...PILL.
TOSS
NOT THIS...
TOSS
NOT THIS...
THE PINK CANDY? YOU NEED THAT?
IT'S NOT THERE...
I WANTED CANDY, SO I WANTED TO OPEN THE JAR...
HUH?
HUH?
...BUT I BROKE IT.
IT WAS REALLY BAD~.
BLECH~
BITTER AND NASTY...
COLD MEDICINE... IS NOT CANDY...
WOBBLE
WOBBLE

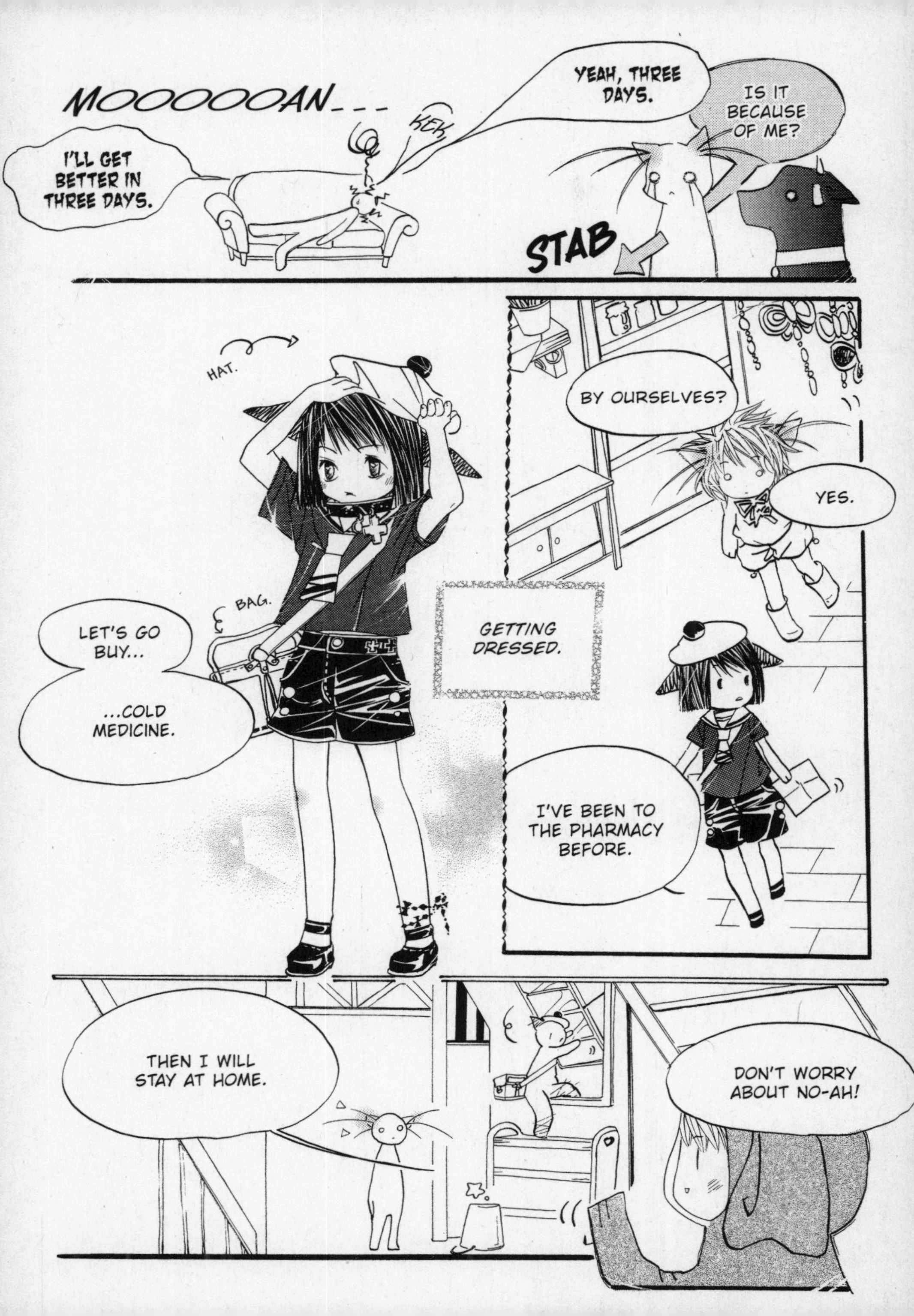
MOOOOOAN...
I'LL GET BETTER IN THREE DAYS.
KEK,
YEAH, THREE DAYS.
IS IT BECAUSE OF ME?
STAB
HAT.
BAG.
LET'S GO BUY...
...COLD MEDICINE.
GETTING DRESSED.
BY OURSELVES?
YES.
I'VE BEEN TO THE PHARMACY BEFORE.
THEN I WILL STAY AT HOME.
DON'T WORRY ABOUT NO-AH!

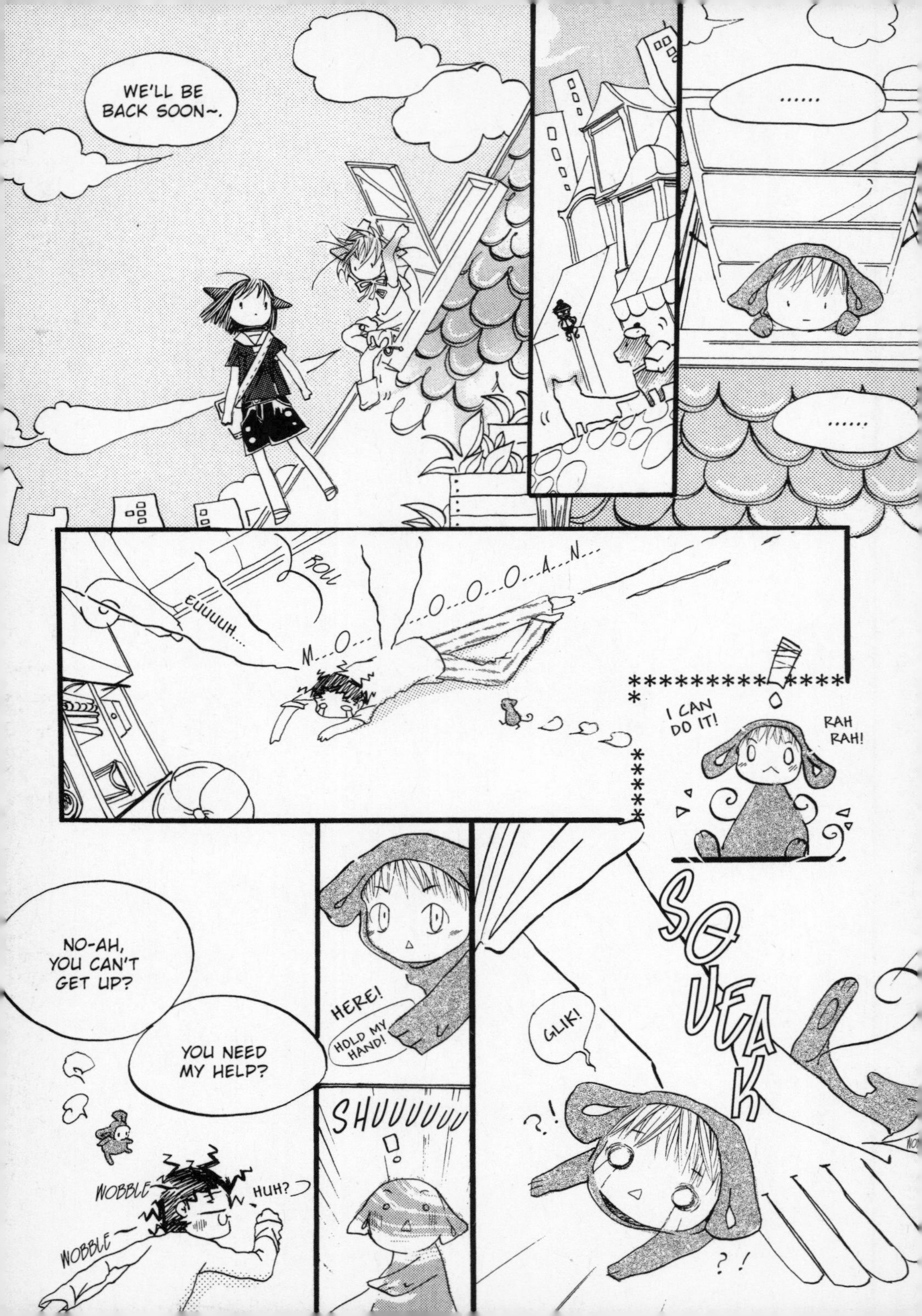
WE'LL BE BACK SOON~.
......
......
ROLL
EUUUUH...
M...O...O...O...O...A...N...
I CAN DO IT!
RAH RAH!
NO-AH, YOU CAN'T GET UP?
YOU NEED MY HELP?
WOBBLE
HUH?
WOBBLE
HERE!
HOLD MY HAND!
SHUUUUUU
!
SQUEAK
GLIK!
?!
?!

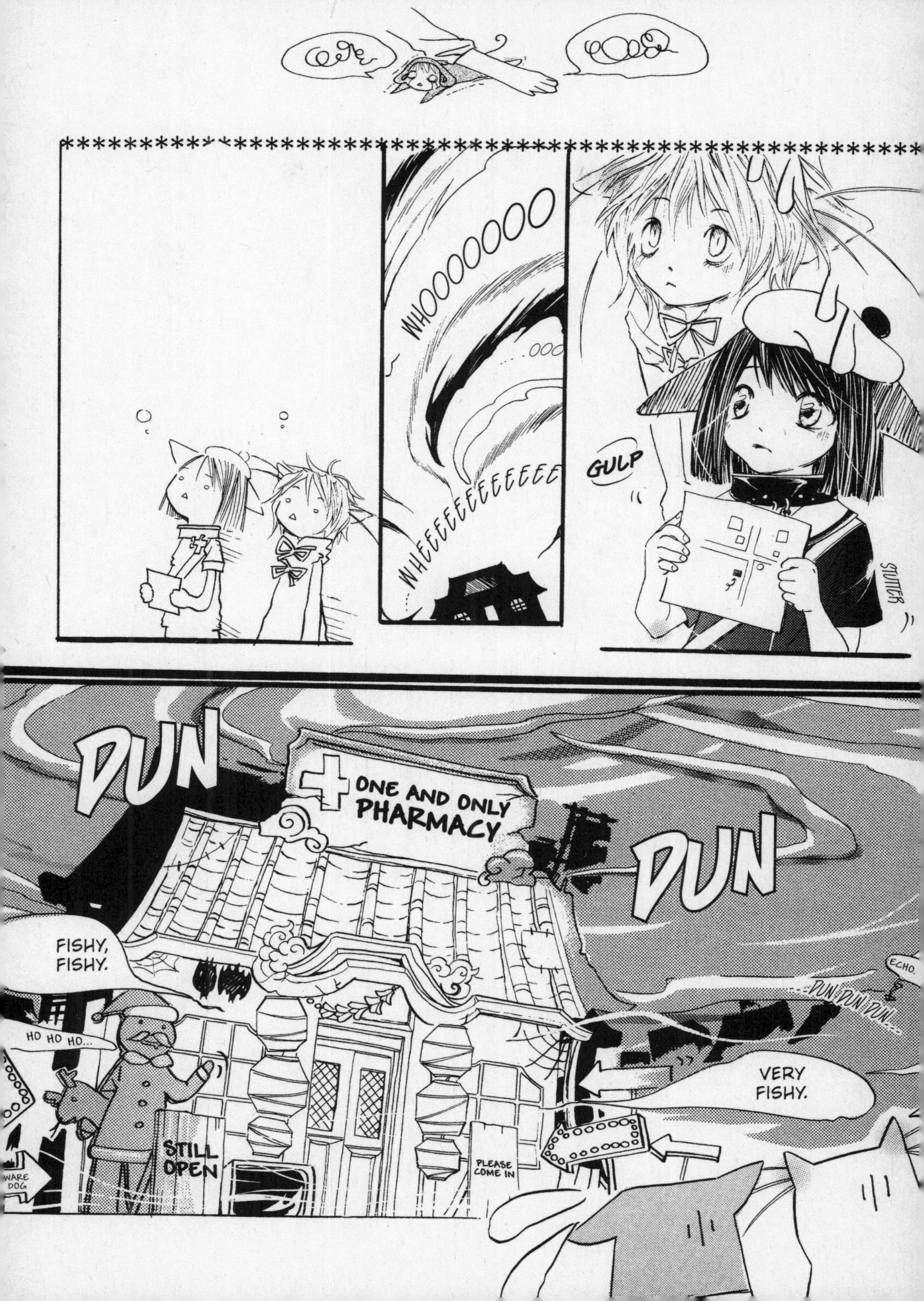
WHOOOOOOOO
...OOO
WHEEEEEEEEEEEE
GULP
STUTTER
DUN
ONE AND ONLY PHARMACY
DUN
FISHY, FISHY.
ECHO.
DUN DUN DUN...
HO HO HO...
VERY FISHY.
STILL OPEN
PLEASE COME IN

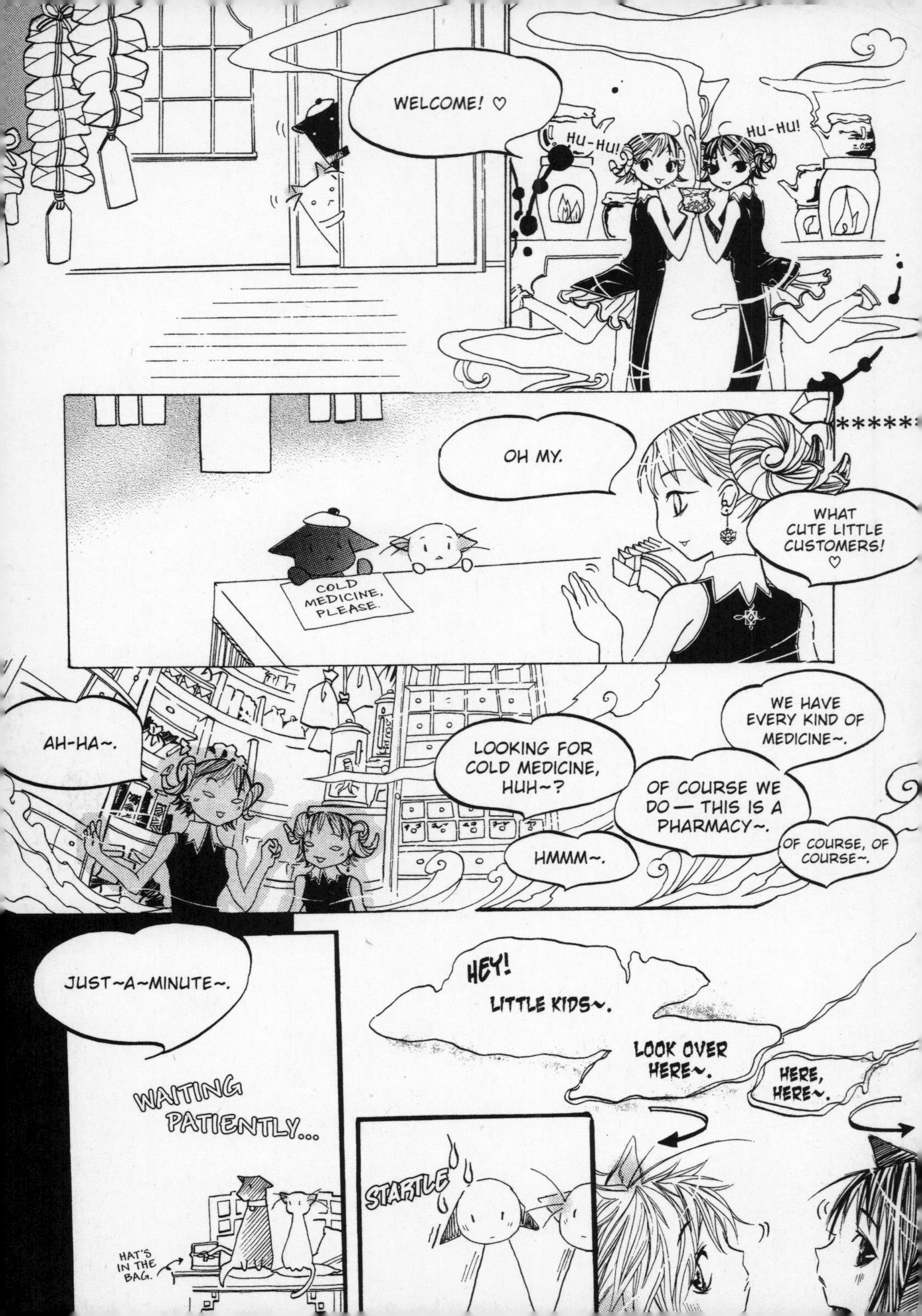
WELCOME! ♡
HU-HU!
HU-HU!
OH MY.
COLD MEDICINE, PLEASE.
WHAT CUTE LITTLE CUSTOMERS! ♡
AH-HA~.
LOOKING FOR COLD MEDICINE, HUH~?
WE HAVE EVERY KIND OF MEDICINE~.
OF COURSE WE DO — THIS IS A PHARMACY~.
HMMM~.
OF COURSE, OF COURSE~.
JUST~A~MINUTE~.
WAITING PATIENTLY...
HAT'S IN THE BAG.
HEY!
LITTLE KIDS~.
LOOK OVER HERE~.
HERE, HERE~.
STARTLE

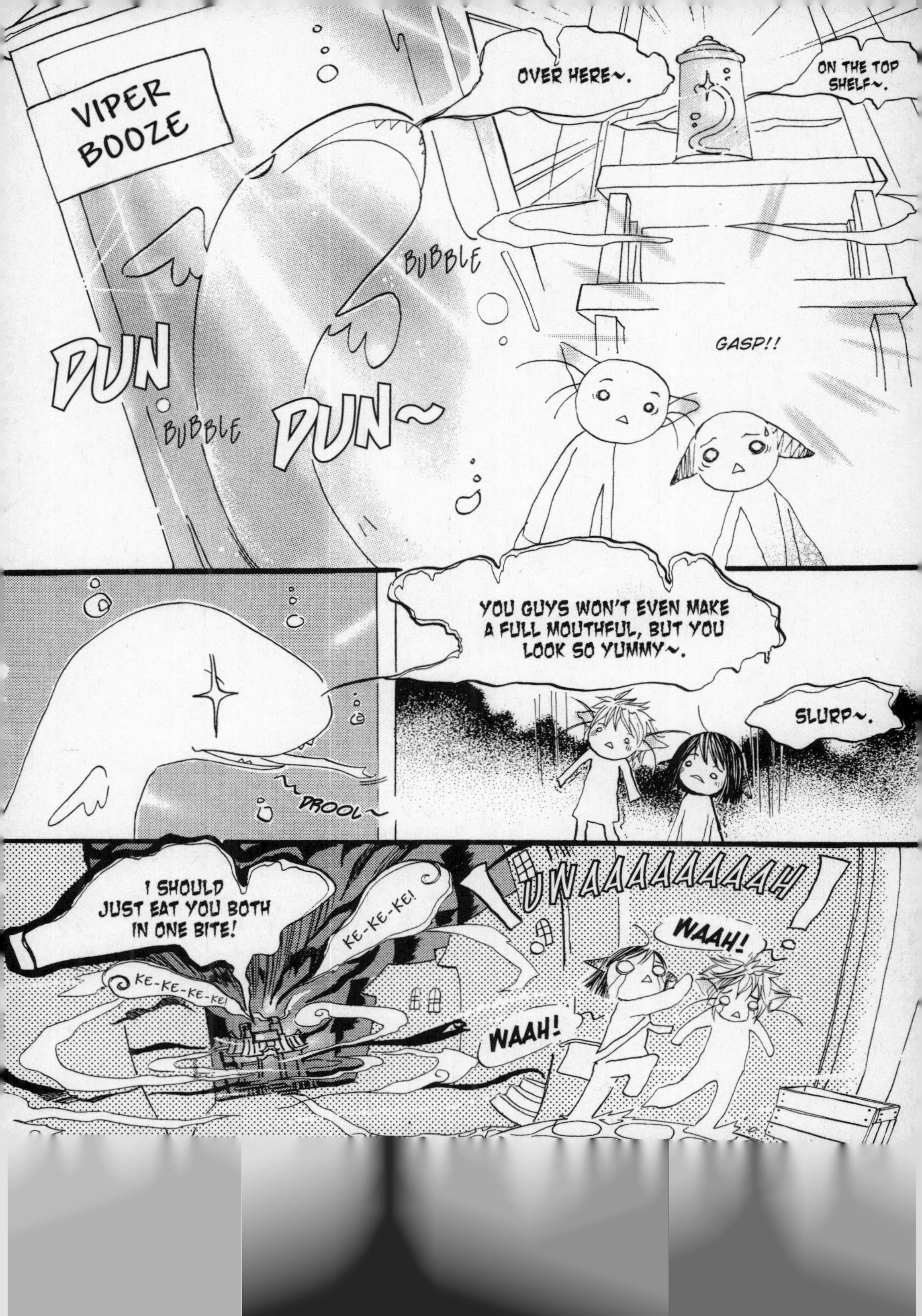
VIPER BOOZE
OVER HERE~.
ON THE TOP SHELF~.
BUBBLE
DUN
BUBBLE
DUN~
GASP!!
YOU GUYS WON'T EVEN MAKE A FULL MOUTHFUL, BUT YOU LOOK SO YUMMY~.
DROOL~
SLURP~.
I SHOULD JUST EAT YOU BOTH IN ONE BITE!
KE-KE-KE!
KE-KE-KE-KE!
UWAAAAAAAAAH!
WAAH!
WAAH!

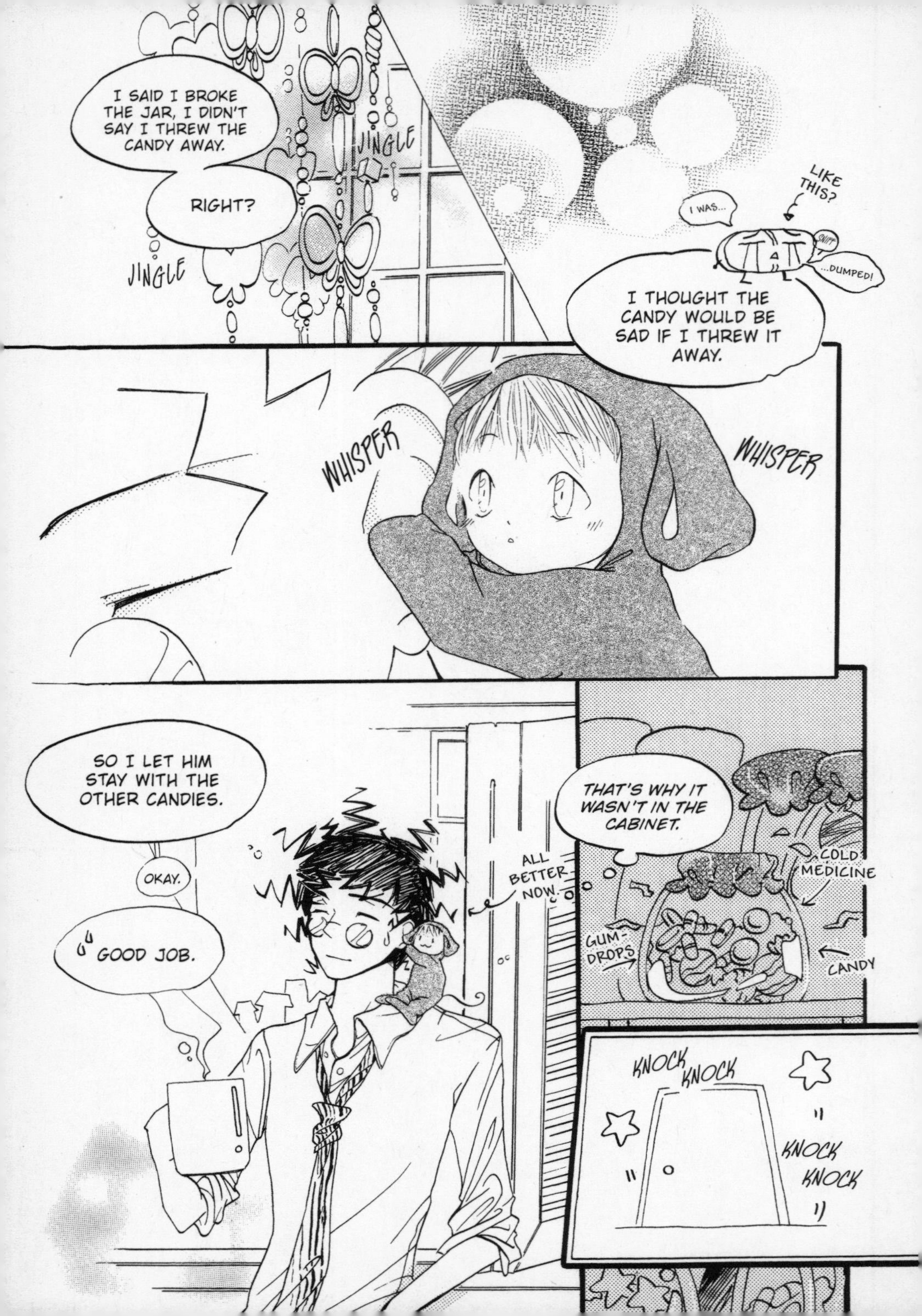
I SAID I BROKE THE JAR, I DIDN'T SAY I THREW THE CANDY AWAY.
JINGLE
RIGHT?
JINGLE
I WAS...
LIKE THIS?
SNIFF
...DUMPED!
I THOUGHT THE CANDY WOULD BE SAD IF I THREW IT AWAY.
WHISPER
WHISPER
SO I LET HIM STAY WITH THE OTHER CANDIES.
OKAY.
GOOD JOB.
ALL BETTER NOW.
THAT'S WHY IT WASN'T IN THE CABINET.
COLD MEDICINE
GUM-DROPS
CANDY
KNOCK KNOCK
KNOCK KNOCK

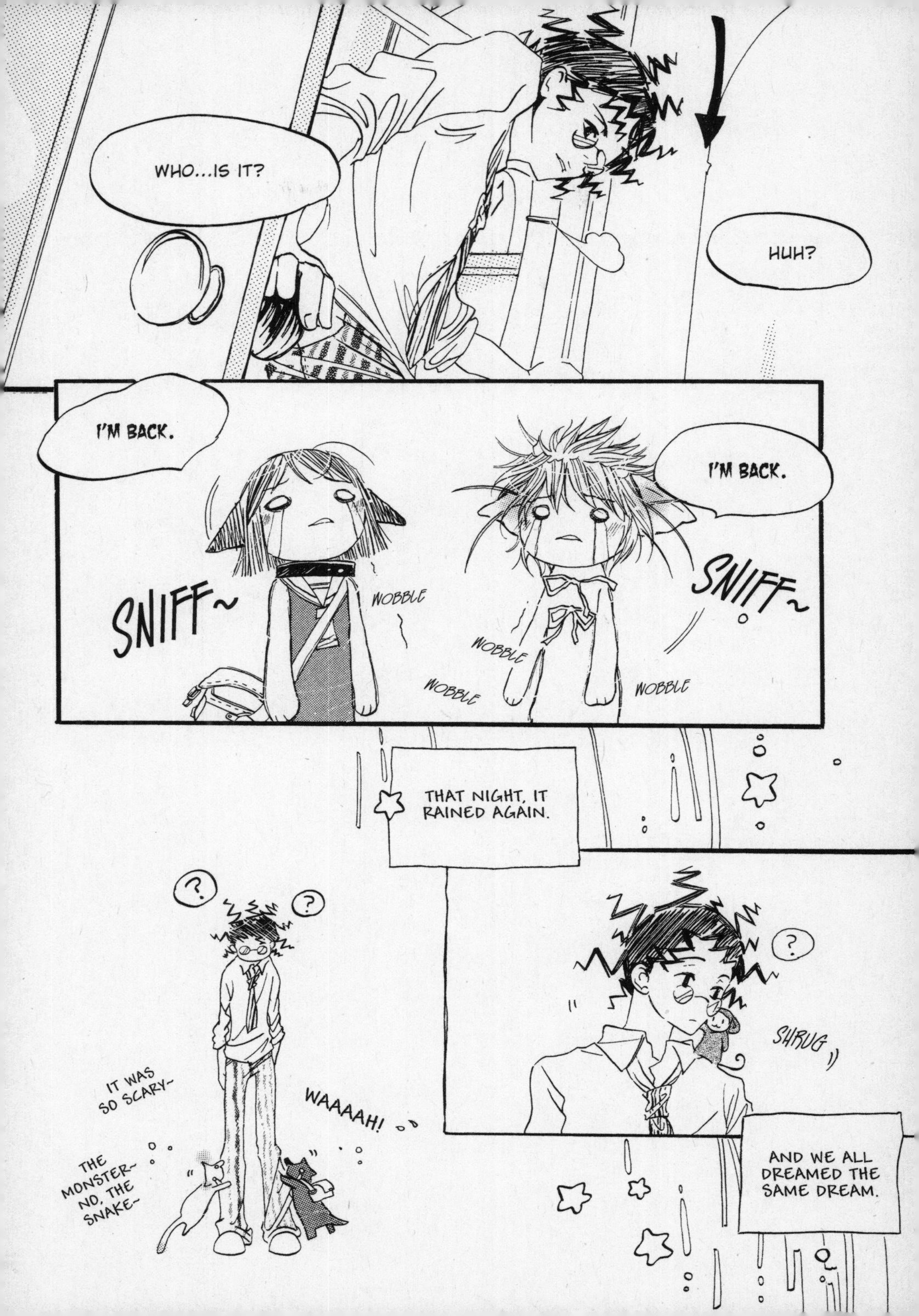
WHO...IS IT?
HUH?
I'M BACK.
I'M BACK.
SNIFF~
WOBBLE
WOBBLE
WOBBLE
WOBBLE
SNIFF~
THAT NIGHT, IT RAINED AGAIN.
IT WAS SO SCARY~
WAAAAH!
THE MONSTER~ NO, THE SNAKE~
SHRUG
AND WE ALL DREAMED THE SAME DREAM.

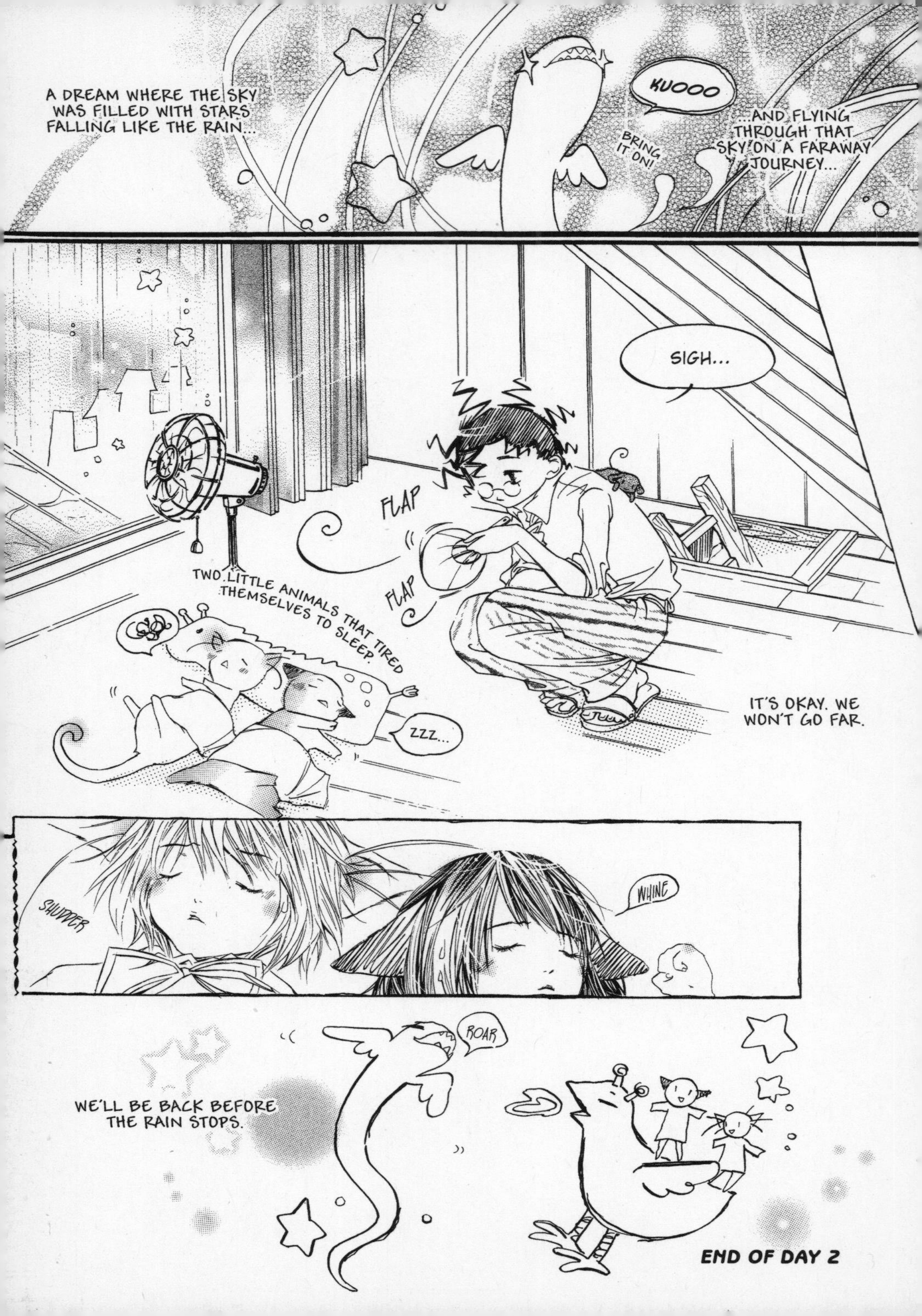
A DREAM WHERE THE SKY WAS FILLED WITH STARS FALLING LIKE THE RAIN...
KUOOO
BRING IT ON!
...AND FLYING THROUGH THAT SKY ON A FARAWAY JOURNEY...
SIGH...
FLAP
FLAP
TWO LITTLE ANIMALS THAT TIRED THEMSELVES TO SLEEP.
ZZZ...
IT'S OKAY. WE WON'T GO FAR.
SHUDDER
WHINE
ROAR
WE'LL BE BACK BEFORE THE RAIN STOPS.
END OF DAY 2

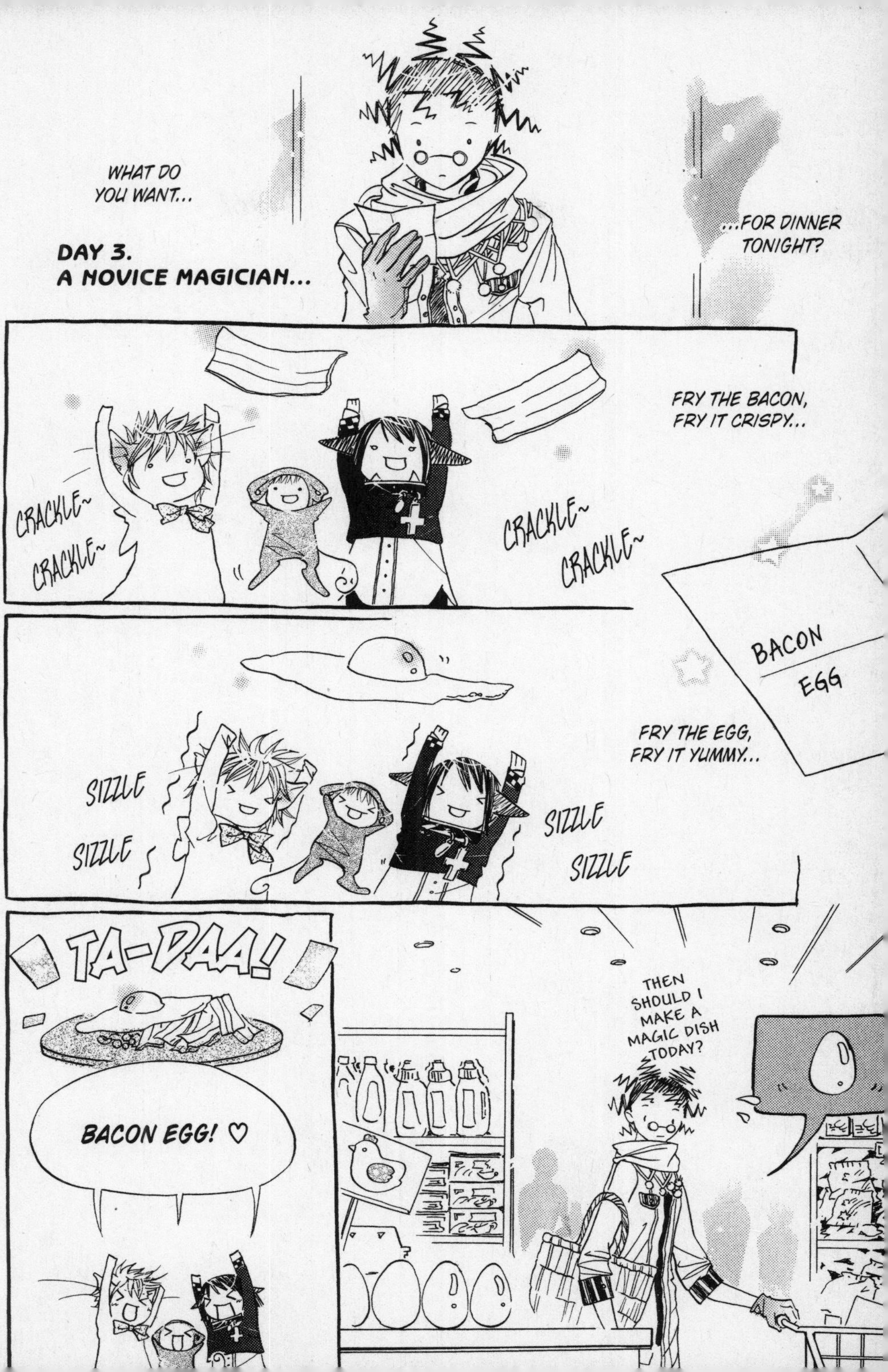
WHAT DO YOU WANT...
DAY 3. A NOVICE MAGICIAN...
...FOR DINNER TONIGHT?
FRY THE BACON, FRY IT CRISPY...
CRACKLE~ CRACKLE~
CRACKLE~ CRACKLE~
BACON
EGG
FRY THE EGG, FRY IT YUMMY...
SIZZLE SIZZLE
SIZZLE SIZZLE
TA-DAA!
BACON EGG! ♡
THEN SHOULD I MAKE A MAGIC DISH TODAY?

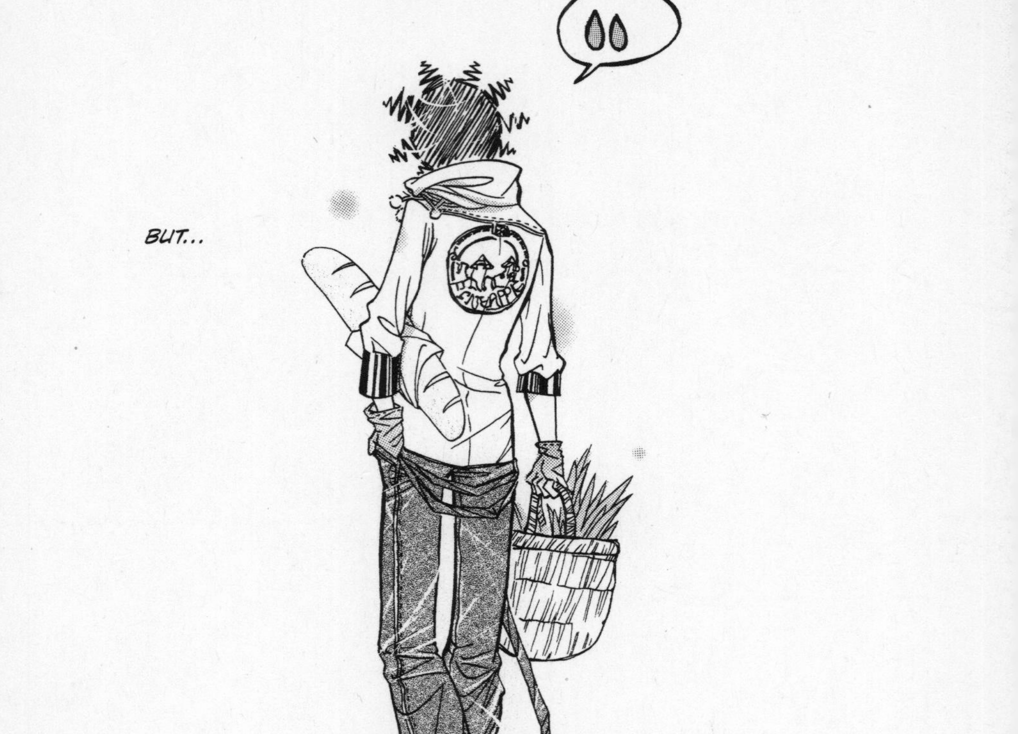
BUT...
...THIS MAN...
...HAD NEVER SUCCEEDED IN MAKING A MAGIC DISH.

# one fine day

DAY 3.
A NOVICE MAGICIAN...

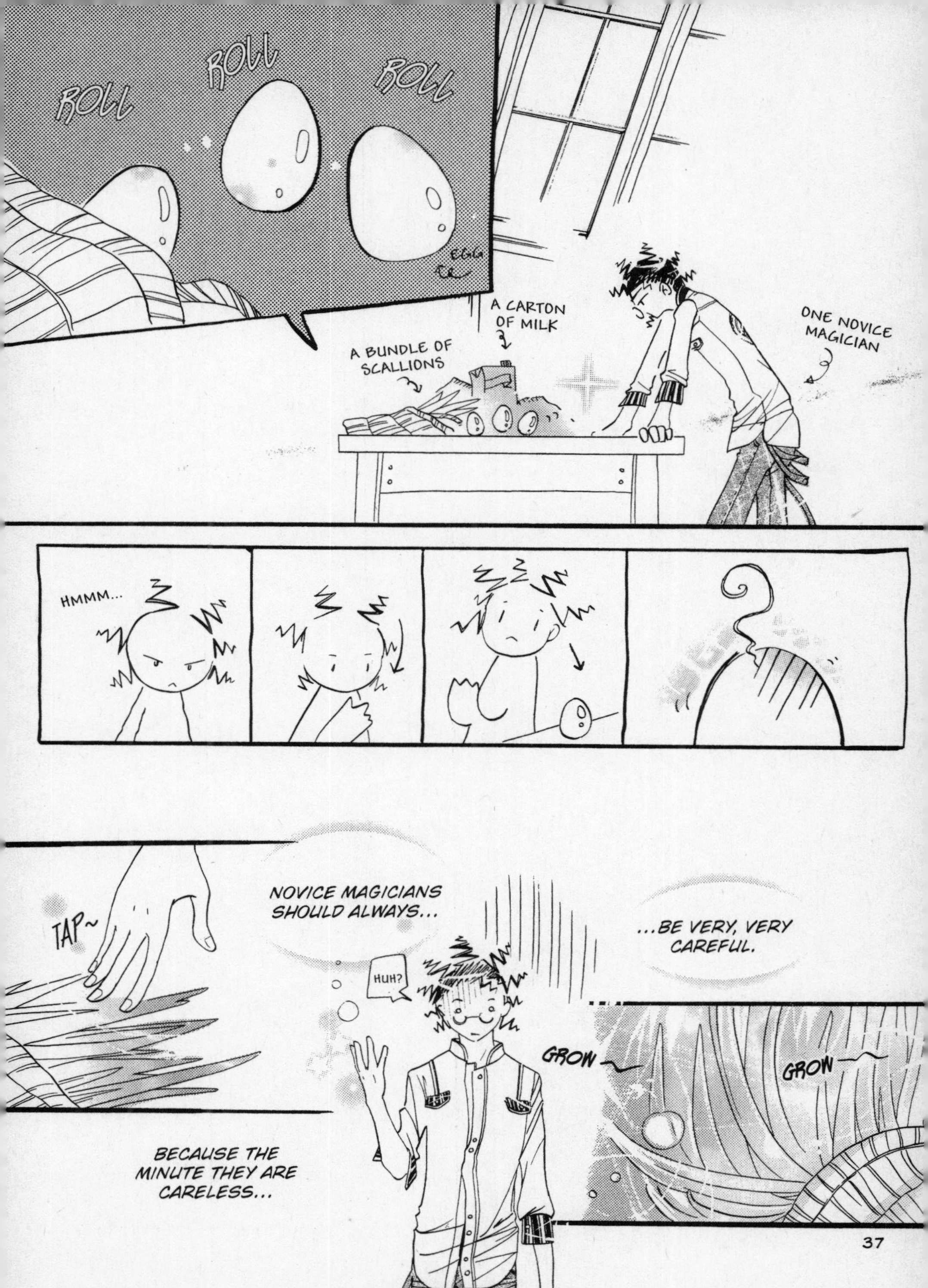
ROLL
ROLL
ROLL
EGG
A BUNDLE OF SCALLIONS
A CARTON OF MILK
ONE NOVICE MAGICIAN
HMMM...
TAP~
NOVICE MAGICIANS SHOULD ALWAYS...
HUH?
...BE VERY, VERY CAREFUL.
GROW
GROW
BECAUSE THE MINUTE THEY ARE CARELESS...

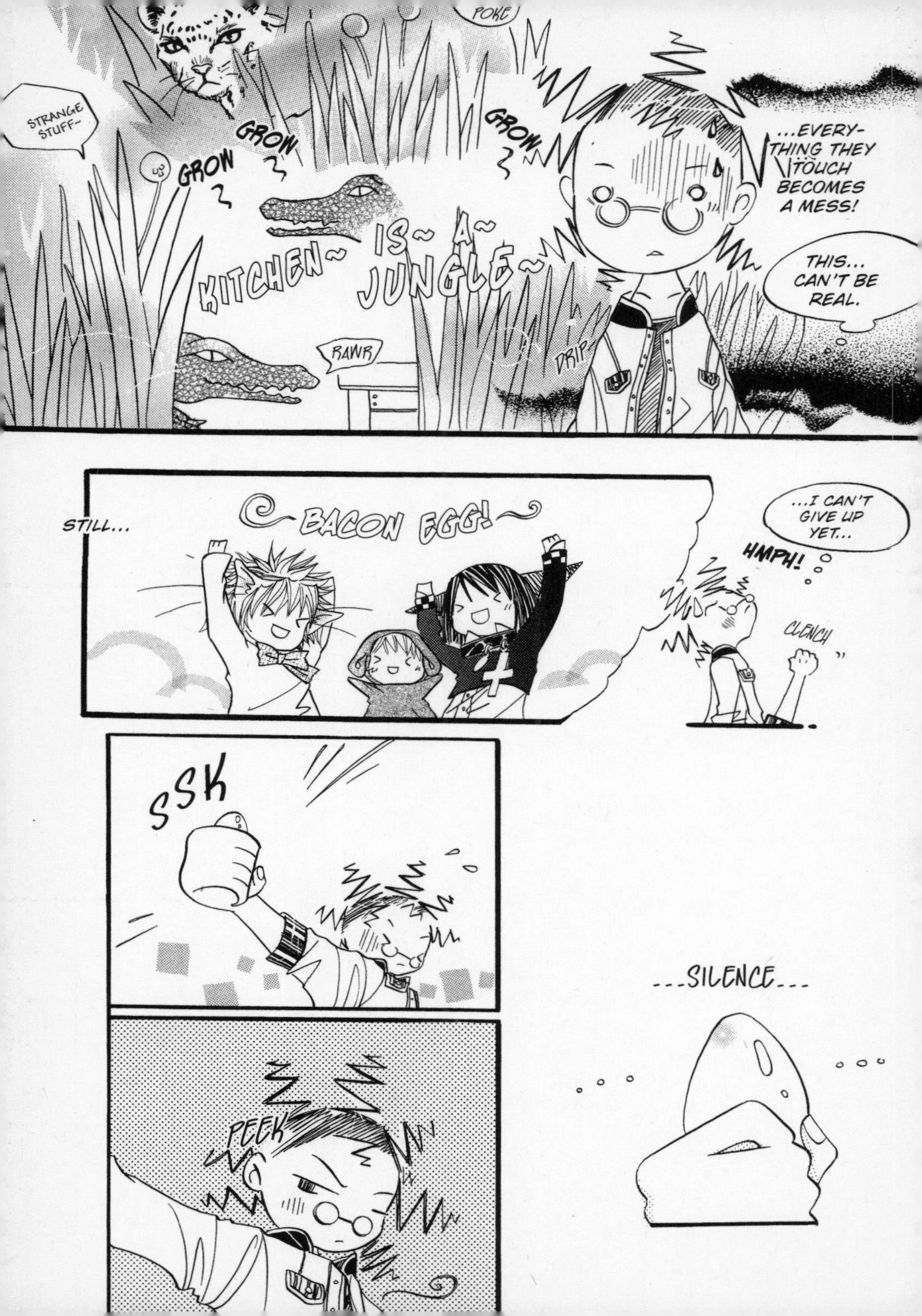
STRANGE STUFF~
POKE
GROW
GROW
GROW
KITCHEN~ IS~ A~ JUNGLE~
RAWR
DRIP
...EVERYTHING THEY TOUCH BECOMES A MESS!
THIS... CAN'T BE REAL.
STILL...
~BACON EGG!~
HMPH!
...I CAN'T GIVE UP YET...
CLENCH
SSK
---SILENCE---
PEEK

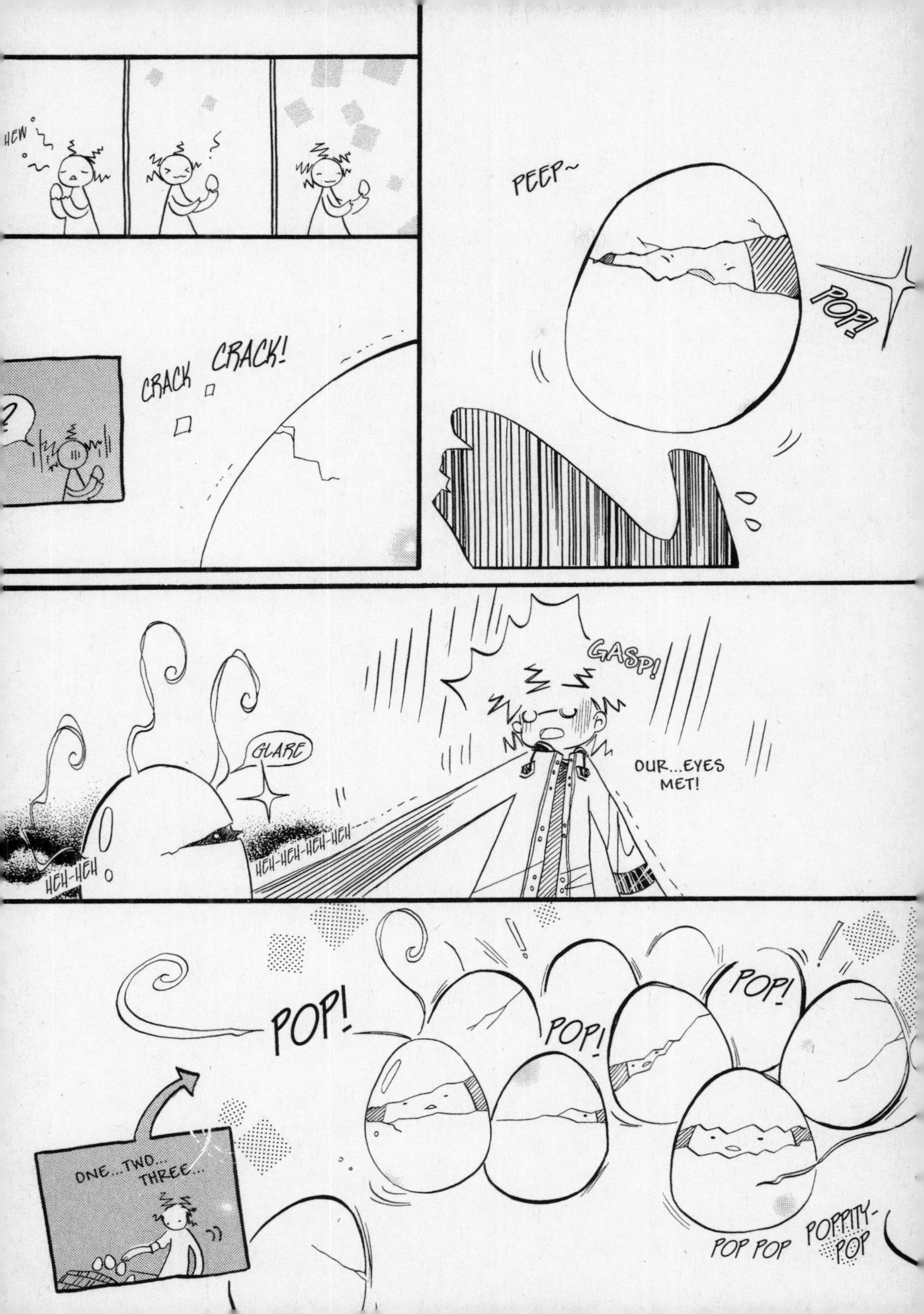
HEW
CRACK CRACK!
PEEP~
POP!
HEH-HEH
GLARE
HEH-HEH-HEH-HEH
GASP!
OUR...EYES MET!
POP!
ONE...TWO... THREE...
POP!
POP!
POP POP
POPPITY-POP

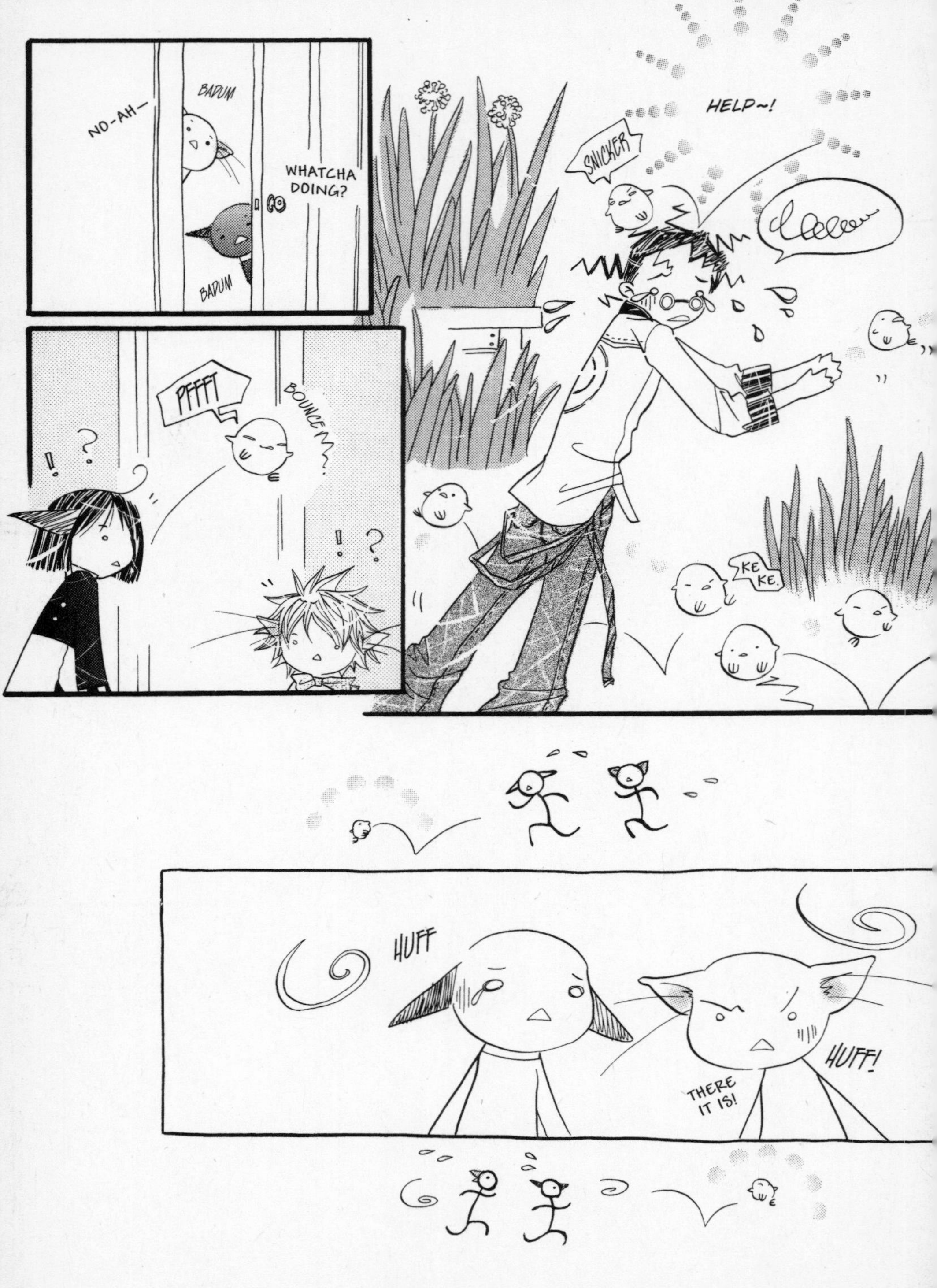
NO-AH—
BADUM
WHATCHA DOING?
BADUM
PFFFT
BOUNCE
HELP~!
SNICKER
KE KE.
HUFF
THERE IT IS!
HUFF!

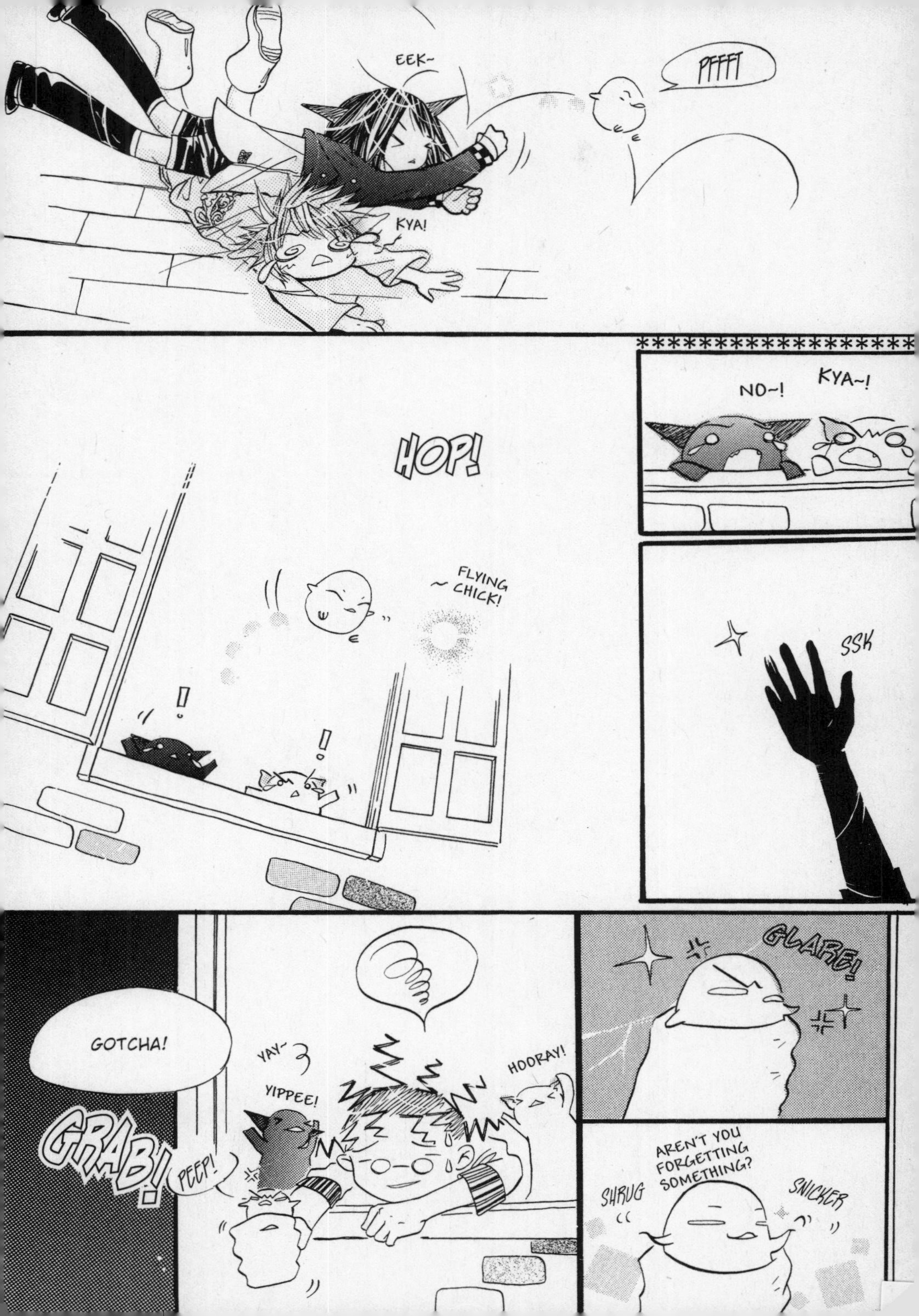
EEK~
PFFFT
KYA!
HOP!
~ FLYING CHICK!
!
!
NO~!
KYA~!
SSK
GOTCHA!
GRAB!
PEEP!
YAY~
YIPPEE!
HOORAY!
GLARE!
ARE'T YOU FORGETTING SOMETHING?
SHRUG
SNICKER

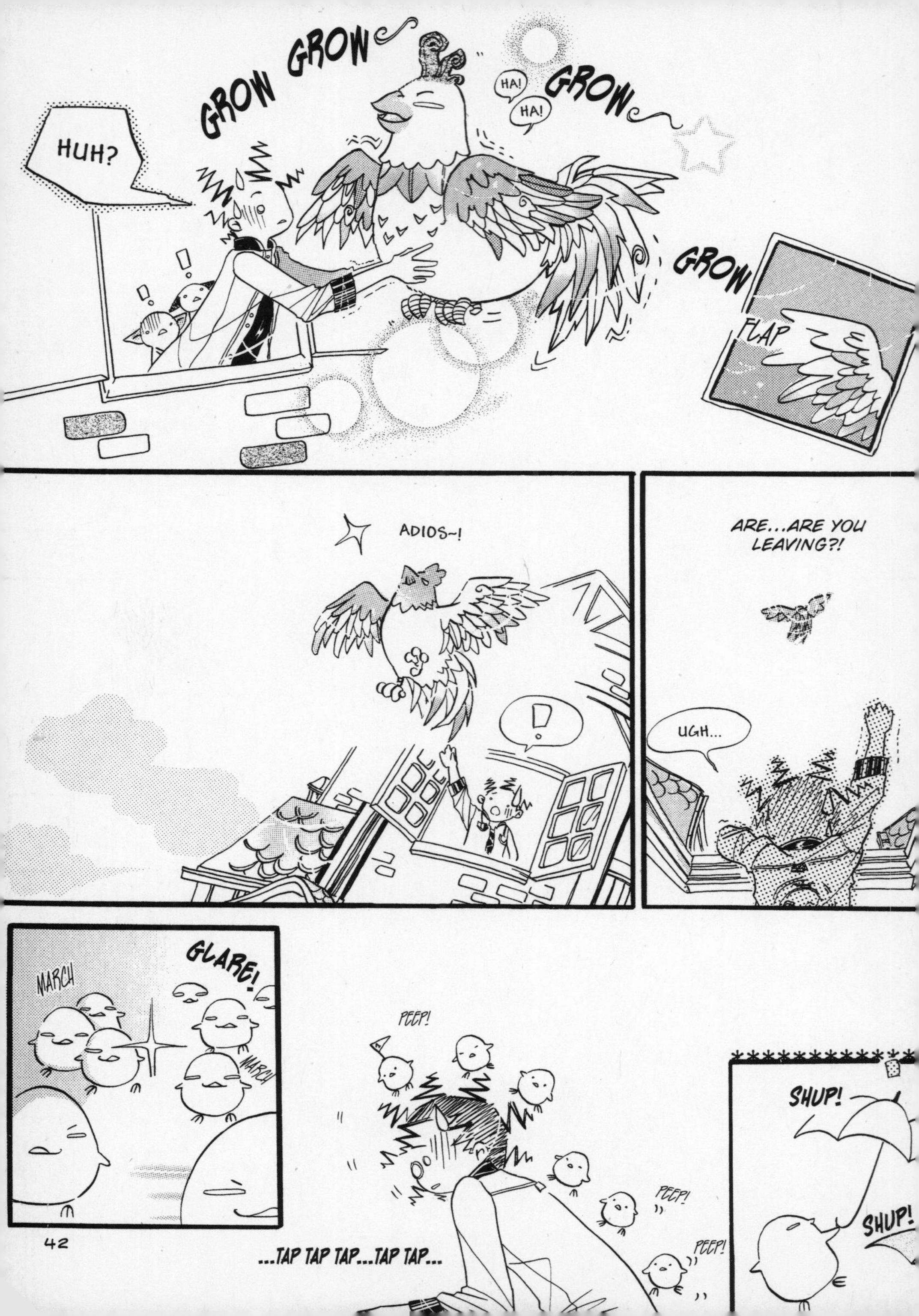
GROW GROW
HA!
HA!
GROW
HUH?
!
!
GROW
FLAP
ADIOS~!
!
ARE...ARE YOU LEAVING?!
UGH...
MARCH
GLARE!
MARCH
PEEP!
PEEP!
PEEP!
...TAP TAP TAP...TAP TAP...
SHUP!
SHUP!

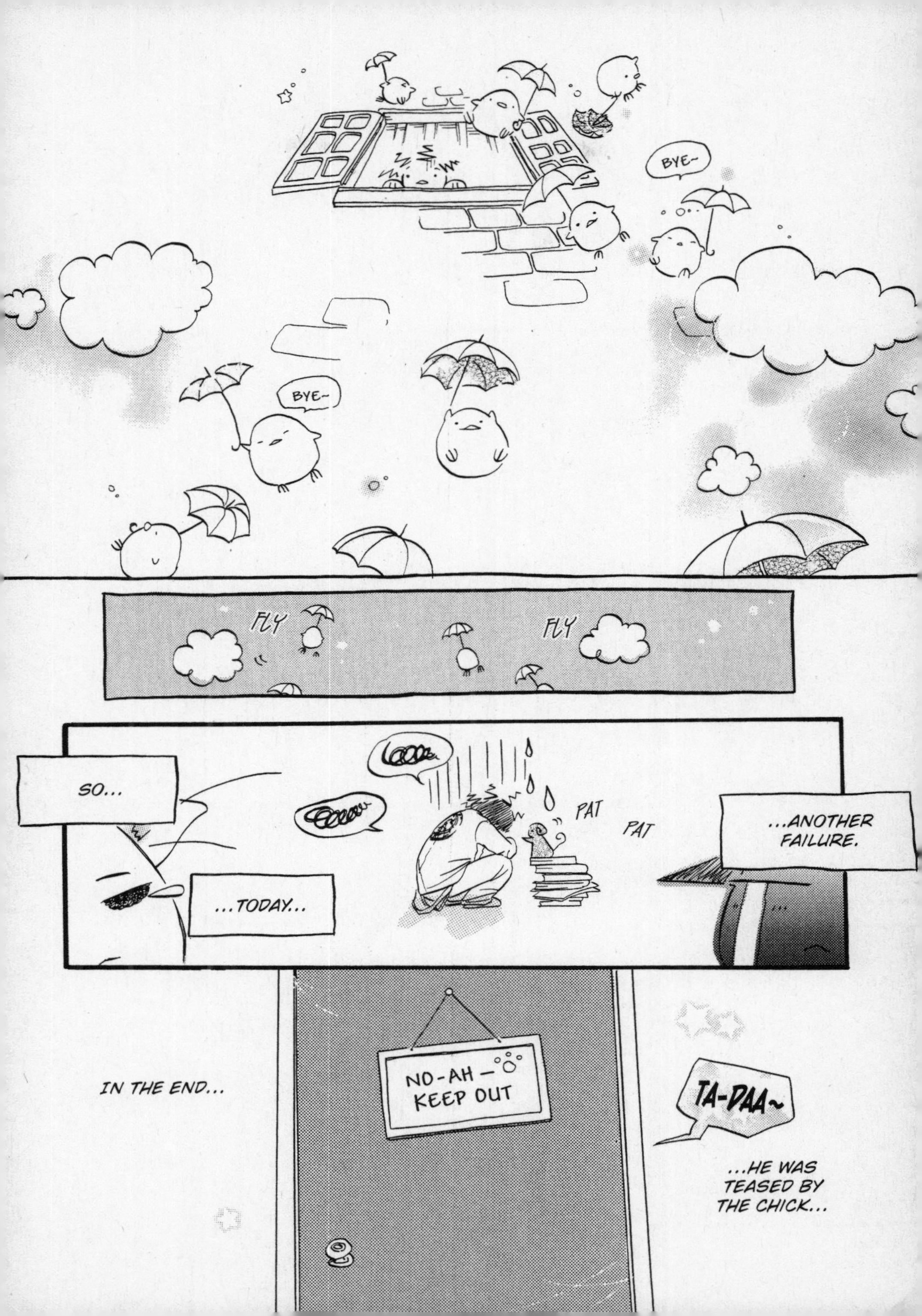
BYE~
BYE~
FLY
FLY
SO...
...TODAY...
PAT
PAT
...ANOTHER FAILURE.
IN THE END...
NO-AH — KEEP OUT
TA-DAA~
...HE WAS TEASED BY THE CHICK...

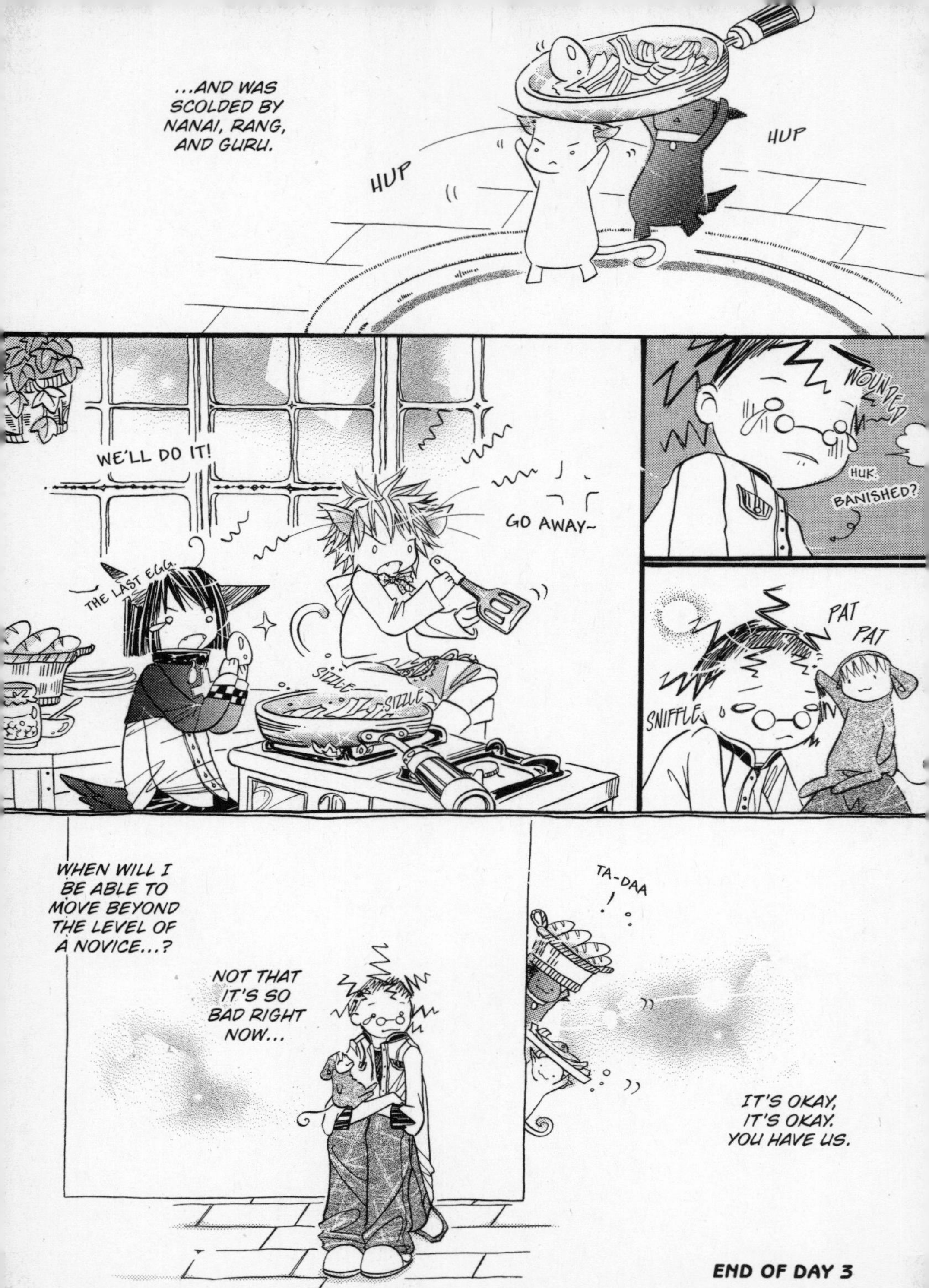
...AND WAS SCOLDED BY NANAI, RANG, AND GURU.
HUP
HUP
WE'LL DO IT!
THE LAST EGG.
SIZZLE
SIZZLE
GO AWAY~
WOUNDED
HUK.
BANISHED?
PAT
PAT
SNIFFLE
WHEN WILL I BE ABLE TO MOVE BEYOND THE LEVEL OF A NOVICE...?
NOT THAT IT'S SO BAD RIGHT NOW...
TA-DAA
IT'S OKAY, IT'S OKAY. YOU HAVE US.

END OF DAY 3

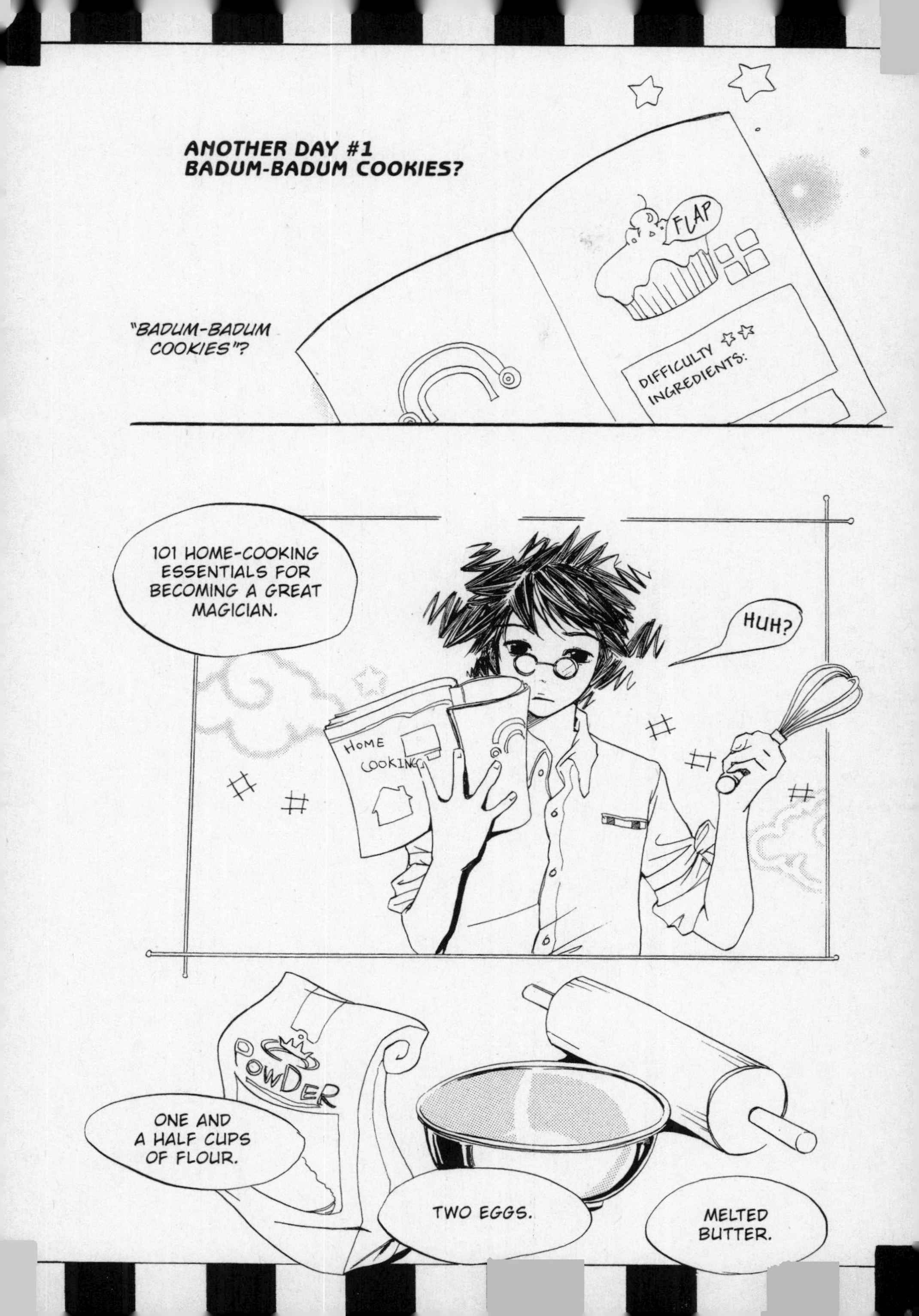
ANOTHER DAY #1
BADUM-BADUM COOKIES?
FLAP
DIFFICULTY
INGREDIENTS:
"BADUM-BADUM COOKIES"?
101 HOME-COOKING ESSENTIALS FOR BECOMING A GREAT MAGICIAN.
HOME COOKING
HUH?
POWDER
ONE AND A HALF CUPS OF FLOUR.
TWO EGGS.
MELTED BUTTER.

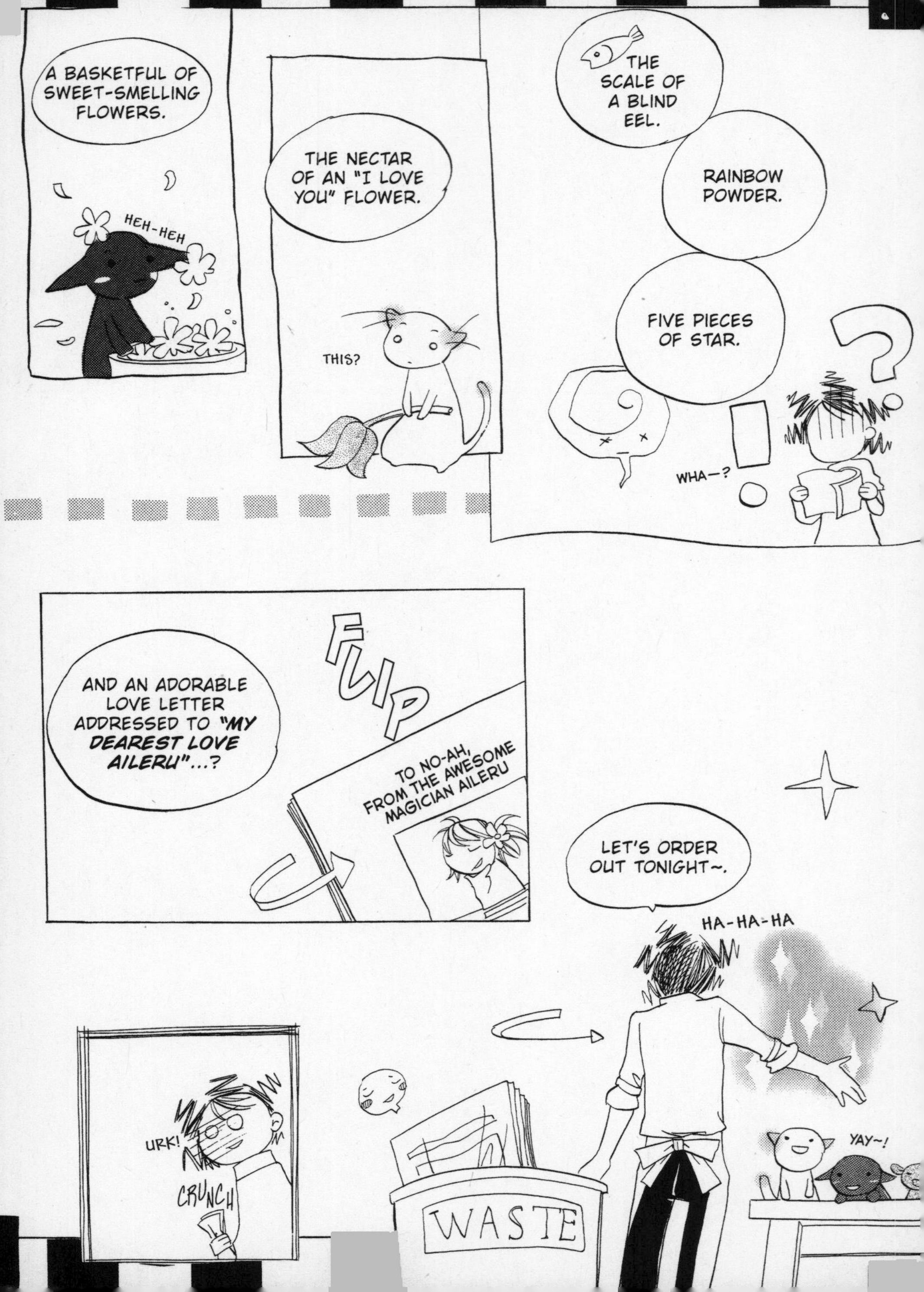
A BASKETFUL OF SWEET-SMELLING FLOWERS.
HEH-HEH
THE NECTAR OF AN "I LOVE YOU" FLOWER.
THIS?
THE SCALE OF A BLIND EEL.
RAINBOW POWDER.
FIVE PIECES OF STAR.
WHA—?
AND AN ADORABLE LOVE LETTER ADDRESSED TO ***"MY DEAREST LOVE AILERU"***...?
FLIP
TO NO-AH, FROM THE AWESOME MAGICIAN AILERU
LET'S ORDER OUT TONIGHT~.
HA-HA-HA
URK!
CRUNCH
WASTE
YAY~!

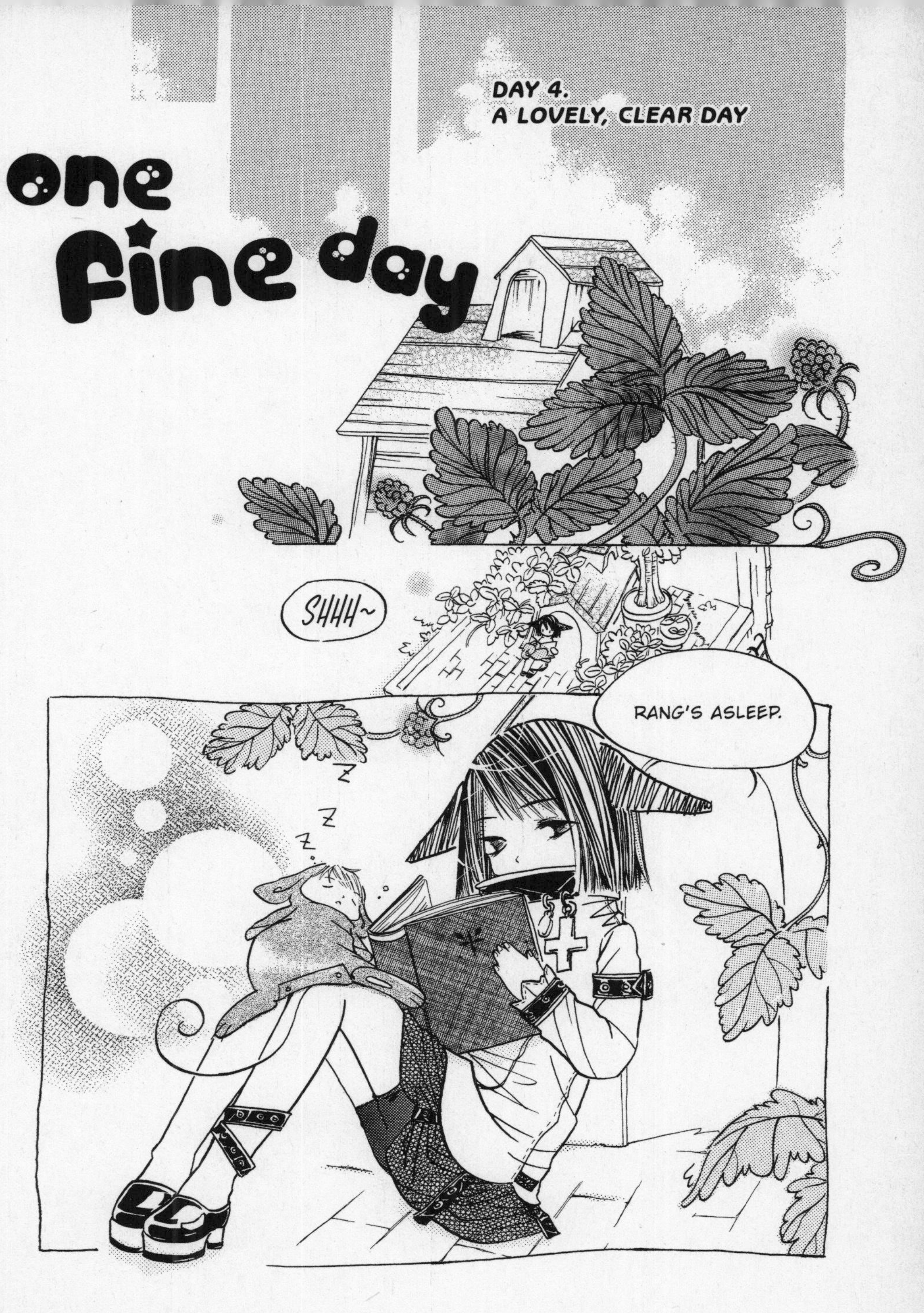
DAY 4.
A LOVELY, CLEAR DAY
one fine day
SHHH~
RANG'S ASLEEP.
Z
Z
Z

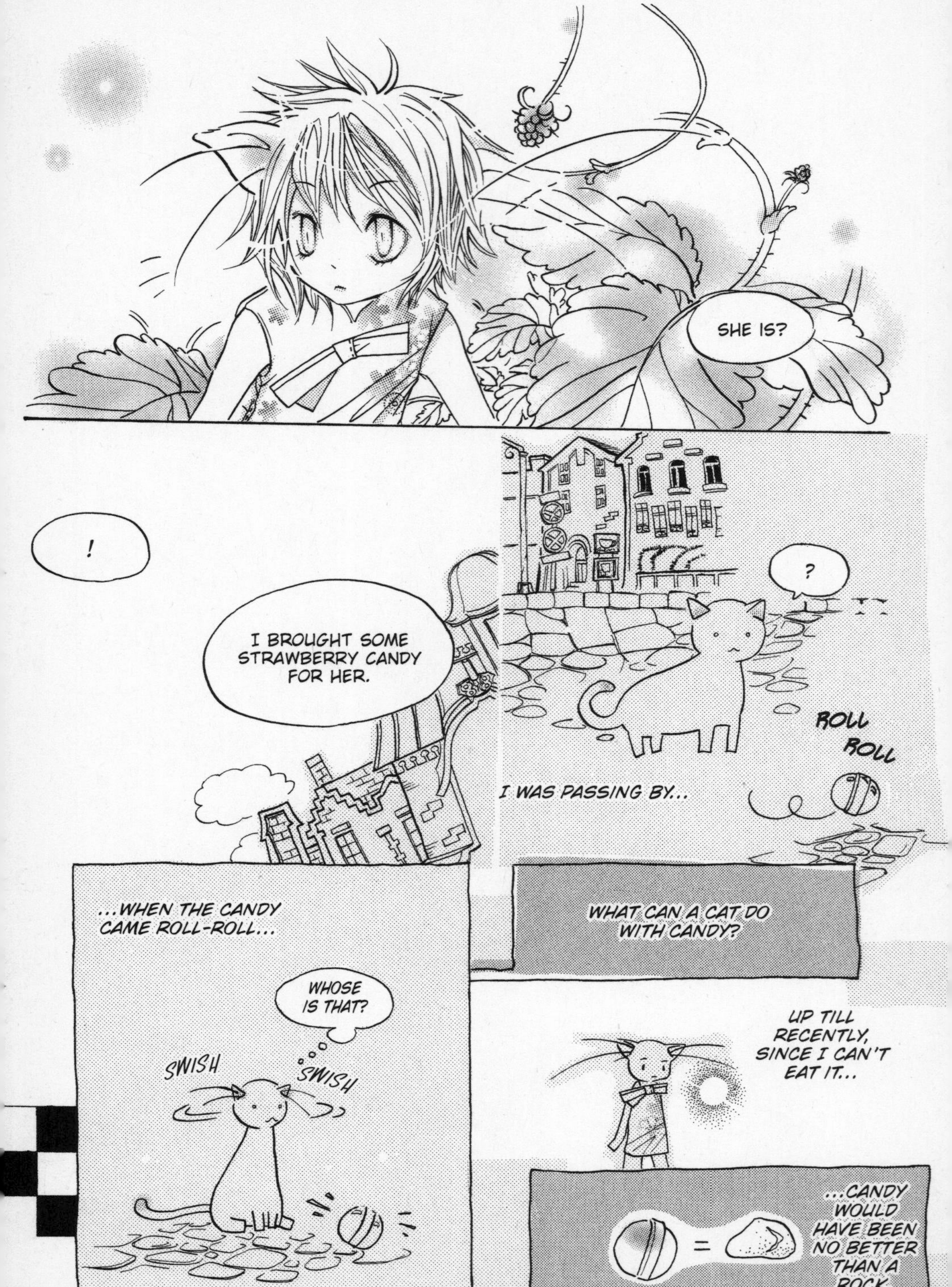
SHE IS?
!
I BROUGHT SOME STRAWBERRY CANDY FOR HER.
?
ROLL ROLL
I WAS PASSING BY...
...WHEN THE CANDY CAME ROLL-ROLL...
WHOSE IS THAT?
SWISH
SWISH
WHAT CAN A CAT DO WITH CANDY?
UP TILL RECENTLY, SINCE I CAN'T EAT IT...
...CANDY WOULD HAVE BEEN NO BETTER THAN A ROCK.
=

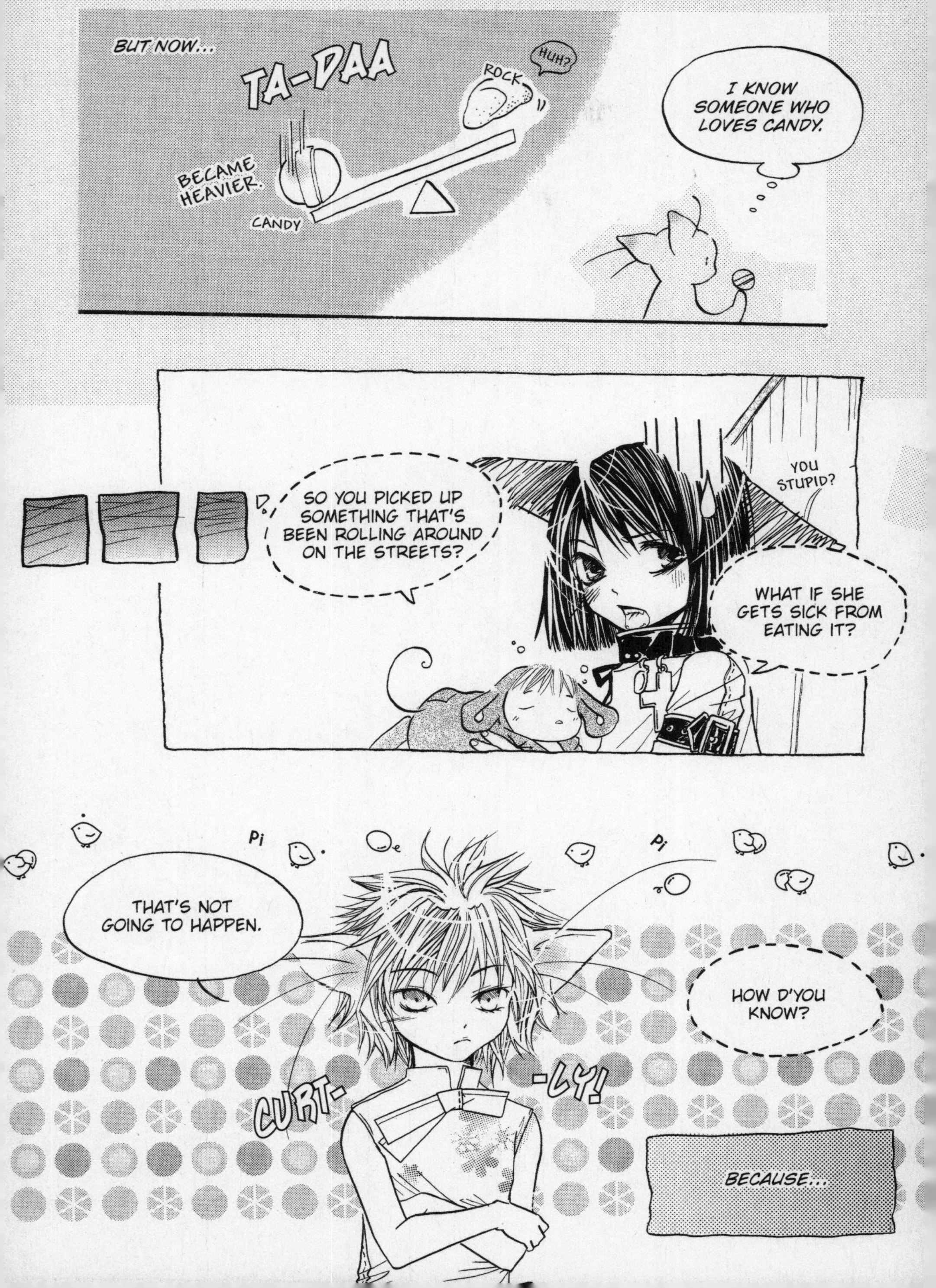
BUT NOW...
TA-DAA
ROCK
HUH?
BECAME HEAVIER.
CANDY
I KNOW SOMEONE WHO LOVES CANDY.
SO YOU PICKED UP SOMETHING THAT'S BEEN ROLLING AROUND ON THE STREETS?
YOU STUPID?
WHAT IF SHE GETS SICK FROM EATING IT?
Pi
Pi
THAT'S NOT GOING TO HAPPEN.
HOW D'YOU KNOW?
CURT-
-LY!
BECAUSE...

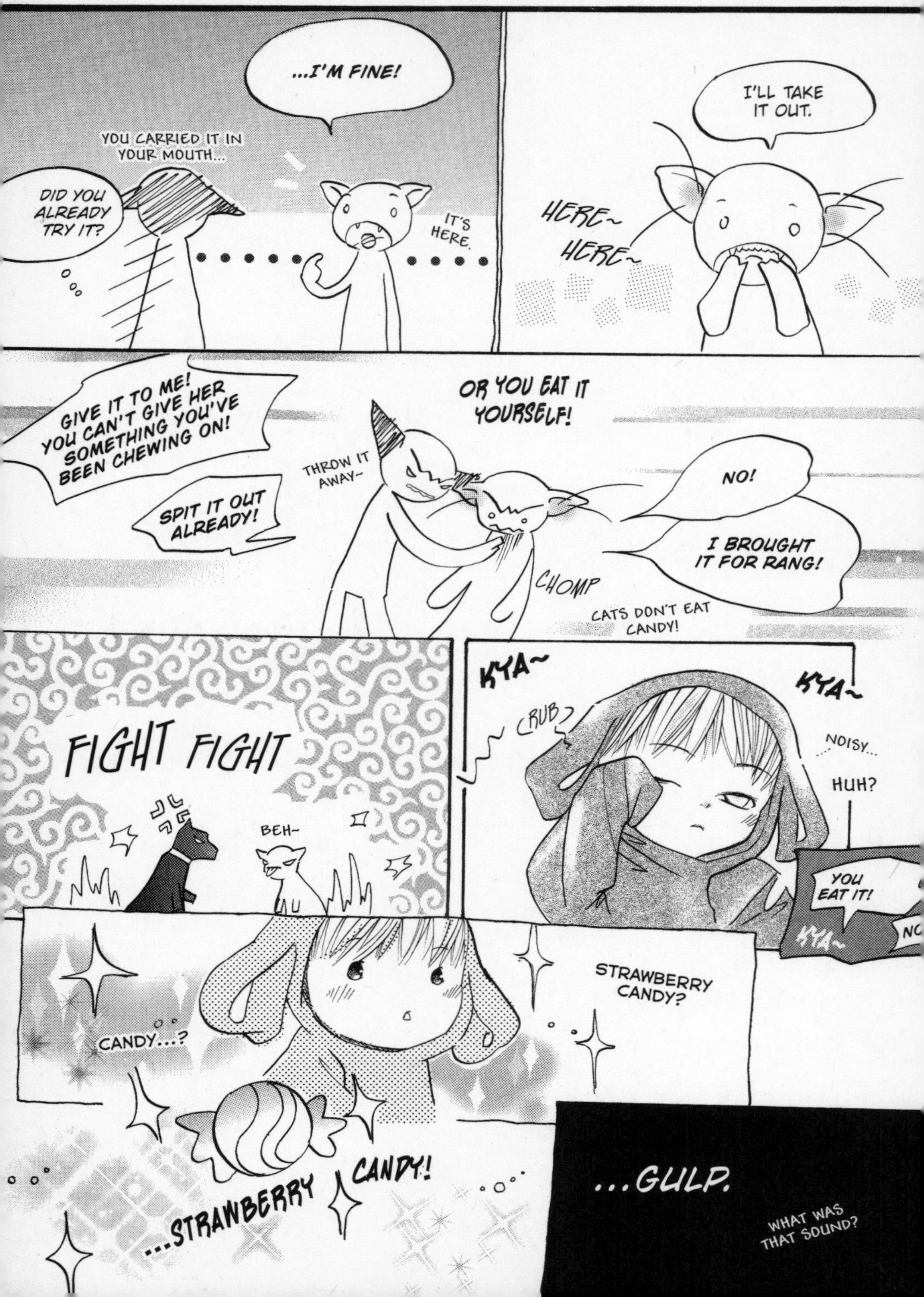
YOU CARRIED IT IN YOUR MOUTH...
DID YOU ALREADY TRY IT?
...I'M FINE!
IT'S HERE.
I'LL TAKE IT OUT.
HERE~
HERE~
GIVE IT TO ME! YOU CAN'T GIVE HER SOMETHING YOU'VE BEEN CHEWING ON!
SPIT IT OUT ALREADY!
THROW IT AWAY~
OR YOU EAT IT YOURSELF!
NO!
I BROUGHT IT FOR RANG!
CHOMP
CATS DON'T EAT CANDY!
FIGHT FIGHT
BEH~
KYA~
KYA~
(RUB)
NOISY...
HUH?
YOU EAT IT!
KYA~
CANDY...?
STRAWBERRY CANDY?
...STRAWBERRY CANDY!
...GULP.
WHAT WAS THAT SOUND?

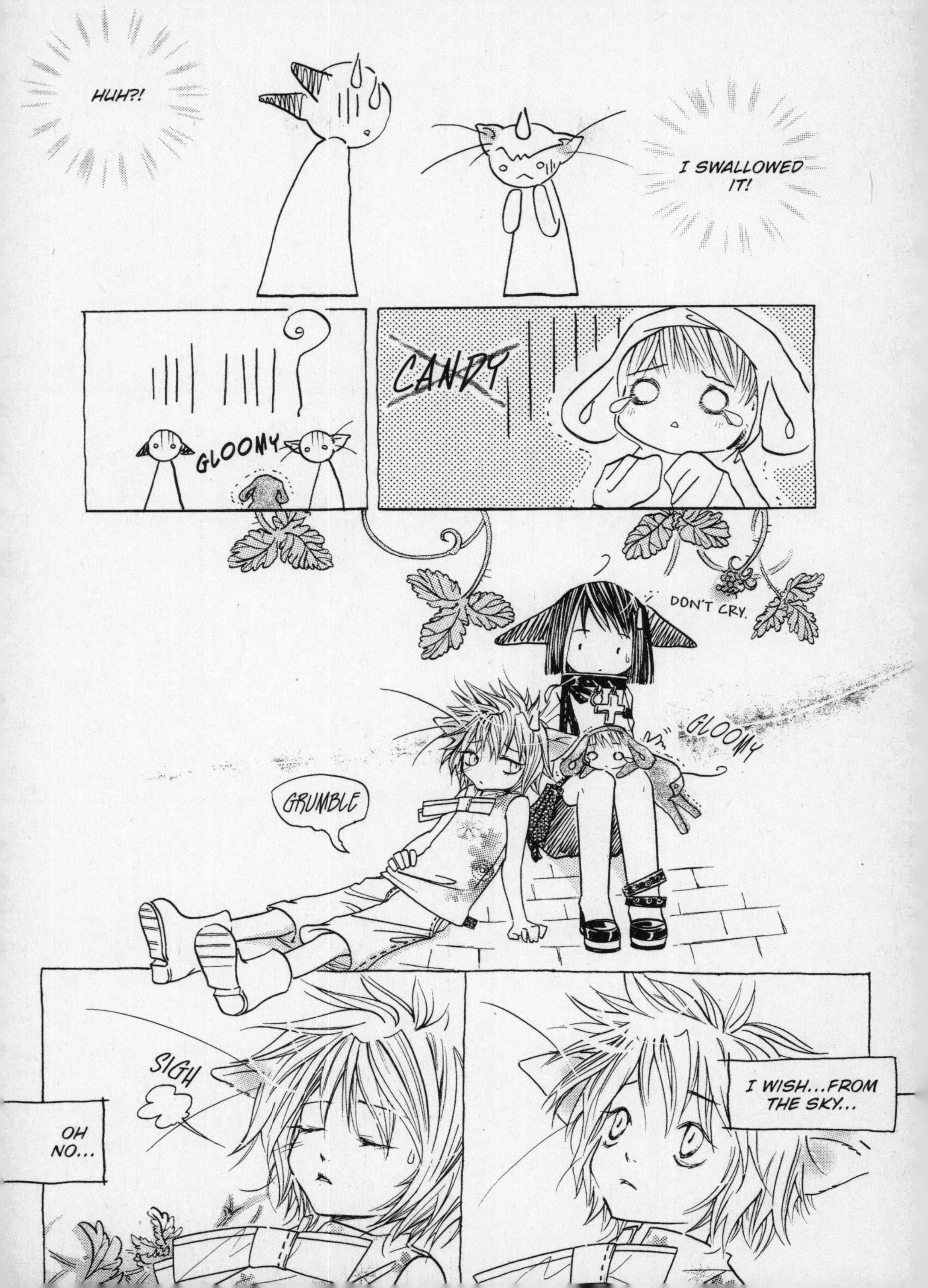
HUH?!
I SWALLOWED IT!
GLOOMY
CANDY
DON'T CRY.
GRUMBLE
GLOOMY
SIGH
OH NO...
I WISH...FROM THE SKY...

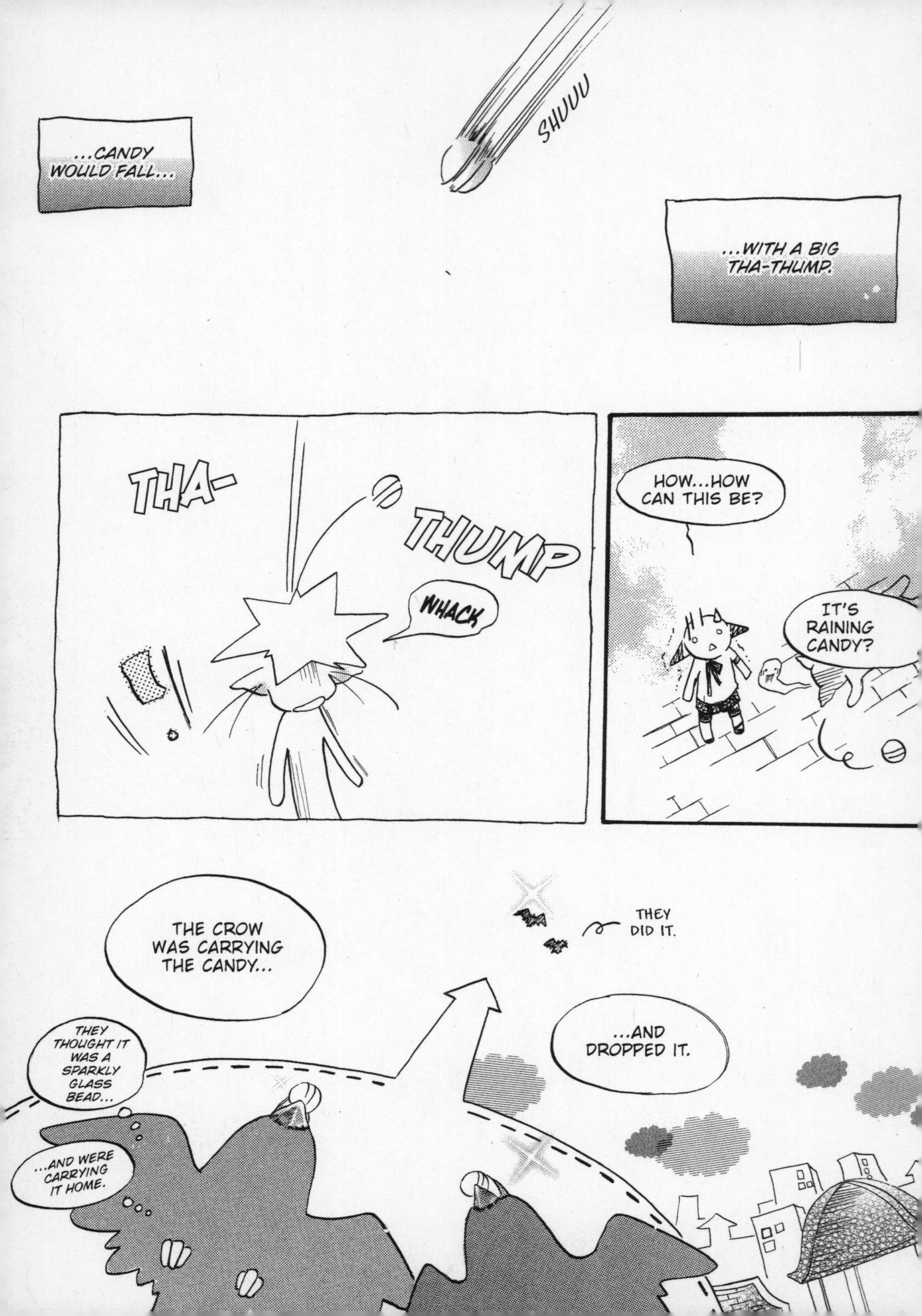
...CANDY WOULD FALL...
SHUUU
...WITH A BIG THA-THUMP.
THA-
THUMP
WHACK
HOW...HOW CAN THIS BE?
IT'S RAINING CANDY?
THE CROW WAS CARRYING THE CANDY...
THEY DID IT.
...AND DROPPED IT.
THEY THOUGHT IT WAS A SPARKLY GLASS BEAD...
...AND WERE CARRYING IT HOME.

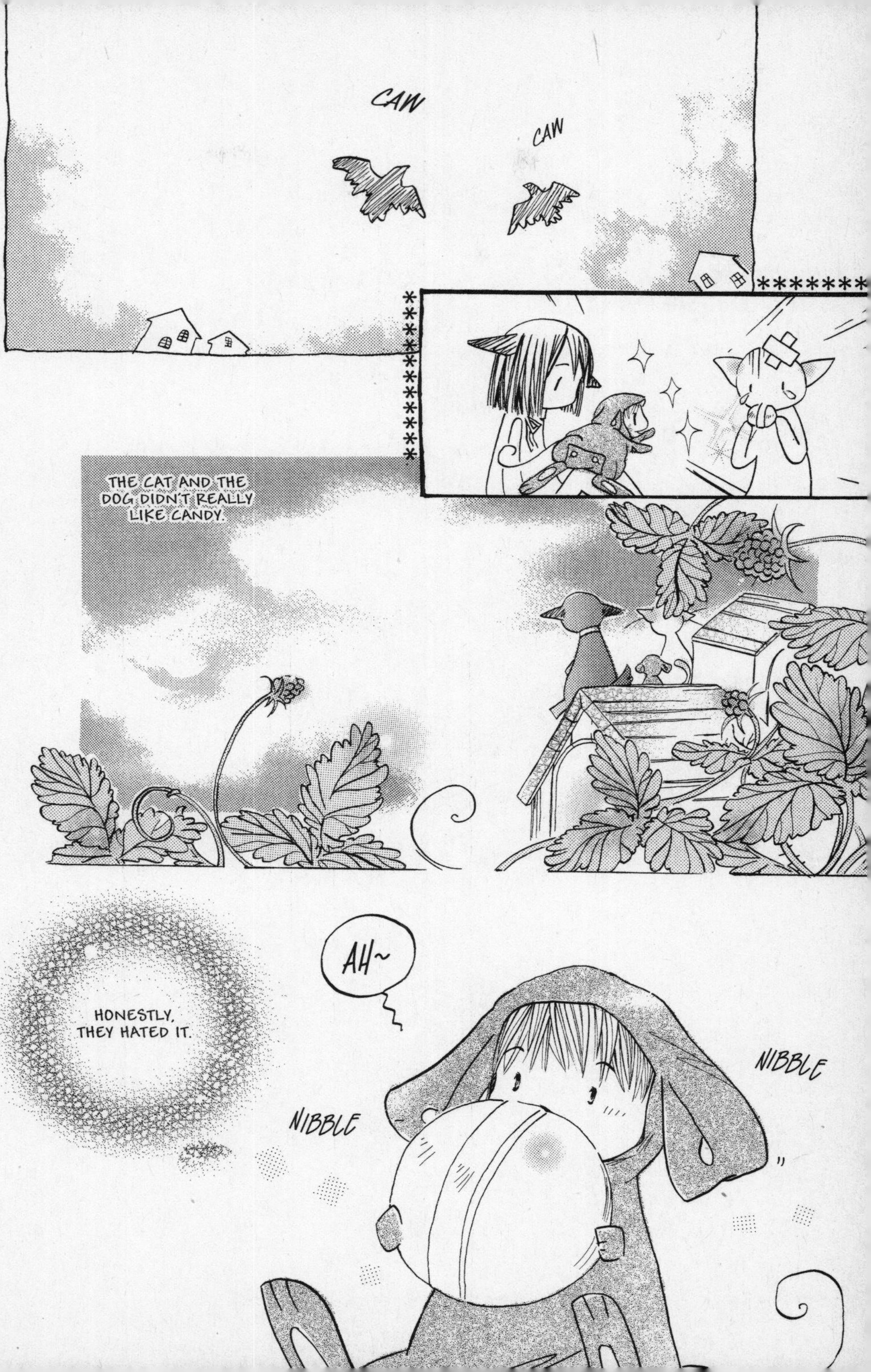
CAW
CAW
THE CAT AND THE DOG DIDN'T REALLY LIKE CANDY.
HONESTLY, THEY HATED IT.
AH~
NIBBLE
NIBBLE

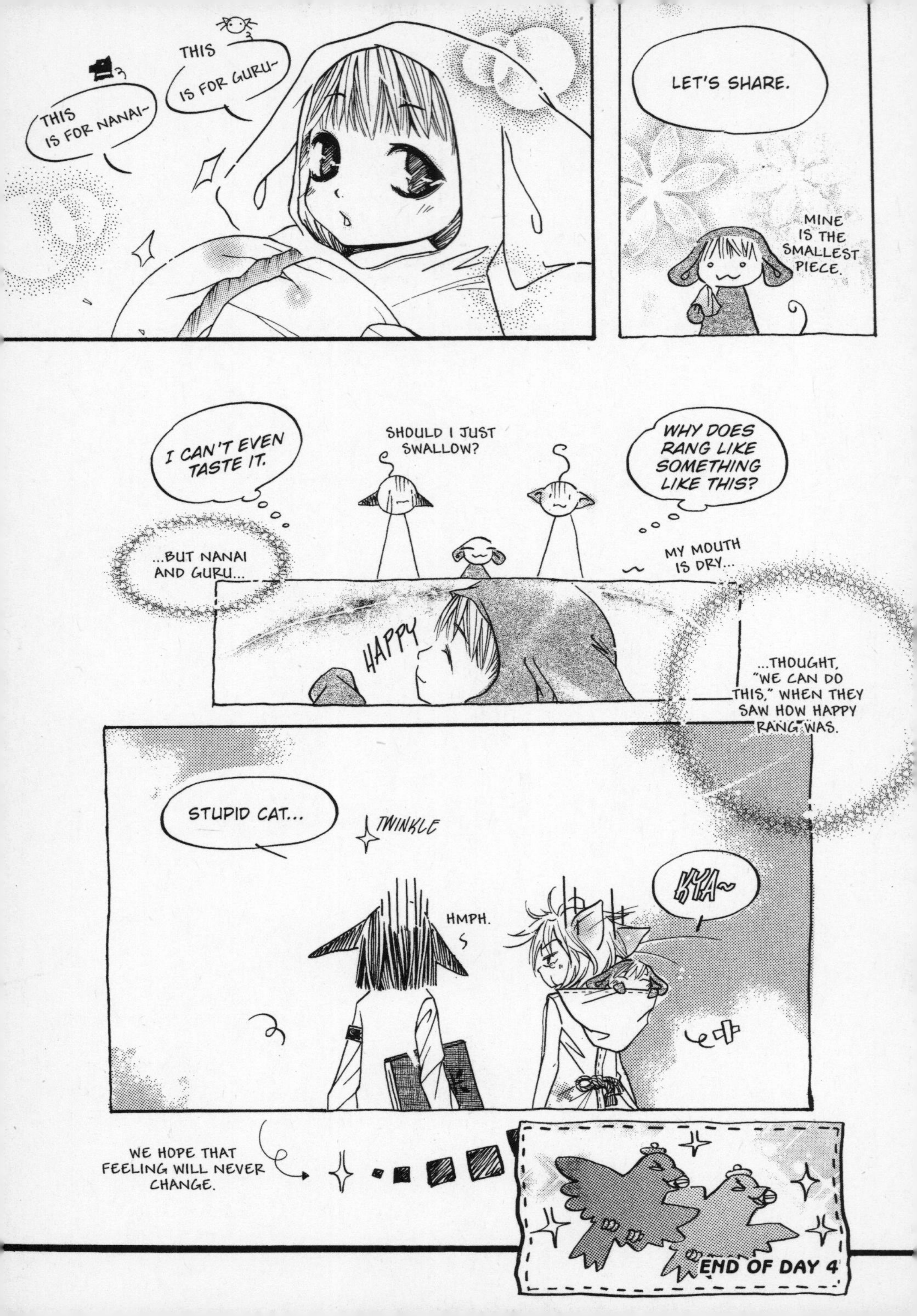
THIS IS FOR NANAI~
THIS IS FOR GURU~
LET'S SHARE.
MINE IS THE SMALLEST PIECE.
I CAN'T EVEN TASTE IT.
SHOULD I JUST SWALLOW?
WHY DOES RANG LIKE SOMETHING LIKE THIS?
...BUT NANAI AND GURU...
MY MOUTH IS DRY...
HAPPY
...THOUGHT, "WE CAN DO THIS," WHEN THEY SAW HOW HAPPY RANG WAS.
STUPID CAT...
TWINKLE
HMPH.
KYA~
WE HOPE THAT FEELING WILL NEVER CHANGE.
END OF DAY 4

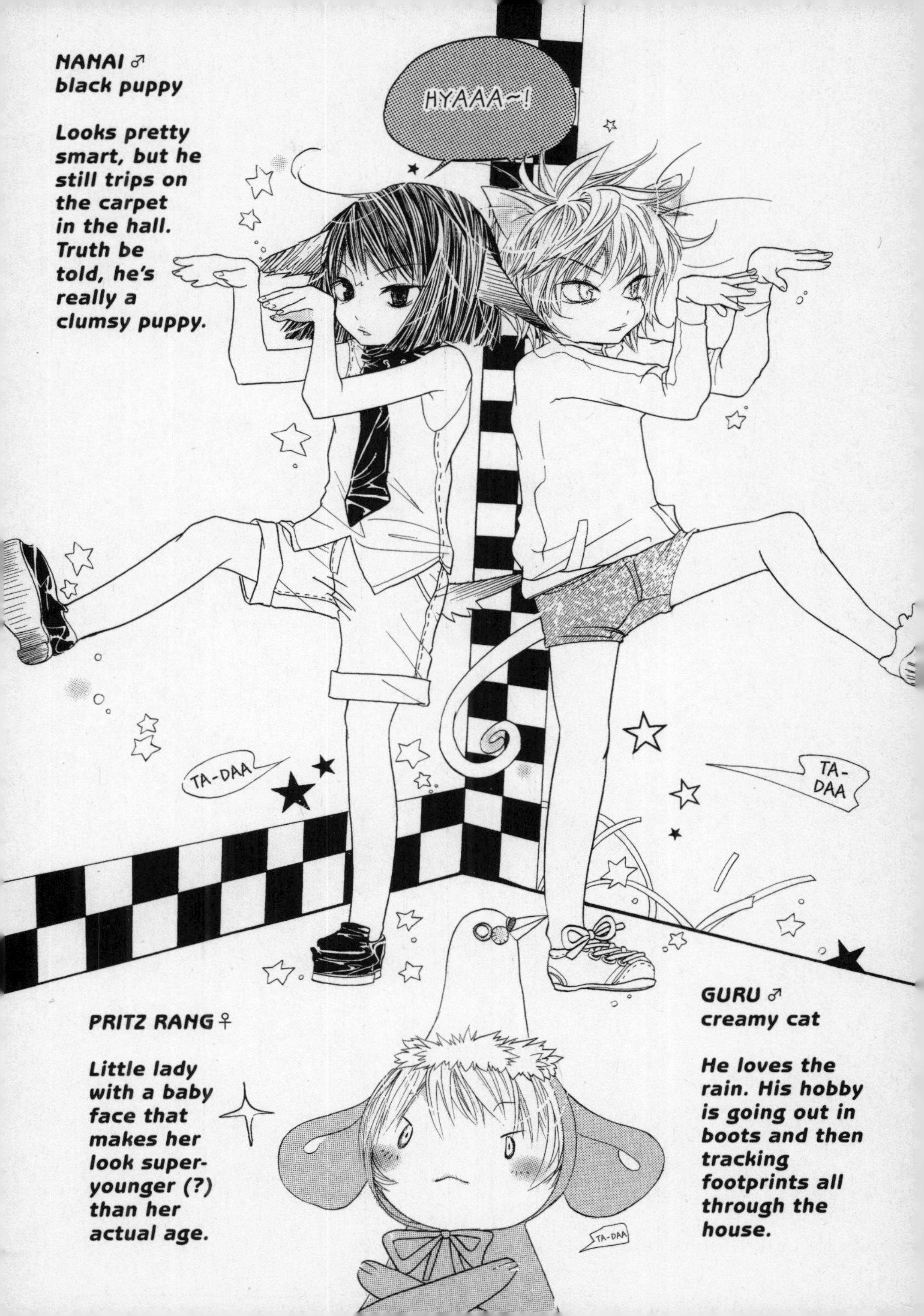
NANAI ♂
black puppy
Looks pretty smart, but he still trips on the carpet in the hall. Truth be told, he's really a clumsy puppy.
HYAAA~!
TA-DAA
TA-DAA
PRITZ RANG ♀
Little lady with a baby face that makes her look super-younger (?) than her actual age.
TA-DAA
GURU ♂
creamy cat
He loves the rain. His hobby is going out in boots and then tracking footprints all through the house.

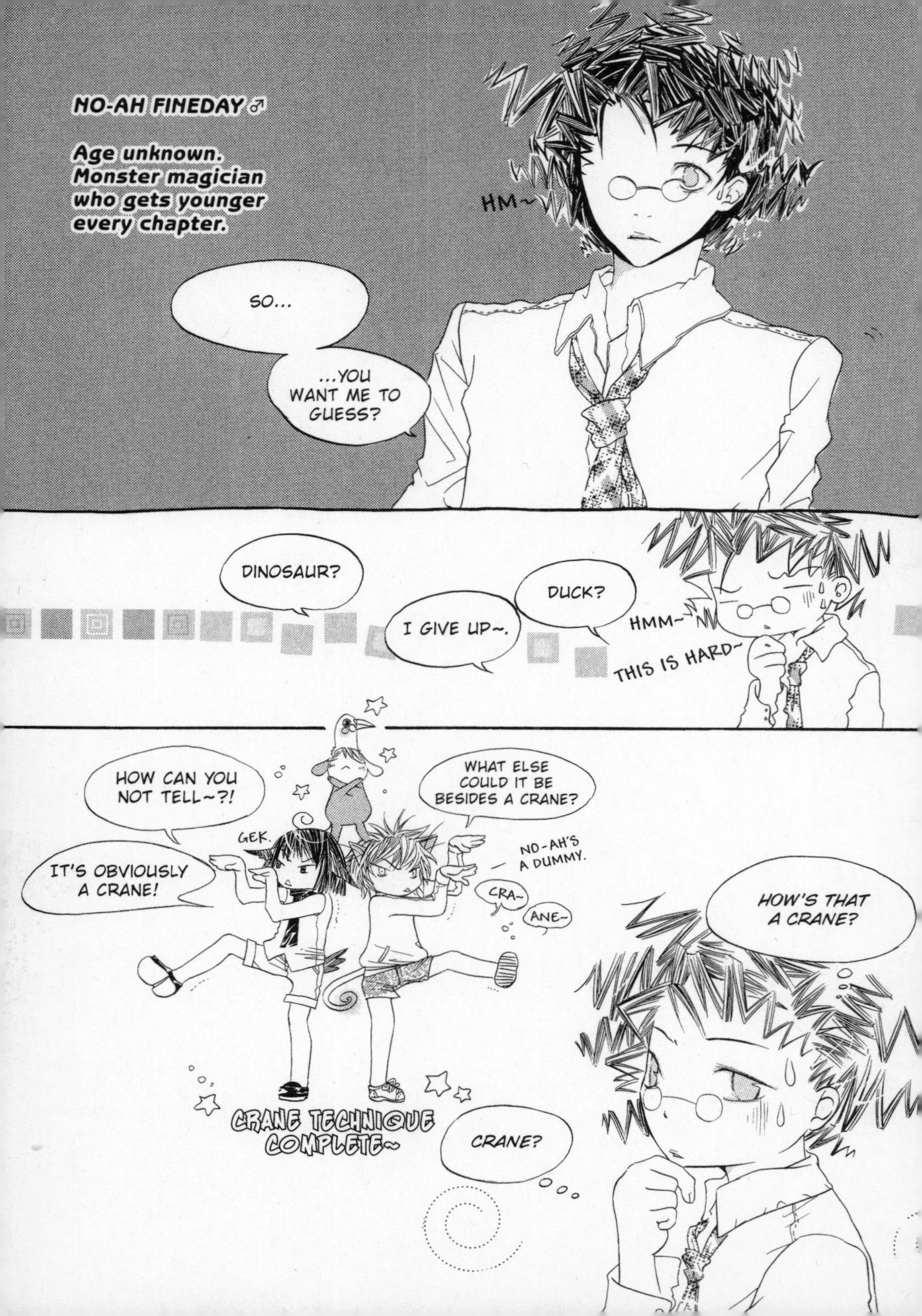
NO-AH FINEDAY ♂
Age unknown. Monster magician who gets younger every chapter.
HM~
SO...
...YOU WANT ME TO GUESS?
DINOSAUR?
I GIVE UP~.
DUCK?
HMM~
THIS IS HARD~
HOW CAN YOU NOT TELL~?!
GEK.
IT'S OBVIOUSLY A CRANE!
WHAT ELSE COULD IT BE BESIDES A CRANE?
NO-AH'S A DUMMY.
CRA~
ANE~
HOW'S THAT A CRANE?
CRANE TECHNIQUE COMPLETE~
CRANE?

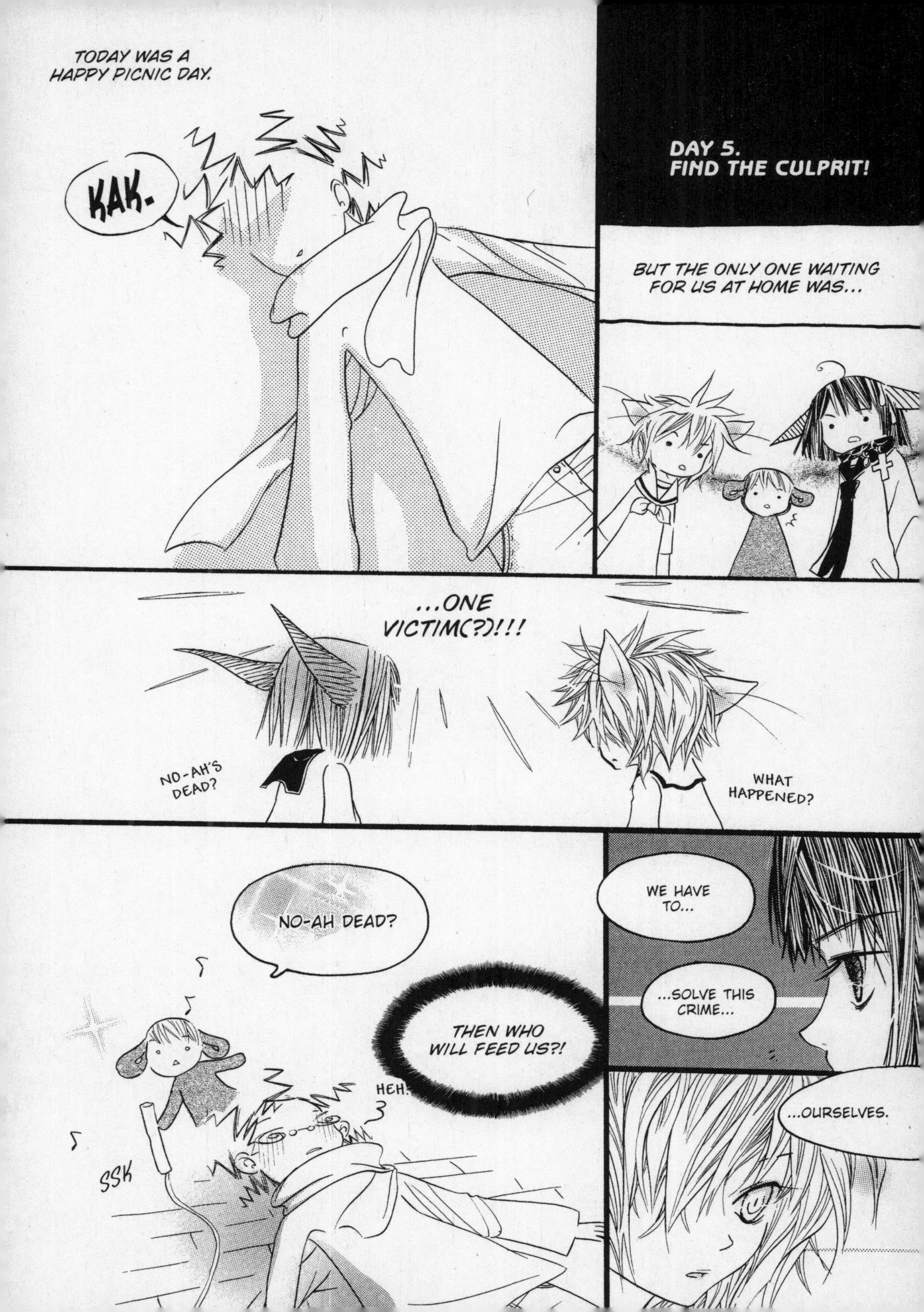
TODAY WAS A HAPPY PICNIC DAY.
KAK.
DAY 5. FIND THE CULPRIT!
BUT THE ONLY ONE WAITING FOR US AT HOME WAS...
...ONE VICTIM(?)!!!
NO-AH'S DEAD?
WHAT HAPPENED?
NO-AH DEAD?
THEN WHO WILL FEED US?!
HEH.
SSK
WE HAVE TO...
...SOLVE THIS CRIME...
...OURSELVES.

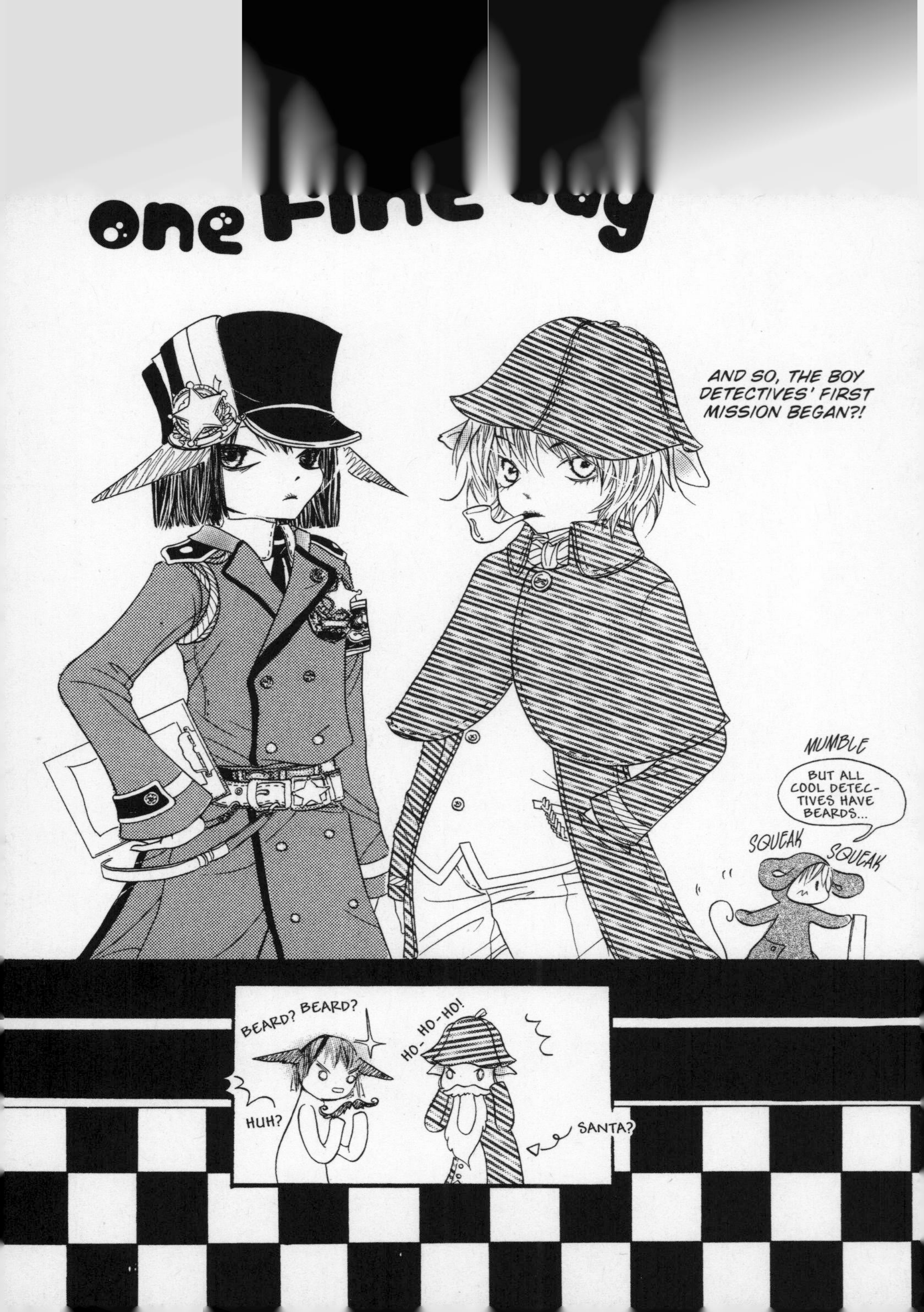
one [redacted]
AND SO, THE BOY DETECTIVES' FIRST MISSION BEGAN?!
MUMBLE
BUT ALL COOL DETEC-TIVES HAVE BEARDS...
SQUEAK
SQUEAK
BEARD? BEARD?
HUH?
HO-HO-HO!
SANTA?

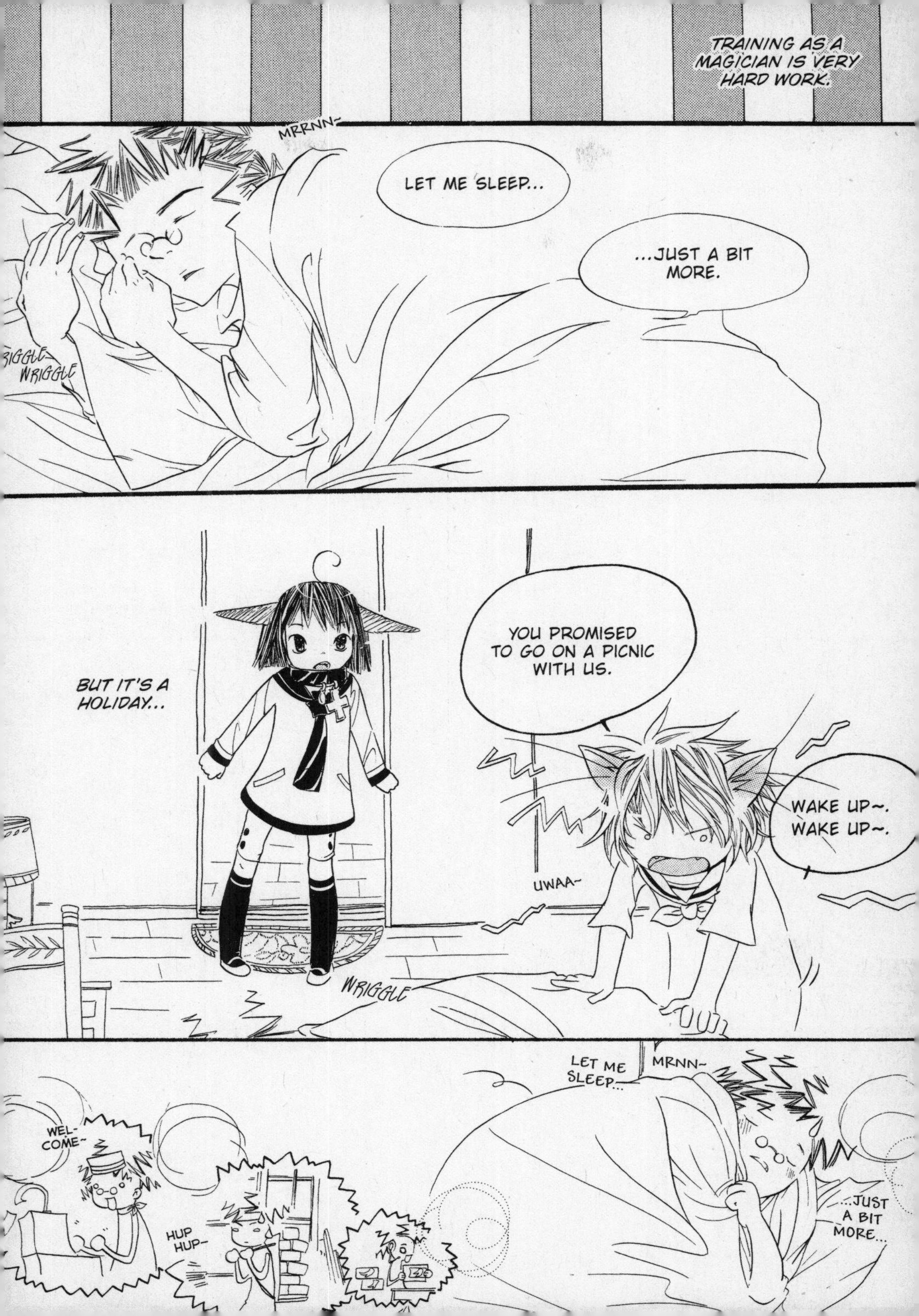
TRAINING AS A MAGICIAN IS VERY HARD WORK.
MRRNN~
LET ME SLEEP...
...JUST A BIT MORE.
RIGGLE WRIGGLE
BUT IT'S A HOLIDAY...
YOU PROMISED TO GO ON A PICNIC WITH US.
WAKE UP~. WAKE UP~.
UWAA~
WRIGGLE
WEL-COME~
HUP HUP~
LET ME SLEEP...
MRNN~
...JUST A BIT MORE...

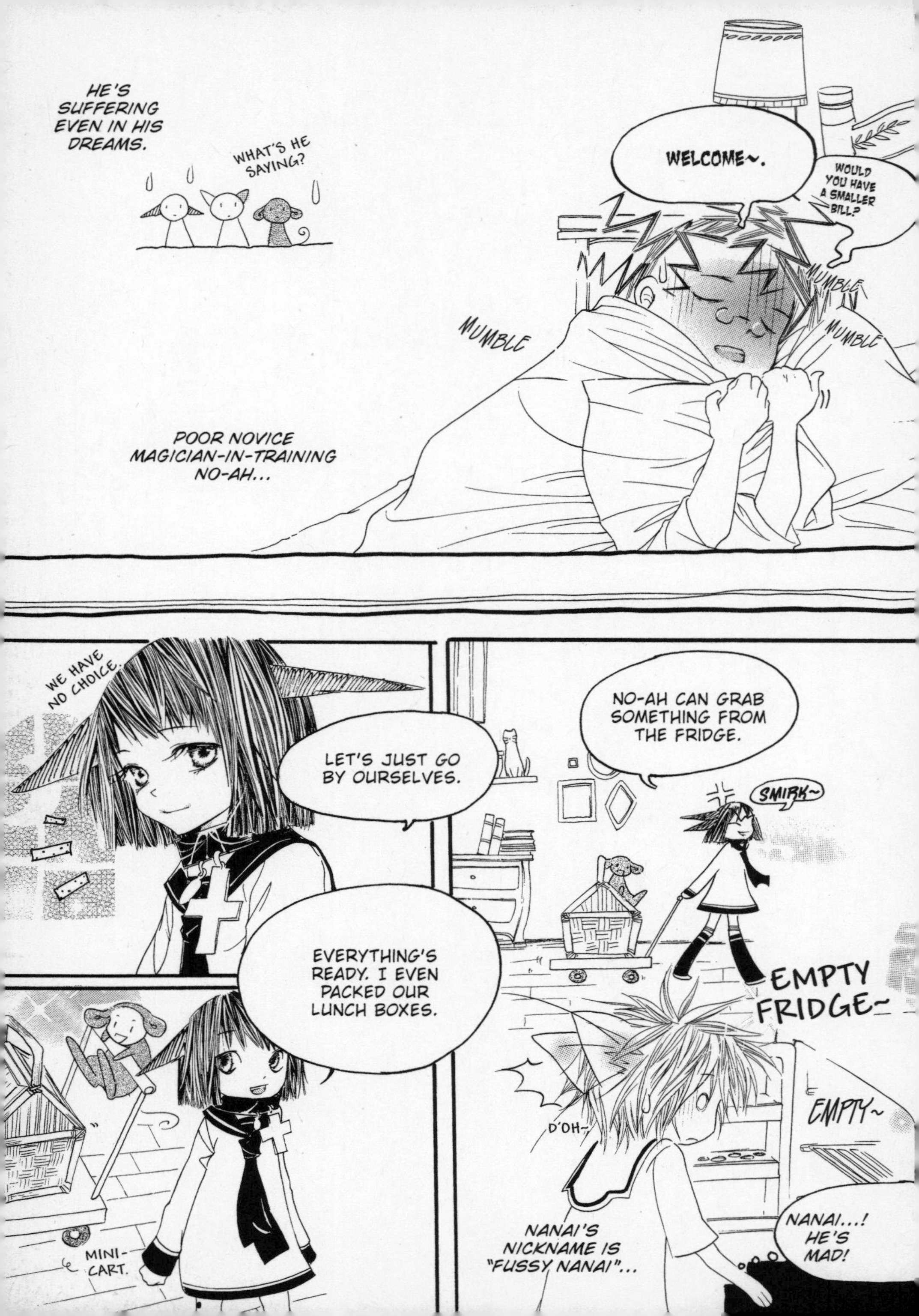
HE'S SUFFERING EVEN IN HIS DREAMS.
WHAT'S HE SAYING?
WELCOME~.
WOULD YOU HAVE A SMALLER BILL?
MUMBLE
MUMBLE
MUMBLE
POOR NOVICE MAGICIAN-IN-TRAINING NO-AH...
WE HAVE NO CHOICE...
LET'S JUST GO BY OURSELVES.
EVERYTHING'S READY. I EVEN PACKED OUR LUNCH BOXES.
MINI-CART.
NO-AH CAN GRAB SOMETHING FROM THE FRIDGE.
SMIRK~
EMPTY FRIDGE~
EMPTY~
D'OH~
NANAI'S NICKNAME IS "FUSSY NANAI"...
NANAI...! HE'S MAD!

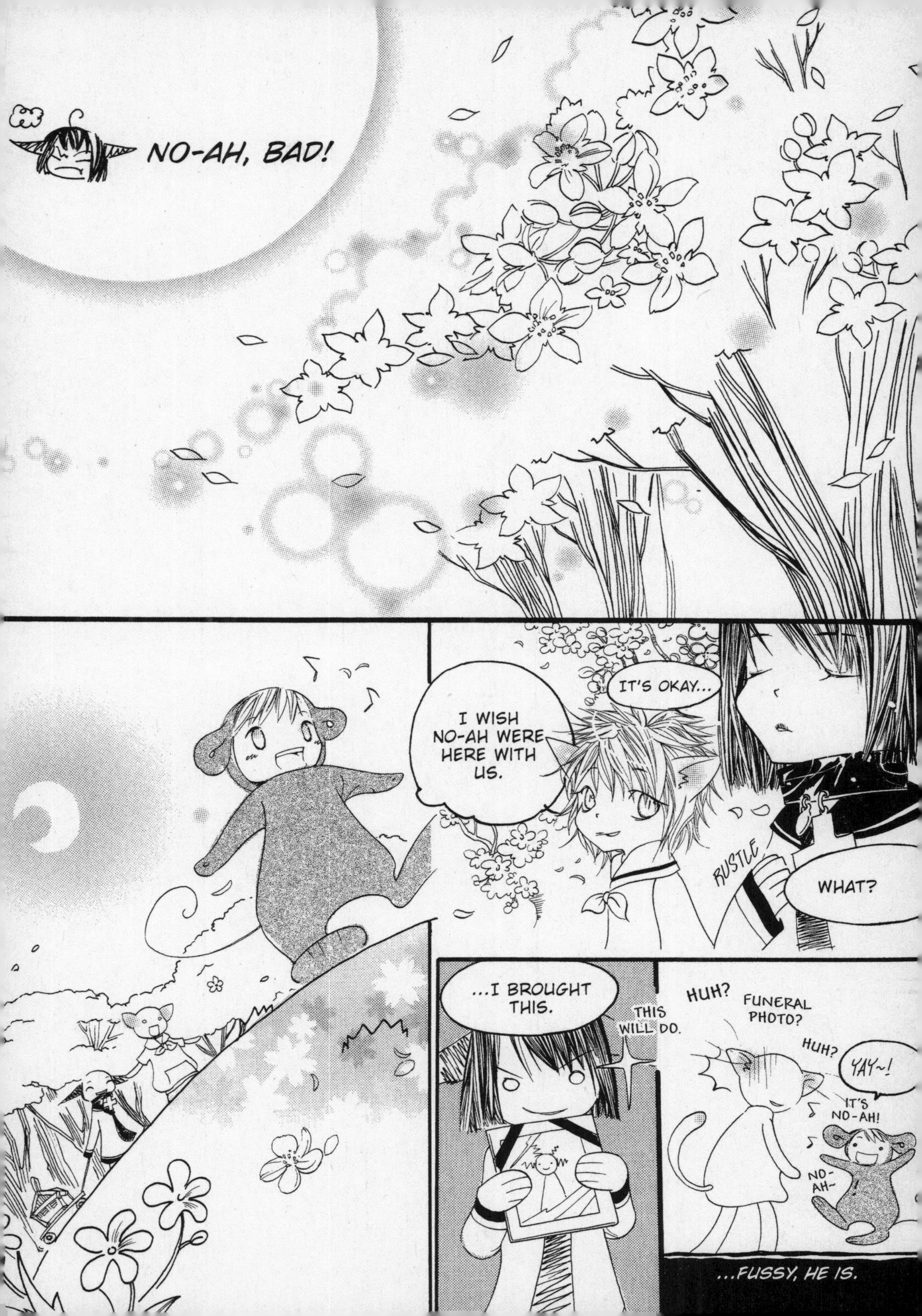
NO-AH, BAD!
I WISH NO-AH WERE HERE WITH US.
IT'S OKAY...
RUSTLE
WHAT?
...I BROUGHT THIS.
THIS WILL DO.
HUH?
FUNERAL PHOTO?
HUH?
YAY~!
IT'S NO-AH!
NO-AH~!
...FUSSY, HE IS.

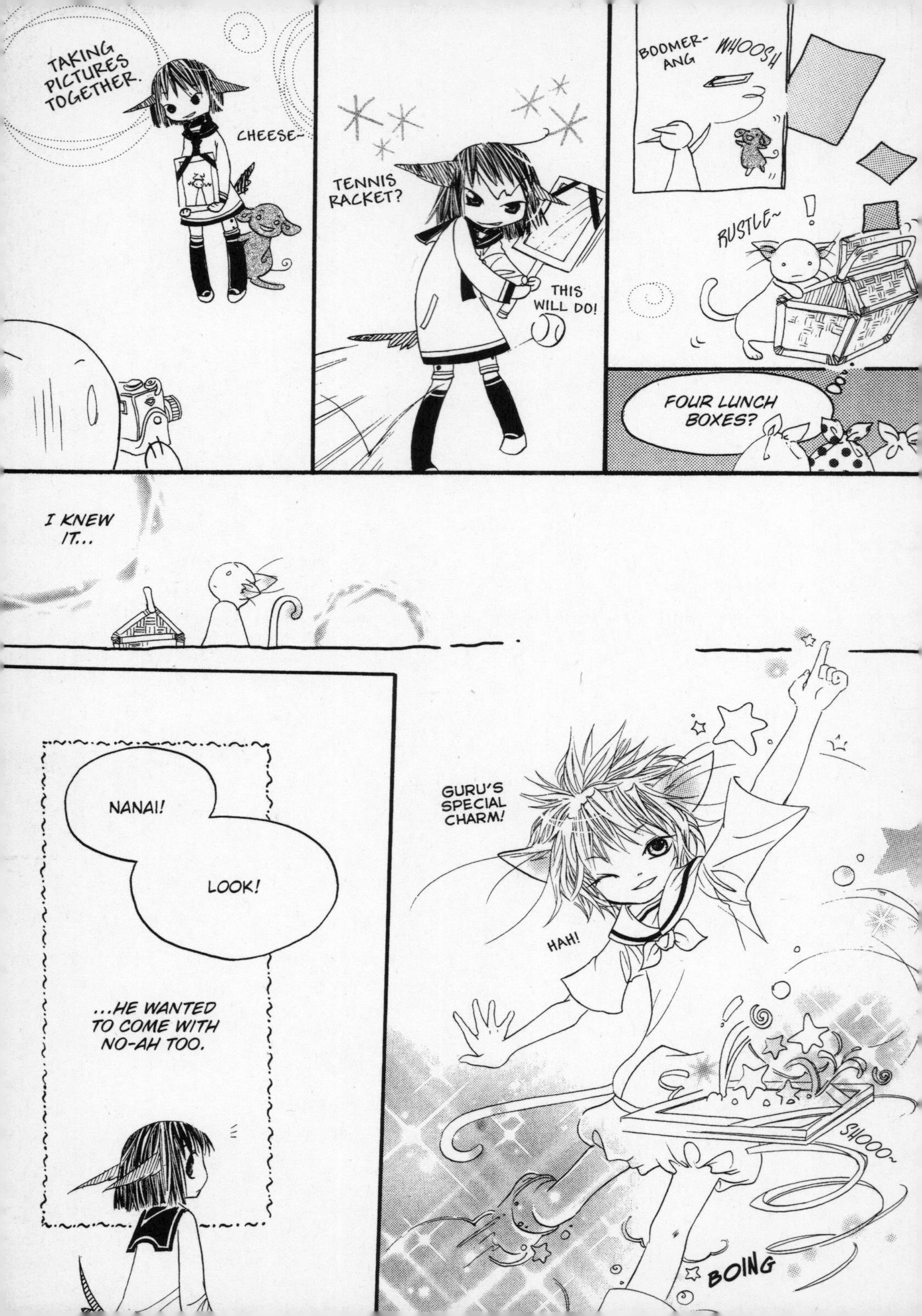

TAKING PICTURES TOGETHER.
CHEESE~
TENNIS RACKET?
THIS WILL DO!
BOOMER-ANG
WHOOSH
RUSTLE~
!
FOUR LUNCH BOXES?
I KNEW IT...
NANAI!
LOOK!
...HE WANTED TO COME WITH NO-AH TOO.
GURU'S SPECIAL CHARM!
HAH!
SHOOO~
BOING

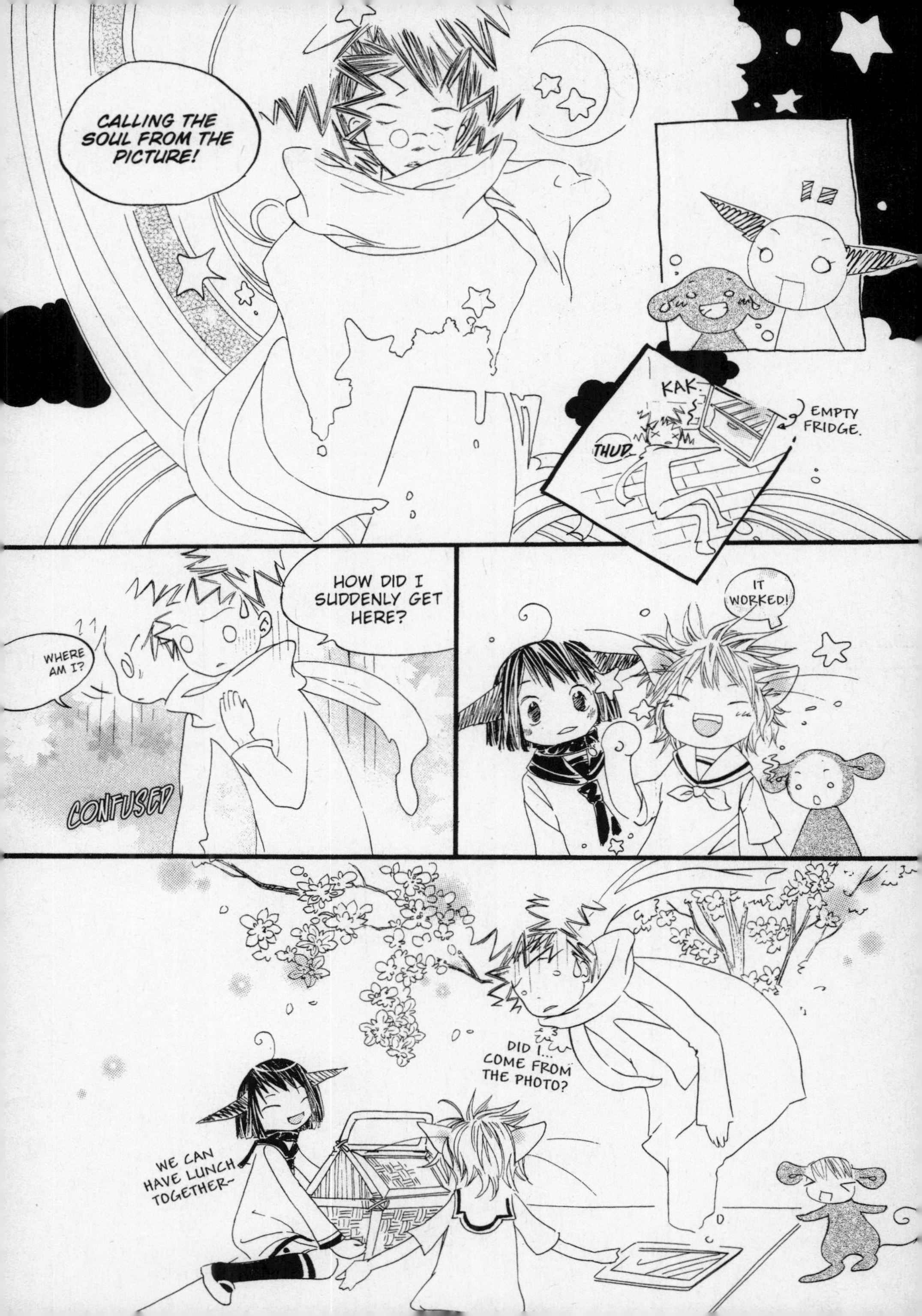
CALLING THE SOUL FROM THE PICTURE!
KAK.
EMPTY FRIDGE.
THUD
WHERE AM I?
HOW DID I SUDDENLY GET HERE?
CONFUSED
IT WORKED!
DID I... COME FROM THE PHOTO?
WE CAN HAVE LUNCH TOGETHER~

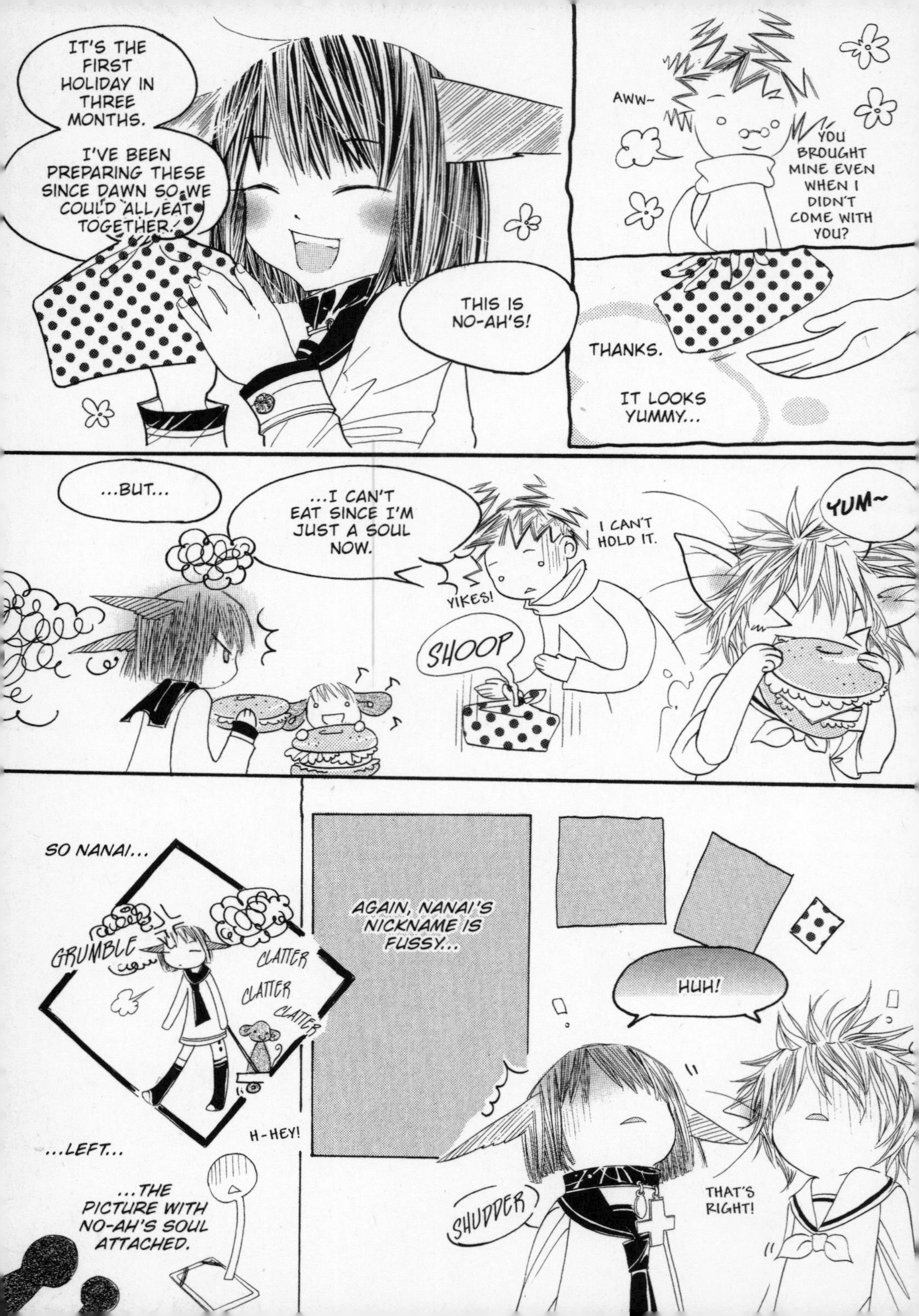
IT'S THE FIRST HOLIDAY IN THREE MONTHS.
I'VE BEEN PREPARING THESE SINCE DAWN SO WE COULD ALL EAT TOGETHER.
THIS IS NO-AH'S!
AWW~
YOU BROUGHT MINE EVEN WHEN I DIDN'T COME WITH YOU?
THANKS.
IT LOOKS YUMMY...
...BUT...
...I CAN'T EAT SINCE I'M JUST A SOUL NOW.
YIKES!
SHOOP
I CAN'T HOLD IT.
YUM~
SO NANAI...
GRUMBLE
CLATTER
CLATTER
CLATTER
...LEFT...
H-HEY!
...THE PICTURE WITH NO-AH'S SOUL ATTACHED.
AGAIN, NANAI'S NICKNAME IS FUSSY...
HUH!
SHUDDER
THAT'S RIGHT!

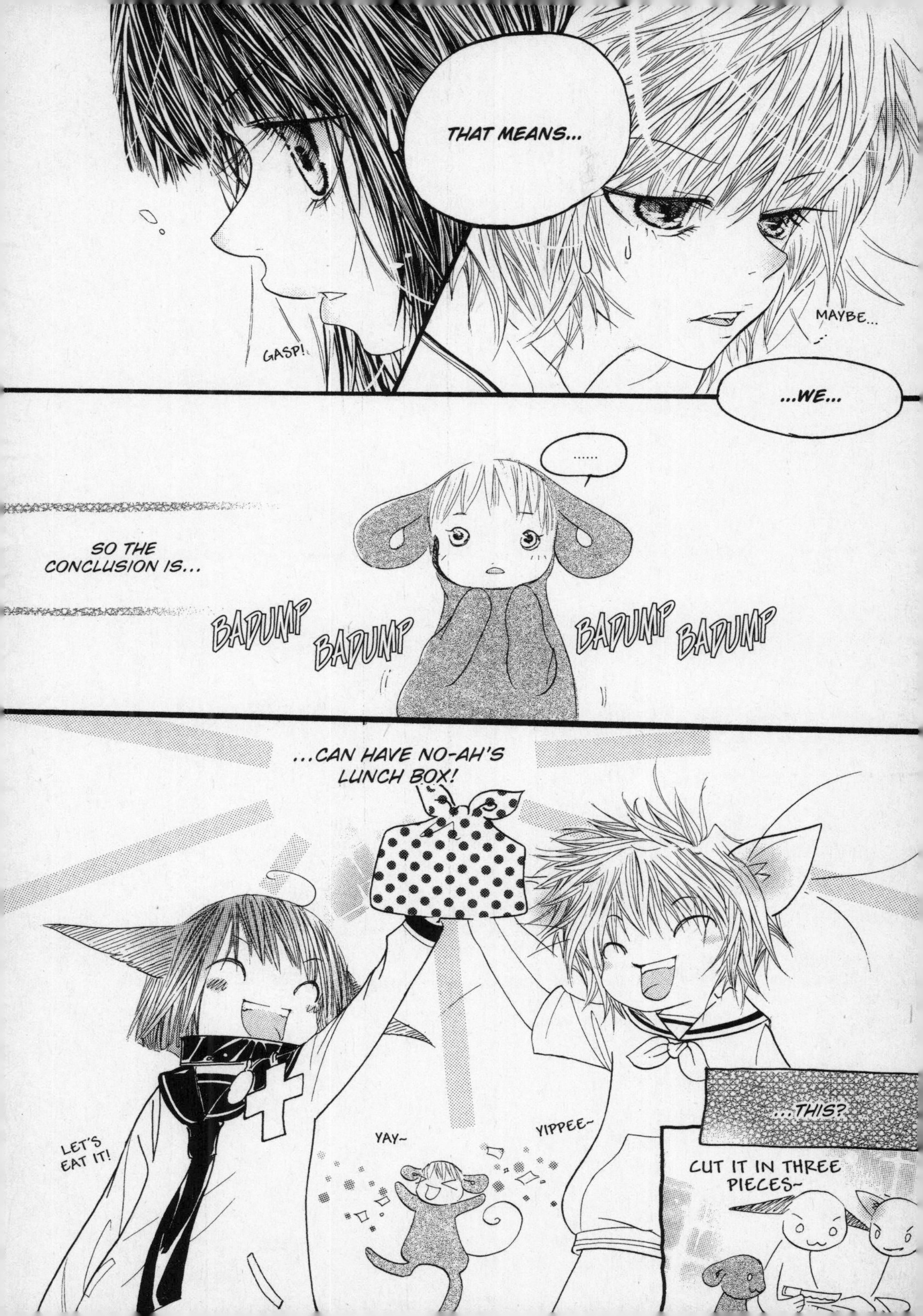
THAT MEANS...
GASP!
MAYBE...
...WE...
......
SO THE CONCLUSION IS...
BADUMP
BADUMP
BADUMP
BADUMP
...CAN HAVE NO-AH'S LUNCH BOX!
LET'S EAT IT!
YAY~
YIPPEE~
...THIS?
CUT IT IN THREE PIECES~

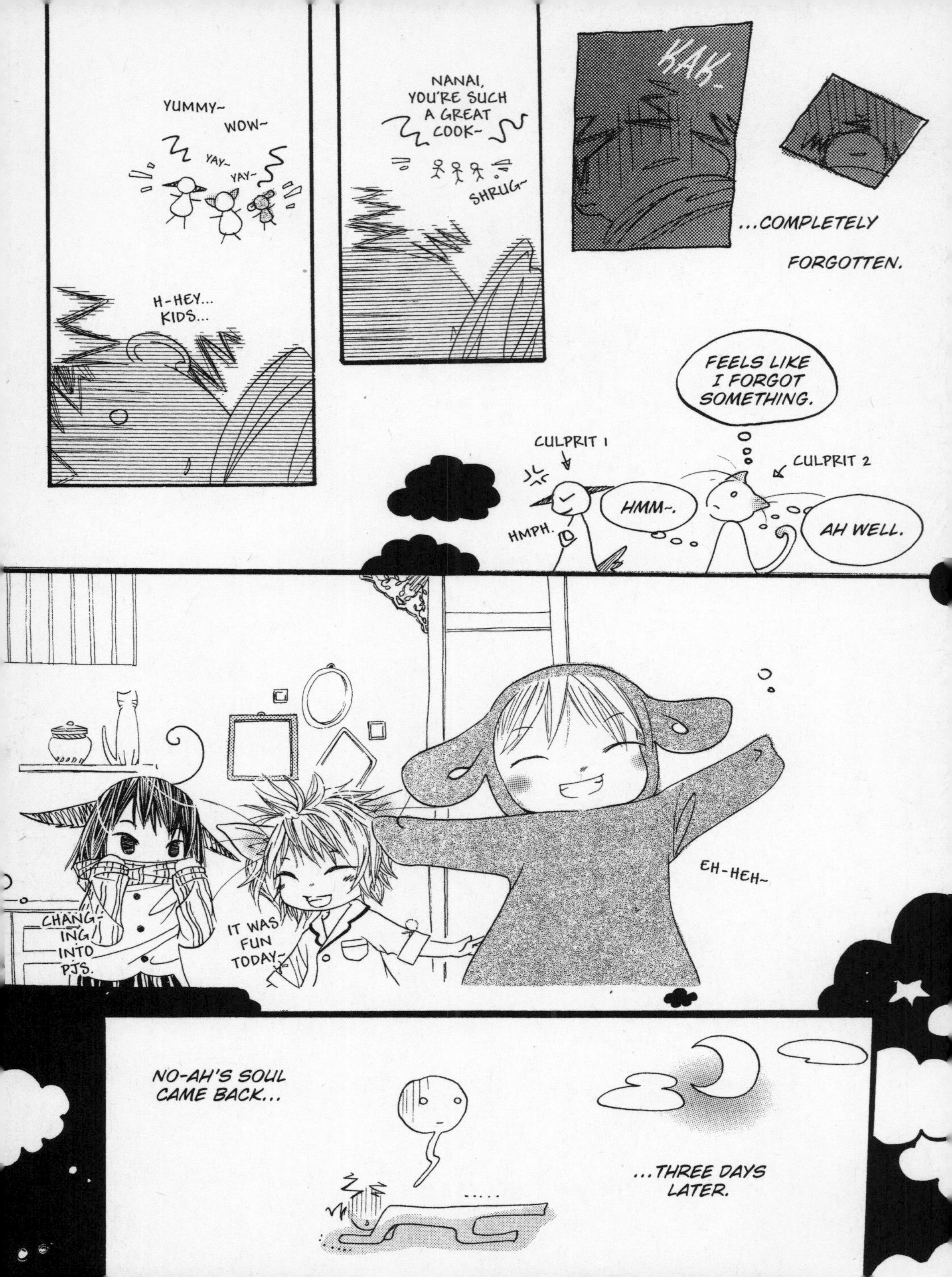
YUMMY~
WOW~
YAY~
YAY~
H-HEY... KIDS...
NANAI, YOU'RE SUCH A GREAT COOK~
SHRUG~
KAK-
...COMPLETELY FORGOTTEN.
CULPRIT 1
HMPH.
HMM~.
FEELS LIKE I FORGOT SOMETHING.
CULPRIT 2
AH WELL.
CHANG-ING INTO PJS.
IT WAS FUN TODAY~
EH-HEH~
NO-AH'S SOUL CAME BACK...
.....
...THREE DAYS LATER.

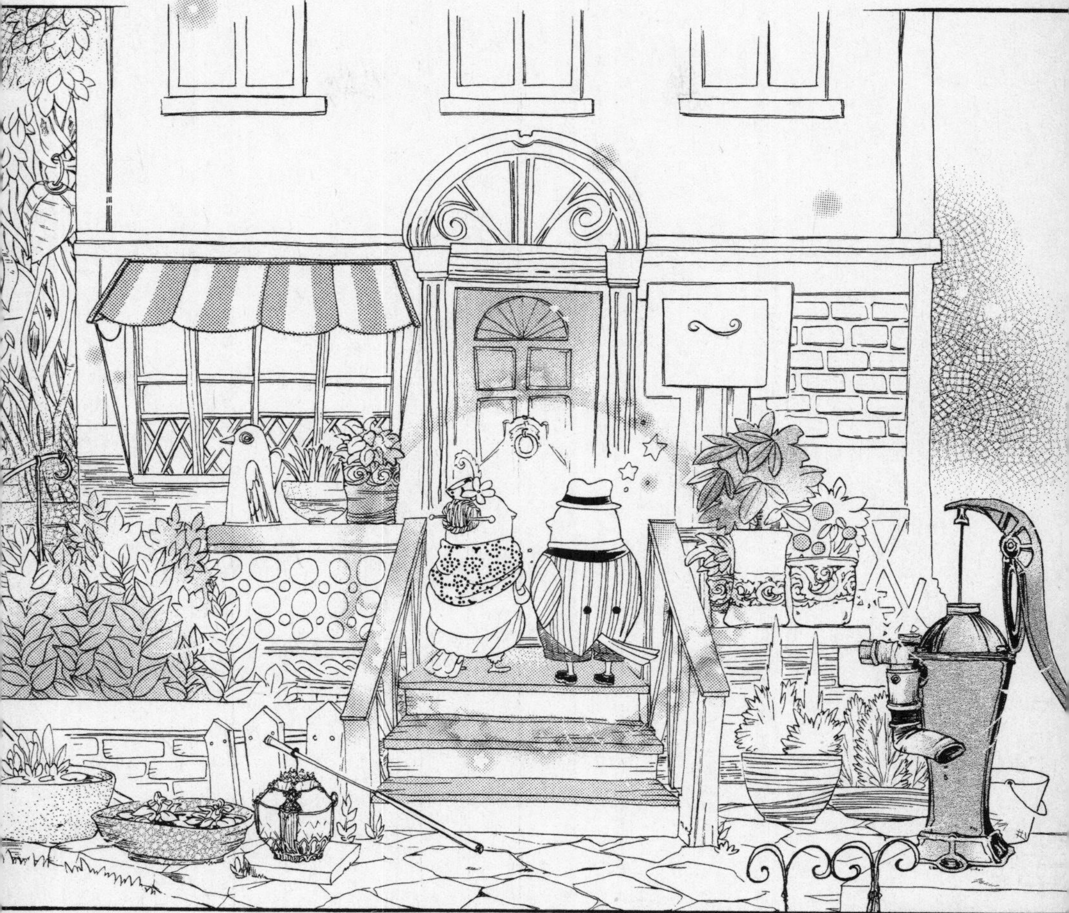

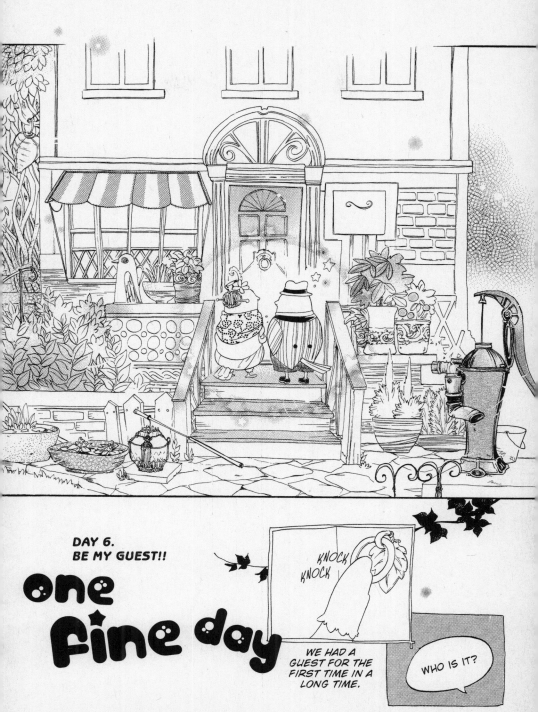

**DAY 6.**
**BE MY GUEST!!**

# one fine day

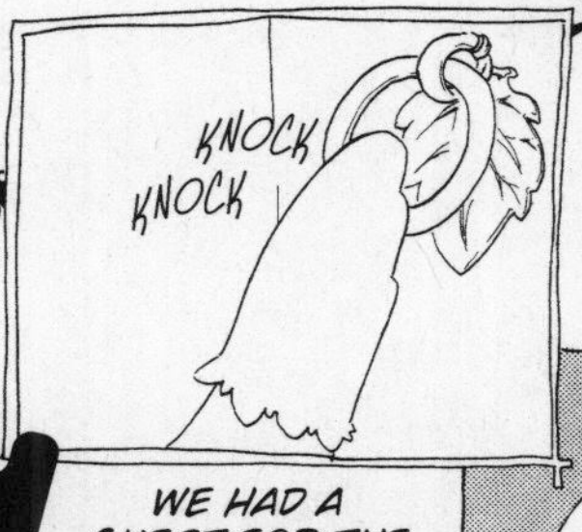
KNOCK
KNOCK

WE HAD A GUEST FOR THE FIRST TIME IN A LONG TIME.

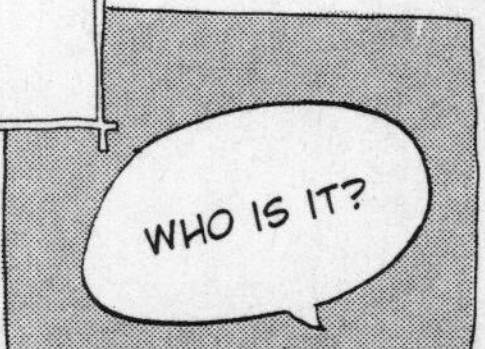
WHO IS IT?

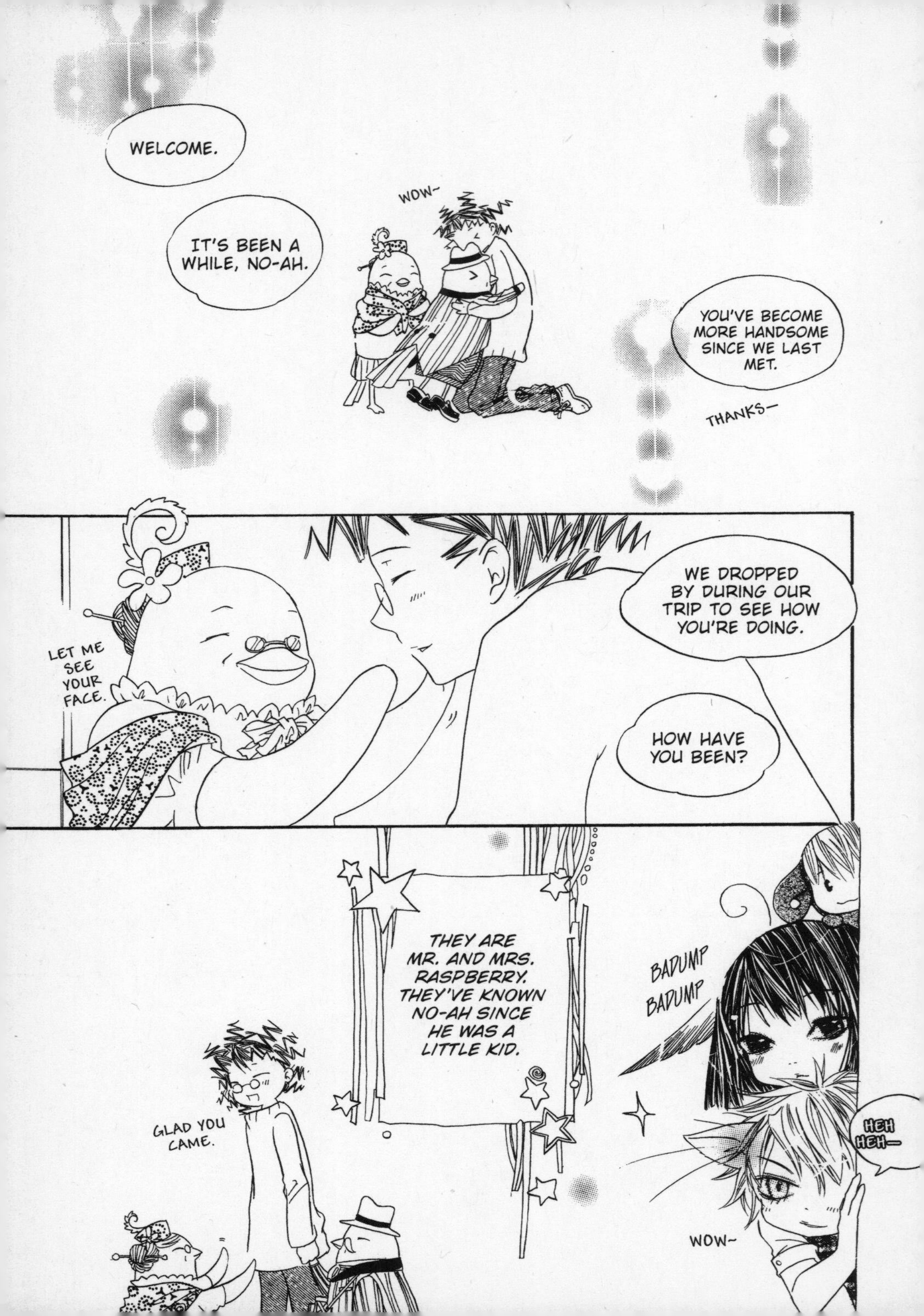
WELCOME.
IT'S BEEN A WHILE, NO-AH.
WOW~
YOU'VE BECOME MORE HANDSOME SINCE WE LAST MET.
THANKS~
LET ME SEE YOUR FACE.
WE DROPPED BY DURING OUR TRIP TO SEE HOW YOU'RE DOING.
HOW HAVE YOU BEEN?
GLAD YOU CAME.
THEY ARE MR. AND MRS. RASPBERRY. THEY'VE KNOWN NO-AH SINCE HE WAS A LITTLE KID.
BADUMP
BADUMP
HEH HEH~
WOW~

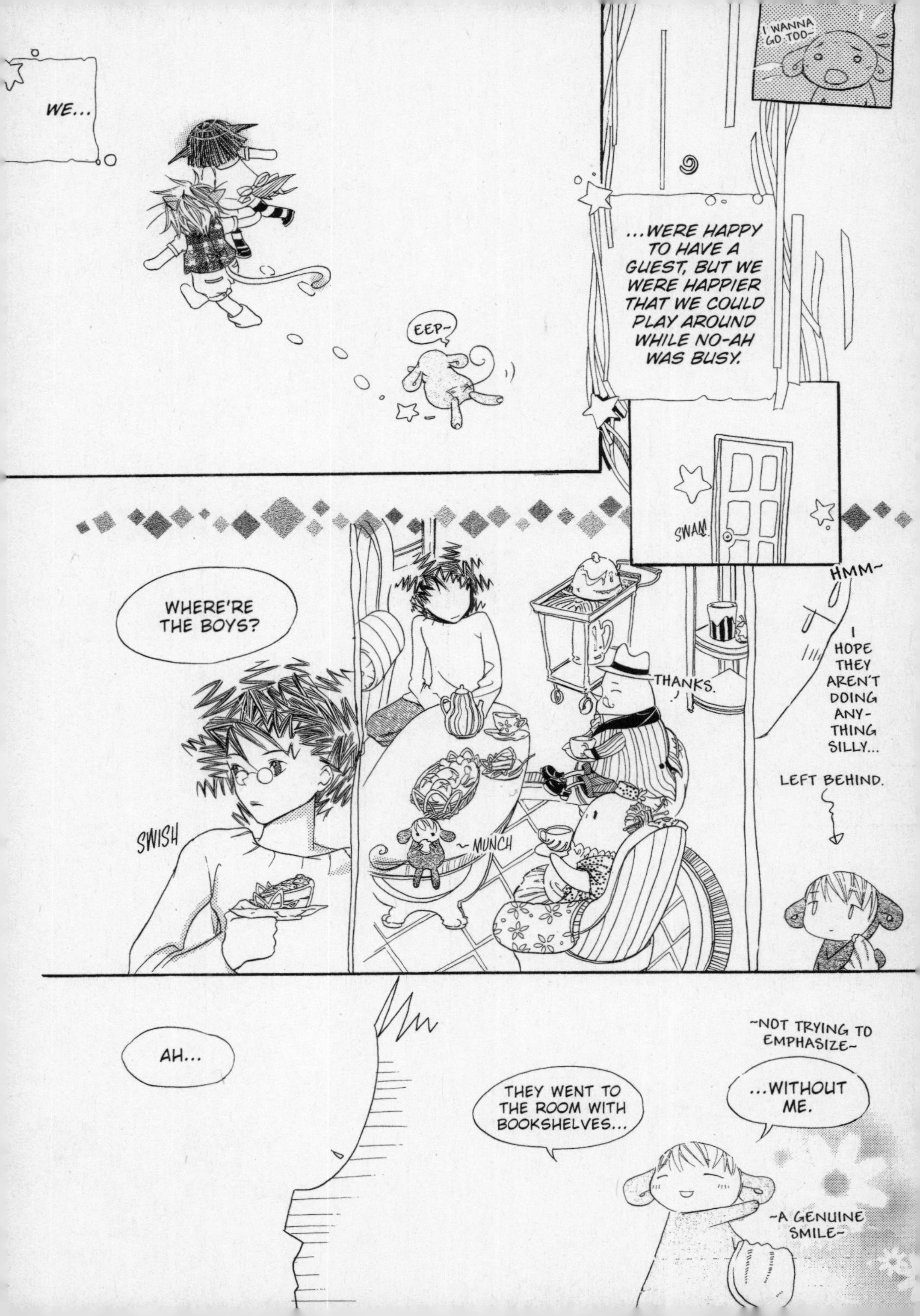
WE...
EEP~
I WANNA GO TOO~
...WERE HAPPY TO HAVE A GUEST, BUT WE WERE HAPPIER THAT WE COULD PLAY AROUND WHILE NO-AH WAS BUSY.
SWAM
WHERE'RE THE BOYS?
SWISH
~MUNCH
THANKS.
HMM~
I HOPE THEY AREN'T DOING ANY-THING SILLY...
LEFT BEHIND.
AH...
THEY WENT TO THE ROOM WITH BOOKSHELVES...
~NOT TRYING TO EMPHASIZE~
...WITHOUT ME.
~A GENUINE SMILE~

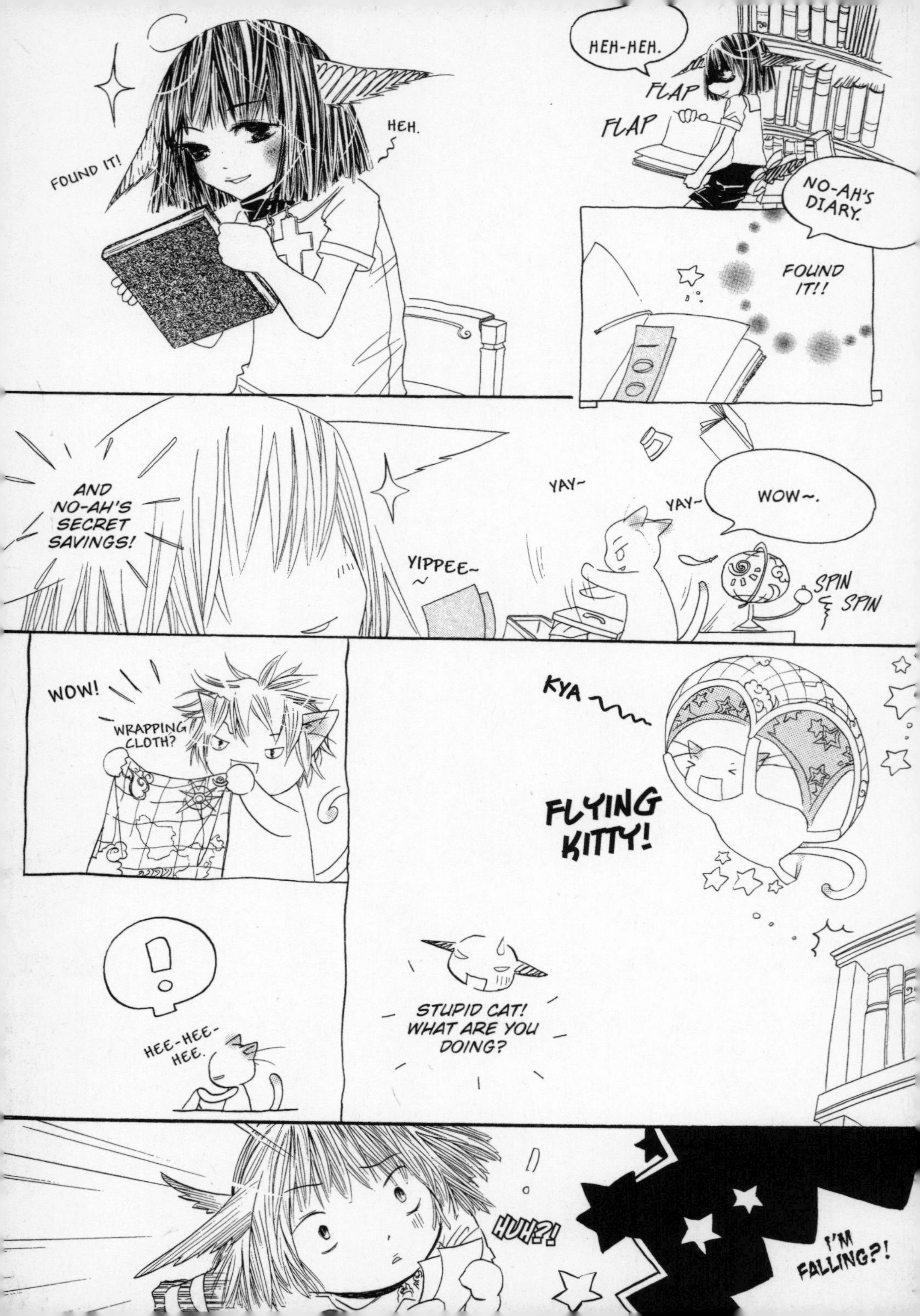
FOUND IT!
HEH.
HEH-HEH.
FLAP
FLAP
NO-AH'S DIARY.
FOUND IT!!
AND NO-AH'S SECRET SAVINGS!
YIPPEE~
YAY~
YAY~
WOW~.
SPIN SPIN
WOW!
WRAPPING CLOTH?
KYA
FLYING KITTY!
!
HEE-HEE-HEE.
STUPID CAT! WHAT ARE YOU DOING?
!
HUH?!
I'M FALLING?!

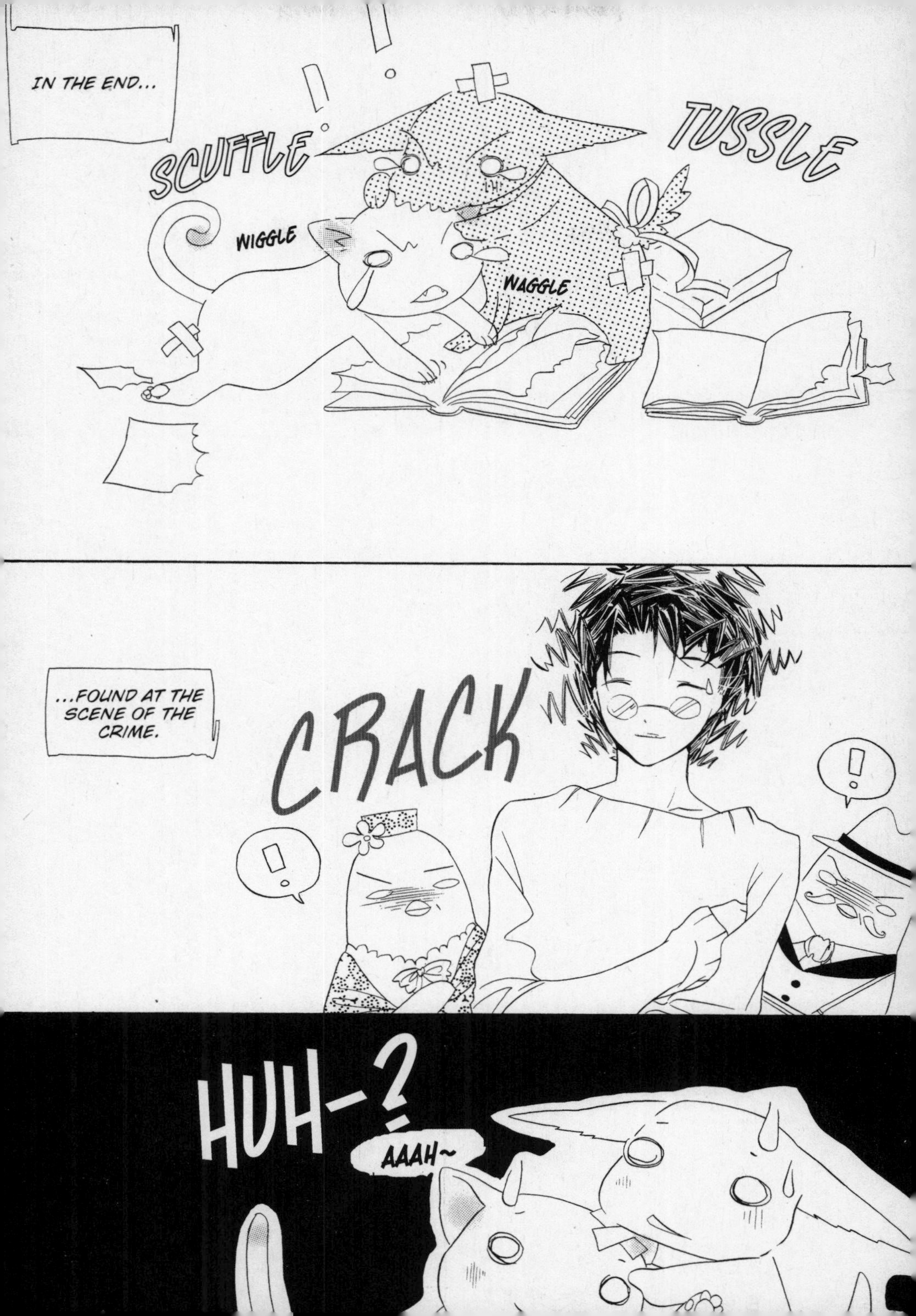
IN THE END...
SCUFFLE
TUSSLE
WIGGLE
WAGGLE
...FOUND AT THE SCENE OF THE CRIME.
CRACK
!
!
HUH-?
AAAH~

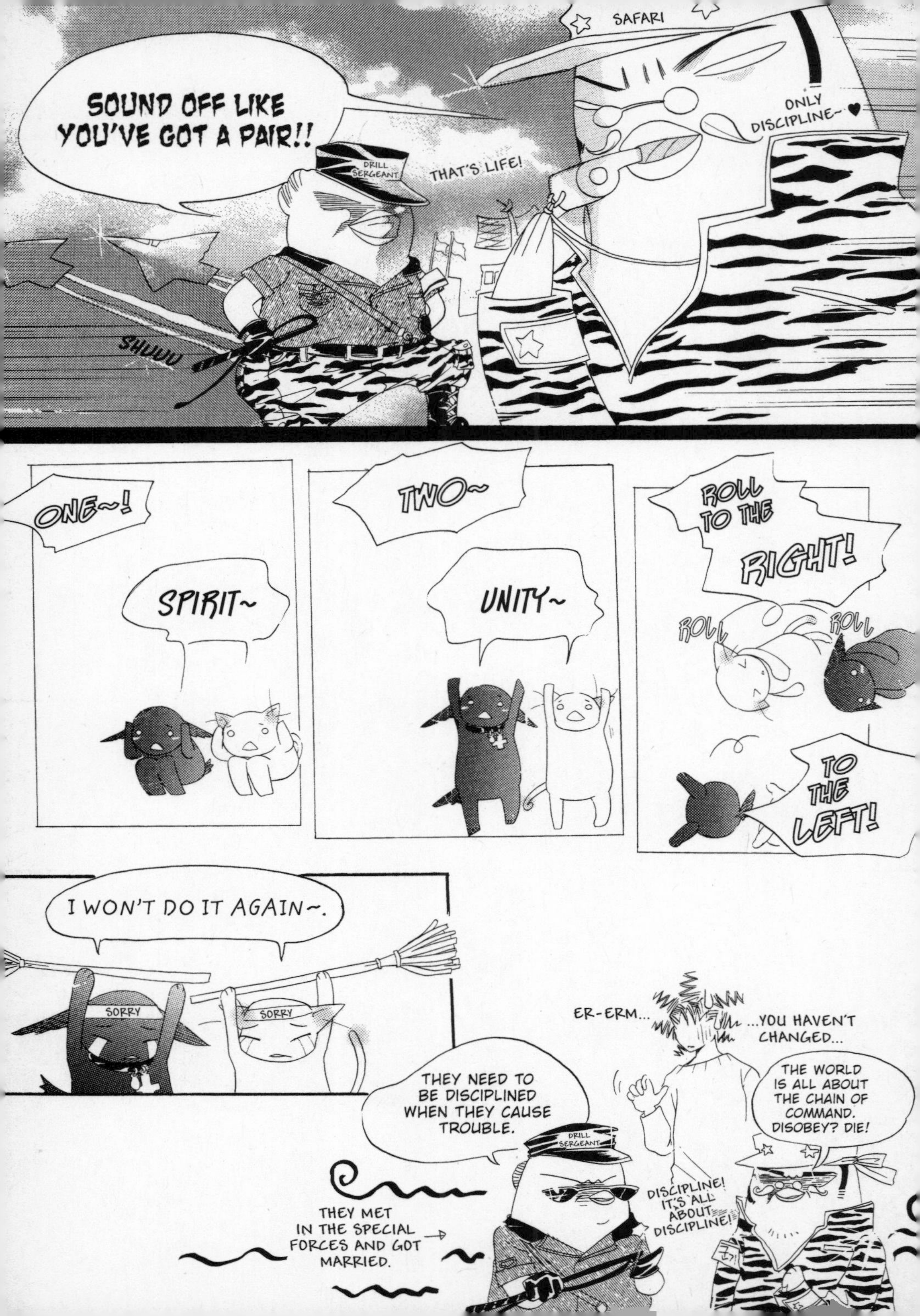
SAFARI
SOUND OFF LIKE YOU'VE GOT A PAIR!!
DRILL SERGEANT
THAT'S LIFE!
ONLY DISCIPLINE~♥
SHUUU
ONE~!
SPIRIT~
TWO~
UNITY~
ROLL TO THE RIGHT!
ROLL
ROLL
TO THE LEFT!
I WON'T DO IT AGAIN~.
SORRY
SORRY
ER-ERM...
...YOU HAVEN'T CHANGED...
THEY NEED TO BE DISCIPLINED WHEN THEY CAUSE TROUBLE.
THE WORLD IS ALL ABOUT THE CHAIN OF COMMAND. DISOBEY? DIE!
DRILL SERGEANT
DISCIPLINE! IT'S ALL ABOUT DISCIPLINE!
THEY MET IN THE SPECIAL FORCES AND GOT MARRIED.

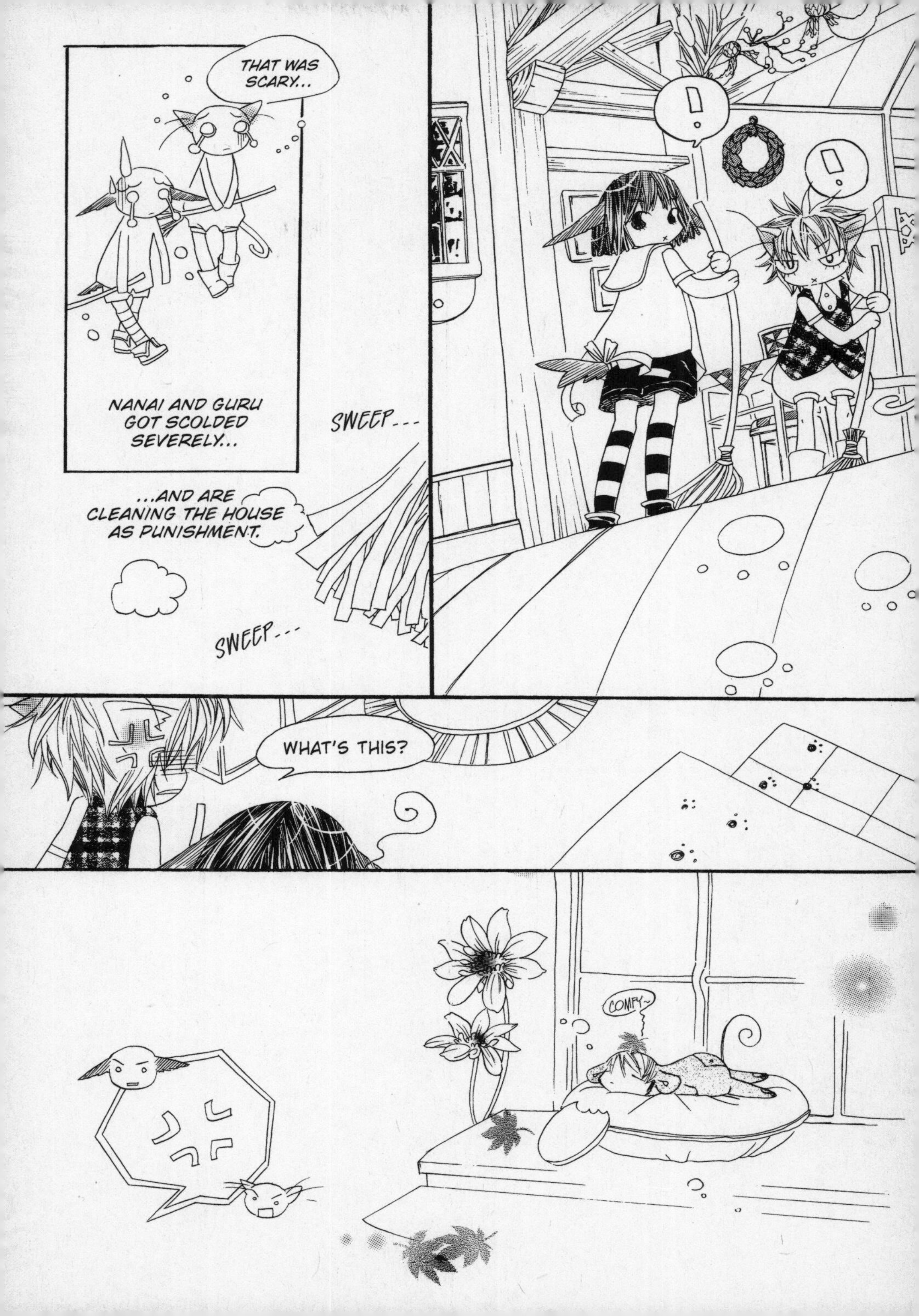
THAT WAS SCARY...
NANAI AND GURU GOT SCOLDED SEVERELY...
...AND ARE CLEANING THE HOUSE AS PUNISHMENT.
SWEEP...
SWEEP...
!
!
WHAT'S THIS?
COMFY~

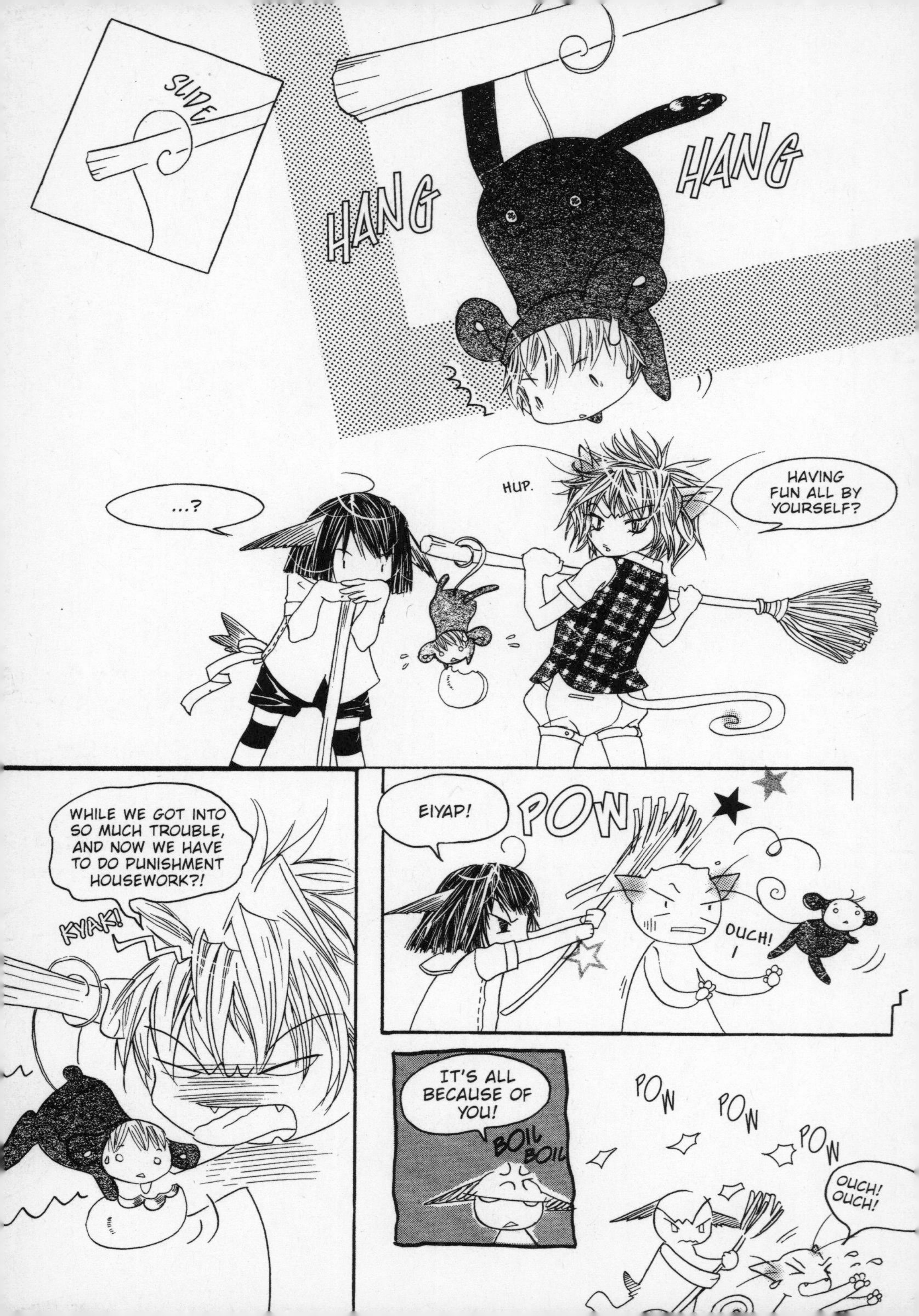

SLIDE
HANG
HANG
...?
HUP.
HAVING FUN ALL BY YOURSELF?
WHILE WE GOT INTO SO MUCH TROUBLE, AND NOW WE HAVE TO DO PUNISHMENT HOUSEWORK?!
KYAK!
EIYAP!
POW
OUCH!
IT'S ALL BECAUSE OF YOU!
BOIL BOIL
POW
POW
POW
OUCH! OUCH!

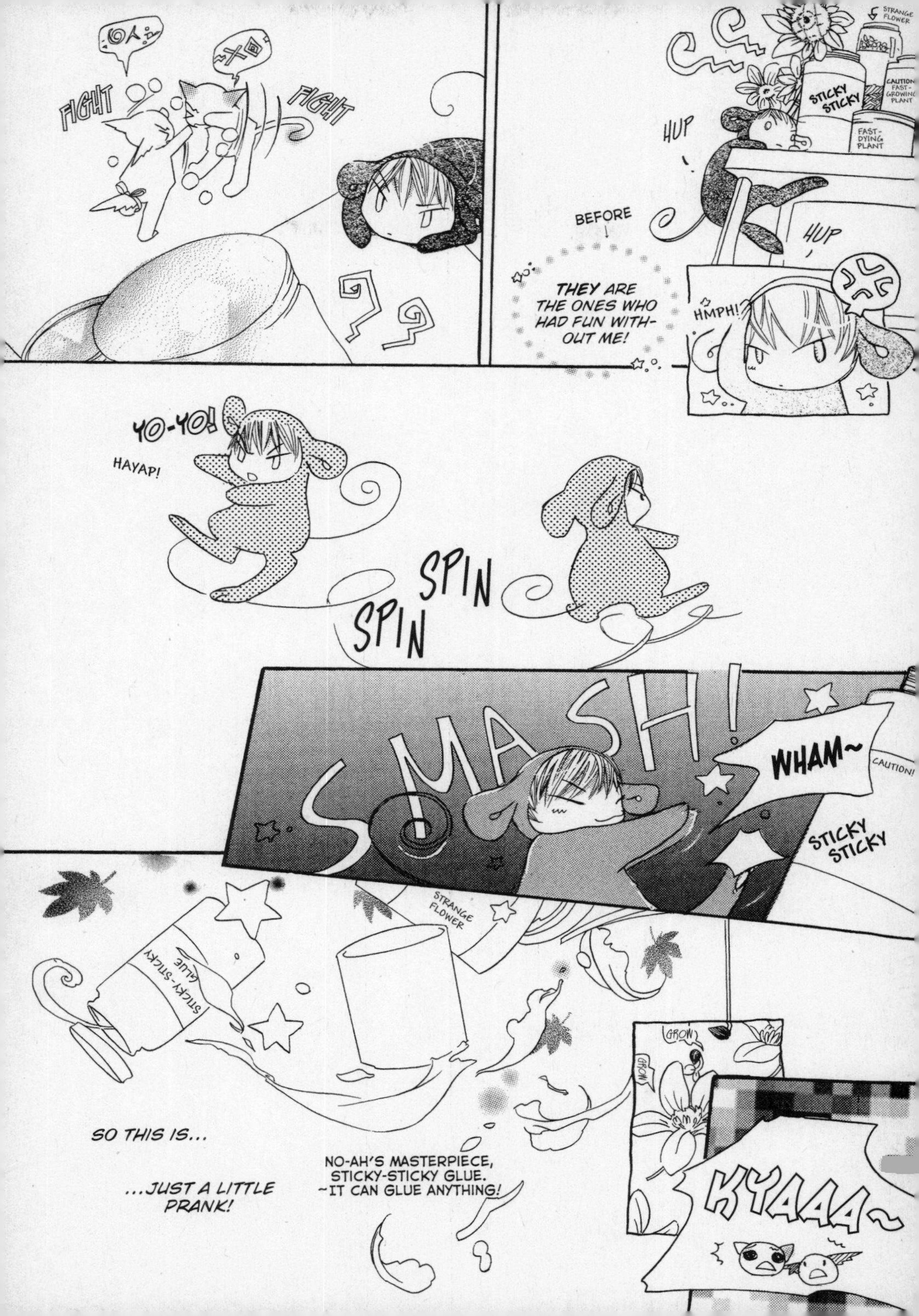
FIGHT
FIGHT
STRANGE FLOWER
STICKY STICKY
CAUTION FAST-GROWING PLANT
FAST-DYING PLANT
HUP
HUP
BEFORE
THEY ARE THE ONES WHO HAD FUN WITH-OUT ME!
HMPH!
YO-YO!
HAYAP!
SPIN
SPIN
SMASH!
WHAM~
CAUTION!
STICKY STICKY
STRANGE FLOWER
STICKY-STICKY GLUE
SO THIS IS...
...JUST A LITTLE PRANK!
NO-AH'S MASTERPIECE, STICKY-STICKY GLUE. ~IT CAN GLUE ANYTHING!
GROW
GROW
KYAAA~

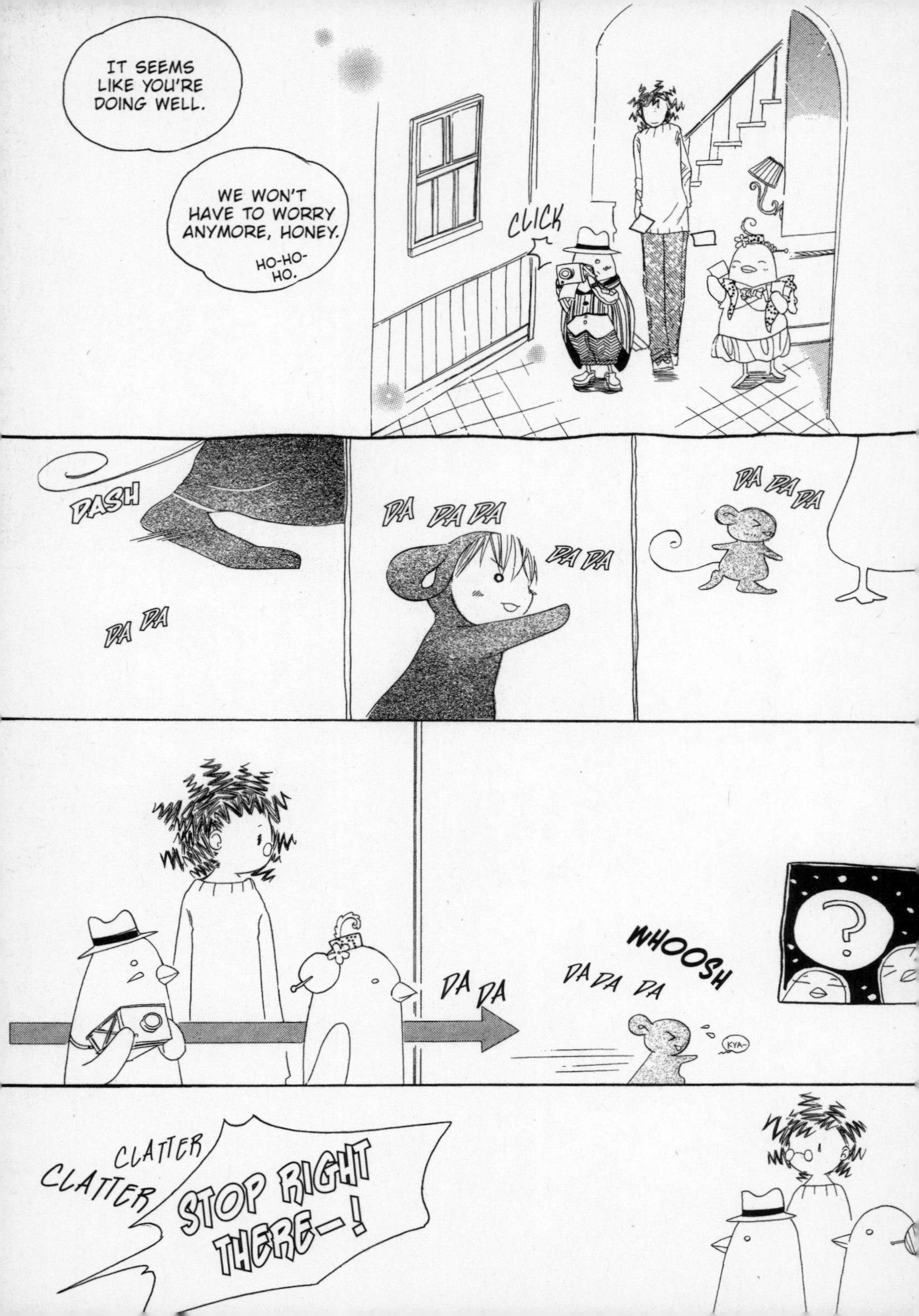
CLICK
IT SEEMS LIKE YOU'RE DOING WELL.
WE WON'T HAVE TO WORRY ANYMORE, HONEY.
HO-HO-HO.
DA DA DA
DA DA DA
DA DA
DASH
DA DA
?
WHOOSH
DA DA DA
KYA-
DA DA
STOP RIGHT THERE-!
CLATTER
CLATTER

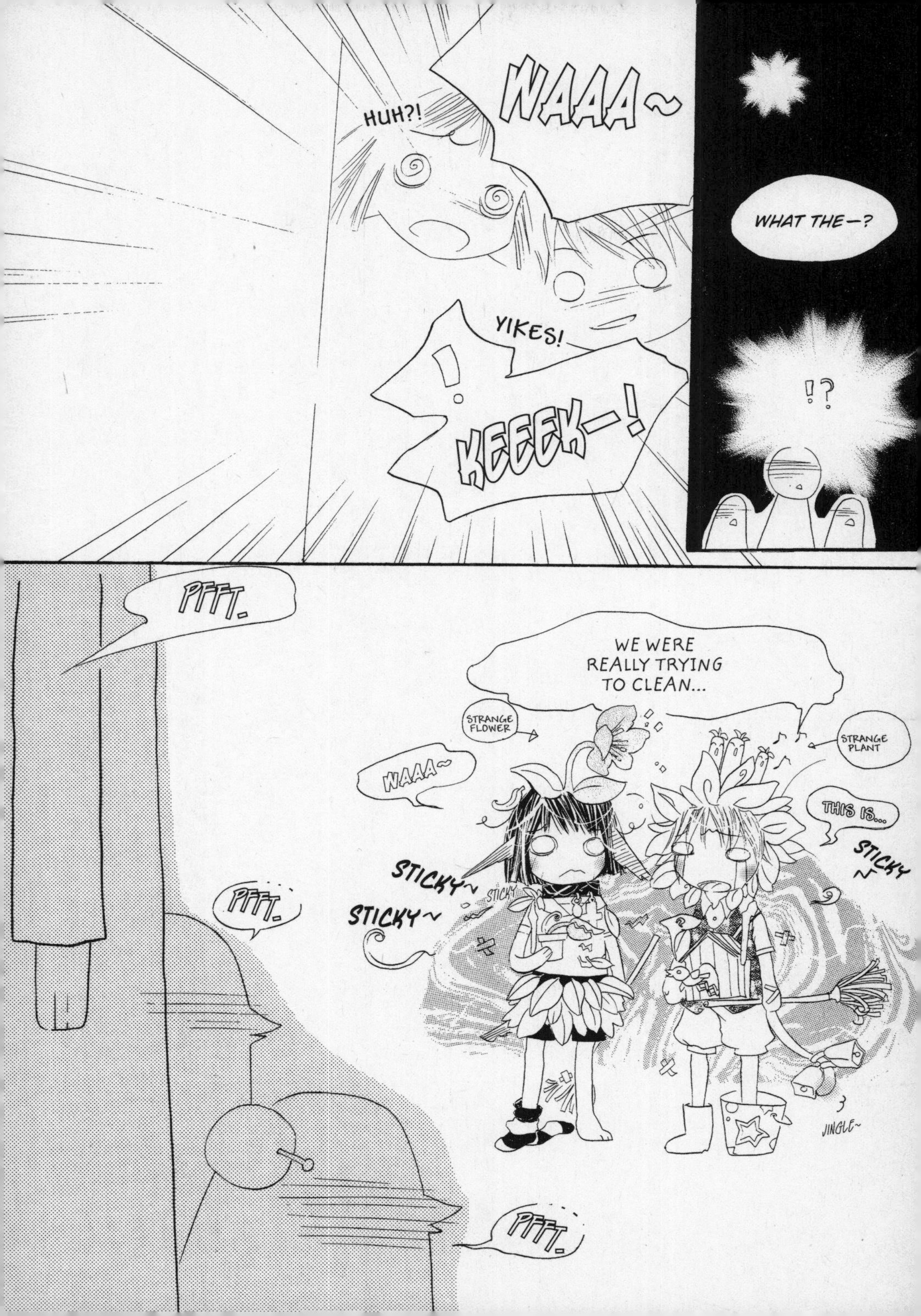
WHAT THE—?
!?
WAAAA~
HUH?!
YIKES!
KEEEK—!
WE WERE REALLY TRYING TO CLEAN...
STRANGE PLANT
THIS IS...
STICKY~
STRANGE FLOWER
WAAA~
STICKY~
STICKY
STICKY~
JINGLE~
PFFT.
PFFT.
PFFT.

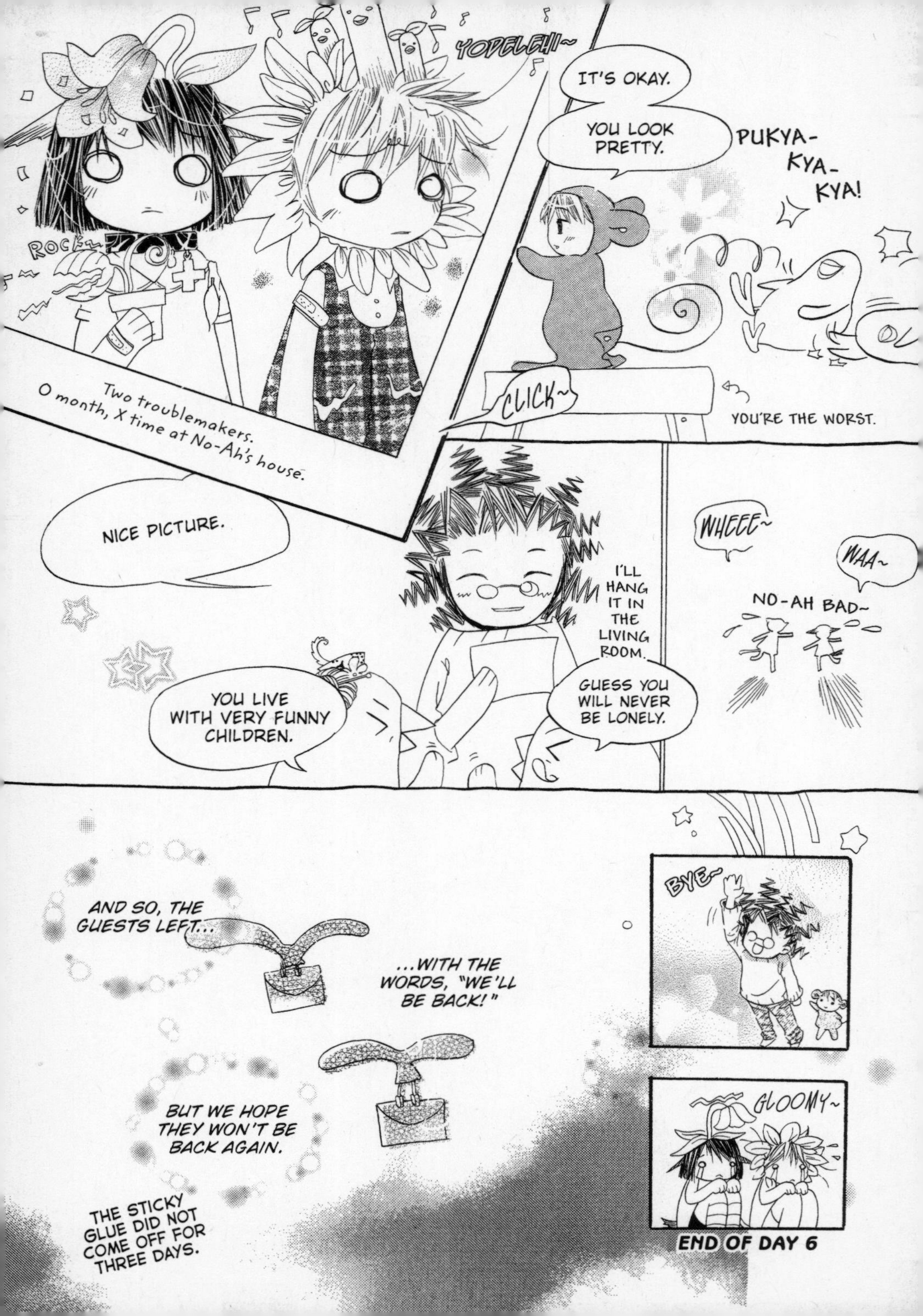
IT'S OKAY.
YOU LOOK PRETTY.
PUKYA-KYA-KYA!
CLICK~
YOU'RE THE WORST.
YODELEHI~
ROCK~
Two troublemakers.
O month, X time at No-Ah's house.
WHEEE~
WAA~
NO-AH BAD~
NICE PICTURE.
I'LL HANG IT IN THE LIVING ROOM.
YOU LIVE WITH VERY FUNNY CHILDREN.
GUESS YOU WILL NEVER BE LONELY.
AND SO, THE GUESTS LEFT...
...WITH THE WORDS, "WE'LL BE BACK!"
BUT WE HOPE THEY WON'T BE BACK AGAIN.
THE STICKY GLUE DID NOT COME OFF FOR THREE DAYS.
BYE~
GLOOMY~
END OF DAY 6

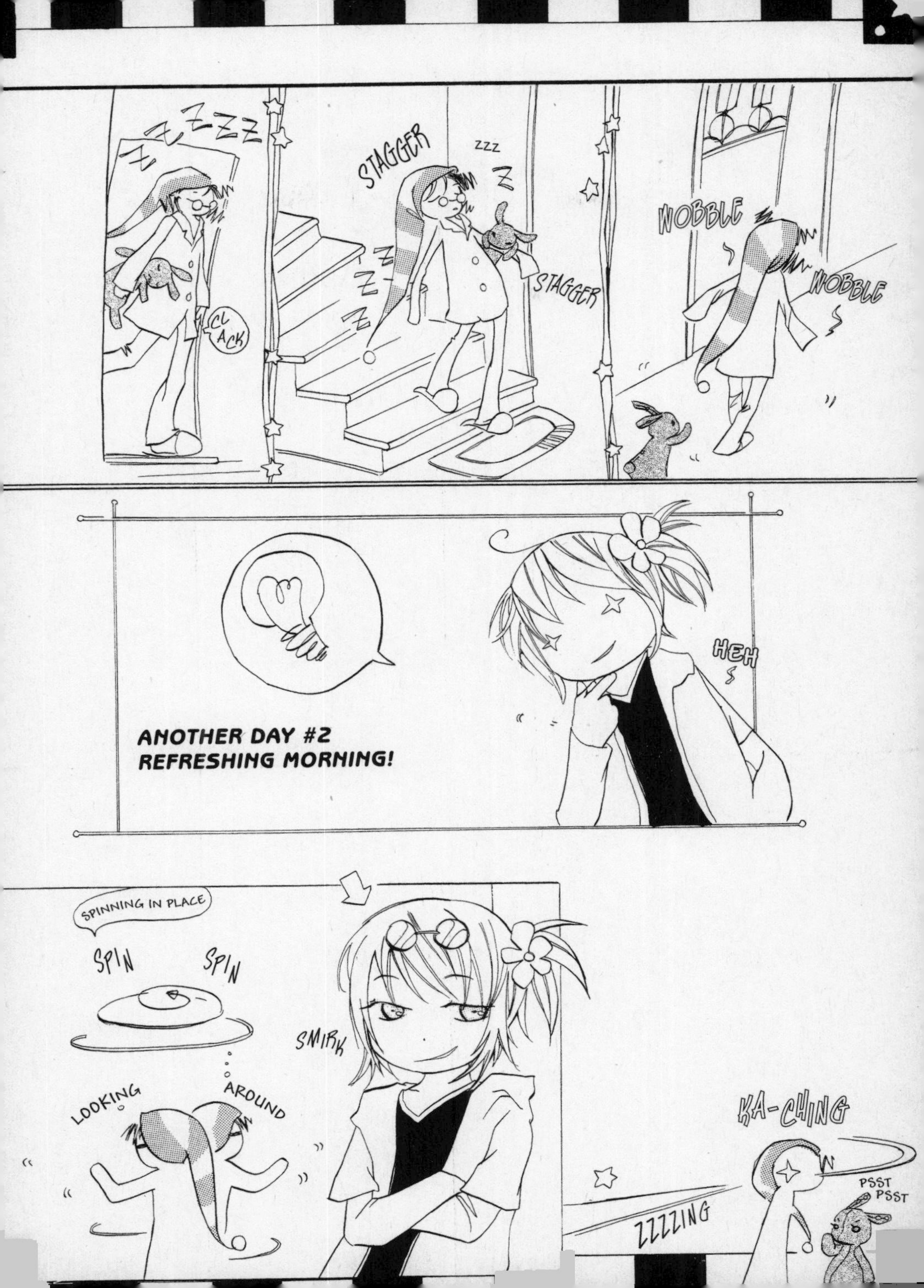
ZZZZZZ
CLACK
STAGGER
ZZZ
Z
ZZZ
STAGGER
WOBBLE
WOBBLE
HEH
ANOTHER DAY #2
REFRESHING MORNING!
SPINNING IN PLACE
SPIN SPIN
LOOKING AROUND
SMIRK
KA-CHING
ZZZZING
PSST PSST

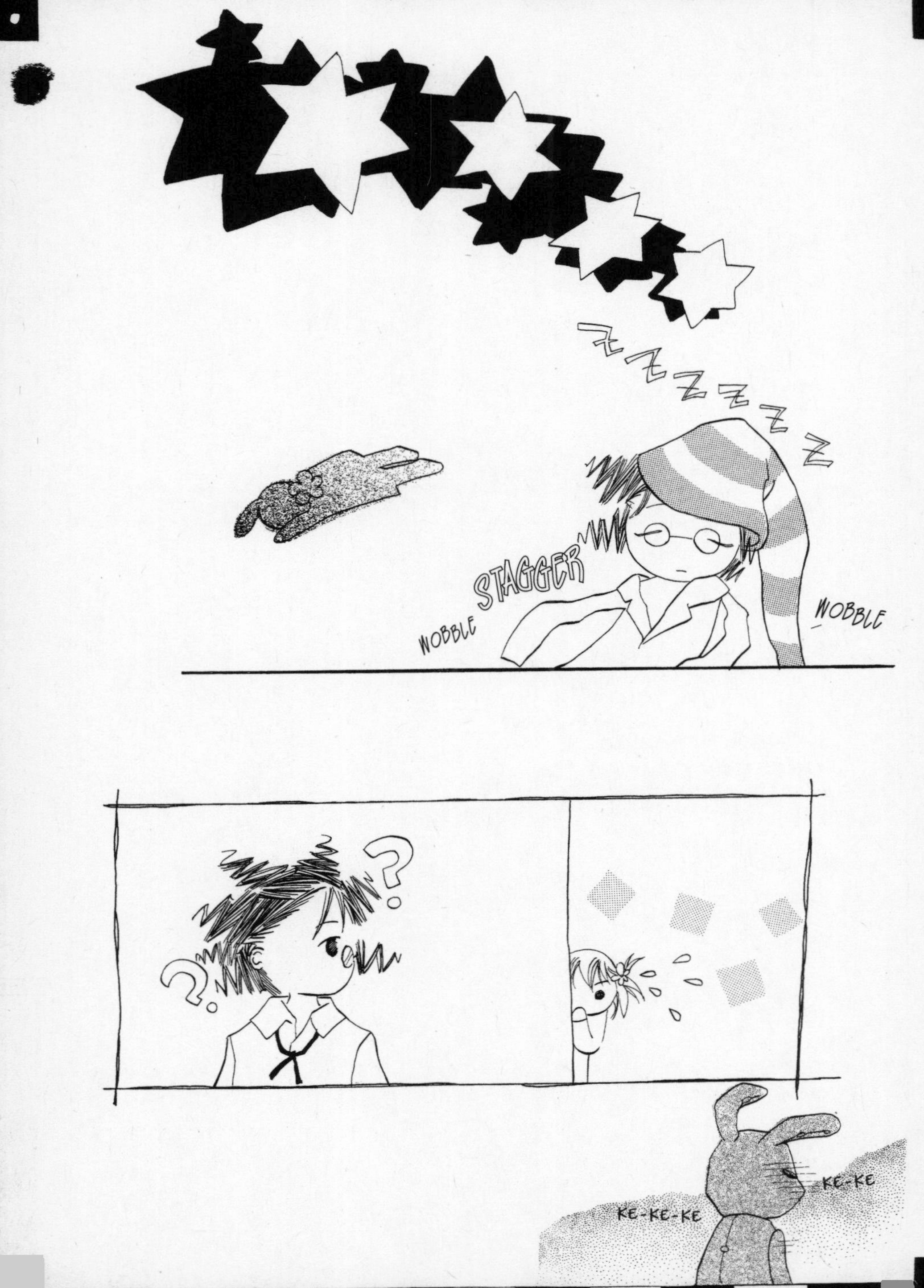
ZZZZZZZ
WOBBLE
STAGGER
WOBBLE
KE-KE
KE-KE-KE

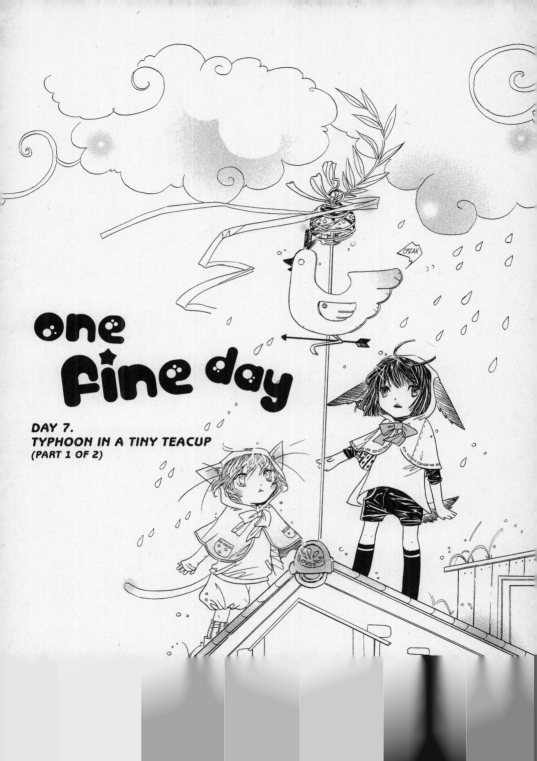

# one fine day

**DAY 7.**
**TYPHOON IN A TINY TEACUP**
**(PART 1 OF 2)**

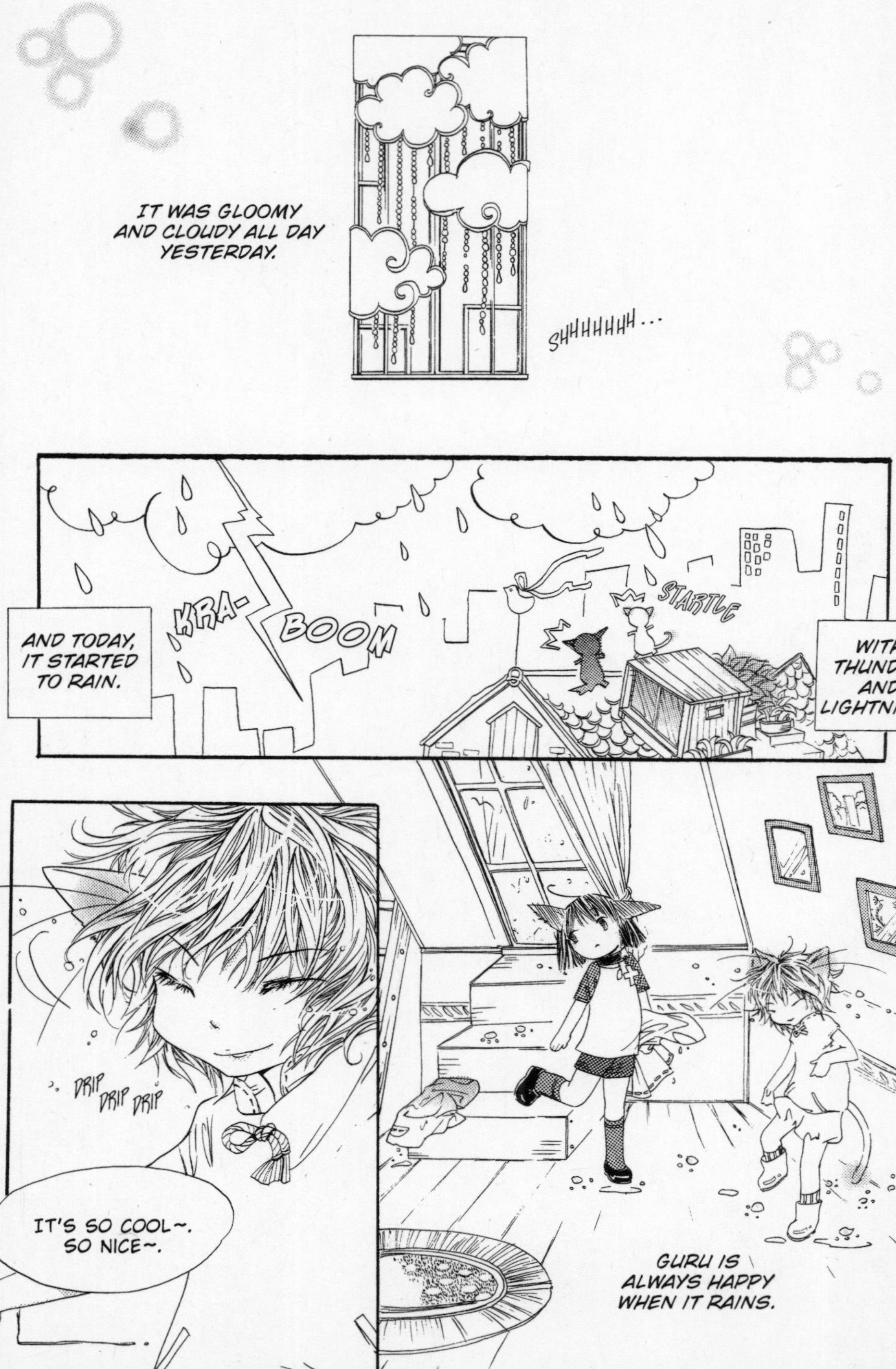
IT WAS GLOOMY AND CLOUDY ALL DAY YESTERDAY.
SHHHHHHH...
AND TODAY, IT STARTED TO RAIN.
KRA-BOOM
STARTLE
WITH THUNDER AND LIGHTNING!
DRIP DRIP DRIP
IT'S SO COOL~. SO NICE~.
GURU IS ALWAYS HAPPY WHEN IT RAINS.

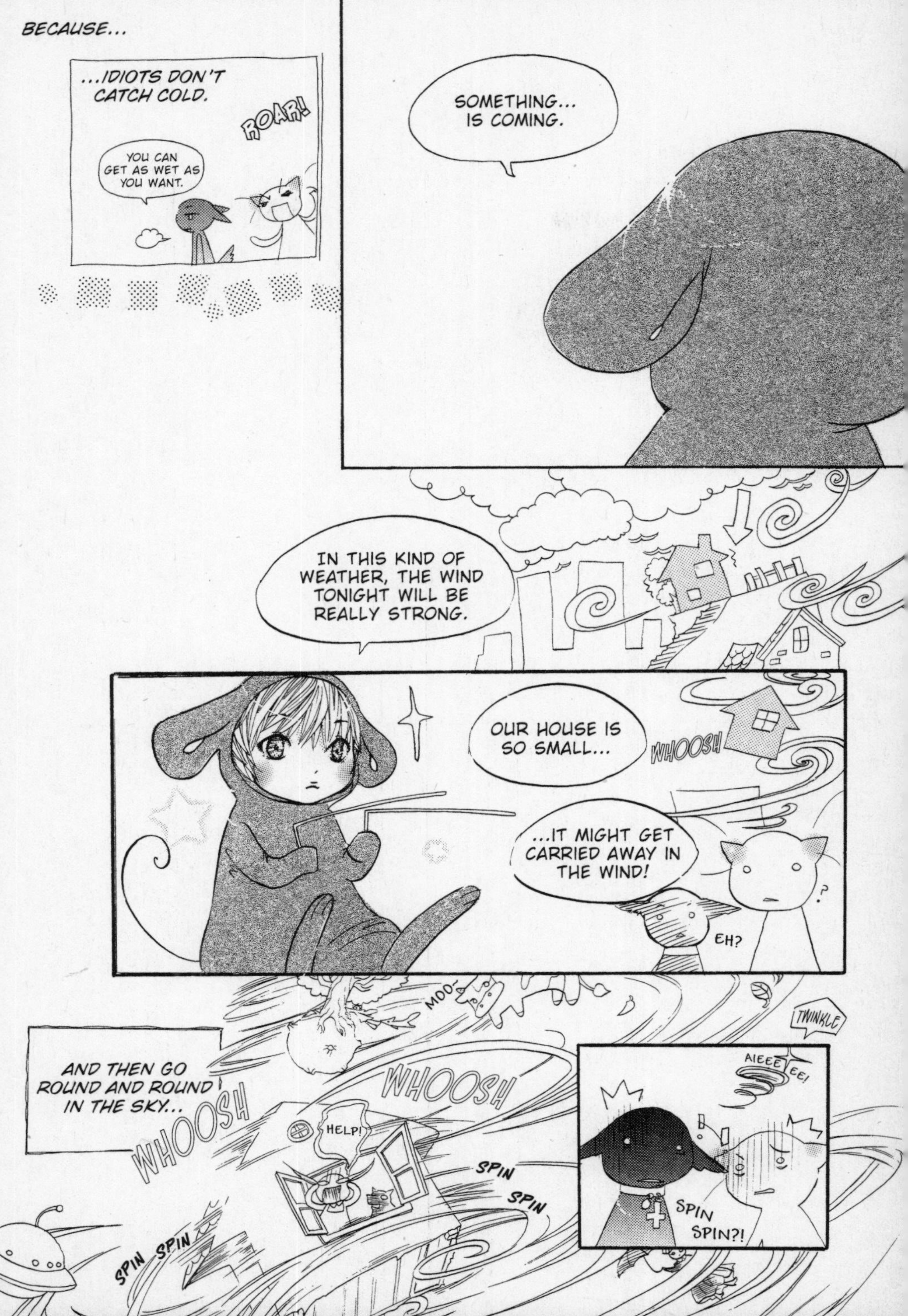
BECAUSE...
...IDIOTS DON'T CATCH COLD.
ROAR!
YOU CAN GET AS WET AS YOU WANT.
SOMETHING... IS COMING.
IN THIS KIND OF WEATHER, THE WIND TONIGHT WILL BE REALLY STRONG.
OUR HOUSE IS SO SMALL...
WHOOSH
...IT MIGHT GET CARRIED AWAY IN THE WIND!
?
EH?
MOO-
AND THEN GO ROUND AND ROUND IN THE SKY...
WHOOSH
WHOOSH
HELP!
SPIN SPIN
SPIN SPIN
TWINKLE
AIEEEEE!
SPIN SPIN?!

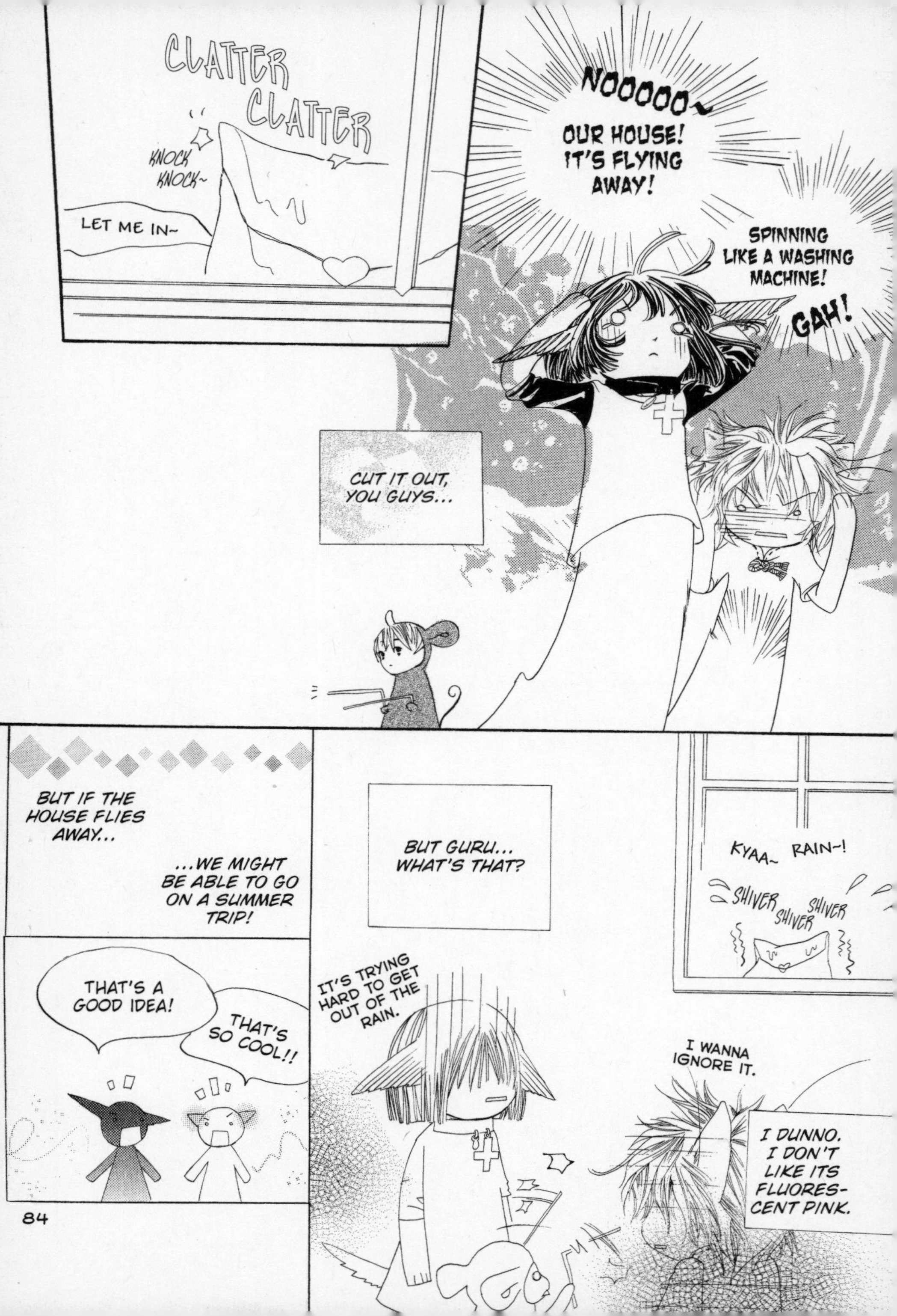
NOOOOO~
OUR HOUSE! IT'S FLYING AWAY!
SPINNING LIKE A WASHING MACHINE!
GAH!
CUT IT OUT, YOU GUYS...
CLATTER CLATTER
KNOCK KNOCK~
LET ME IN~
KYAA~ RAIN~!
SHIVER SHIVER SHIVER
BUT GURU... WHAT'S THAT?
I DUNNO. I DON'T LIKE ITS FLUORES-CENT PINK.
IT'S TRYING HARD TO GET OUT OF THE RAIN.
I WANNA IGNORE IT.
BUT IF THE HOUSE FLIES AWAY...
...WE MIGHT BE ABLE TO GO ON A SUMMER TRIP!
THAT'S SO COOL!!
THAT'S A GOOD IDEA!

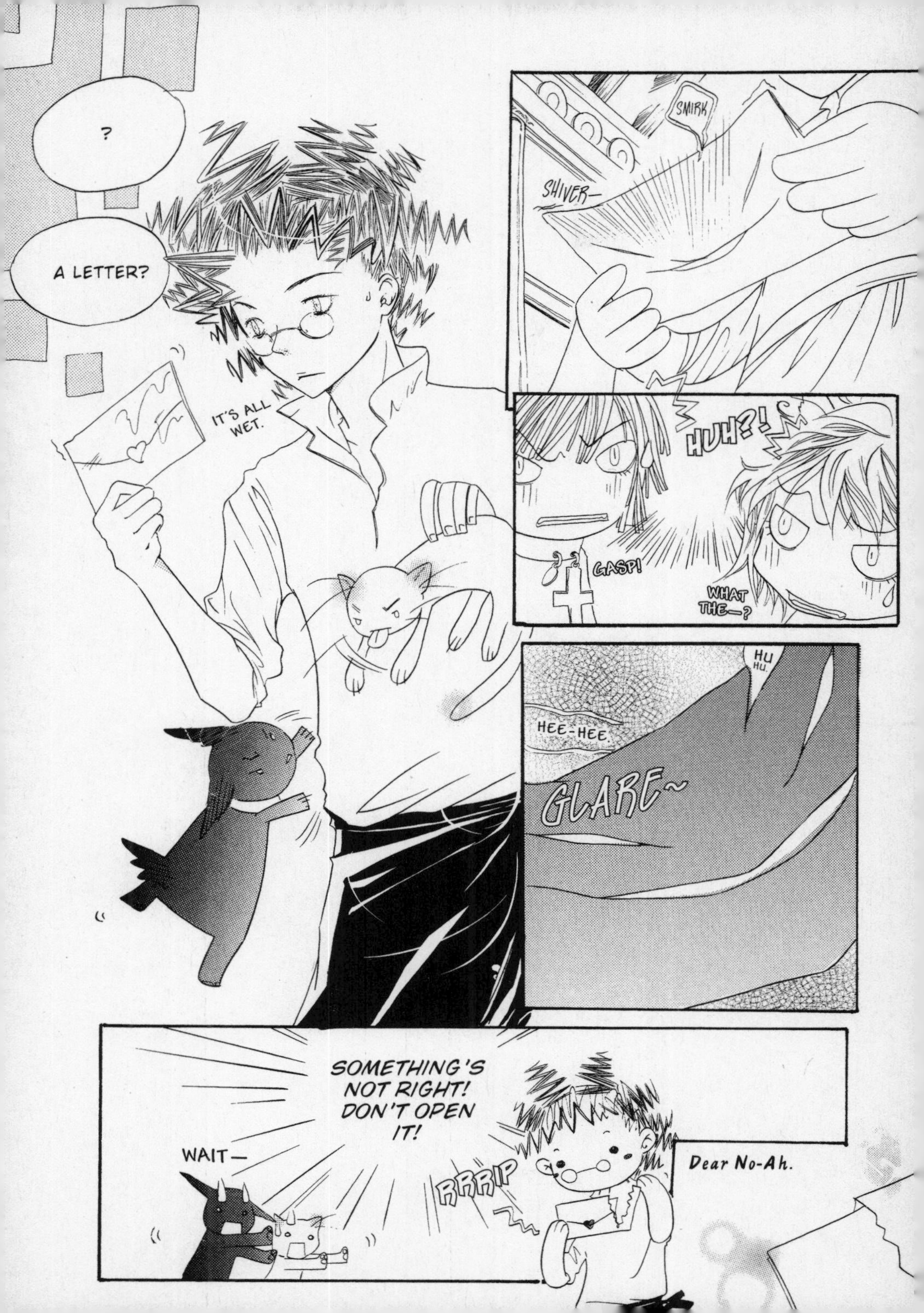

SMIRK
SHIVER—
HUH?!
WHAT THE—?
GASP!
HU HU.
HEE-HEE.
GLARE~
?
A LETTER?
IT'S ALL WET.
SOMETHING'S NOT RIGHT! DON'T OPEN IT!
Dear No-Ah.
RRRIP
WAIT—

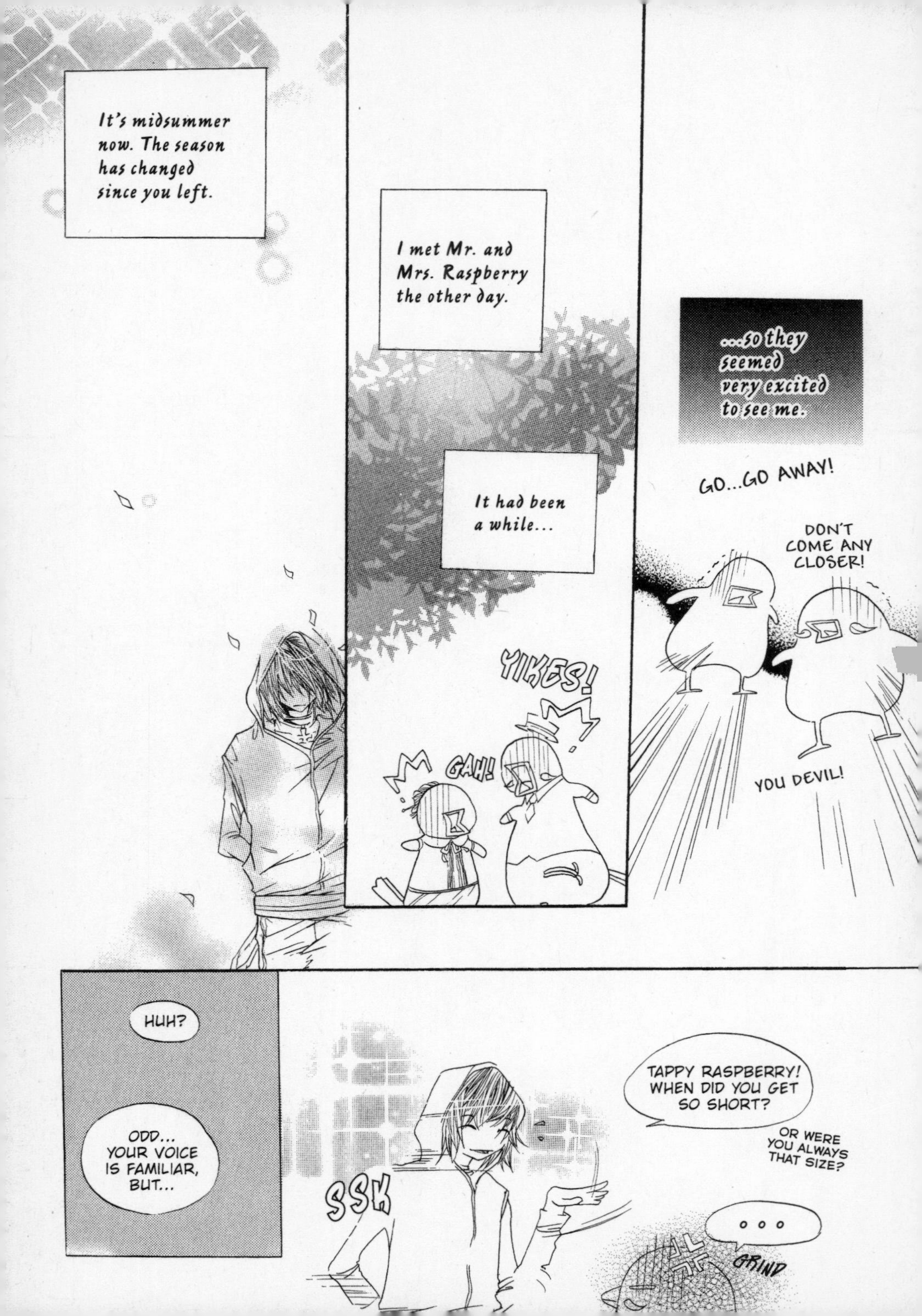
It's midsummer now. The season has changed since you left.
I met Mr. and Mrs. Raspberry the other day.
It had been a while...
YIKES!
GAH!
...so they seemed very excited to see me.
GO...GO AWAY!
DON'T COME ANY CLOSER!
YOU DEVIL!
HUH?
ODD... YOUR VOICE IS FAMILIAR, BUT...
SSK
TAPPY RASPBERRY! WHEN DID YOU GET SO SHORT?
OR WERE YOU ALWAYS THAT SIZE?
...
GRIND

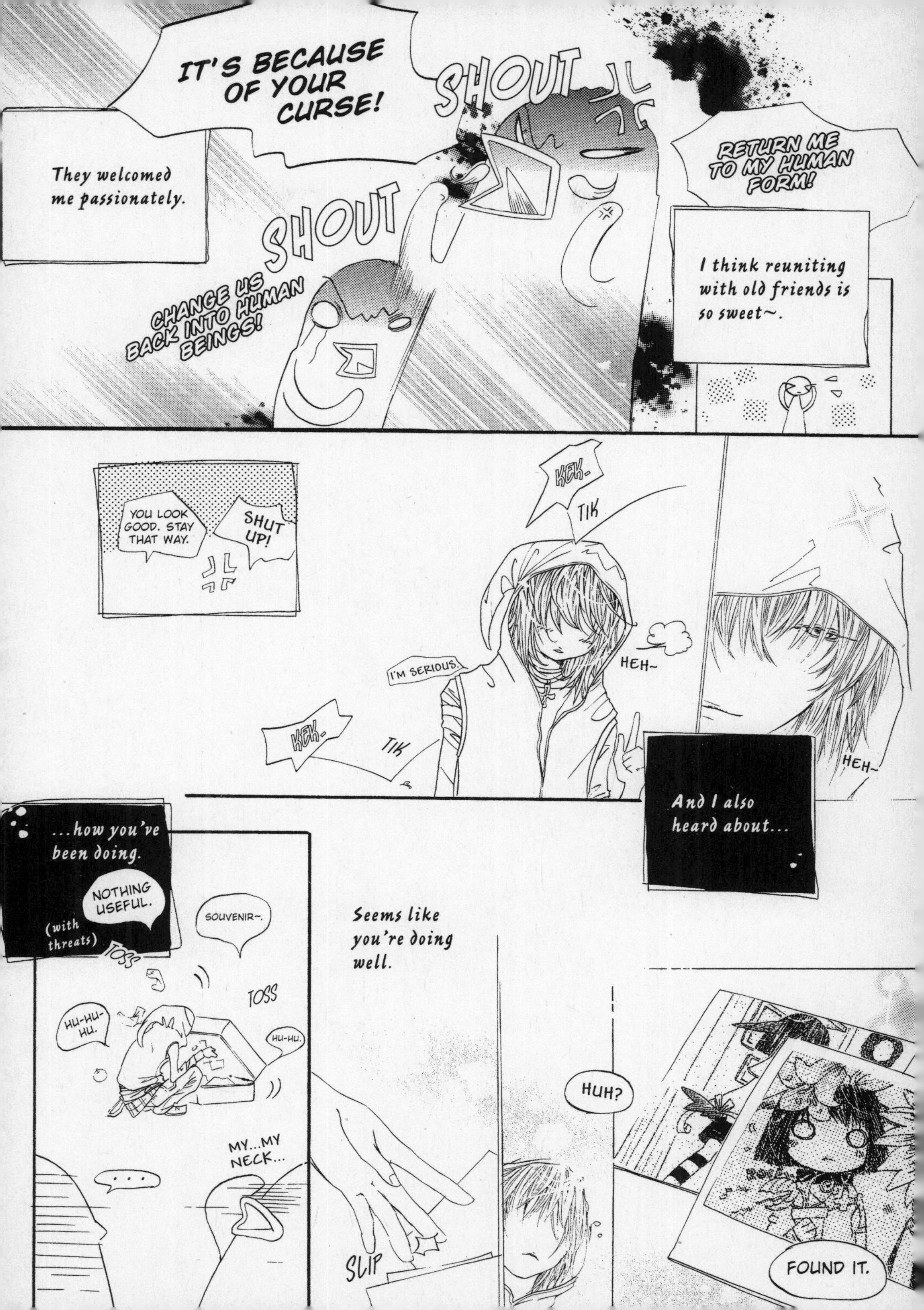

They welcomed me passionately.
IT'S BECAUSE OF YOUR CURSE!
SHOUT
SHOUT
CHANGE US BACK INTO HUMAN BEINGS!
RETURN ME TO MY HUMAN FORM!
I think reuniting with old friends is so sweet~.
YOU LOOK GOOD. STAY THAT WAY.
SHUT UP!
KEK-
TIK
I'M SERIOUS.
KEK-
TIK
HEH~
HEH~
And I also heard about...
...how you've been doing.
NOTHING USEFUL.
(with threats)
SOUVENIR~.
TOSS
TOSS
HU-HU-HU.
HU-HU.
MY...MY NECK...
...
Seems like you're doing well.
SLIP
HUH?
FOUND IT.

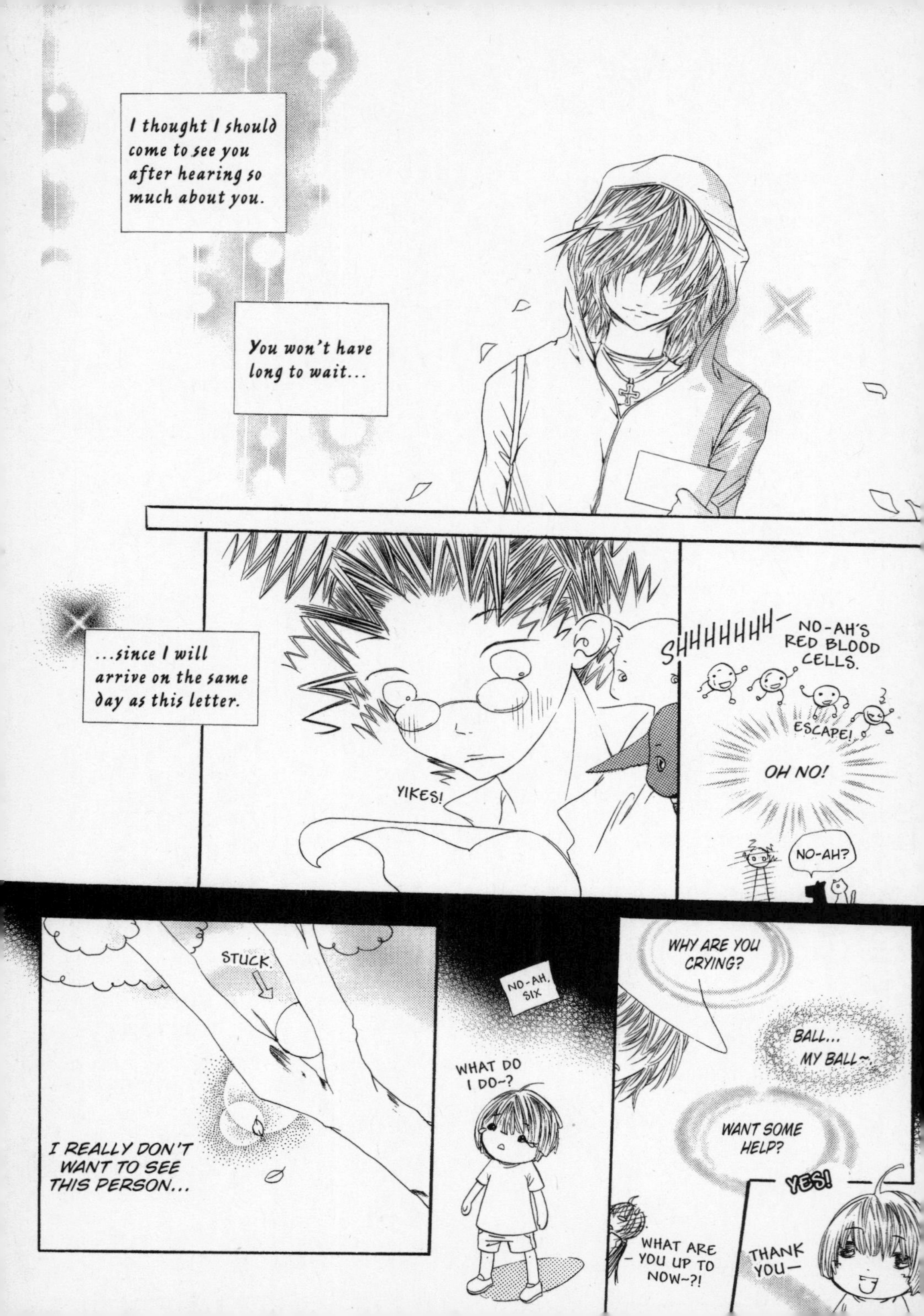

I thought I should come to see you after hearing so much about you.
You won't have long to wait...
...since I will arrive on the same day as this letter.
YIKES!
SHHHHHHH-
NO-AH'S RED BLOOD CELLS.
ESCAPE!
OH NO!
NO-AH?
STUCK.
I REALLY DON'T WANT TO SEE THIS PERSON...
NO-AH, SIX
WHAT DO I DO~?
WHY ARE YOU CRYING?
BALL... MY BALL~.
WANT SOME HELP?
YES!
WHAT ARE YOU UP TO NOW~?!
THANK YOU—

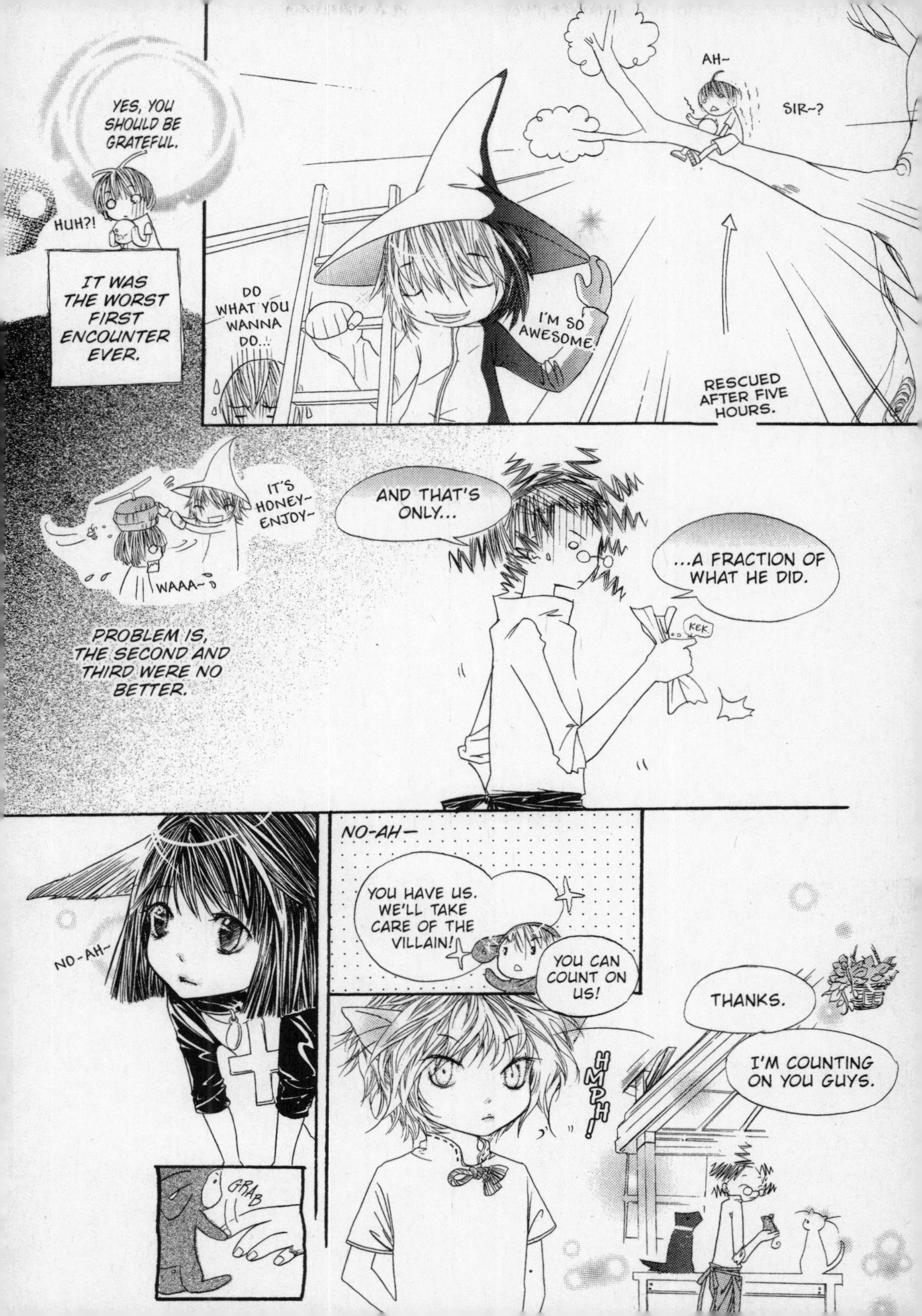
AH~
SIR~?
I'M SO AWESOME.
DO WHAT YOU WANNA DO...
RESCUED AFTER FIVE HOURS.
YES, YOU SHOULD BE GRATEFUL.
HUH?!
IT WAS THE WORST FIRST ENCOUNTER EVER.
AND THAT'S ONLY...
...A FRACTION OF WHAT HE DID.
KEK.
IT'S HONEY-ENJOY~
WAAA~
PROBLEM IS, THE SECOND AND THIRD WERE NO BETTER.
NO-AH—
YOU HAVE US. WE'LL TAKE CARE OF THE VILLAIN!
YOU CAN COUNT ON US!
THANKS.
I'M COUNTING ON YOU GUYS.
HMPH!
NO-AH~
GRAB

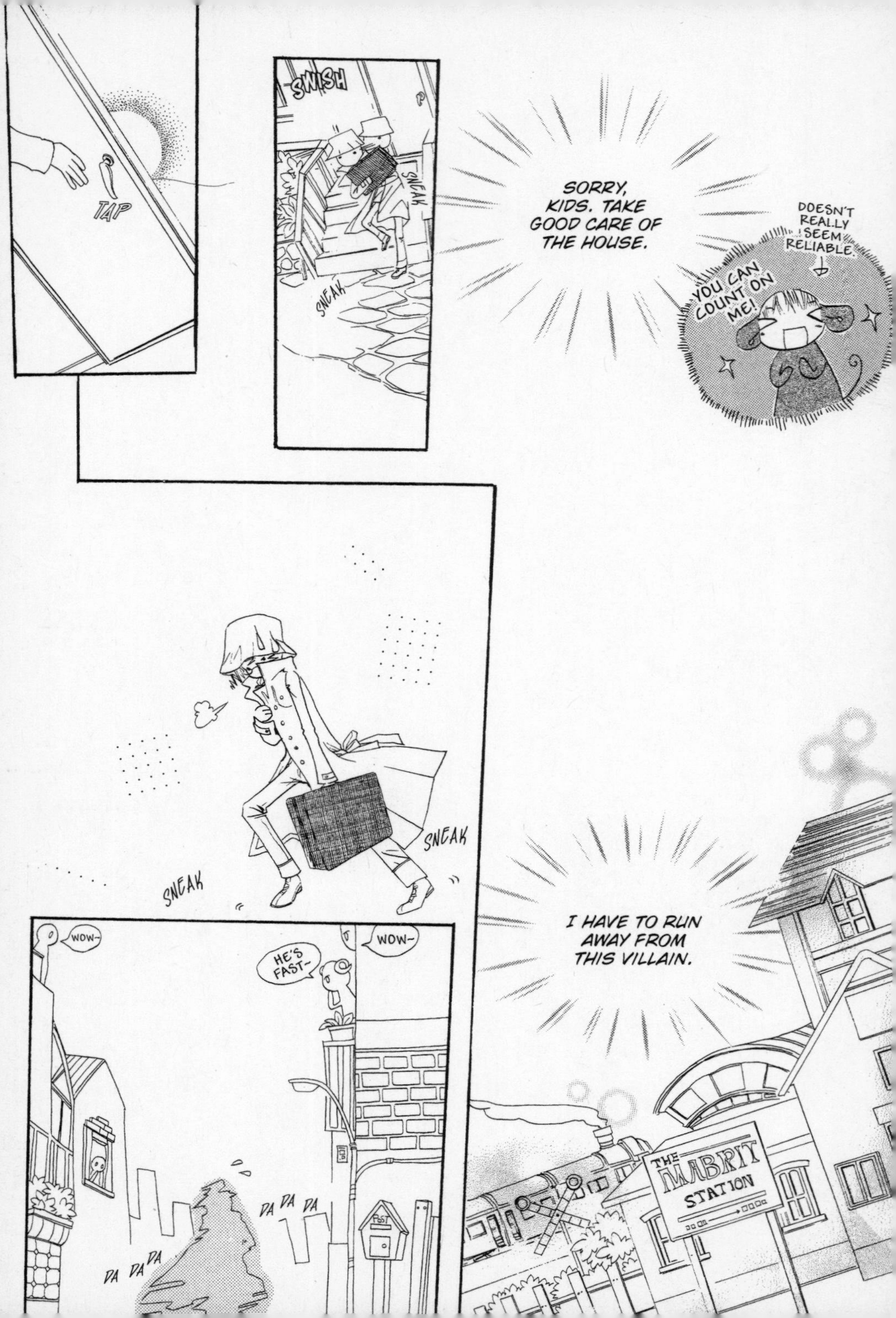
SORRY, KIDS. TAKE GOOD CARE OF THE HOUSE.
YOU CAN COUNT ON ME!
DOESN'T REALLY SEEM RELIABLE.
SWISH
SNEAK
SNEAK
TAP
SNEAK
SNEAK
I HAVE TO RUN AWAY FROM THIS VILLAIN.
THE MABRIT STATION
WOW-
HE'S FAST-
WOW-
DA DA DA
DA DA DA
POST

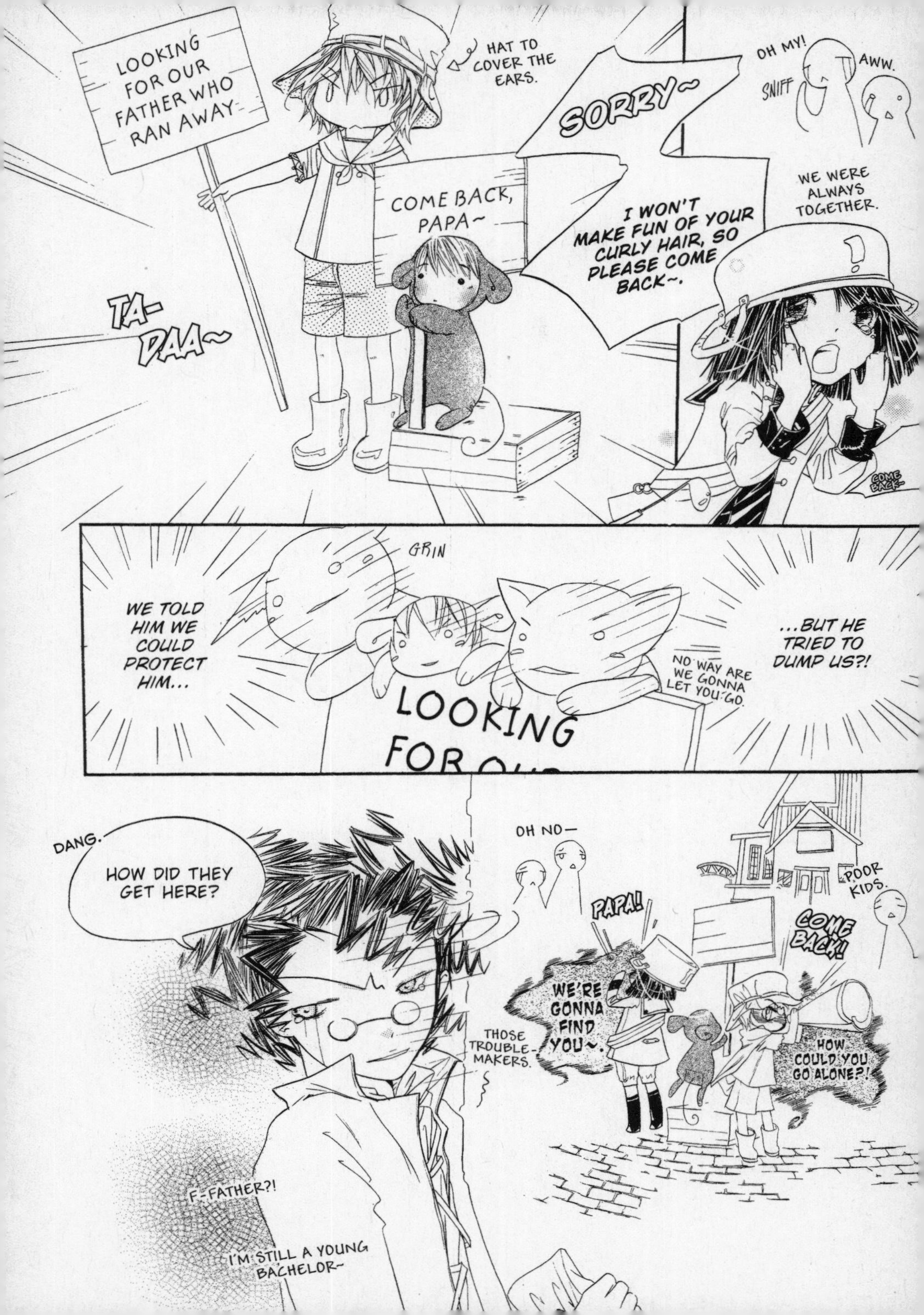
LOOKING FOR OUR FATHER WHO RAN AWAY
HAT TO COVER THE EARS.
TA-DAA~
COME BACK, PAPA~
SORRY~
I WON'T MAKE FUN OF YOUR CURLY HAIR, SO PLEASE COME BACK~.
OH MY!
SNIFF
AWW.
WE WERE ALWAYS TOGETHER.
COME BACK~
GRIN
WE TOLD HIM WE COULD PROTECT HIM...
LOOKING FOR OU
NO WAY ARE WE GONNA LET YOU GO.
...BUT HE TRIED TO DUMP US?!
DANG.
HOW DID THEY GET HERE?
F-FATHER?!
I'M STILL A YOUNG BACHELOR~
THOSE TROUBLE-MAKERS.
OH NO—
PAPA!
WE'RE GONNA FIND YOU~.
POOR KIDS.
COME BACK!
HOW COULD YOU GO ALONE?!

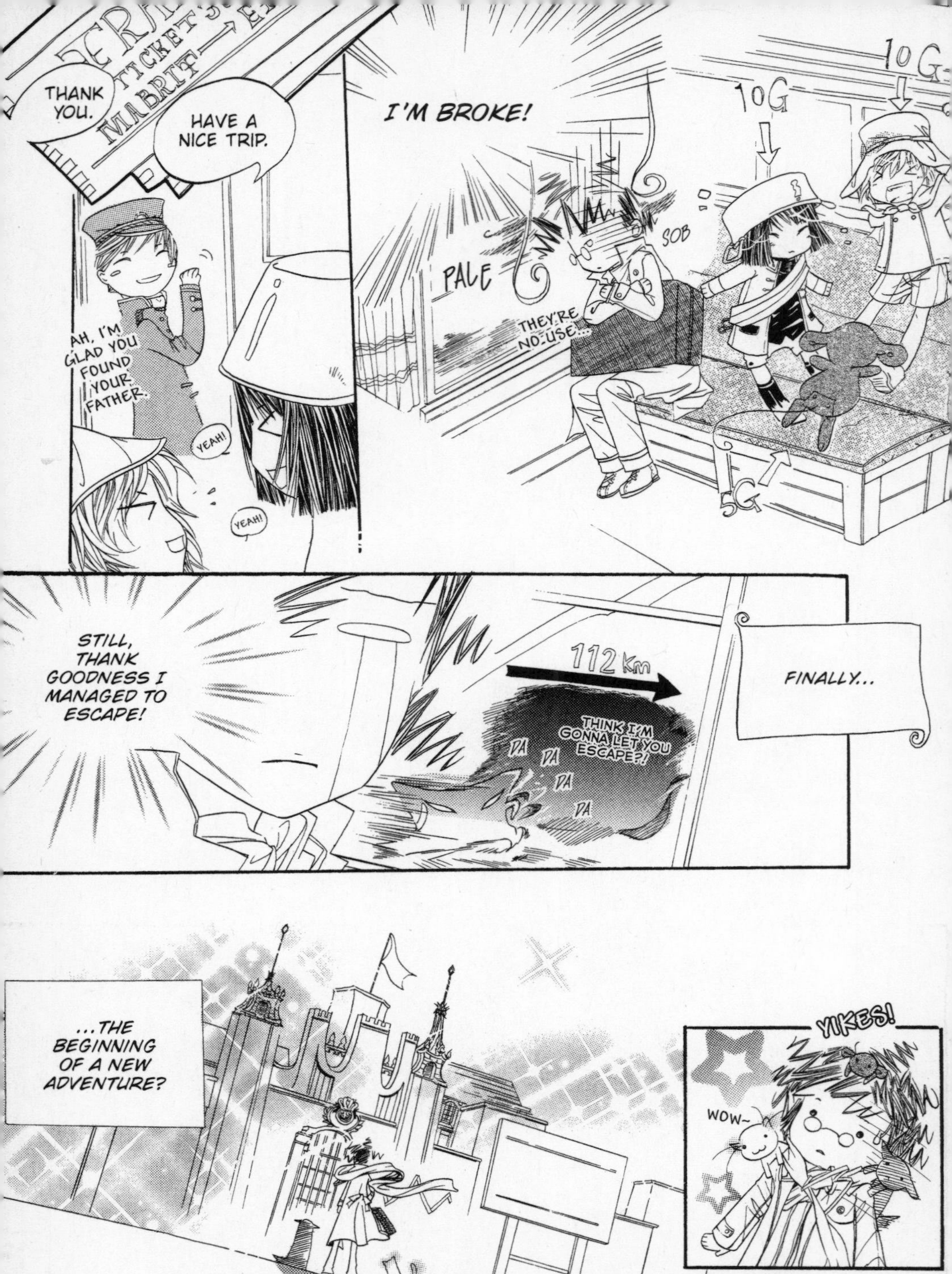
TICKETS
MABRIF
THANK YOU.
HAVE A NICE TRIP.
AH, I'M GLAD YOU FOUND YOUR FATHER.
YEAH!
YEAH!
I'M BROKE!
10G
10G
PALE
SOB
THEY'RE NO USE...
5G
STILL, THANK GOODNESS I MANAGED TO ESCAPE!
112 Km
THINK I'M GONNA LET YOU ESCAPE?!
DA DA DA DA
FINALLY...
...THE BEGINNING OF A NEW ADVENTURE?
YIKES!
WOW~

TO BE CONTINUED

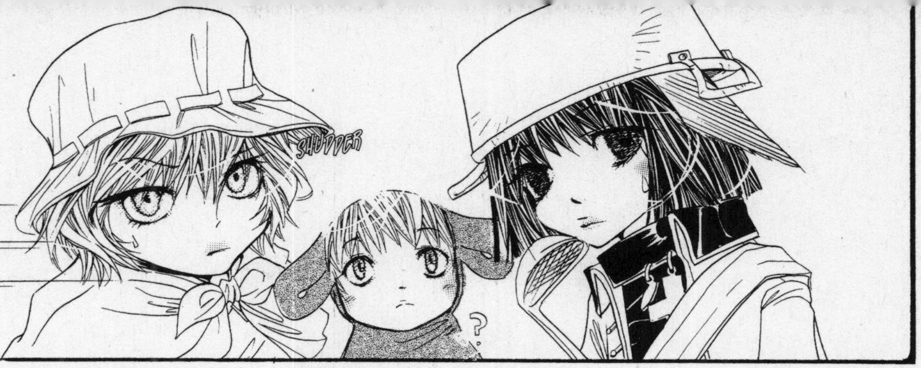
SHUDDER
?

# one fine day

**DAY 8.**
**TYPHOON IN A TINY TEACUP**
**(PART 2 OF 2)**

WE WERE ON THE TRAIN ALL DAY AND ALL NIGHT BEFORE WE FINALLY GOT HERE.

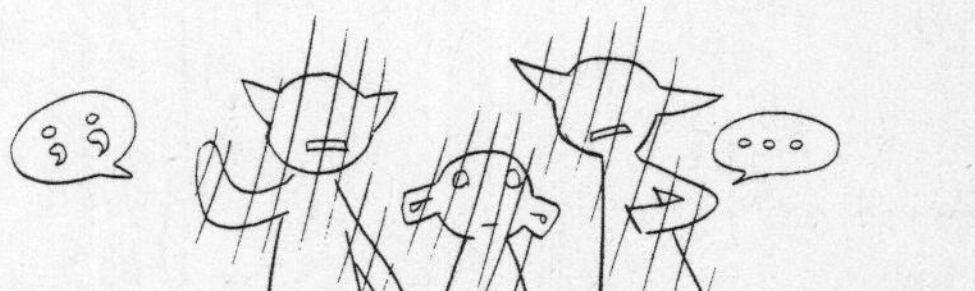

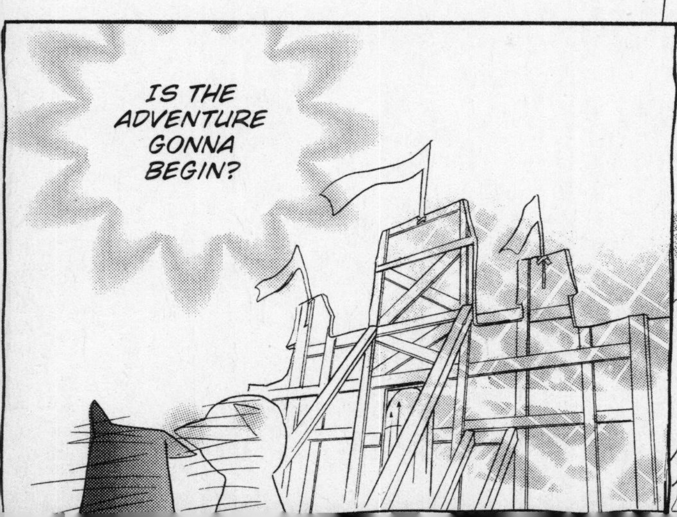
IS THE ADVENTURE GONNA BEGIN?

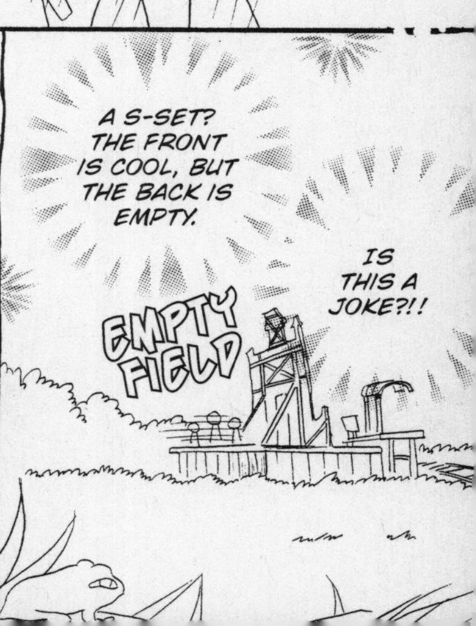
A S-SET? THE FRONT IS COOL, BUT THE BACK IS EMPTY.
EMPTY FIELD
IS THIS A JOKE?!!

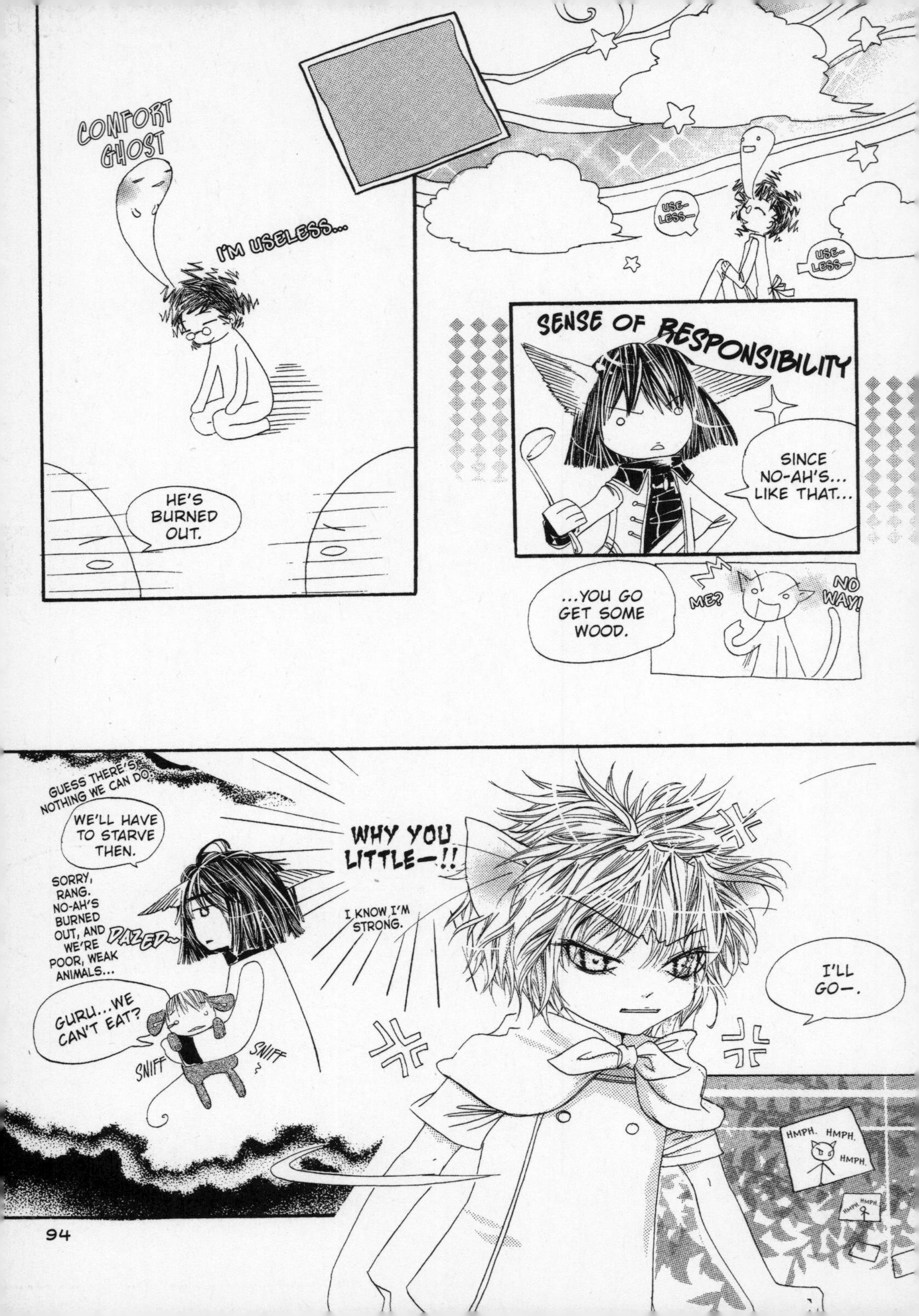
COMFORT GHOST
I'M USELESS...
HE'S BURNED OUT.
USE-LESS—
USE-LESS—
SENSE OF RESPONSIBILITY
SINCE NO-AH'S... LIKE THAT...
...YOU GO GET SOME WOOD.
ME?
NO WAY!
GUESS THERE'S NOTHING WE CAN DO.
WE'LL HAVE TO STARVE THEN.
SORRY, RANG. NO-AH'S BURNED OUT, AND WE'RE POOR, WEAK ANIMALS...
DAZED~
GURU...WE CAN'T EAT?
SNIFF
SNIFF
WHY YOU LITTLE—!!
I KNOW I'M STRONG.
I'LL GO—.
HMPH. HMPH. HMPH.
HMPH. HMPH.

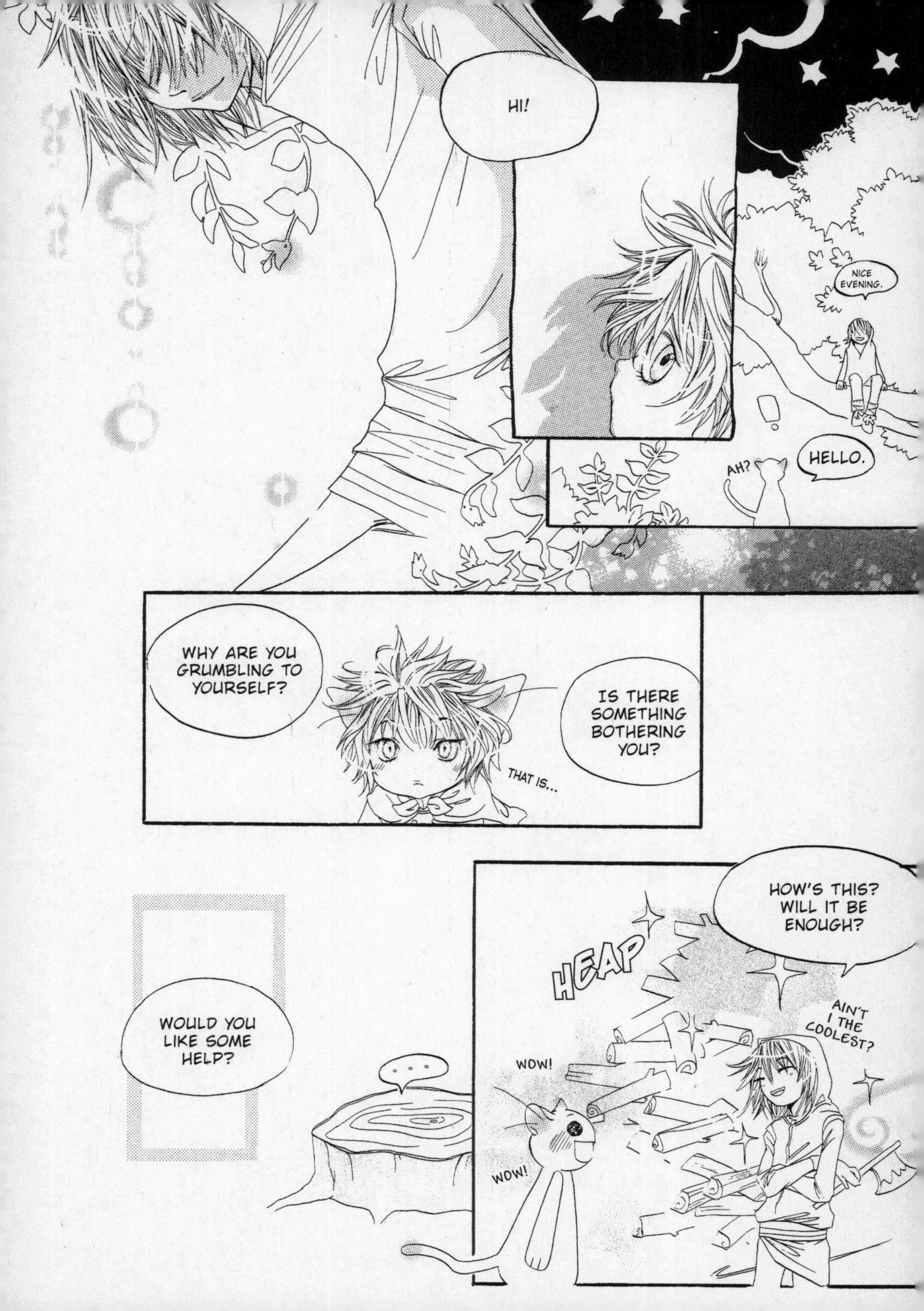
HI!
NICE EVENING.
HELLO.
AH?
WHY ARE YOU GRUMBLING TO YOURSELF?
IS THERE SOMETHING BOTHERING YOU?
THAT IS...
HOW'S THIS? WILL IT BE ENOUGH?
HEAP
AIN'T I THE COOLEST?
WOW!
WOW!
...
WOULD YOU LIKE SOME HELP?

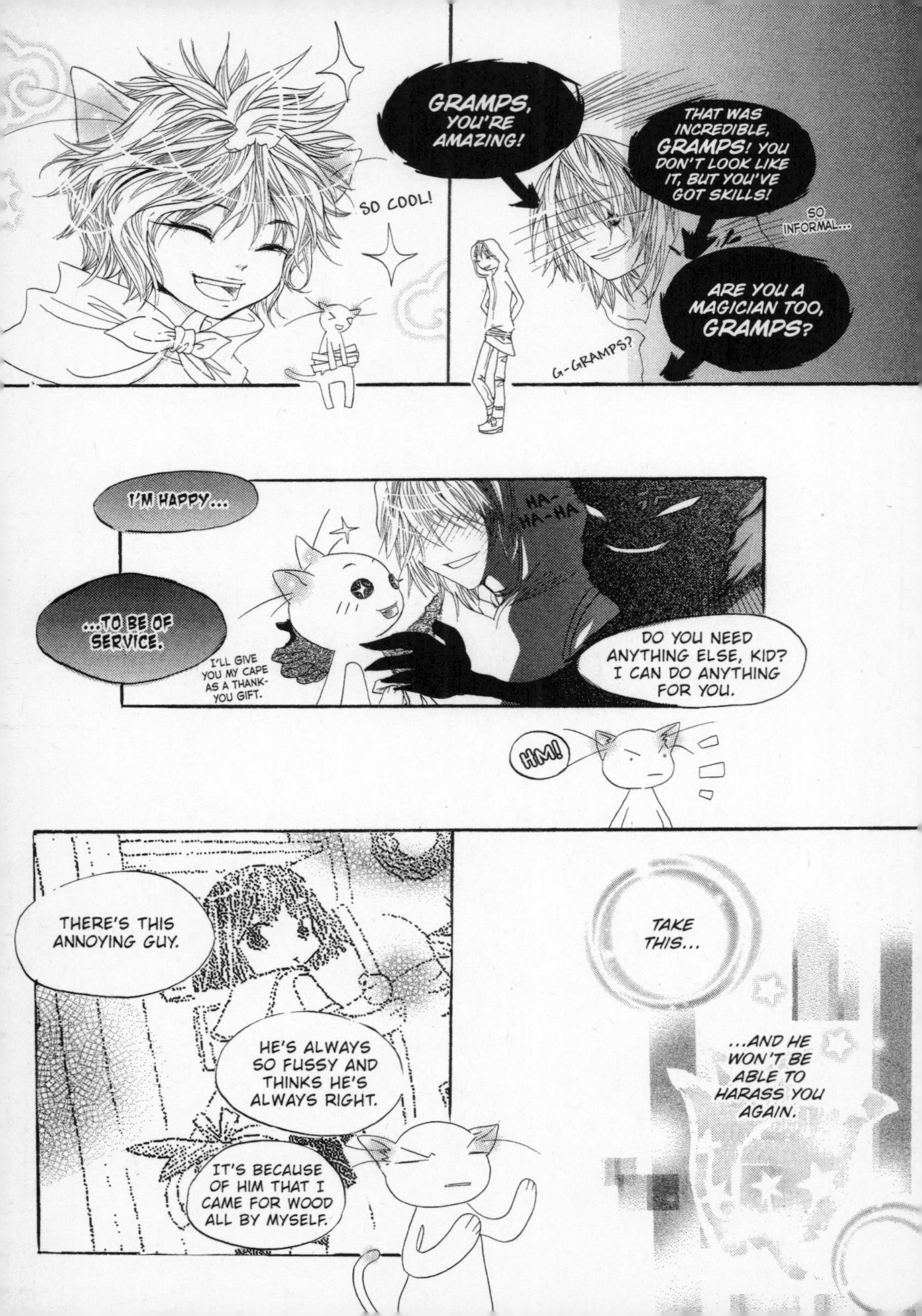
SO COOL!
GRAMPS, YOU'RE AMAZING!
THAT WAS INCREDIBLE, GRAMPS! YOU DON'T LOOK LIKE IT, BUT YOU'VE GOT SKILLS!
SO INFORMAL...
ARE YOU A MAGICIAN TOO, GRAMPS?
G-GRAMPS?
I'M HAPPY...
...TO BE OF SERVICE.
I'LL GIVE YOU MY CAPE AS A THANK-YOU GIFT.
HA-HA-HA
DO YOU NEED ANYTHING ELSE, KID? I CAN DO ANYTHING FOR YOU.
HM!
THERE'S THIS ANNOYING GUY.
HE'S ALWAYS SO FUSSY AND THINKS HE'S ALWAYS RIGHT.
IT'S BECAUSE OF HIM THAT I CAME FOR WOOD ALL BY MYSELF.
TAKE THIS...
...AND HE WON'T BE ABLE TO HARASS YOU AGAIN.

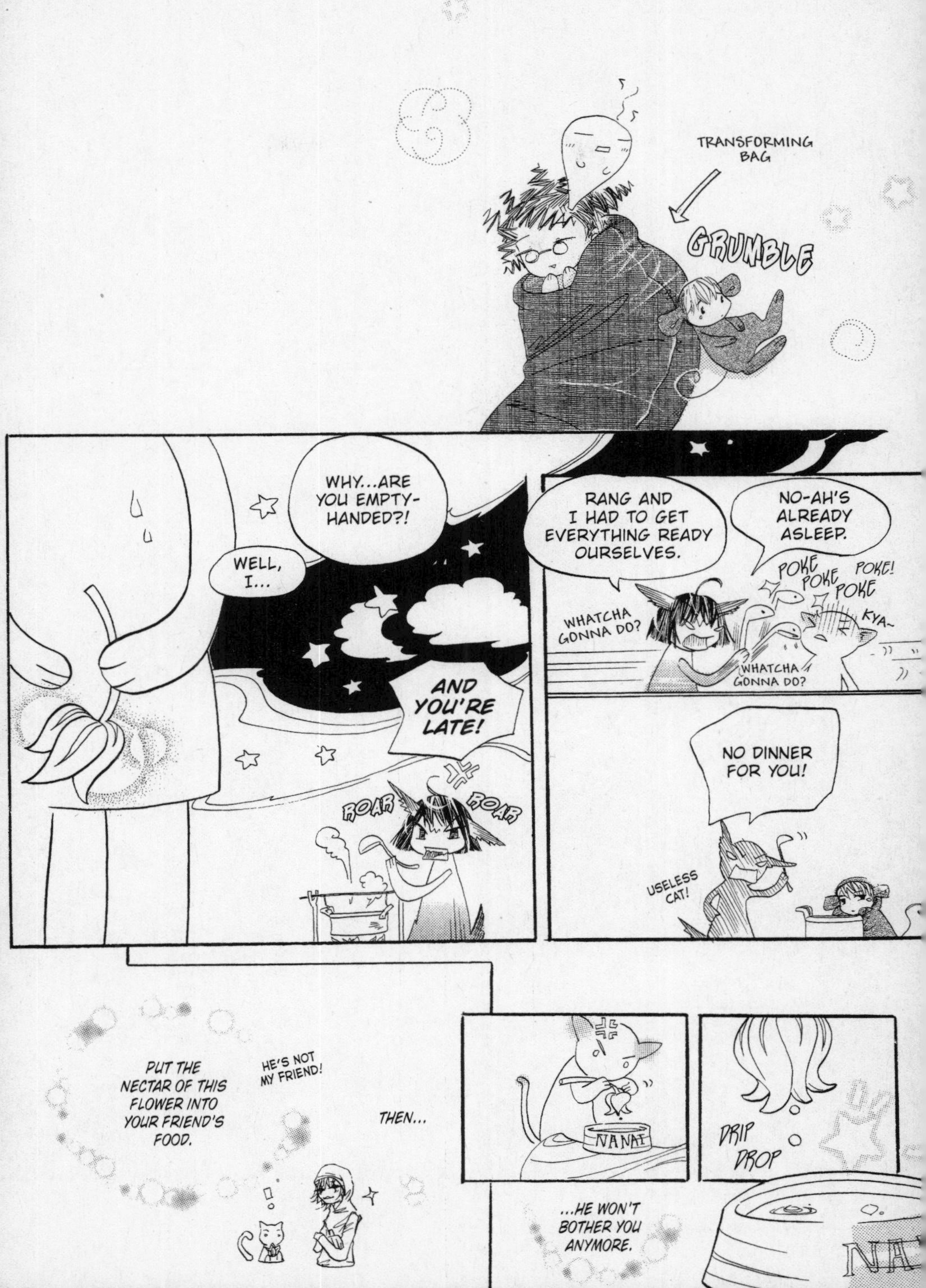
TRANSFORMING BAG
GRUMBLE
WHY...ARE YOU EMPTY-HANDED?!
WELL, I...
AND YOU'RE LATE!
ROAR
ROAR
RANG AND I HAD TO GET EVERYTHING READY OURSELVES.
NO-AH'S ALREADY ASLEEP.
POKE
POKE
POKE!
POKE
KYA~
WHATCHA GONNA DO?
WHATCHA GONNA DO?
NO DINNER FOR YOU!
USELESS CAT!
PUT THE NECTAR OF THIS FLOWER INTO YOUR FRIEND'S FOOD.
HE'S NOT MY FRIEND!
THEN...
NANAI
DRIP
DROP
...HE WON'T BOTHER YOU ANYMORE.

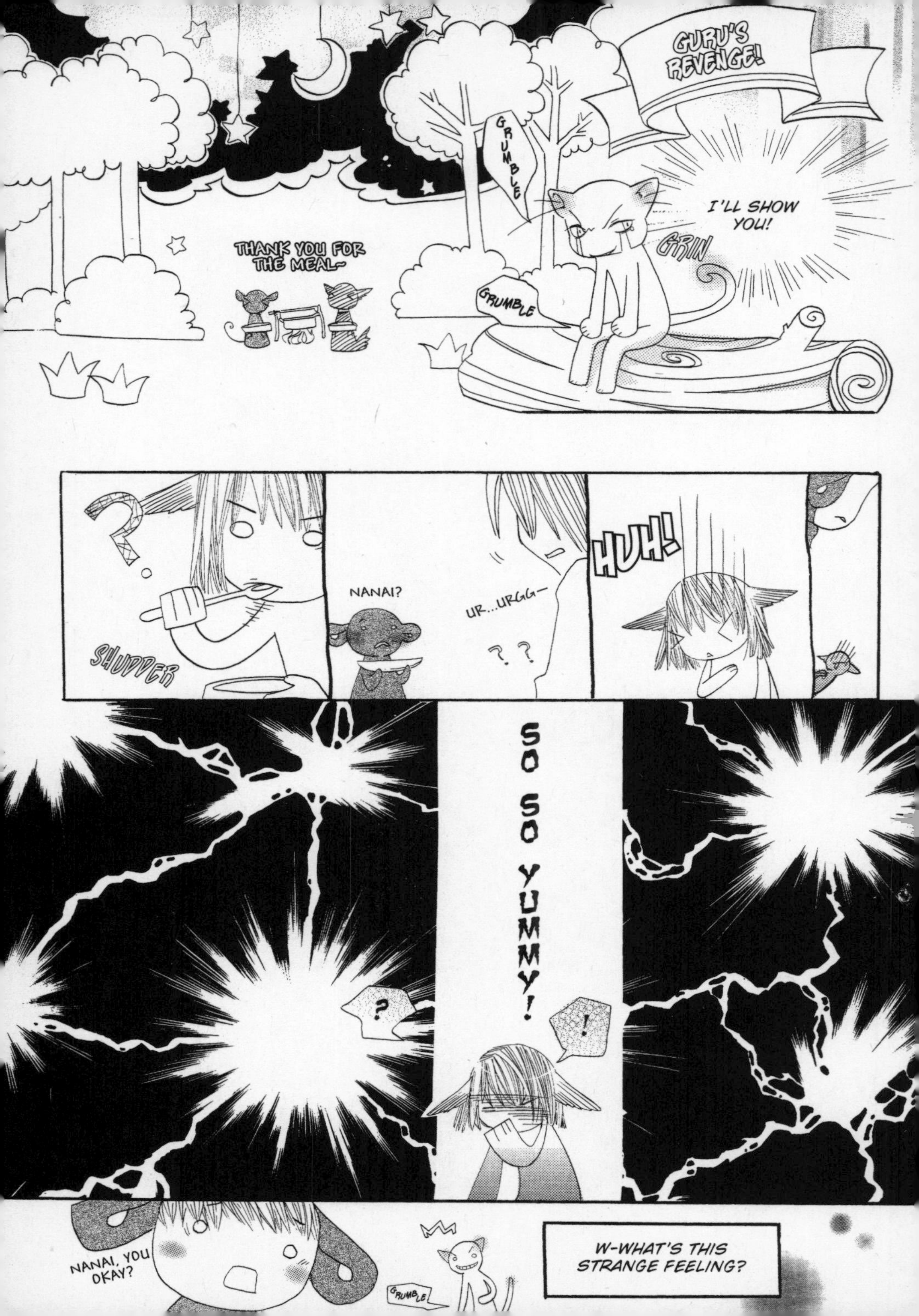
GURU'S REVENGE!
THANK YOU FOR THE MEAL~
GRUMBLE
GRUMBLE
I'LL SHOW YOU!
GRIN
SHUDDER
NANAI?
UR...URGG--
? ?
HUH!
SO SO YUMMY!
?
!
NANAI, YOU OKAY?
GRUMBLE
W-WHAT'S THIS STRANGE FEELING?

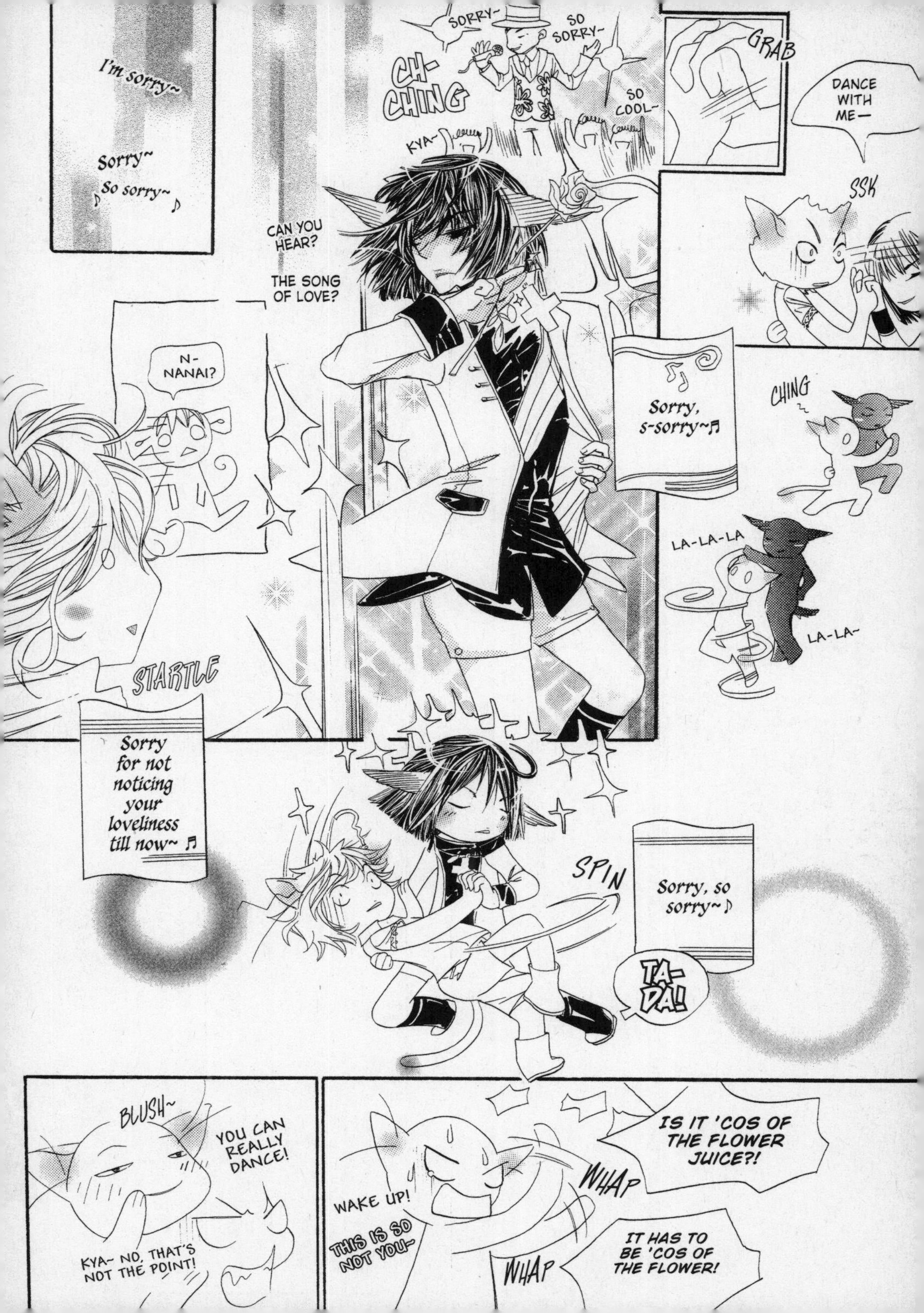

I'm sorry~
Sorry~
So sorry~ ♪
SORRY~
SO SORRY~
CH-CHING
SO COOL~
KYA~
CAN YOU HEAR?
THE SONG OF LOVE?
GRAB
DANCE WITH ME—
SSK
N-NANAI?
STARTLE
Sorry, s-sorry~♪
CHING
LA-LA-LA
LA-LA~
Sorry for not noticing your loveliness till now~ ♪
SPIN
Sorry, so sorry~♪
TA-DA!
BLUSH~
YOU CAN REALLY DANCE!
KYA~ NO, THAT'S NOT THE POINT!
IS IT 'COS OF THE FLOWER JUICE?!
WHAP
WAKE UP!
THIS IS SO NOT YOU~
IT HAS TO BE 'COS OF THE FLOWER!
WHAP

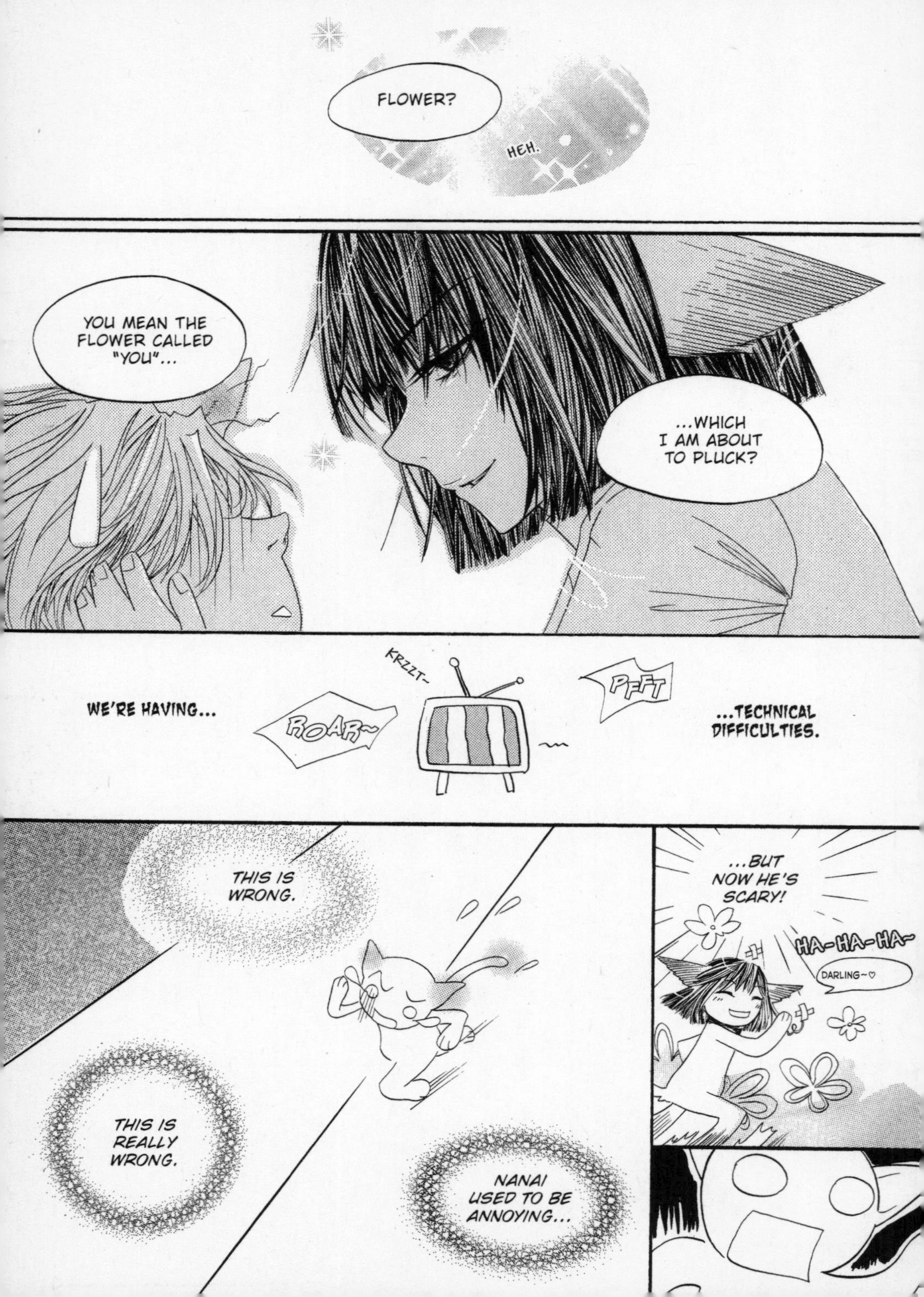
FLOWER?
HEH.
YOU MEAN THE FLOWER CALLED "YOU"...
...WHICH I AM ABOUT TO PLUCK?
WE'RE HAVING...
KRZZT-
ROAR~
PFFT
...TECHNICAL DIFFICULTIES.
THIS IS WRONG.
THIS IS REALLY WRONG.
NANAI USED TO BE ANNOYING...
...BUT NOW HE'S SCARY!
HA-HA-HA-
DARLING~♡

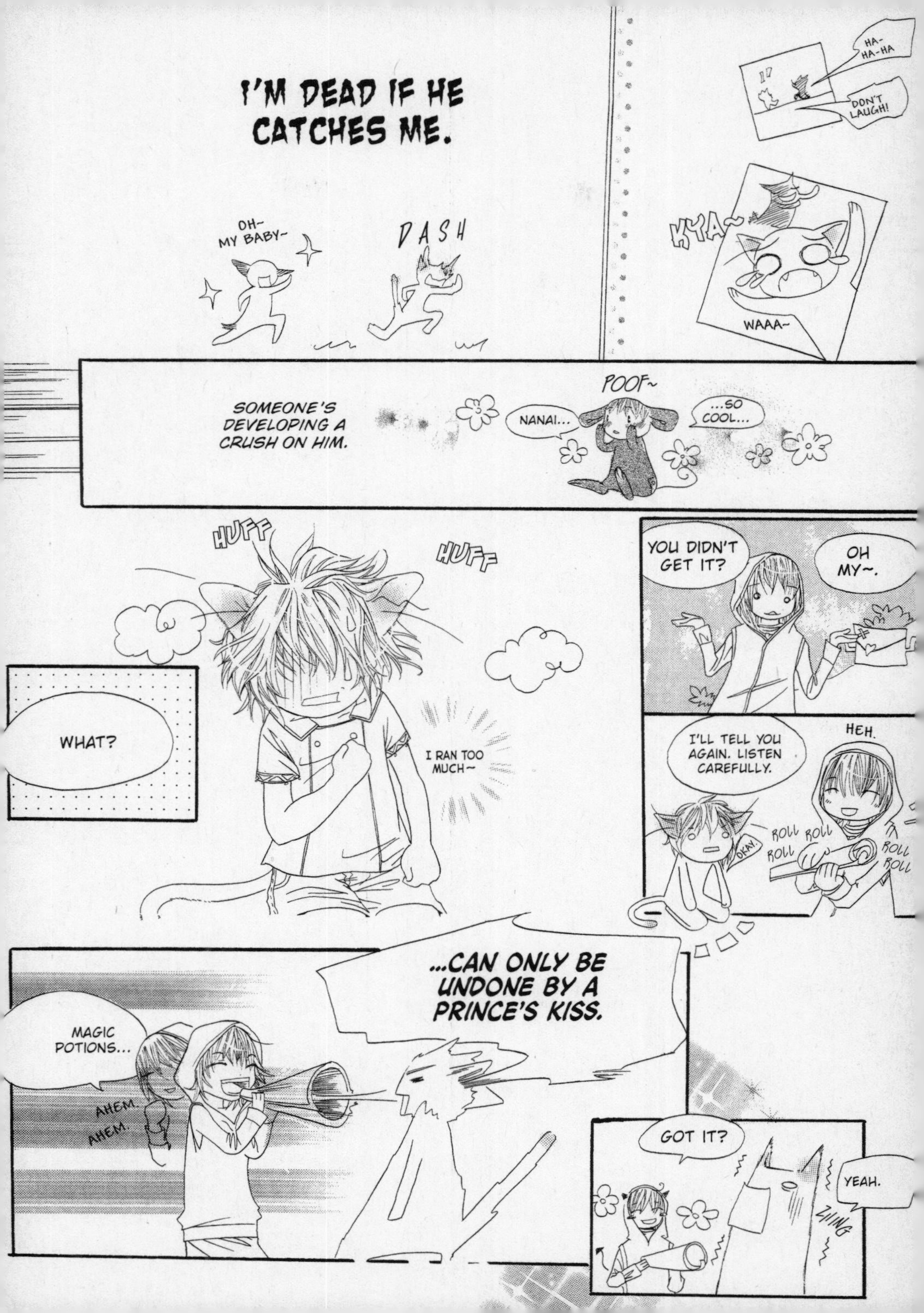
I'M DEAD IF HE CATCHES ME.
OH~ MY BABY~
DASH
HA-HA-HA
DON'T LAUGH!
KYA~
WAAA~
SOMEONE'S DEVELOPING A CRUSH ON HIM.
POOF~
NANAI...
...SO COOL...
HUFF
HUFF
WHAT?
I RAN TOO MUCH~
YOU DIDN'T GET IT?
OH MY~.
I'LL TELL YOU AGAIN. LISTEN CAREFULLY.
HEH.
OKAY.
ROLL ROLL ROLL ROLL ROLL ROLL
MAGIC POTIONS...
AHEM. AHEM.
...CAN ONLY BE UNDONE BY A PRINCE'S KISS.
GOT IT?
YEAH.
ZING

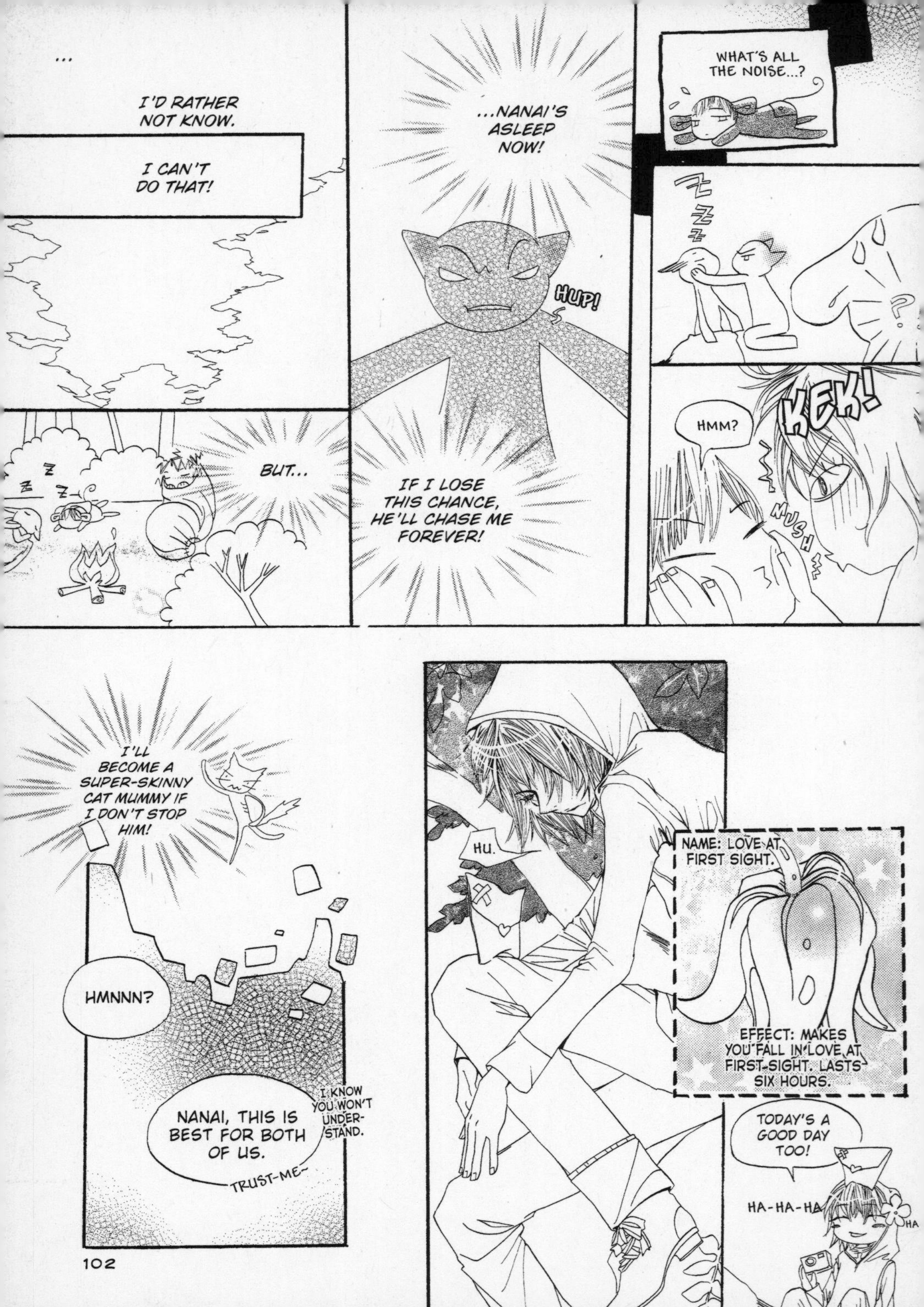
...
I'D RATHER NOT KNOW.
I CAN'T DO THAT!
BUT...
Z
Z
Z
...NANAI'S ASLEEP NOW!
HUP!
IF I LOSE THIS CHANCE, HE'LL CHASE ME FOREVER!
WHAT'S ALL THE NOISE...?
?
HMM?
KEK!
MUSH
I'LL BECOME A SUPER-SKINNY CAT MUMMY IF I DON'T STOP HIM!
HMNNN?
NANAI, THIS IS BEST FOR BOTH OF US.
I KNOW YOU WON'T UNDER-STAND.
TRUST-ME~
HU.
NAME: LOVE AT FIRST SIGHT.
EFFECT: MAKES YOU FALL IN LOVE AT FIRST SIGHT. LASTS SIX HOURS.
TODAY'S A GOOD DAY TOO!
HA-HA-HA
HA

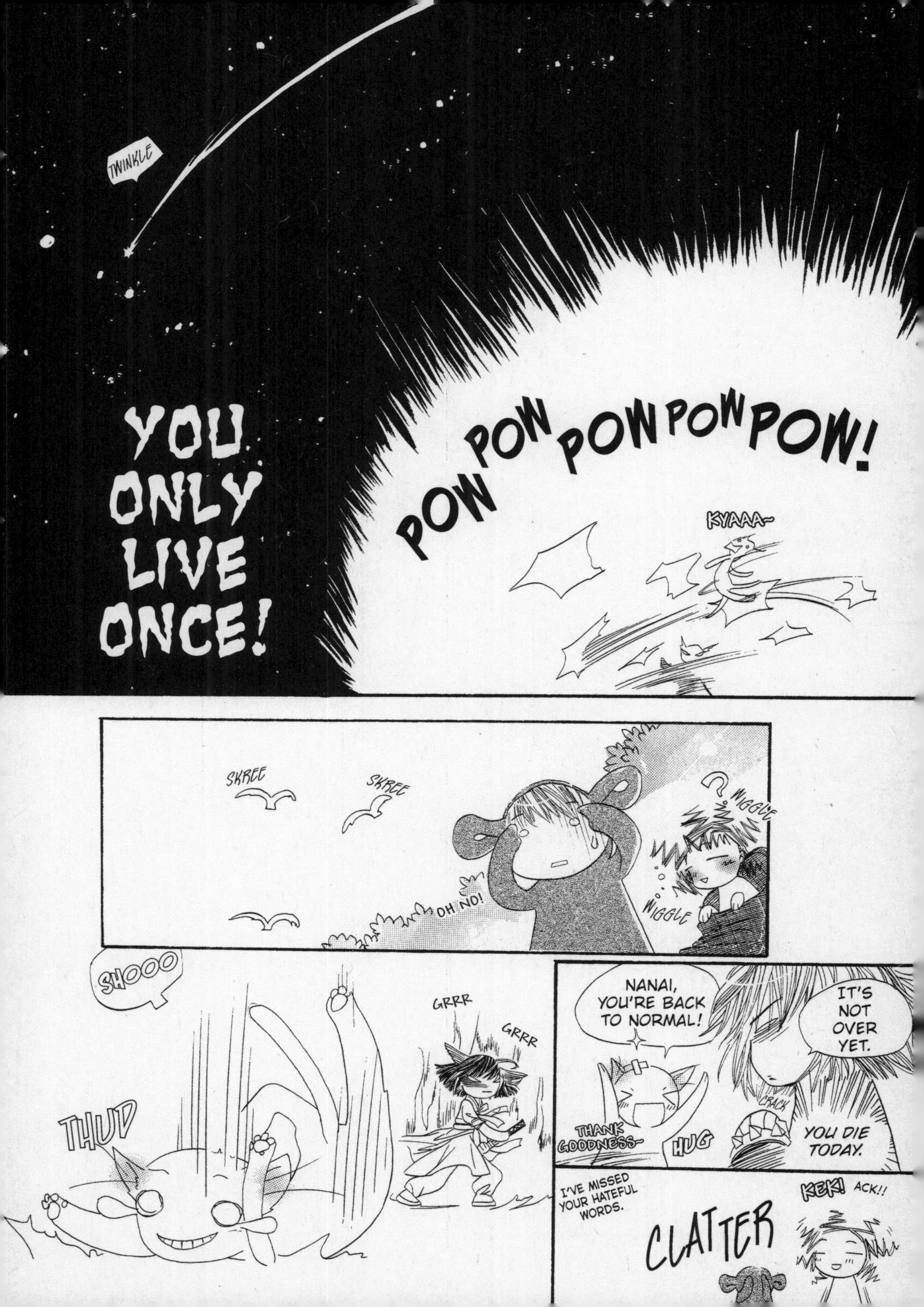
TWINKLE
YOU ONLY LIVE ONCE!
POW POW POW POW POW!
KYAAA~
SKREE
SKREE
OH NO!
WIGGLE
WIGGLE
SHOOO
THUD
GRRR
GRRR
NANAI, YOU'RE BACK TO NORMAL!
THANK GOODNESS~
HUG
IT'S NOT OVER YET.
CRACK
YOU DIE TODAY.
I'VE MISSED YOUR HATEFUL WORDS.
CLATTER
KEK!
ACK!!

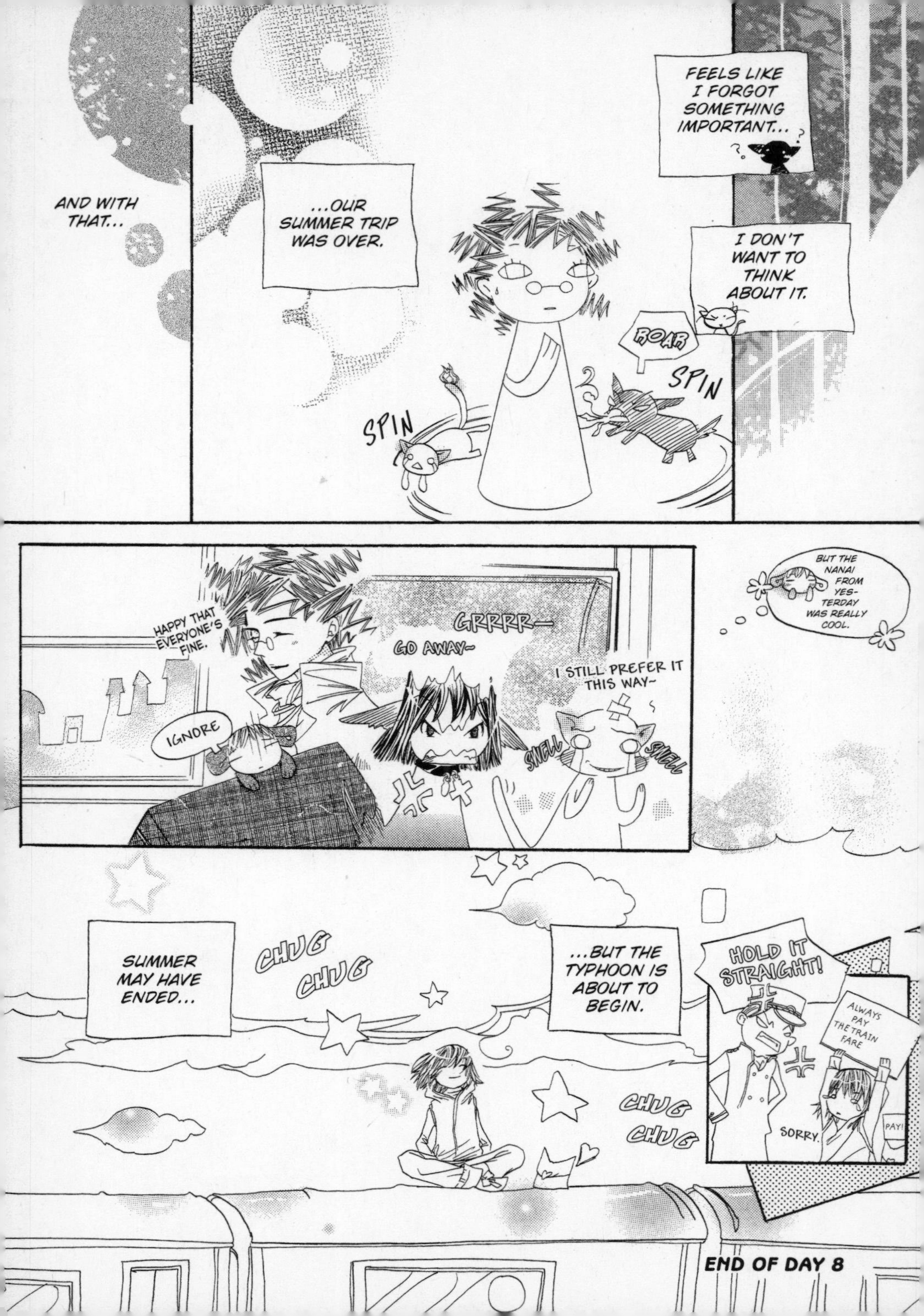
AND WITH THAT...
...OUR SUMMER TRIP WAS OVER.
FEELS LIKE I FORGOT SOMETHING IMPORTANT...
I DON'T WANT TO THINK ABOUT IT.
ROAR
SPIN
SPIN
HAPPY THAT EVERYONE'S FINE.
GRRRR—
GO AWAY~
I STILL PREFER IT THIS WAY~
IGNORE
SNIFF SNIFF
BUT THE NANAI FROM YESTERDAY WAS REALLY COOL.
SUMMER MAY HAVE ENDED...
CHUG CHUG
...BUT THE TYPHOON IS ABOUT TO BEGIN.
CHUG CHUG
HOLD IT STRAIGHT!
ALWAYS PAY THE TRAIN FARE
SORRY.
PAY!

END OF DAY 8

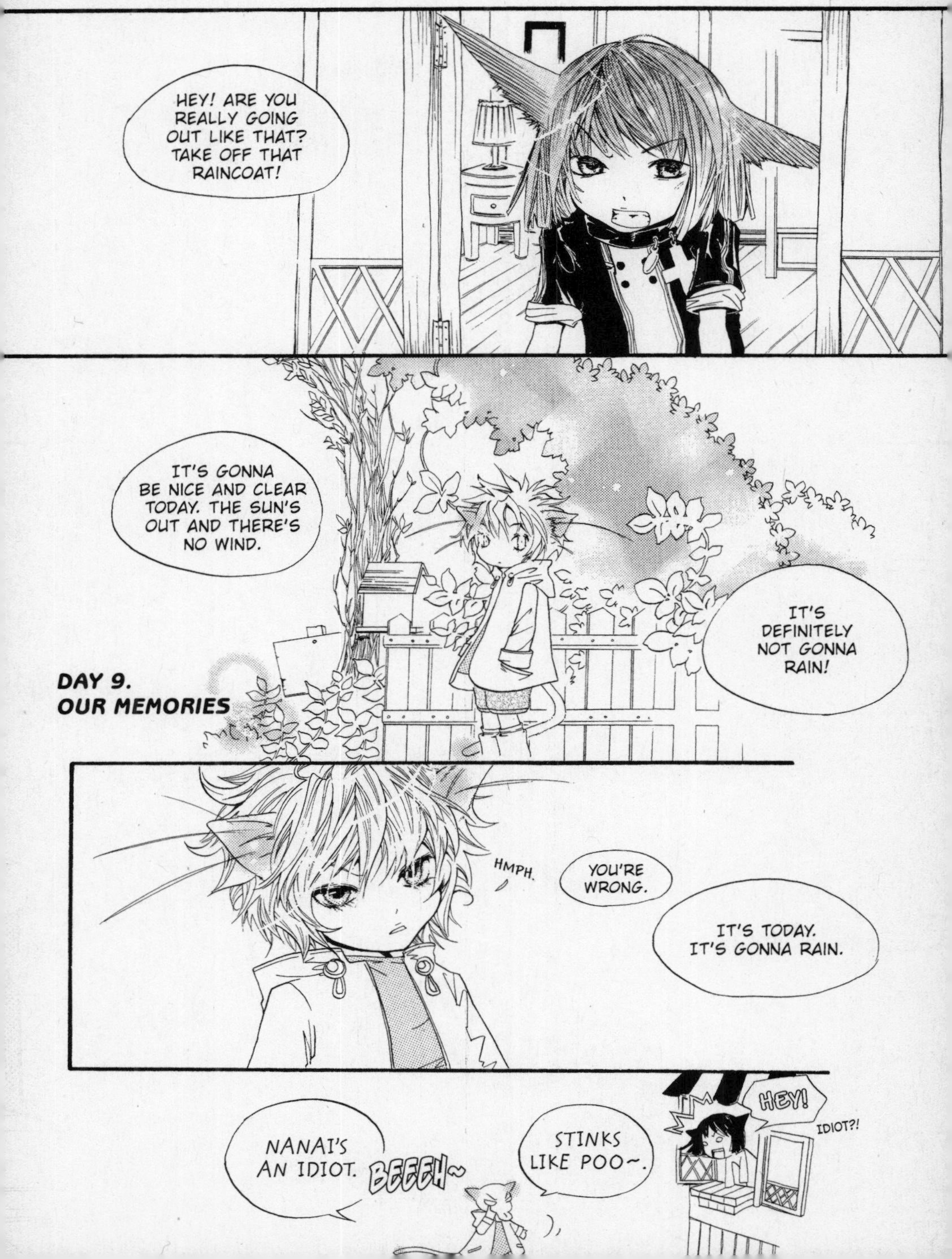
HEY! ARE YOU REALLY GOING OUT LIKE THAT? TAKE OFF THAT RAINCOAT!
IT'S GONNA BE NICE AND CLEAR TODAY. THE SUN'S OUT AND THERE'S NO WIND.
IT'S DEFINITELY NOT GONNA RAIN!
DAY 9.
OUR MEMORIES
HMPH.
YOU'RE WRONG.
IT'S TODAY. IT'S GONNA RAIN.
NANAI'S AN IDIOT.
BEEEH~
STINKS LIKE POO~.
HEY!
IDIOT?!

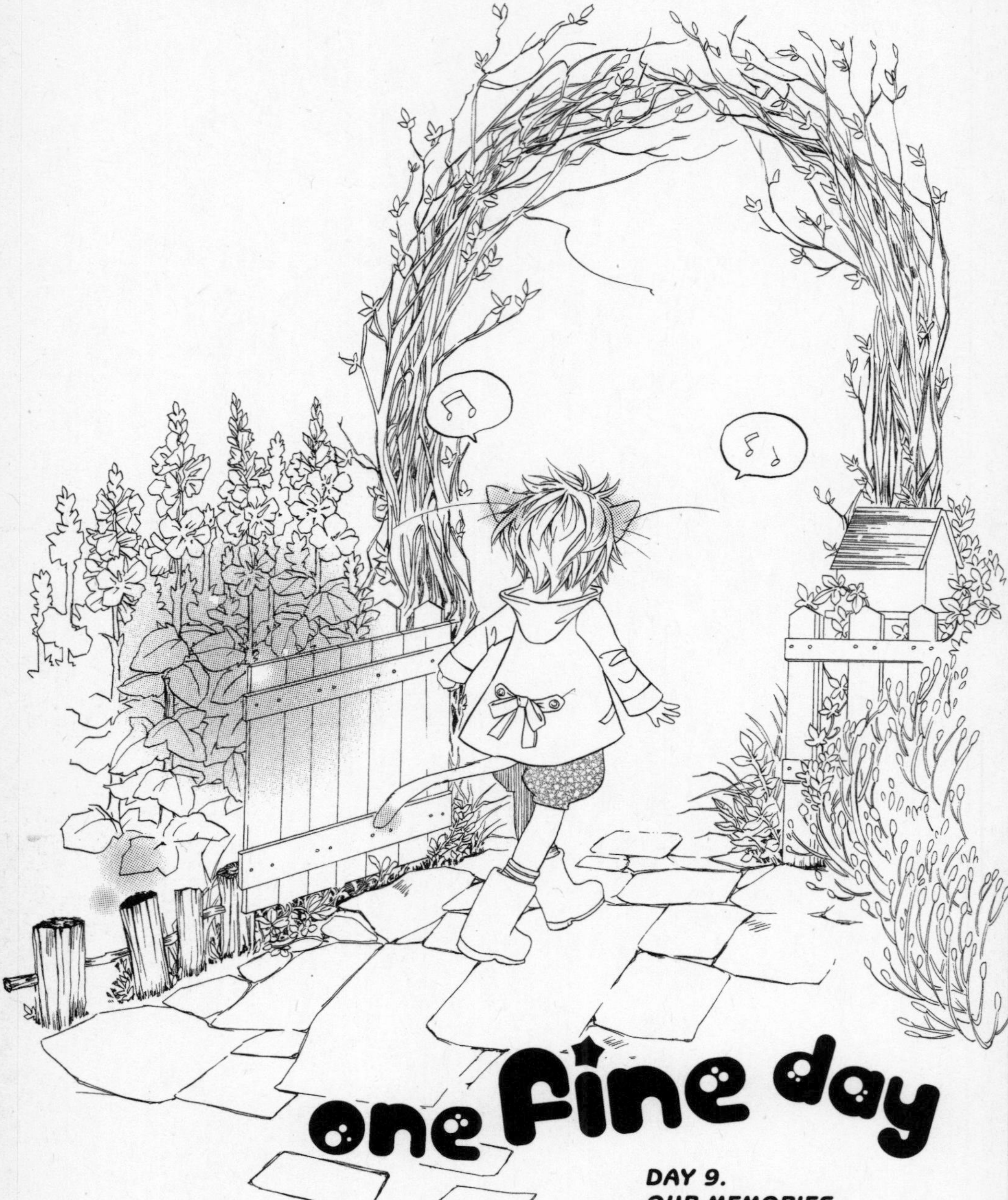

# one fine day

## DAY 9.
## OUR MEMORIES

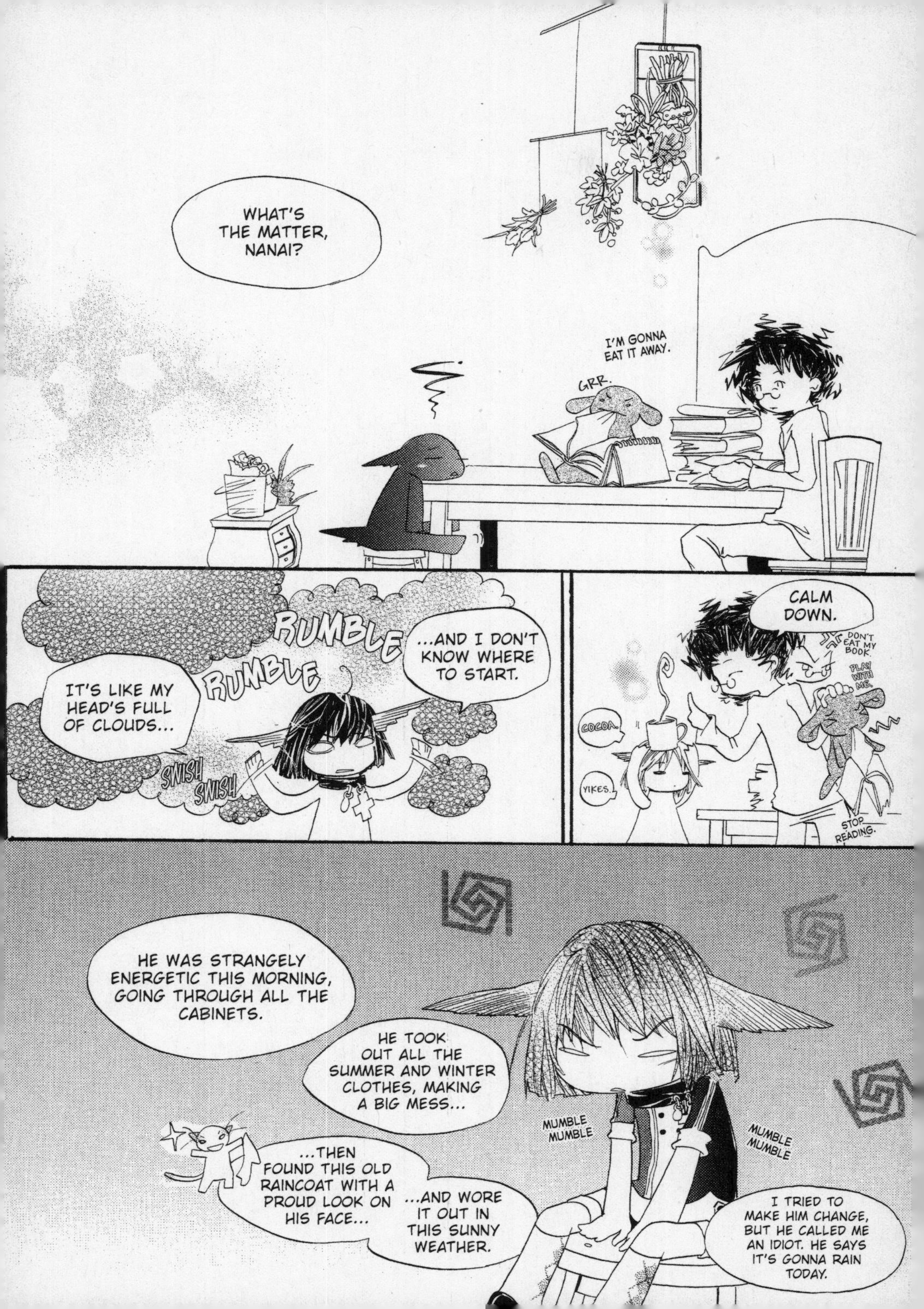
WHAT'S THE MATTER, NANAI?
I'M GONNA EAT IT AWAY.
GRR.
IT'S LIKE MY HEAD'S FULL OF CLOUDS...
RUMBLE
RUMBLE
...AND I DON'T KNOW WHERE TO START.
SWISH
SWISH
CALM DOWN.
DON'T EAT MY BOOK.
PLAY WITH ME.
COCOA.
YIKES.
STOP READING.
HE WAS STRANGELY ENERGETIC THIS MORNING, GOING THROUGH ALL THE CABINETS.
HE TOOK OUT ALL THE SUMMER AND WINTER CLOTHES, MAKING A BIG MESS...
MUMBLE MUMBLE
MUMBLE MUMBLE
...THEN FOUND THIS OLD RAINCOAT WITH A PROUD LOOK ON HIS FACE...
...AND WORE IT OUT IN THIS SUNNY WEATHER.
I TRIED TO MAKE HIM CHANGE, BUT HE CALLED ME AN IDIOT. HE SAYS IT'S GONNA RAIN TODAY.

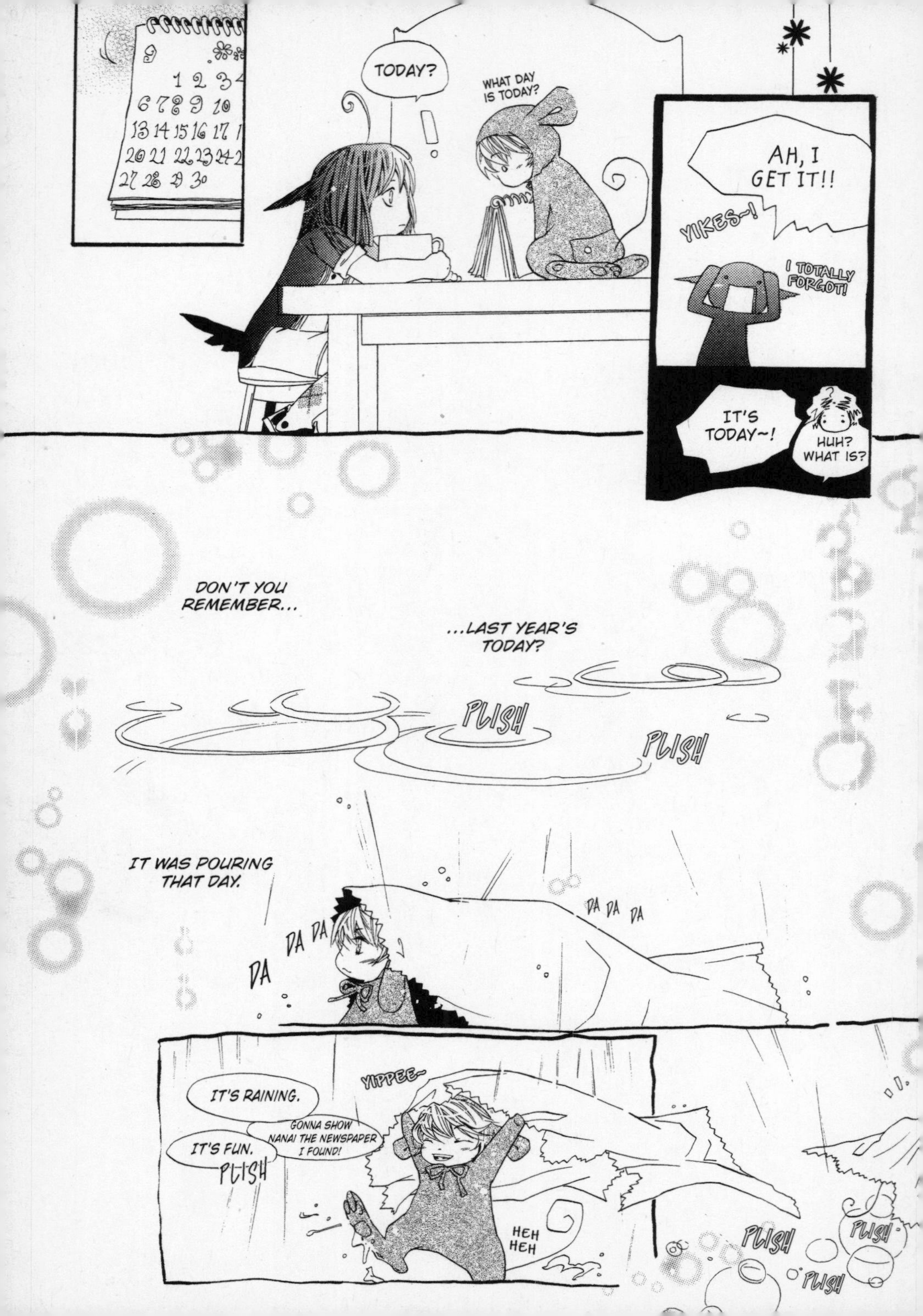
TODAY?
WHAT DAY IS TODAY?
AH, I GET IT!!
YIKES~!
I TOTALLY FORGOT!
IT'S TODAY~!
HUH? WHAT IS?
DON'T YOU REMEMBER...
...LAST YEAR'S TODAY?
PLISH
PLISH
IT WAS POURING THAT DAY.
DA DA DA
DA DA DA
YIPPEE~
IT'S RAINING.
GONNA SHOW NANAI THE NEWSPAPER I FOUND!
IT'S FUN.
PLISH
HEH HEH
PLISH
PLISH
PLISH

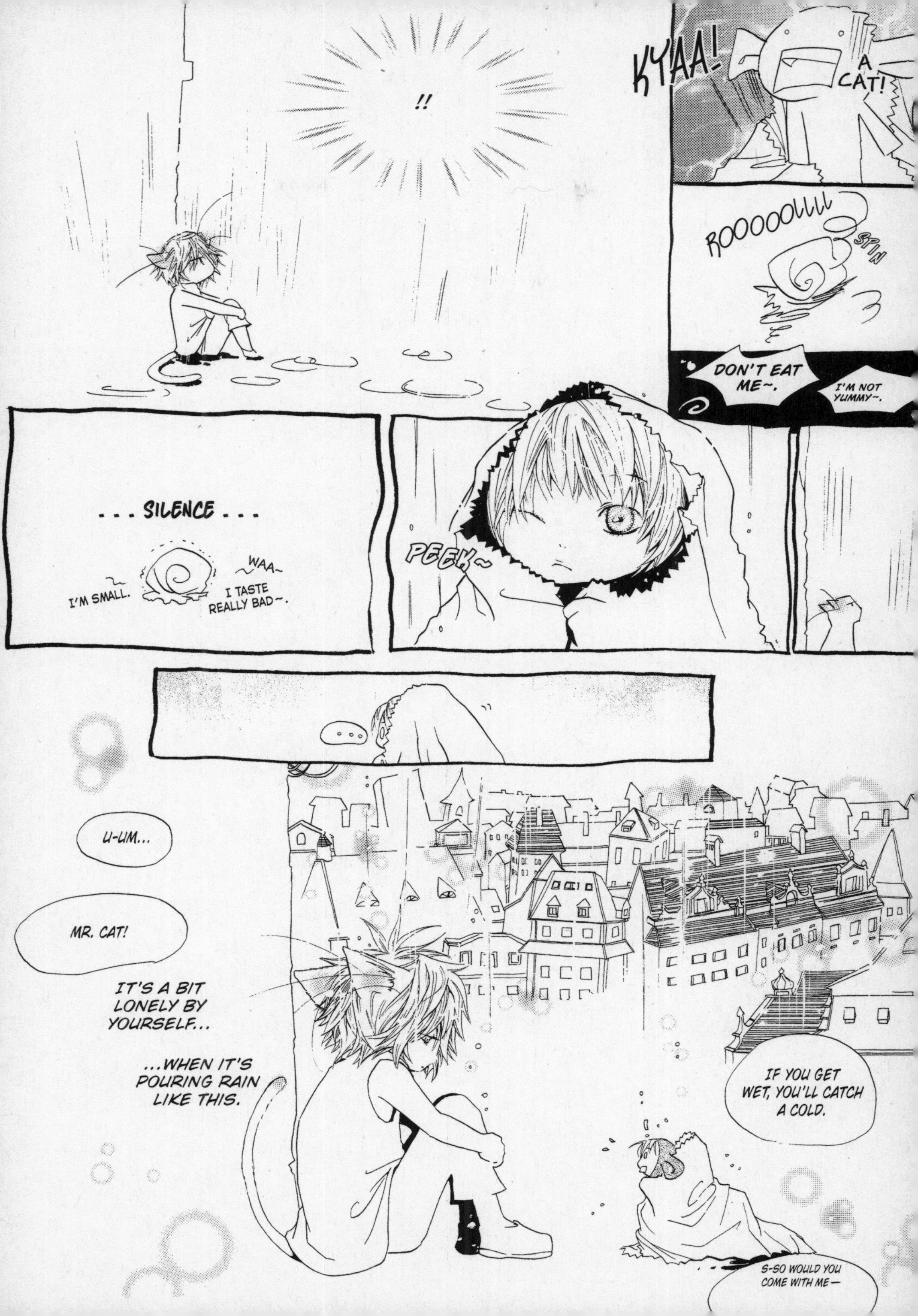
KYAA!
A CAT!
!!
ROOOOOLLLL
SPIN
DON'T EAT ME~.
I'M NOT YUMMY~.
PEEK~
...SILENCE...
I'M SMALL.
WAA~
I TASTE REALLY BAD~.
...
U-UM...
MR. CAT!
IT'S A BIT LONELY BY YOURSELF...
...WHEN IT'S POURING RAIN LIKE THIS.
IF YOU GET WET, YOU'LL CATCH A COLD.
S-SO WOULD YOU COME WITH ME—

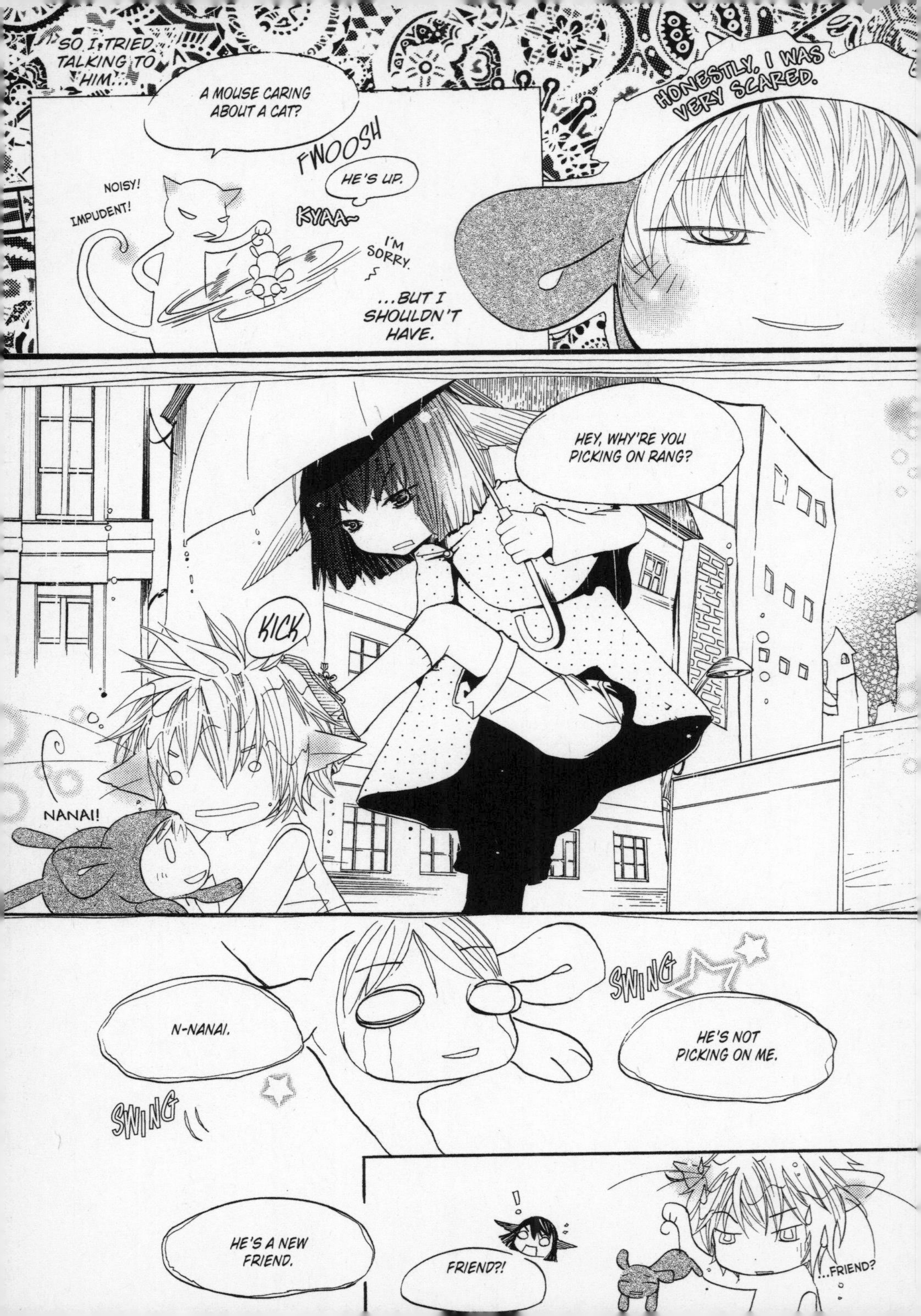

SO I TRIED TALKING TO HIM...
A MOUSE CARING ABOUT A CAT?
FWOOSH
HE'S UP.
NOISY!
IMPUDENT!
KYAA~
I'M SORRY.
...BUT I SHOULDN'T HAVE.
HONESTLY, I WAS VERY SCARED.
HEY, WHY'RE YOU PICKING ON RANG?
KICK
NANAI!
SWING
N-NANAI.
HE'S NOT PICKING ON ME.
SWING
HE'S A NEW FRIEND.
FRIEND?!
...FRIEND?

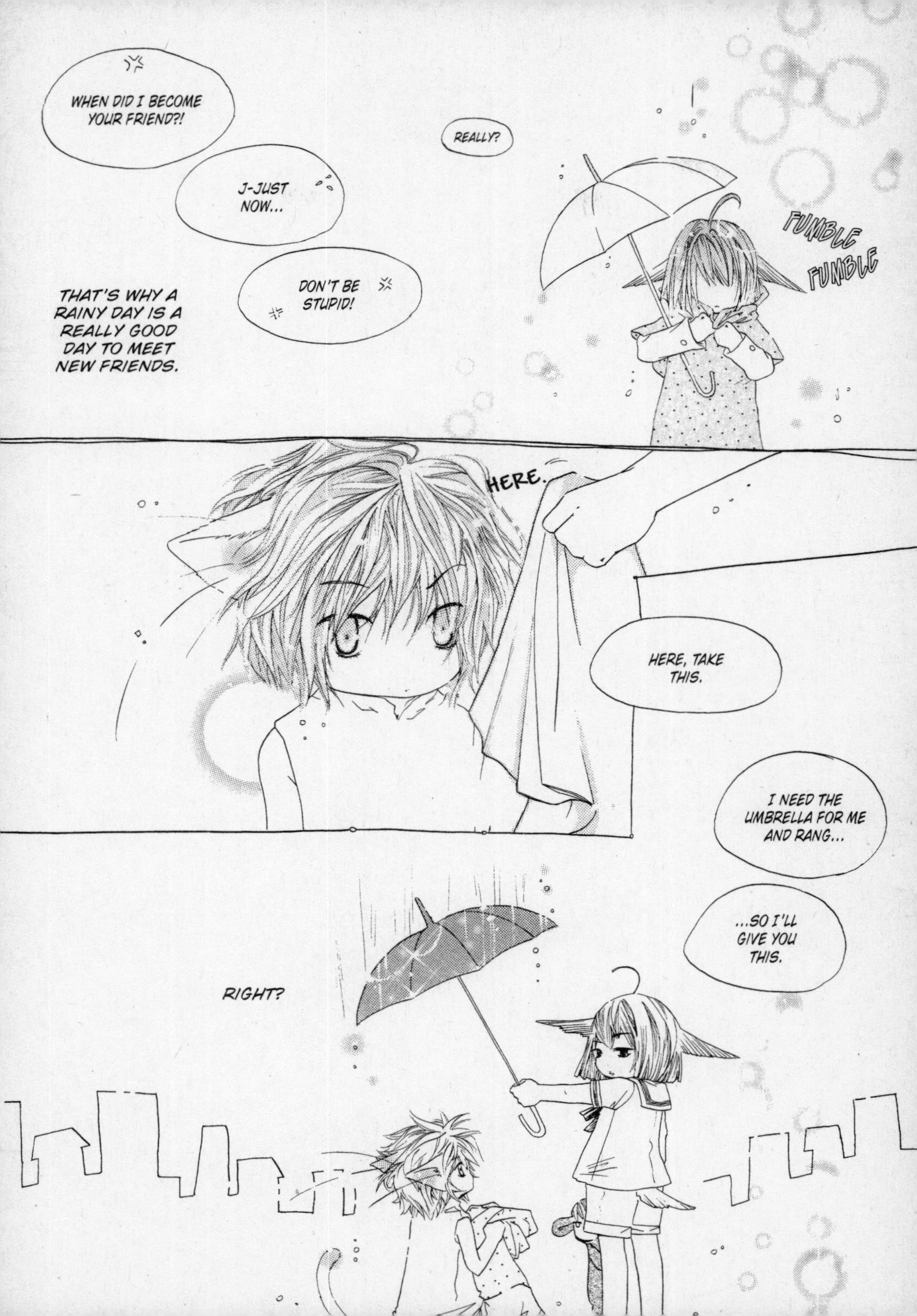

WHEN DID I BECOME YOUR FRIEND?!
REALLY?
J-JUST NOW...
DON'T BE STUPID!
THAT'S WHY A RAINY DAY IS A REALLY GOOD DAY TO MEET NEW FRIENDS.
FUMBLE FUMBLE
HERE.
HERE, TAKE THIS.
I NEED THE UMBRELLA FOR ME AND RANG...
...SO I'LL GIVE YOU THIS.
RIGHT?

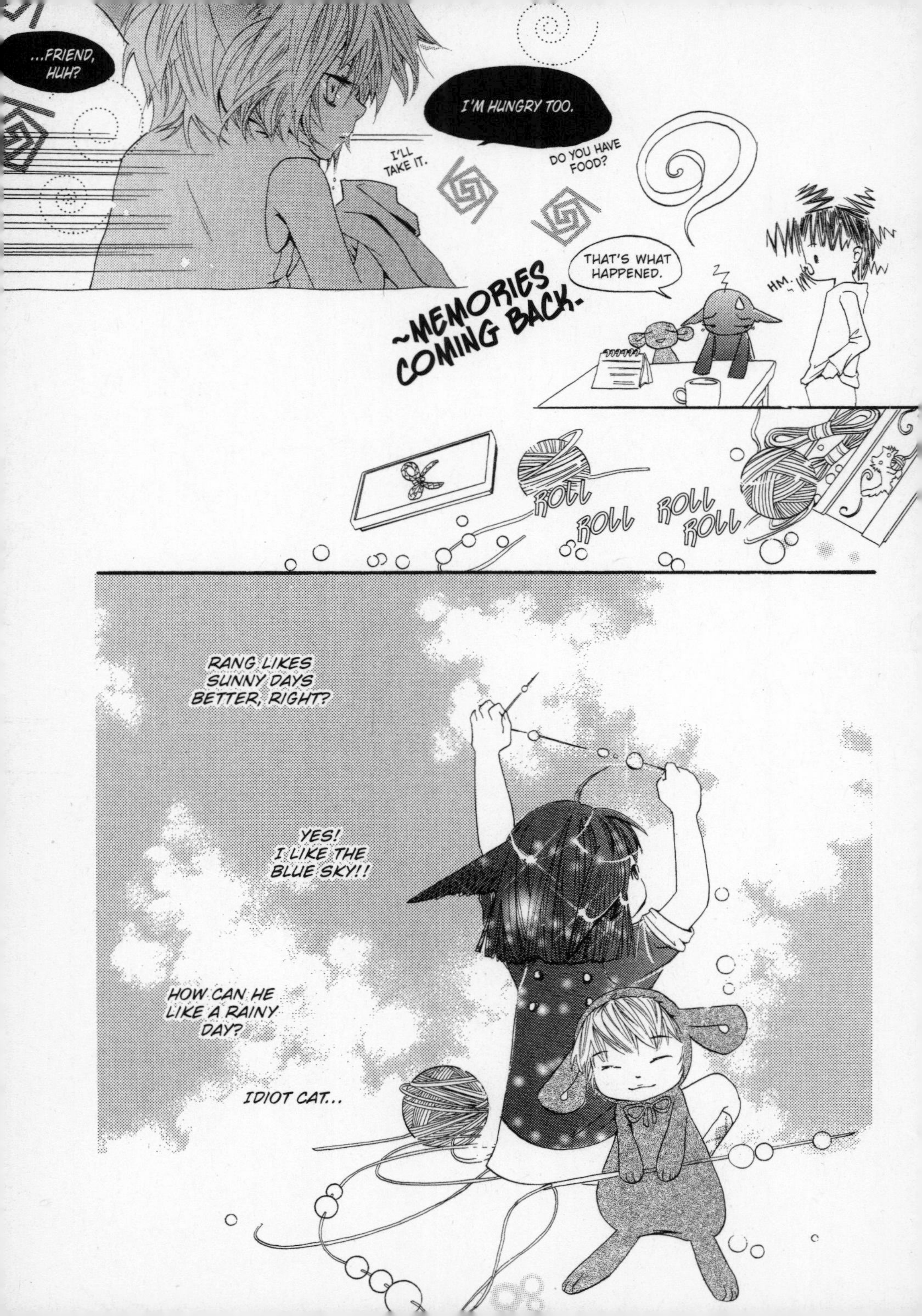
...FRIEND, HUH?
I'M HUNGRY TOO.
I'LL TAKE IT.
DO YOU HAVE FOOD?
~MEMORIES COMING BACK.
THAT'S WHAT HAPPENED.
HM.
ROLL
ROLL
ROLL
ROLL
RANG LIKES SUNNY DAYS BETTER, RIGHT?
YES! I LIKE THE BLUE SKY!!
HOW CAN HE LIKE A RAINY DAY?
IDIOT CAT...

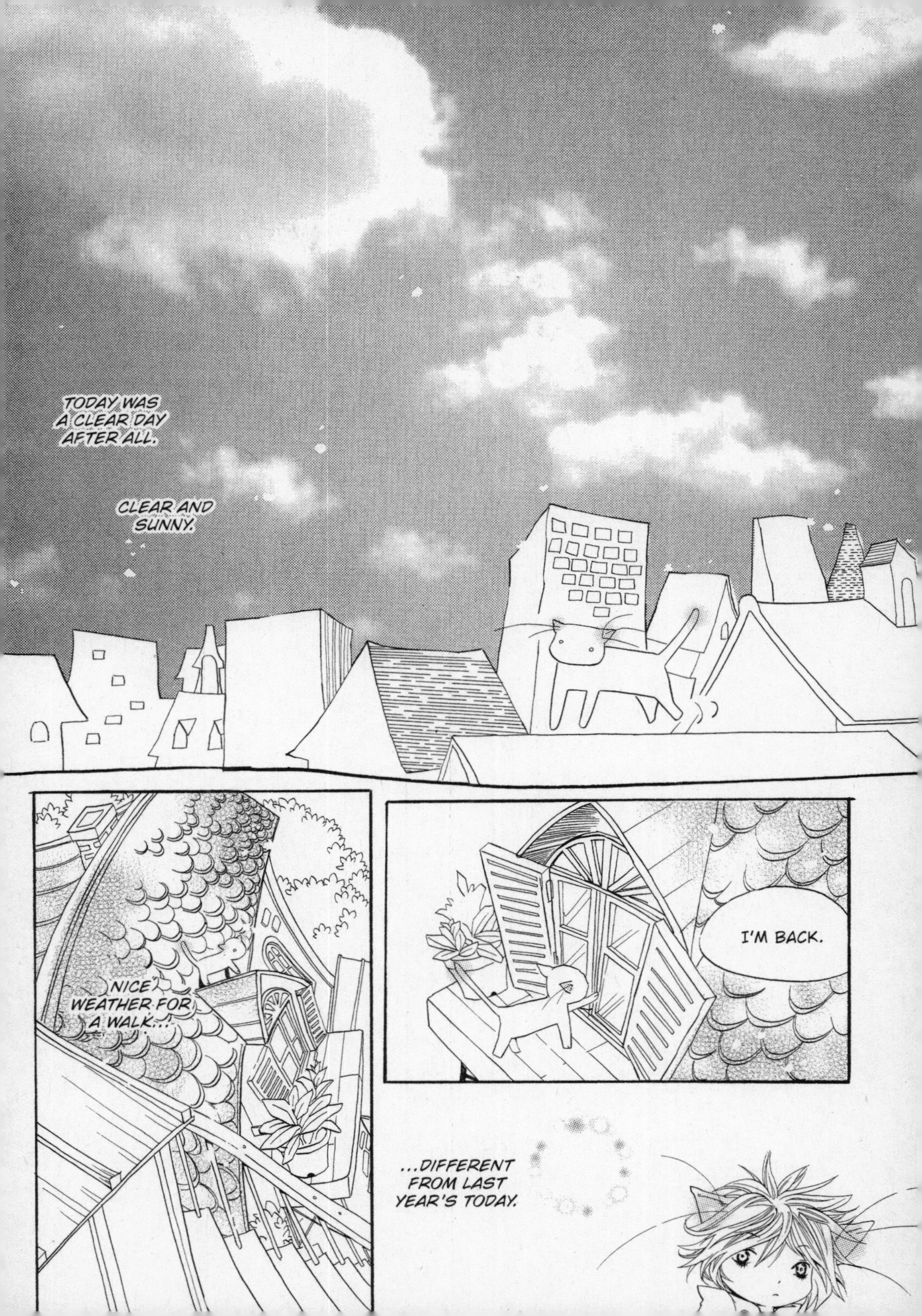
TODAY WAS A CLEAR DAY AFTER ALL.
CLEAR AND SUNNY.
NICE WEATHER FOR A WALK...
I'M BACK.
...DIFFERENT FROM LAST YEAR'S TODAY.

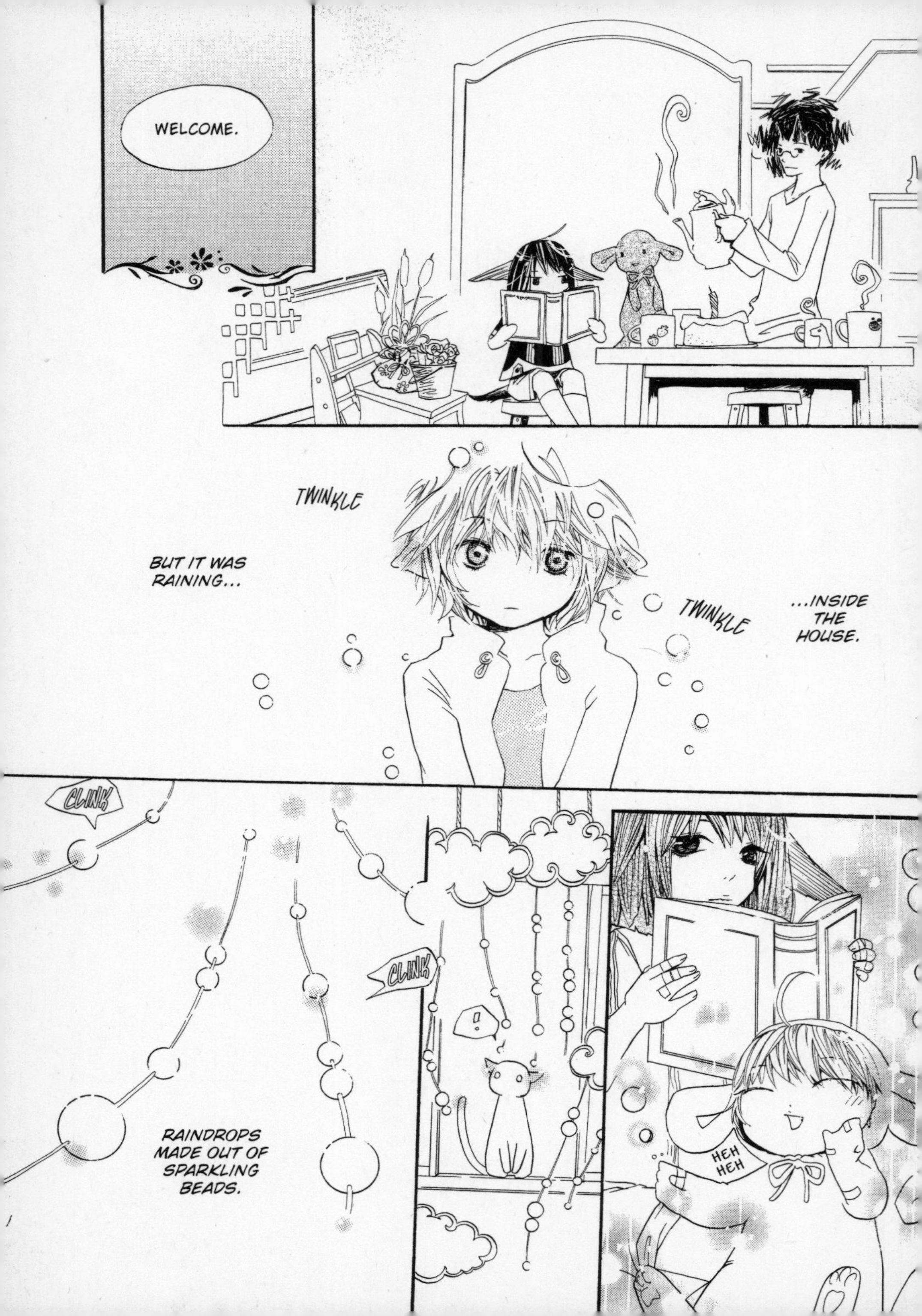
WELCOME.
TWINKLE
BUT IT WAS RAINING...
TWINKLE
...INSIDE THE HOUSE.
CLINK
RAINDROPS MADE OUT OF SPARKLING BEADS.
CLINK
!
HEH HEH

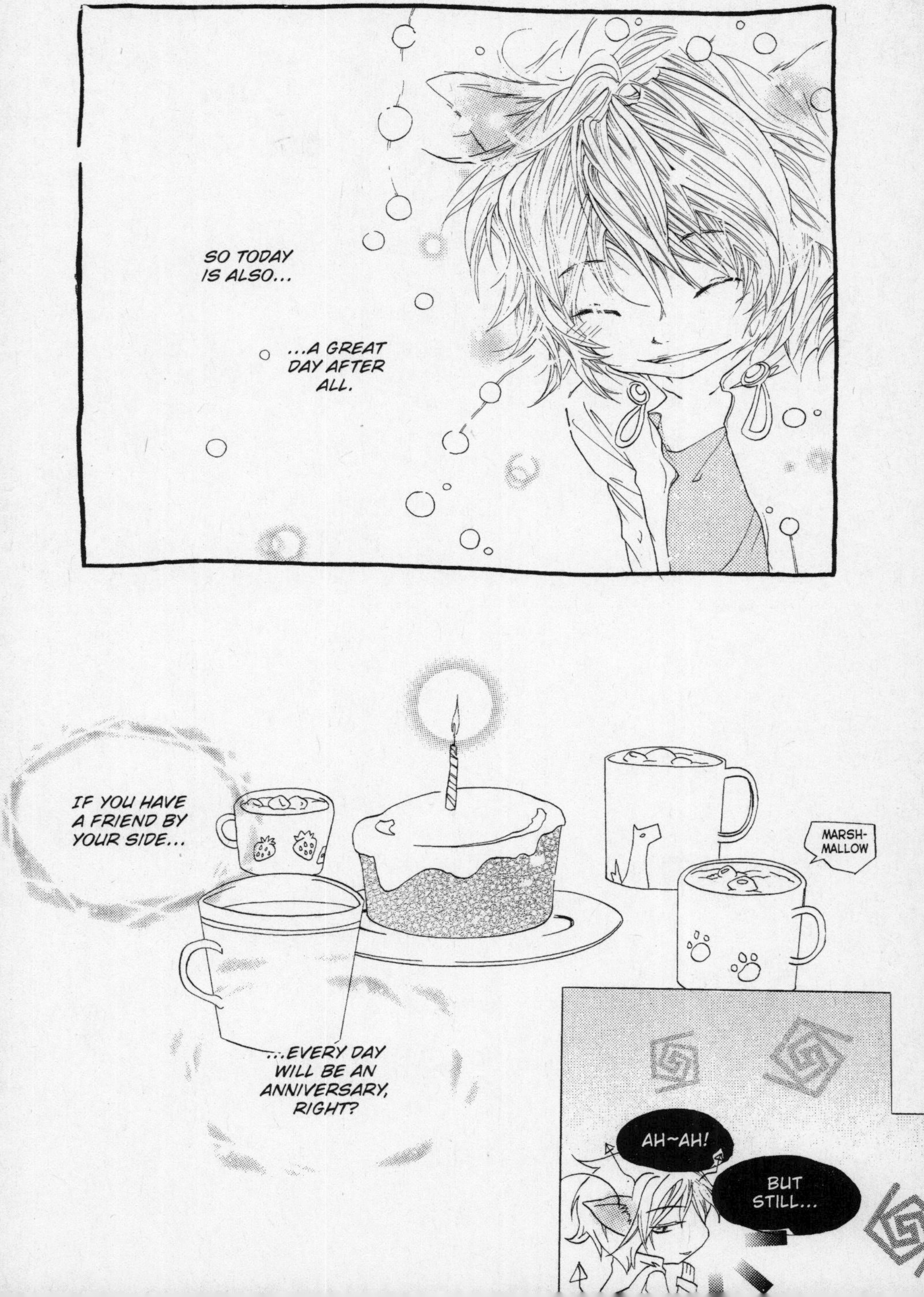
SO TODAY IS ALSO...
...A GREAT DAY AFTER ALL.
IF YOU HAVE A FRIEND BY YOUR SIDE...
MARSH-MALLOW
...EVERY DAY WILL BE AN ANNIVERSARY, RIGHT?
AH~AH!
BUT STILL...

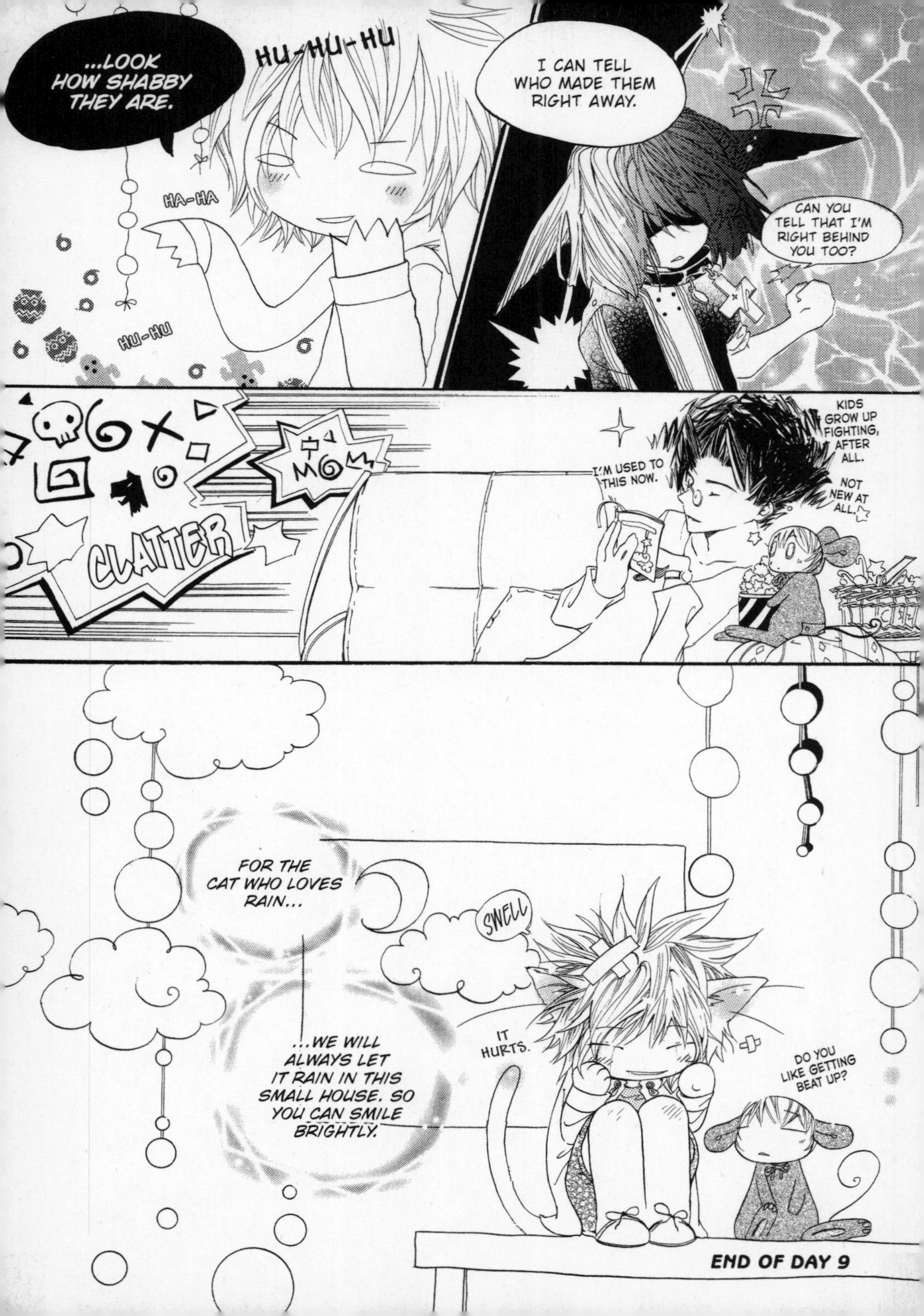

...LOOK HOW SHABBY THEY ARE.
HU-HU-HU
HA-HA
HU-HU
I CAN TELL WHO MADE THEM RIGHT AWAY.
CAN YOU TELL THAT I'M RIGHT BEHIND YOU TOO?
CLATTER
I'M USED TO THIS NOW.
KIDS GROW UP FIGHTING, AFTER ALL.
NOT NEW AT ALL.
FOR THE CAT WHO LOVES RAIN...
...WE WILL ALWAYS LET IT RAIN IN THIS SMALL HOUSE. SO YOU CAN SMILE BRIGHTLY.
SWELL
IT HURTS.
DO YOU LIKE GETTING BEAT UP?
END OF DAY 9

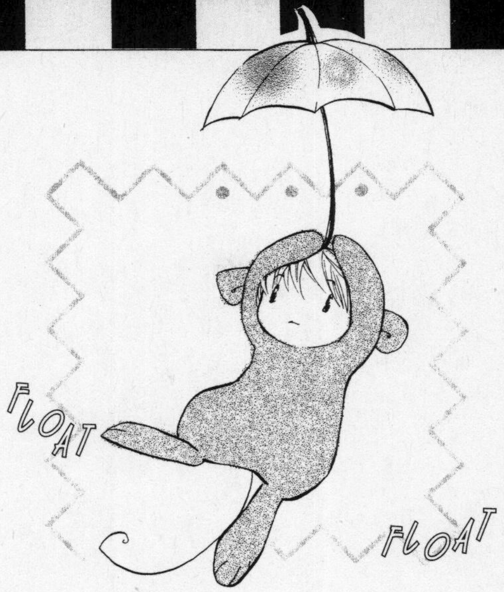
FLOAT
FLOAT

**ANOTHER DAY #3**
**SWEET LUNCH**

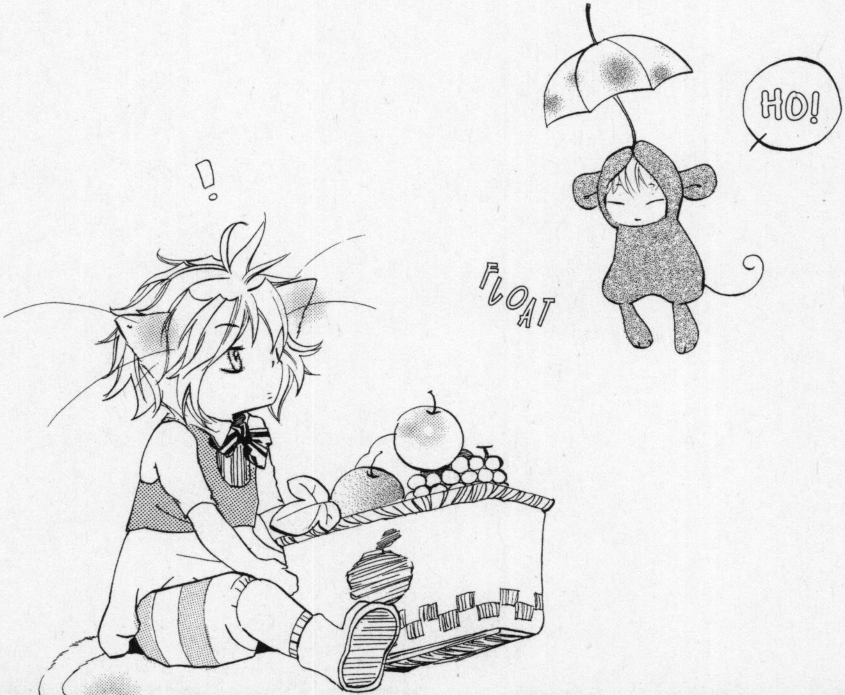
HO!
FLOAT
!

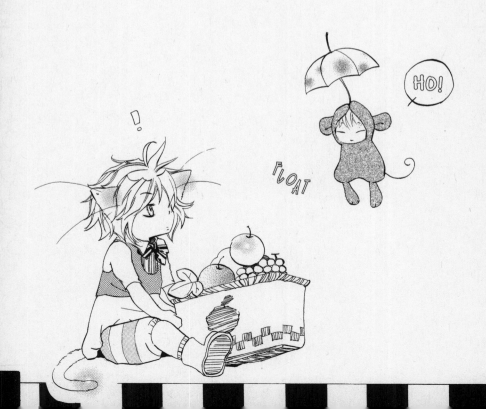

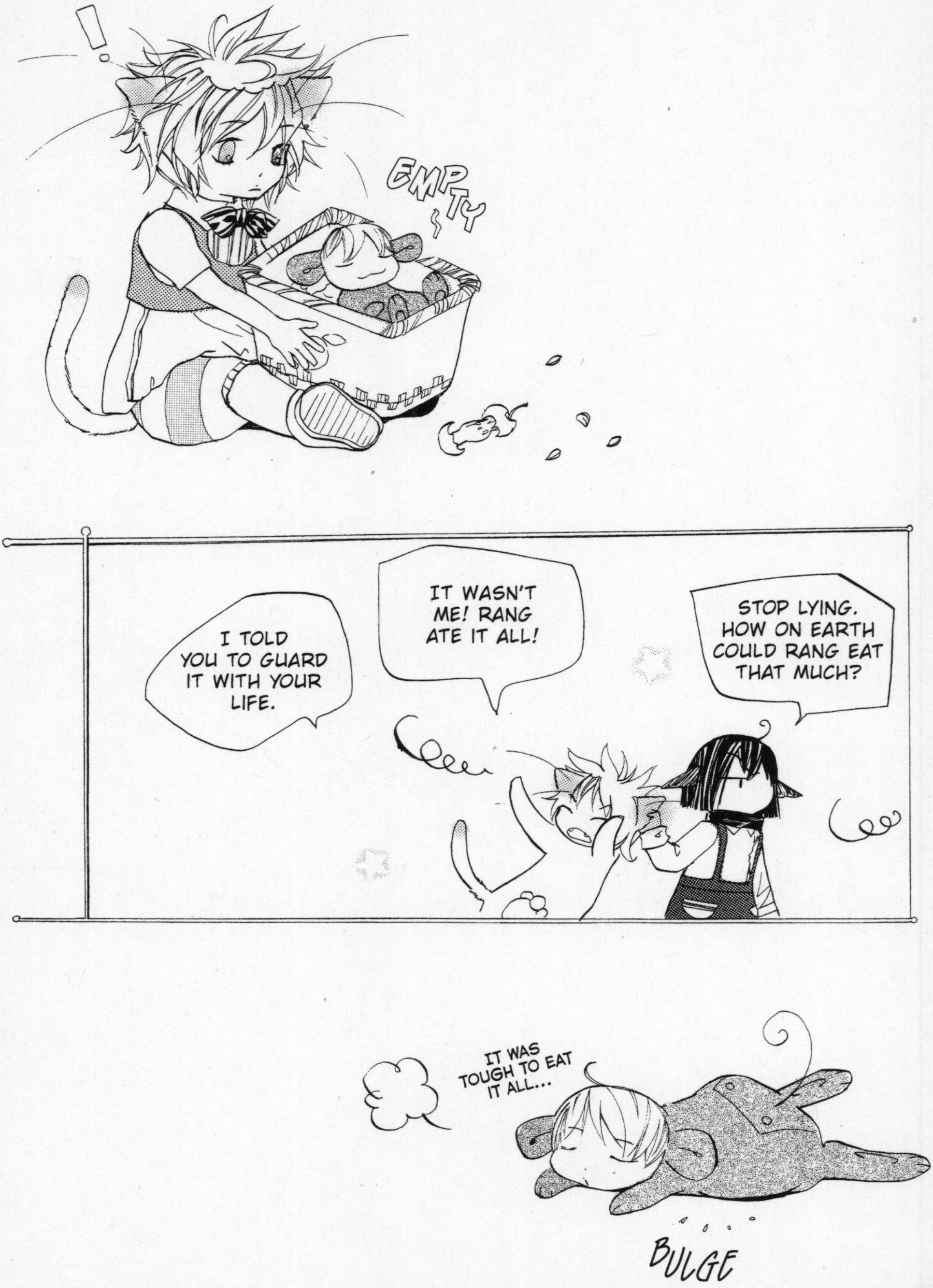
!
EMPTY
I TOLD YOU TO GUARD IT WITH YOUR LIFE.
IT WASN'T ME! RANG ATE IT ALL!
STOP LYING. HOW ON EARTH COULD RANG EAT THAT MUCH?
IT WAS TOUGH TO EAT IT ALL...
BULGE

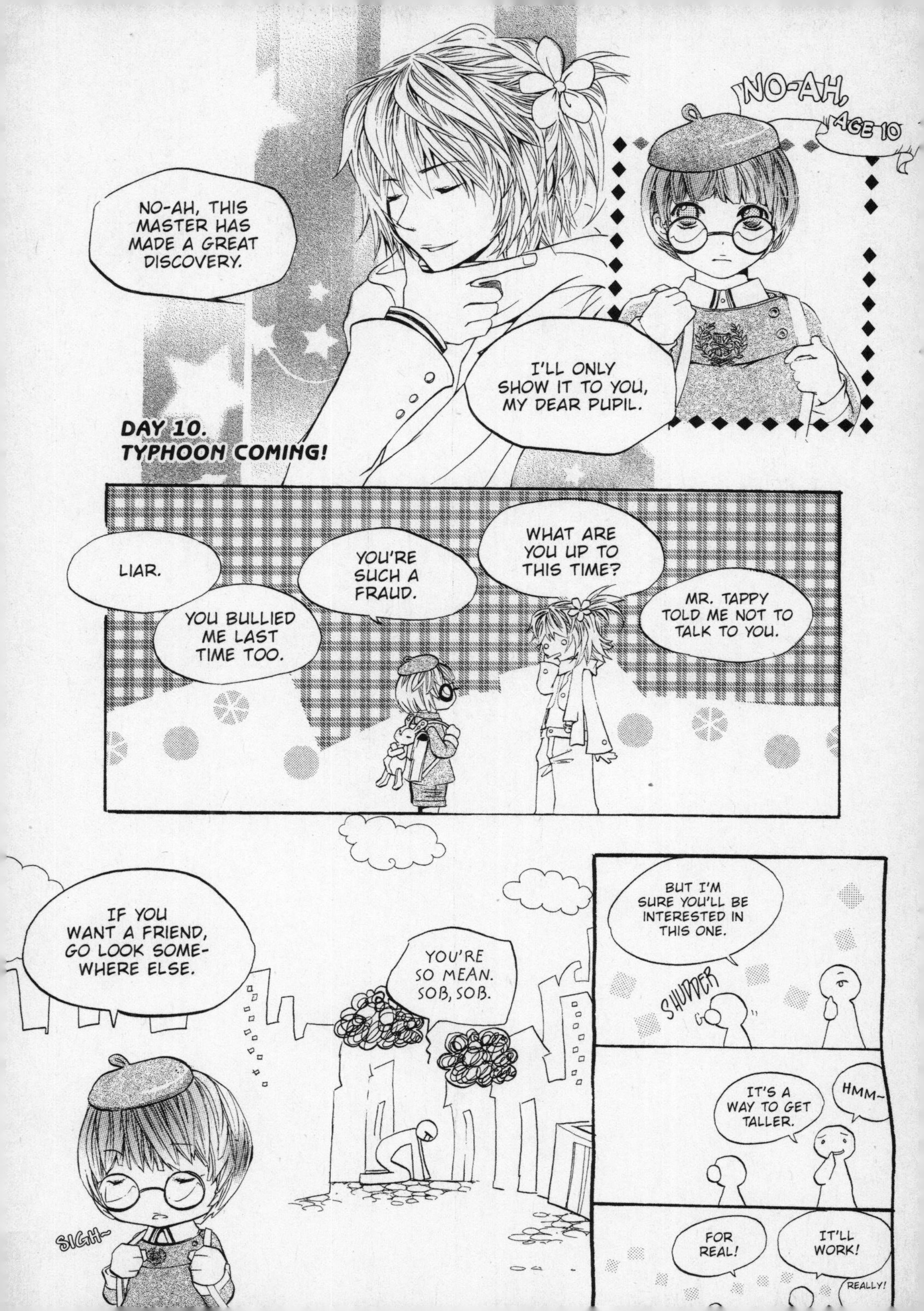
NO-AH, THIS MASTER HAS MADE A GREAT DISCOVERY.
NO-AH, AGE 10
I'LL ONLY SHOW IT TO YOU, MY DEAR PUPIL.
DAY 10. TYPHOON COMING!
LIAR.
YOU BULLIED ME LAST TIME TOO.
YOU'RE SUCH A FRAUD.
WHAT ARE YOU UP TO THIS TIME?
MR. TAPPY TOLD ME NOT TO TALK TO YOU.
IF YOU WANT A FRIEND, GO LOOK SOME-WHERE ELSE.
SIGH~
YOU'RE SO MEAN. SOB, SOB.
BUT I'M SURE YOU'LL BE INTERESTED IN THIS ONE.
SHUDDER
IT'S A WAY TO GET TALLER.
HMM~
FOR REAL!
IT'LL WORK!
REALLY!

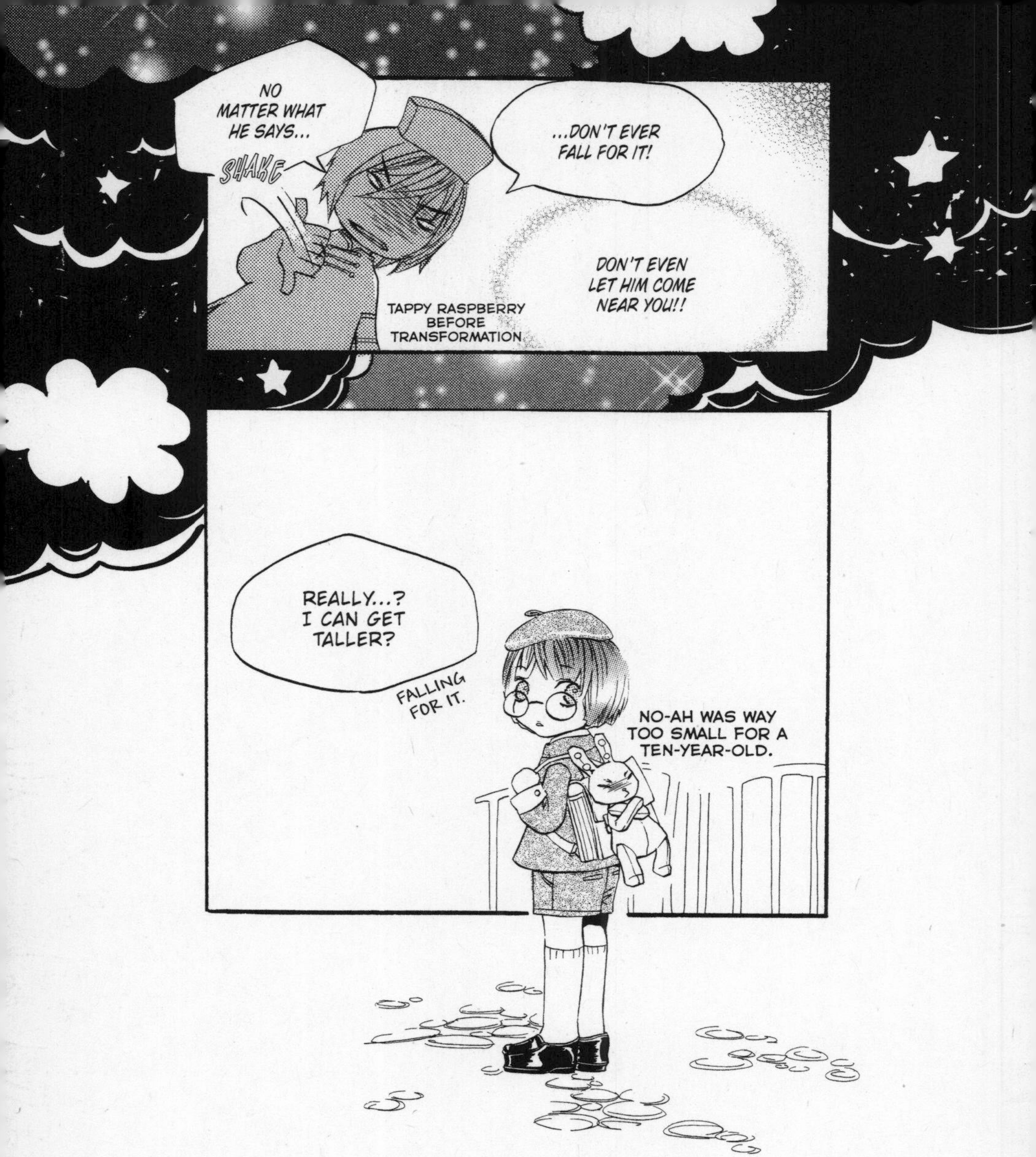
NO MATTER WHAT HE SAYS...
SHAKE
...DON'T EVER FALL FOR IT!
DON'T EVEN LET HIM COME NEAR YOU!!
TAPPY RASPBERRY BEFORE TRANSFORMATION
REALLY...? I CAN GET TALLER?
FALLING FOR IT.
NO-AH WAS WAY TOO SMALL FOR A TEN-YEAR-OLD.

# one fine day

**DAY 10.**
**TYPHOON COMING!**

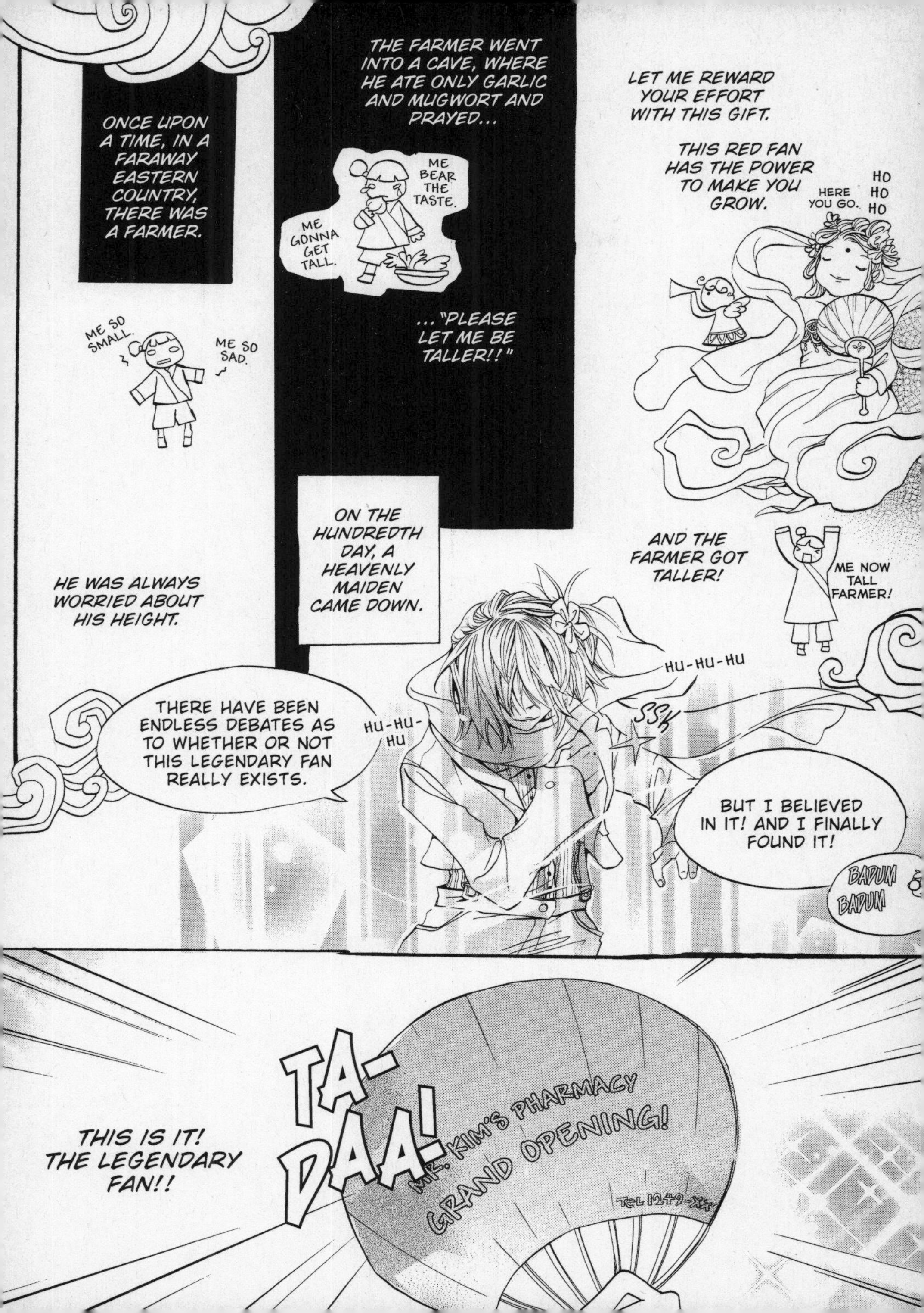
ONCE UPON A TIME, IN A FARAWAY EASTERN COUNTRY, THERE WAS A FARMER.
ME SO SMALL.
ME SO SAD.
HE WAS ALWAYS WORRIED ABOUT HIS HEIGHT.
THE FARMER WENT INTO A CAVE, WHERE HE ATE ONLY GARLIC AND MUGWORT AND PRAYED...
ME BEAR THE TASTE.
ME GONNA GET TALL.
..."PLEASE LET ME BE TALLER!!"
ON THE HUNDREDTH DAY, A HEAVENLY MAIDEN CAME DOWN.
LET ME REWARD YOUR EFFORT WITH THIS GIFT.
THIS RED FAN HAS THE POWER TO MAKE YOU GROW.
HERE YOU GO.
HO HO HO
AND THE FARMER GOT TALLER!
ME NOW TALL FARMER!
THERE HAVE BEEN ENDLESS DEBATES AS TO WHETHER OR NOT THIS LEGENDARY FAN REALLY EXISTS.
HU-HU-HU
HU-HU-HU
SSK
BUT I BELIEVED IN IT! AND I FINALLY FOUND IT!
BADUM BADUM
THIS IS IT! THE LEGENDARY FAN!!
TA-DAA!
MR. KIM'S PHARMACY
GRAND OPENING!
Tel 1249-XX

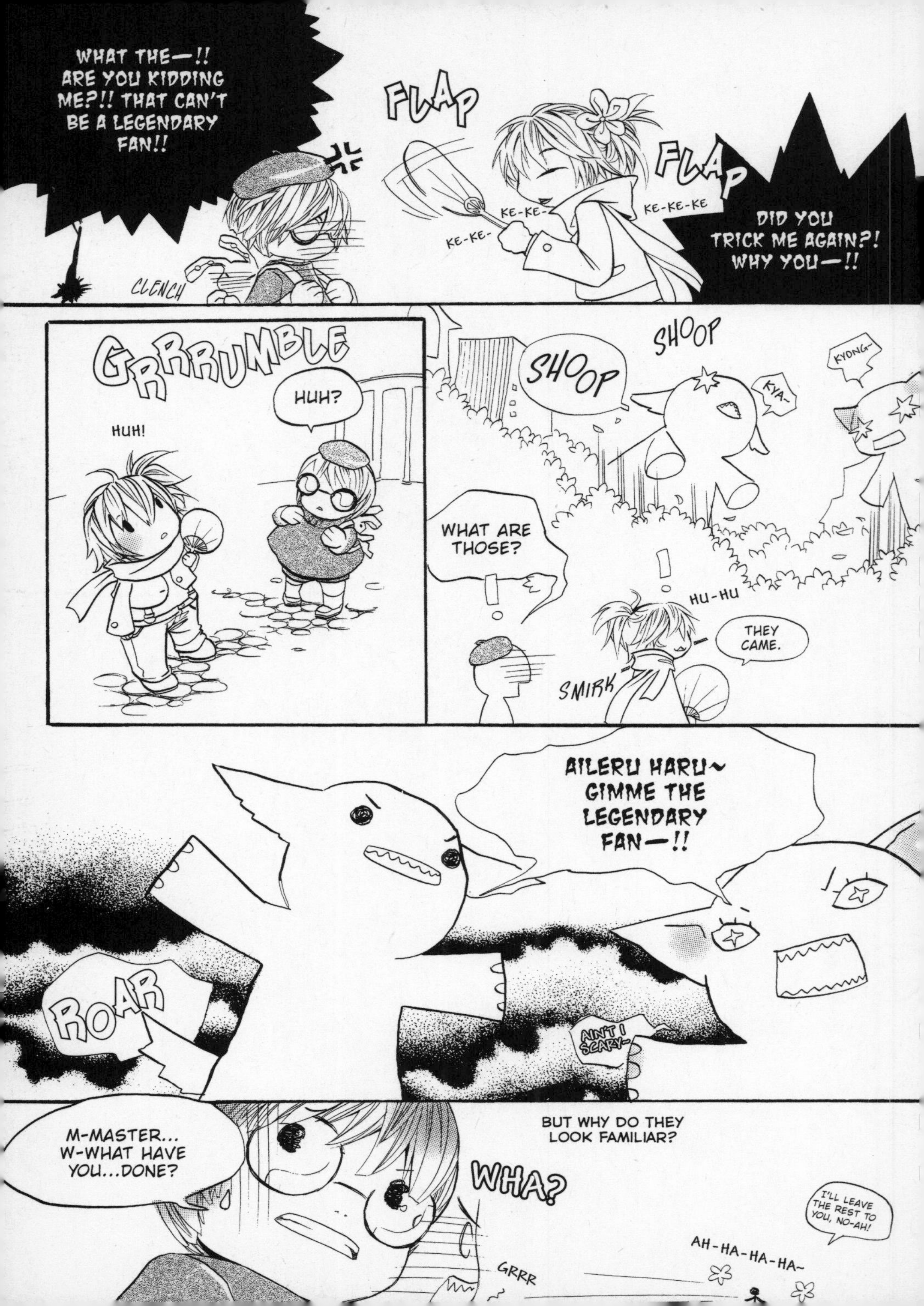
WHAT THE—!! ARE YOU KIDDING ME?!! THAT CAN'T BE A LEGENDARY FAN!!
FLAP
FLAP
KE-KE-
KE-KE-
KE-KE-KE
DID YOU TRICK ME AGAIN?! WHY YOU—!!
CLENCH
GRRRUMBLE
HUH?
HUH!
SHOOP
SHOOP
KYA-
KYONG-
WHAT ARE THOSE?
HU-HU
THEY CAME.
SMIRK
AILERU HARU~ GIMME THE LEGENDARY FAN—!!
ROAR
AIN'T I SCARY~
M-MASTER... W-WHAT HAVE YOU...DONE?
BUT WHY DO THEY LOOK FAMILIAR?
WHA?
I'LL LEAVE THE REST TO YOU, NO-AH!
AH-HA-HA-HA~
GRRR

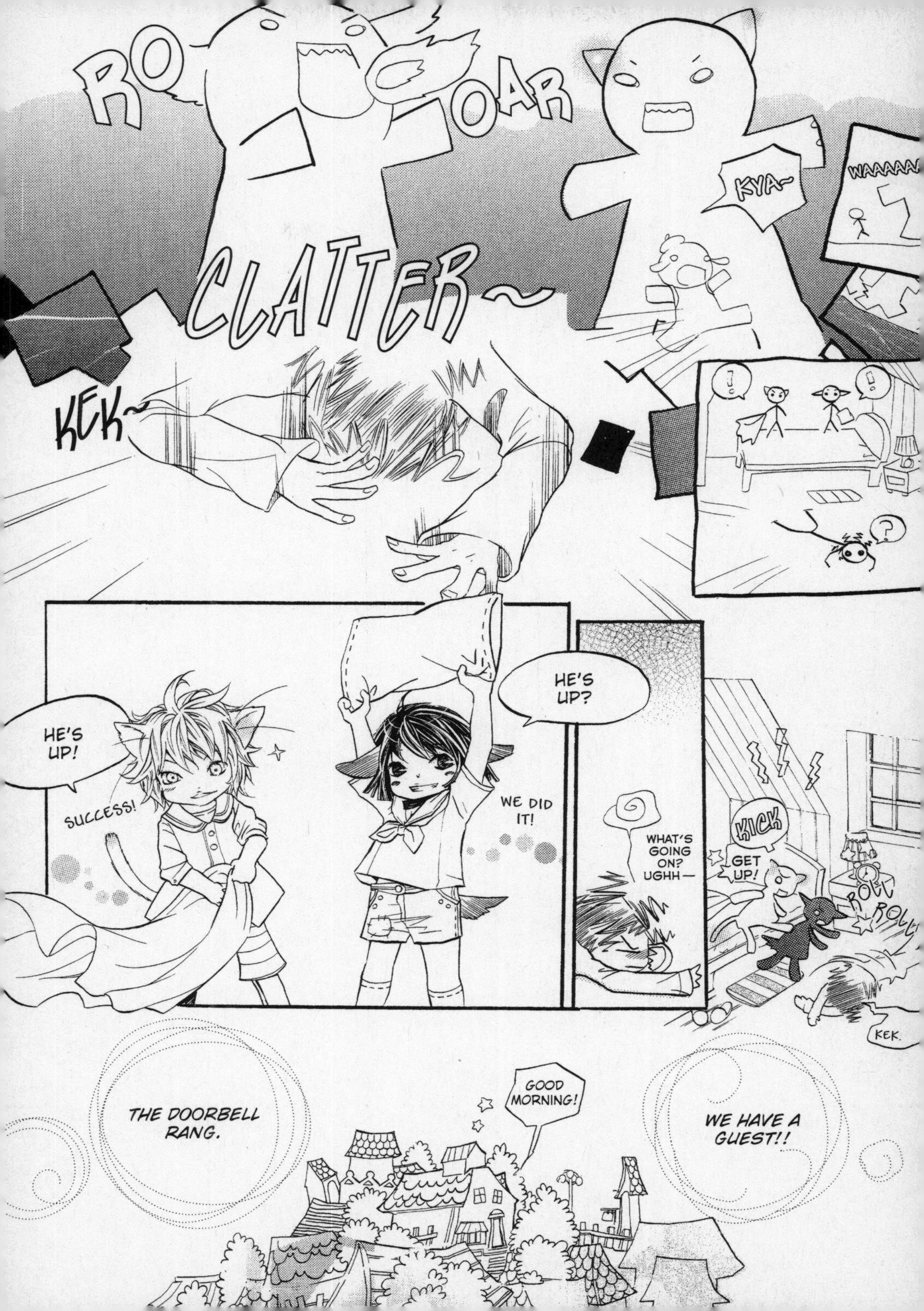

RO
OAR
KYA~
WAAAAA
CLATTER~
KEK~
!
!
?
HE'S UP!
SUCCESS!
HE'S UP?
WE DID IT!
WHAT'S GOING ON? UGHH—
KICK
GET UP!
ROLL ROLL
KEK.
THE DOORBELL RANG.
GOOD MORNING!
WE HAVE A GUEST!!

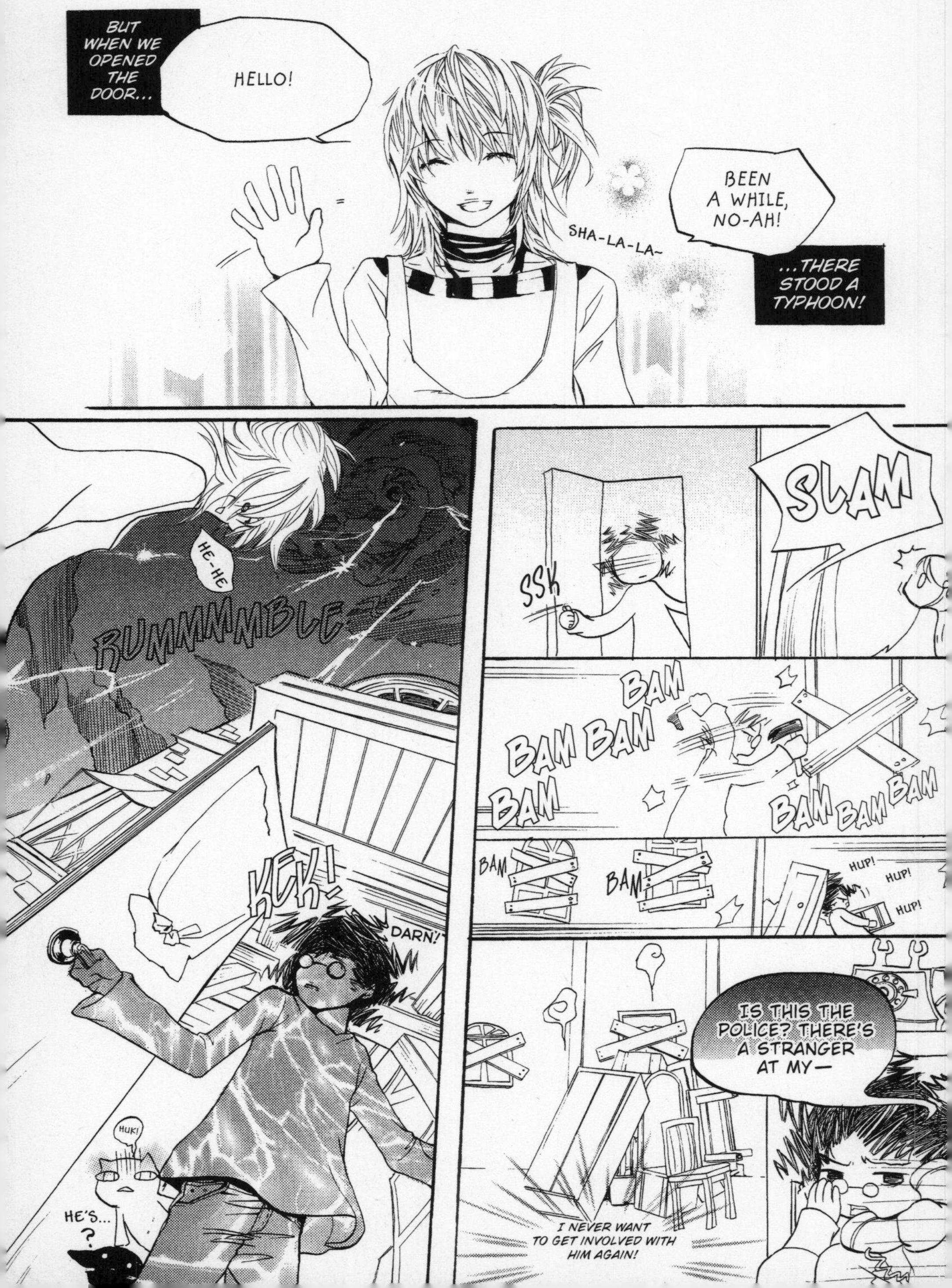
BUT WHEN WE OPENED THE DOOR...
HELLO!
SHA-LA-LA~
BEEN A WHILE, NO-AH!
...THERE STOOD A TYPHOON!
HE-HE
RUMMMMBLE
KEK!
DARN!
HUK!
HE'S... ?
SSK
SLAM
BAM BAM BAM BAM BAM BAM BAM
BAM
BAM
HUP! HUP! HUP!
IS THIS THE POLICE? THERE'S A STRANGER AT MY—
I NEVER WANT TO GET INVOLVED WITH HIM AGAIN!

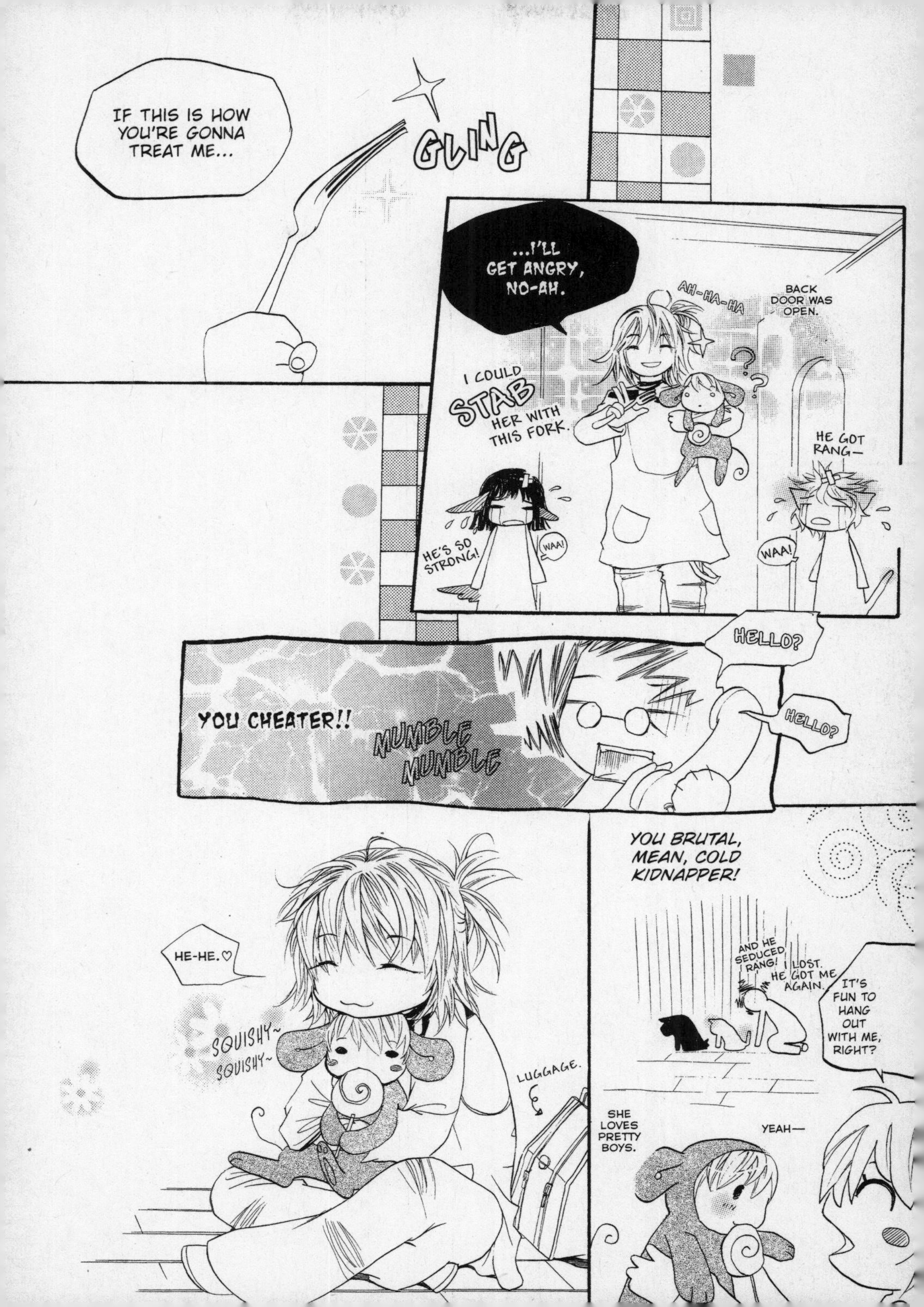
IF THIS IS HOW YOU'RE GONNA TREAT ME...
GLING
...I'LL GET ANGRY, NO-AH.
AH-HA-HA
BACK DOOR WAS OPEN.
I COULD STAB HER WITH THIS FORK.
HE GOT RANG—
HE'S SO STRONG!
WAA!
WAA!
YOU CHEATER!!
MUMBLE MUMBLE
HELLO?
HELLO?
HE-HE.♡
SQUISHY~ SQUISHY~
LUGGAGE.
YOU BRUTAL, MEAN, COLD KIDNAPPER!
AND HE SEDUCED RANG!
I LOST. HE GOT ME AGAIN.
IT'S FUN TO HANG OUT WITH ME, RIGHT?
SHE LOVES PRETTY BOYS.
YEAH—

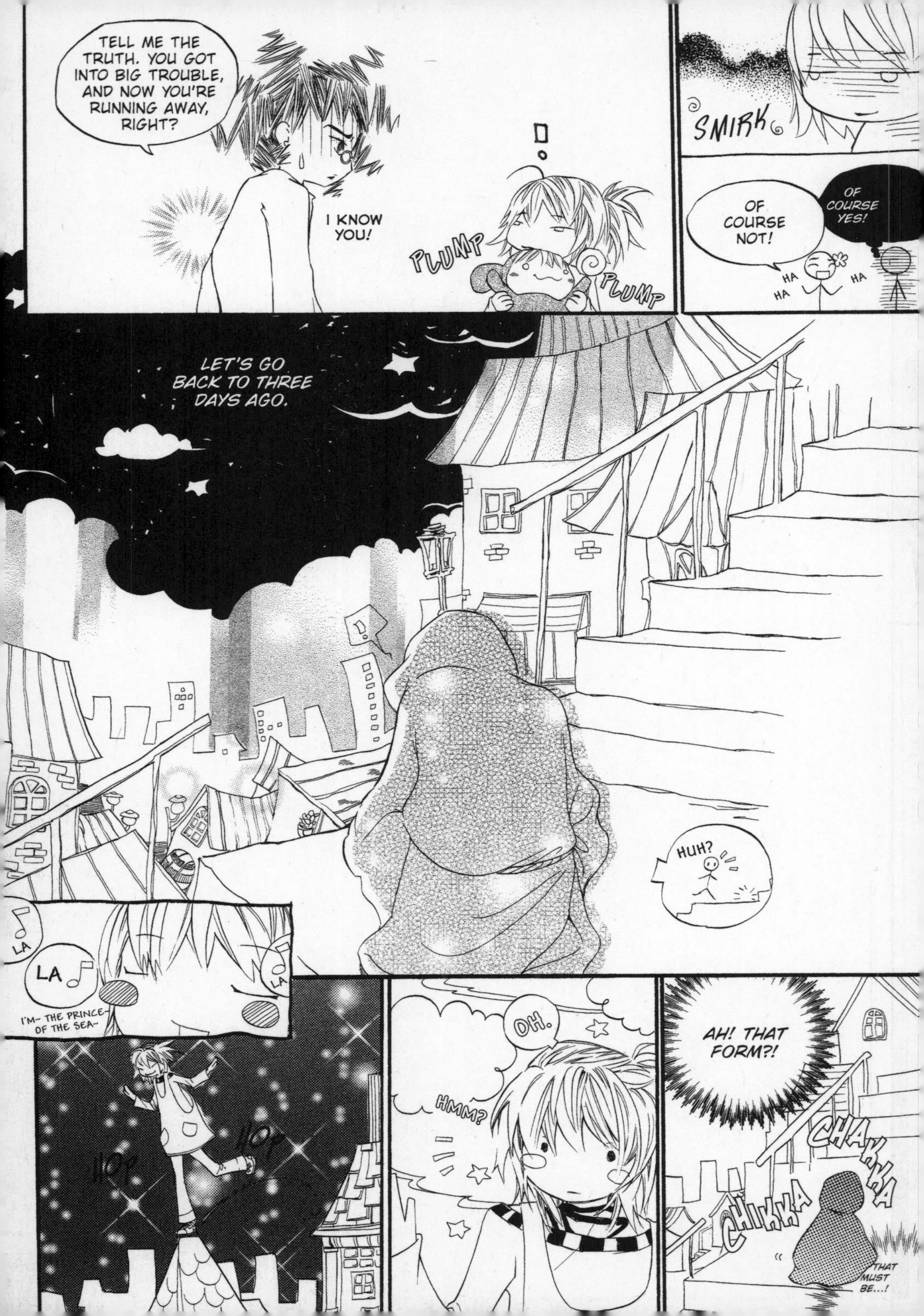
TELL ME THE TRUTH. YOU GOT INTO BIG TROUBLE, AND NOW YOU'RE RUNNING AWAY, RIGHT?
I KNOW YOU!
PLUMP
PLUMP
SMIRK
OF COURSE NOT!
OF COURSE YES!
HA
HA
HA
LET'S GO BACK TO THREE DAYS AGO.
HUH?
LA
LA
LA
I'M~ THE PRINCE OF THE SEA~
HOP
HOP
OH.
HMM?
AH! THAT FORM?!
CHAKKA
CHIKKA
THAT MUST BE...!

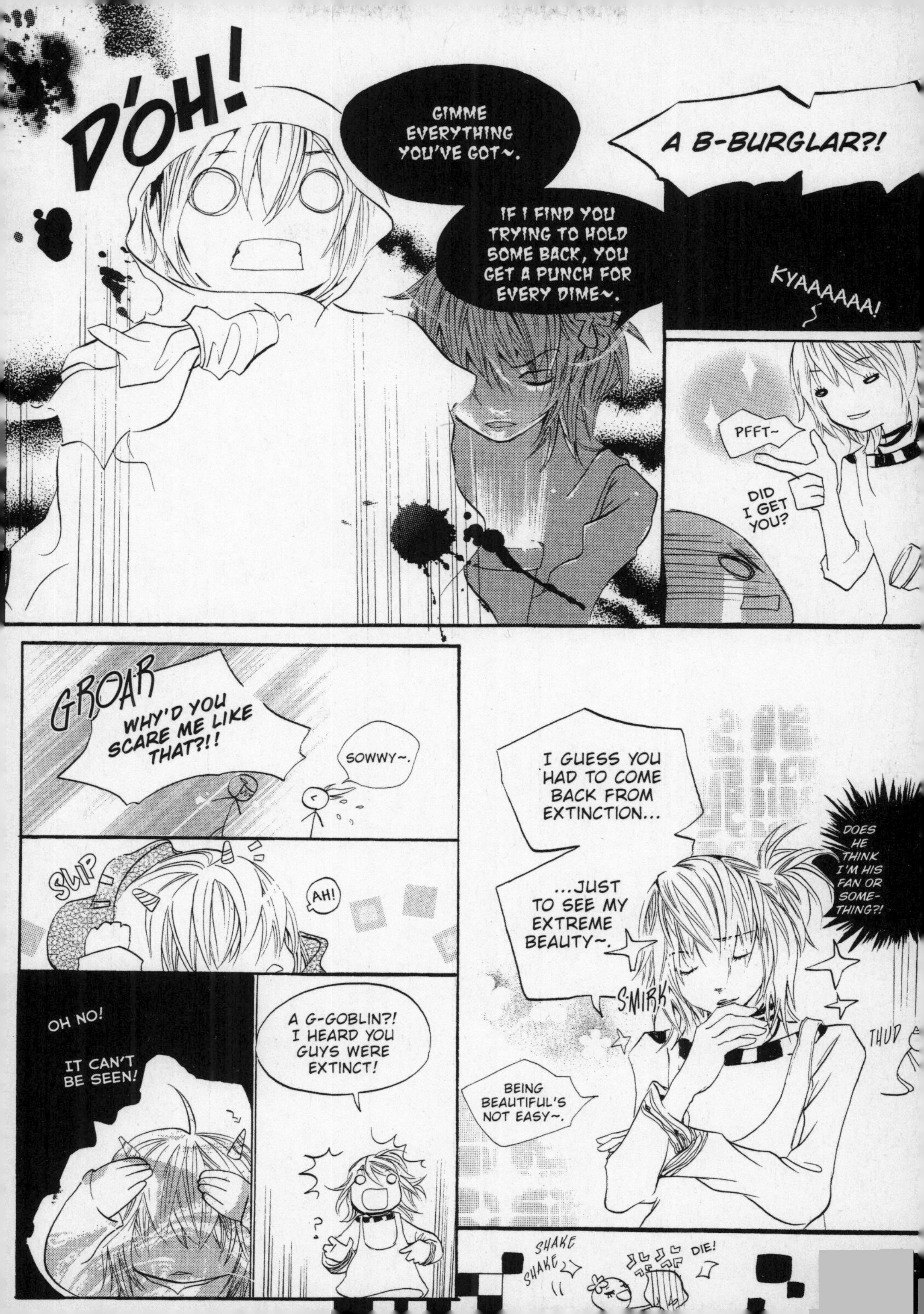
D'OH!
GIMME EVERYTHING YOU'VE GOT~.
IF I FIND YOU TRYING TO HOLD SOME BACK, YOU GET A PUNCH FOR EVERY DIME~.
A B-BURGLAR?!
KYAAAAAAA!
PFFT~
DID I GET YOU?
GROAR
WHY'D YOU SCARE ME LIKE THAT?!!
SOWWY~.
SLIP
AH!
OH NO!
IT CAN'T BE SEEN!
A G-GOBLIN?! I HEARD YOU GUYS WERE EXTINCT!
I GUESS YOU HAD TO COME BACK FROM EXTINCTION...
...JUST TO SEE MY EXTREME BEAUTY~.
DOES HE THINK I'M HIS FAN OR SOME-THING?!
SMIRK
BEING BEAUTIFUL'S NOT EASY~.
THUD
SHAKE
SHAKE
DIE!

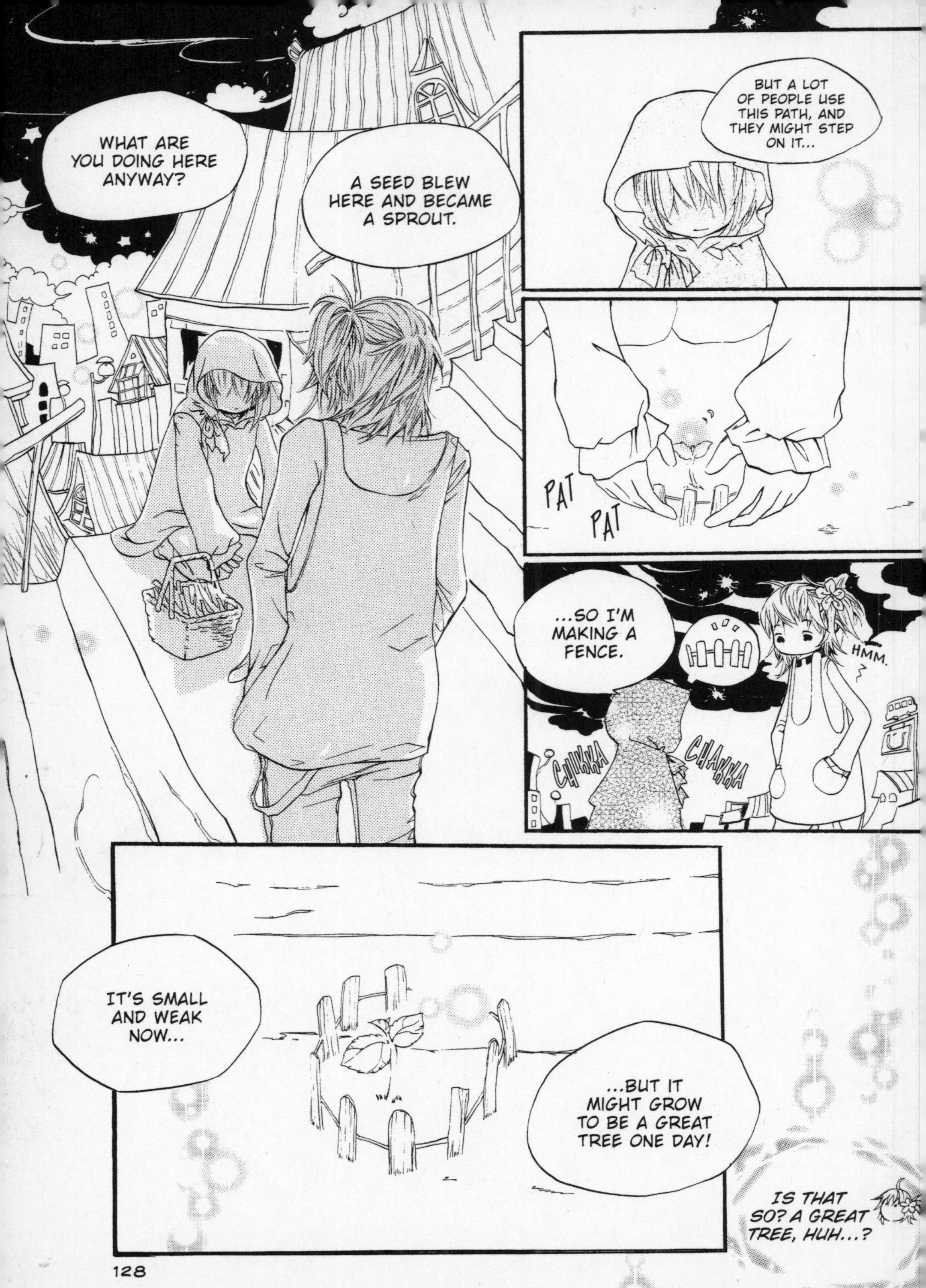
WHAT ARE YOU DOING HERE ANYWAY?
A SEED BLEW HERE AND BECAME A SPROUT.
BUT A LOT OF PEOPLE USE THIS PATH, AND THEY MIGHT STEP ON IT...
PAT PAT
...SO I'M MAKING A FENCE.
HMM.
CHAKKA
CHAKKA
IT'S SMALL AND WEAK NOW...
...BUT IT MIGHT GROW TO BE A GREAT TREE ONE DAY!
IS THAT SO? A GREAT TREE, HUH...?

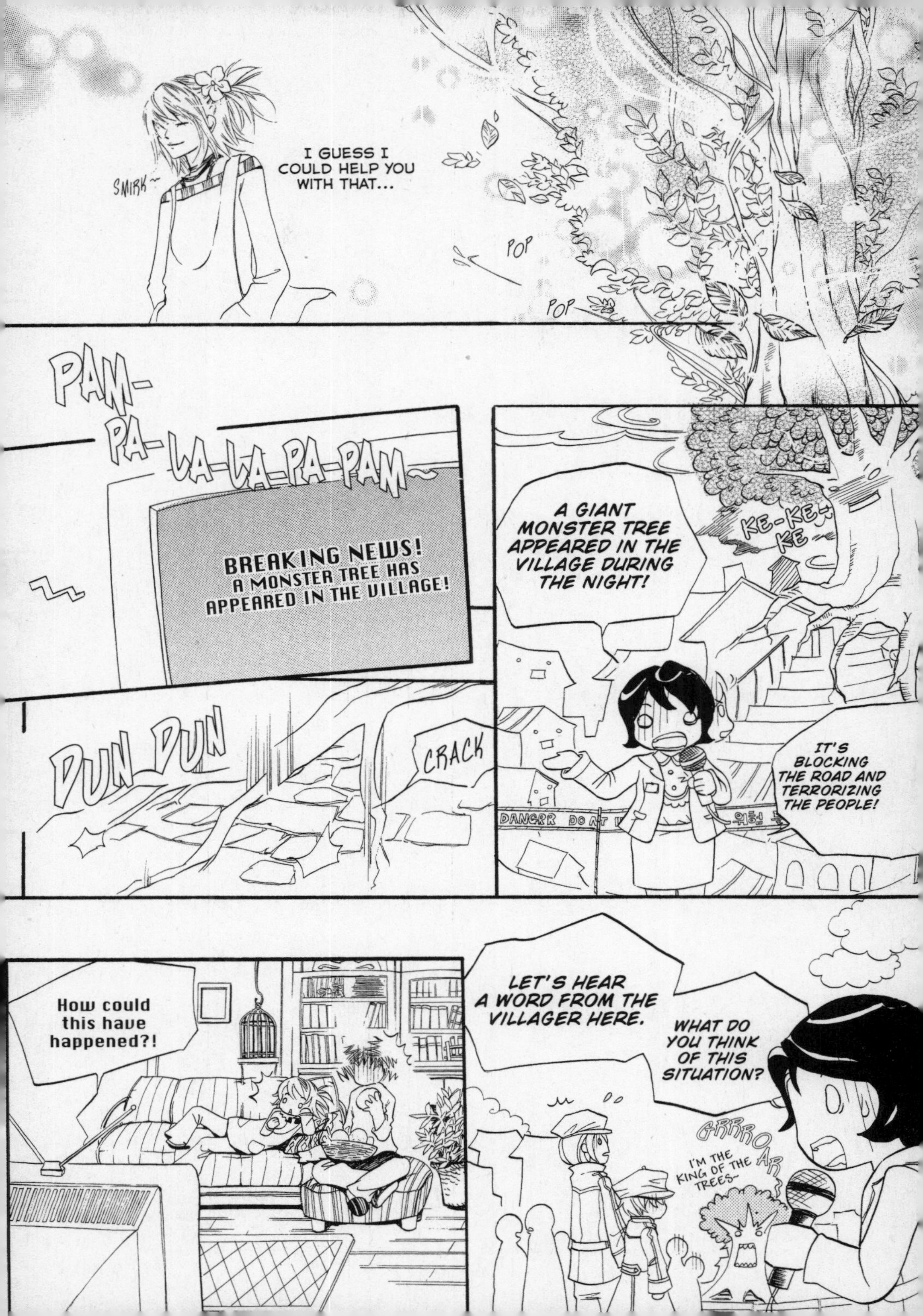
SMIRK~
I GUESS I COULD HELP YOU WITH THAT...
POP
POP
PAM-PA-LA-LA-PA-PAM~
BREAKING NEWS! A MONSTER TREE HAS APPEARED IN THE VILLAGE!
DUN DUN
CRACK
A GIANT MONSTER TREE APPEARED IN THE VILLAGE DURING THE NIGHT!
KE-KE-KE
IT'S BLOCKING THE ROAD AND TERRORIZING THE PEOPLE!
How could this have happened?!
LET'S HEAR A WORD FROM THE VILLAGER HERE.
WHAT DO YOU THINK OF THIS SITUATION?
GRRROAR
I'M THE KING OF THE TREES~

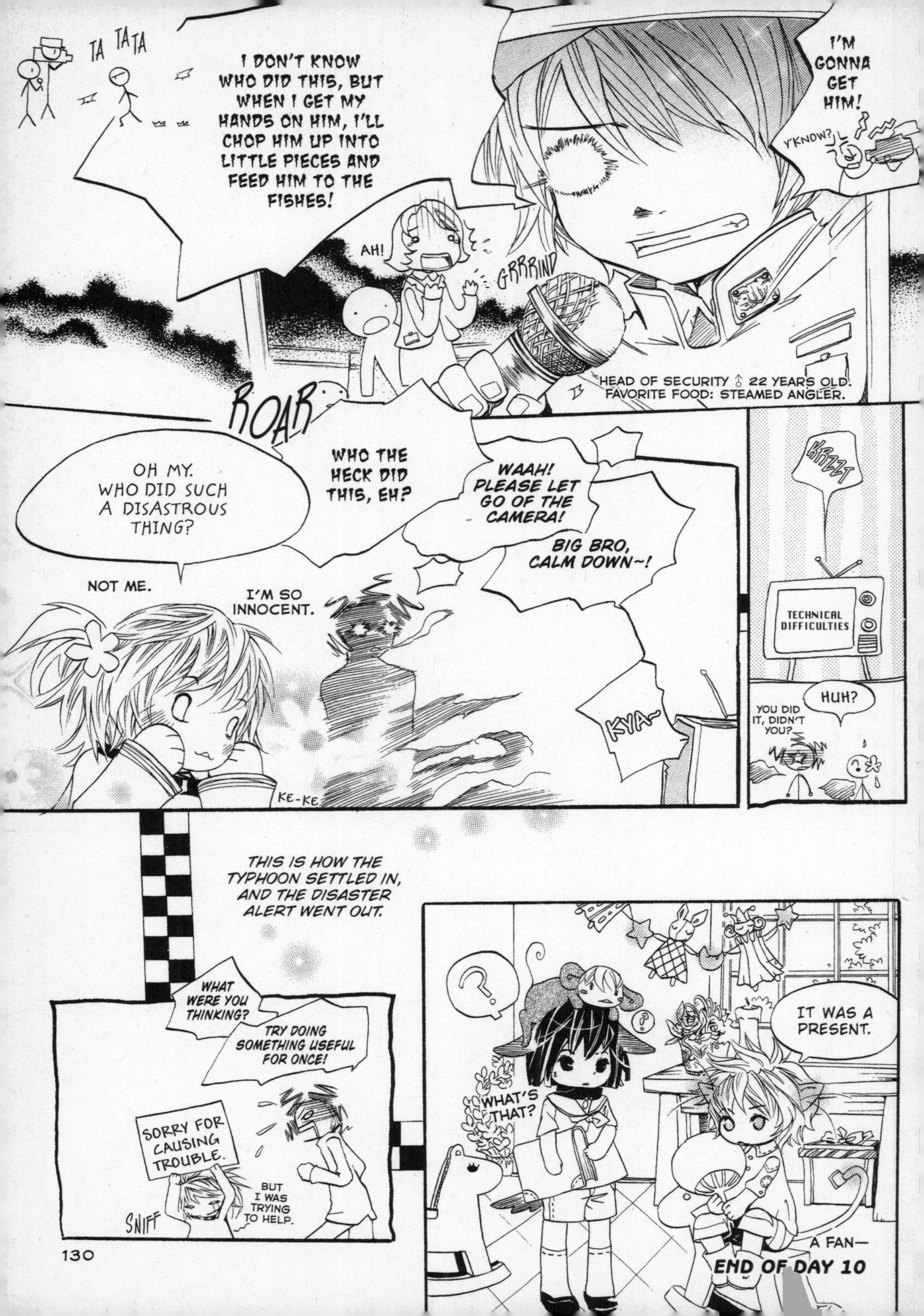
TA TA TA
I DON'T KNOW WHO DID THIS, BUT WHEN I GET MY HANDS ON HIM, I'LL CHOP HIM UP INTO LITTLE PIECES AND FEED HIM TO THE FISHES!
I'M GONNA GET HIM!
Y'KNOW?
AH!
GRRRIND
ROAR
HEAD OF SECURITY ♂ 22 YEARS OLD.
FAVORITE FOOD: STEAMED ANGLER.
OH MY. WHO DID SUCH A DISASTROUS THING?
WHO THE HECK DID THIS, EH?
WAAH! PLEASE LET GO OF THE CAMERA!
BIG BRO, CALM DOWN~!
NOT ME.
I'M SO INNOCENT.
KYA~
KE-KE
KRZZZT
TECHNICAL DIFFICULTIES
HUH?
YOU DID IT, DIDN'T YOU?
THIS IS HOW THE TYPHOON SETTLED IN, AND THE DISASTER ALERT WENT OUT.
WHAT WERE YOU THINKING?
TRY DOING SOMETHING USEFUL FOR ONCE!
SORRY FOR CAUSING TROUBLE.
BUT I WAS TRYING TO HELP.
SNIFF
?
?
WHAT'S THAT?
IT WAS A PRESENT.
A FAN—
END OF DAY 10

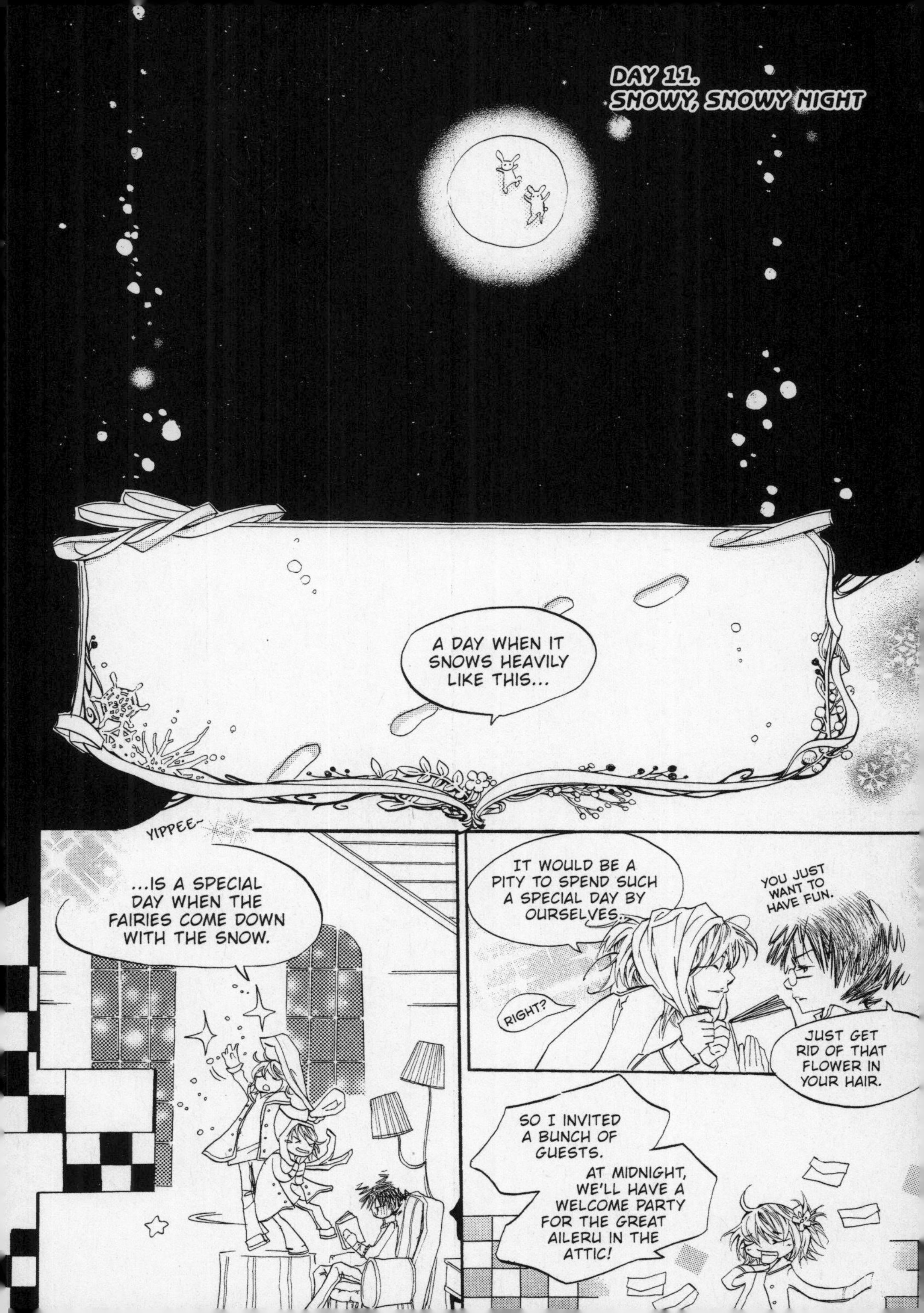
DAY 11.
SNOWY, SNOWY NIGHT
A DAY WHEN IT SNOWS HEAVILY LIKE THIS...
YIPPEE~
...IS A SPECIAL DAY WHEN THE FAIRIES COME DOWN WITH THE SNOW.
IT WOULD BE A PITY TO SPEND SUCH A SPECIAL DAY BY OURSELVES.
RIGHT?
YOU JUST WANT TO HAVE FUN.
JUST GET RID OF THAT FLOWER IN YOUR HAIR.
SO I INVITED A BUNCH OF GUESTS.
AT MIDNIGHT, WE'LL HAVE A WELCOME PARTY FOR THE GREAT AILERU IN THE ATTIC!

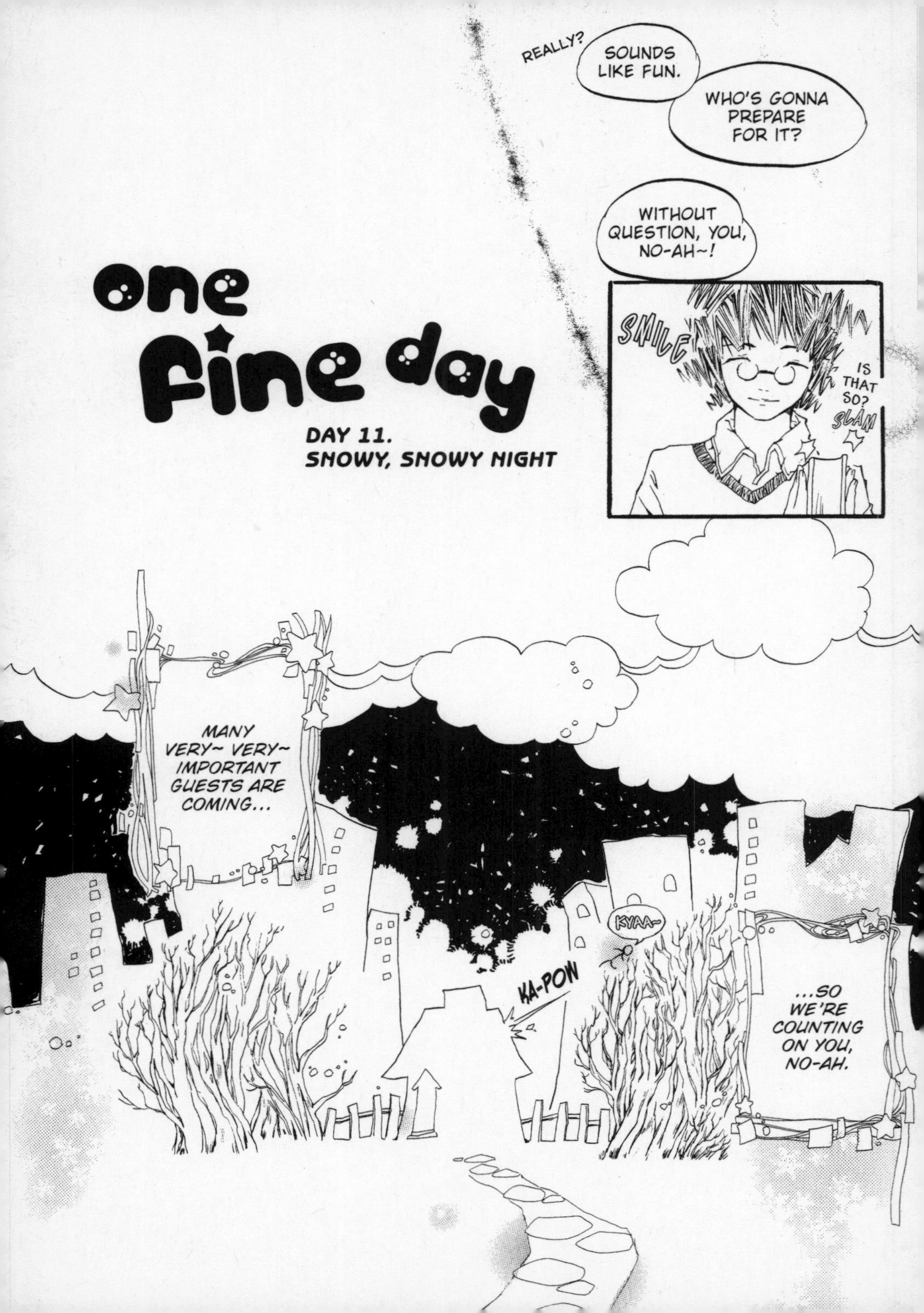
REALLY?
SOUNDS LIKE FUN.
WHO'S GONNA PREPARE FOR IT?
WITHOUT QUESTION, YOU, NO-AH~!
one fine day
DAY 11.
SNOWY, SNOWY NIGHT
SMILE
IS THAT SO?
SLAM
MANY VERY~ VERY~ IMPORTANT GUESTS ARE COMING...
KYAA~
KA-POW
...SO WE'RE COUNTING ON YOU, NO-AH.

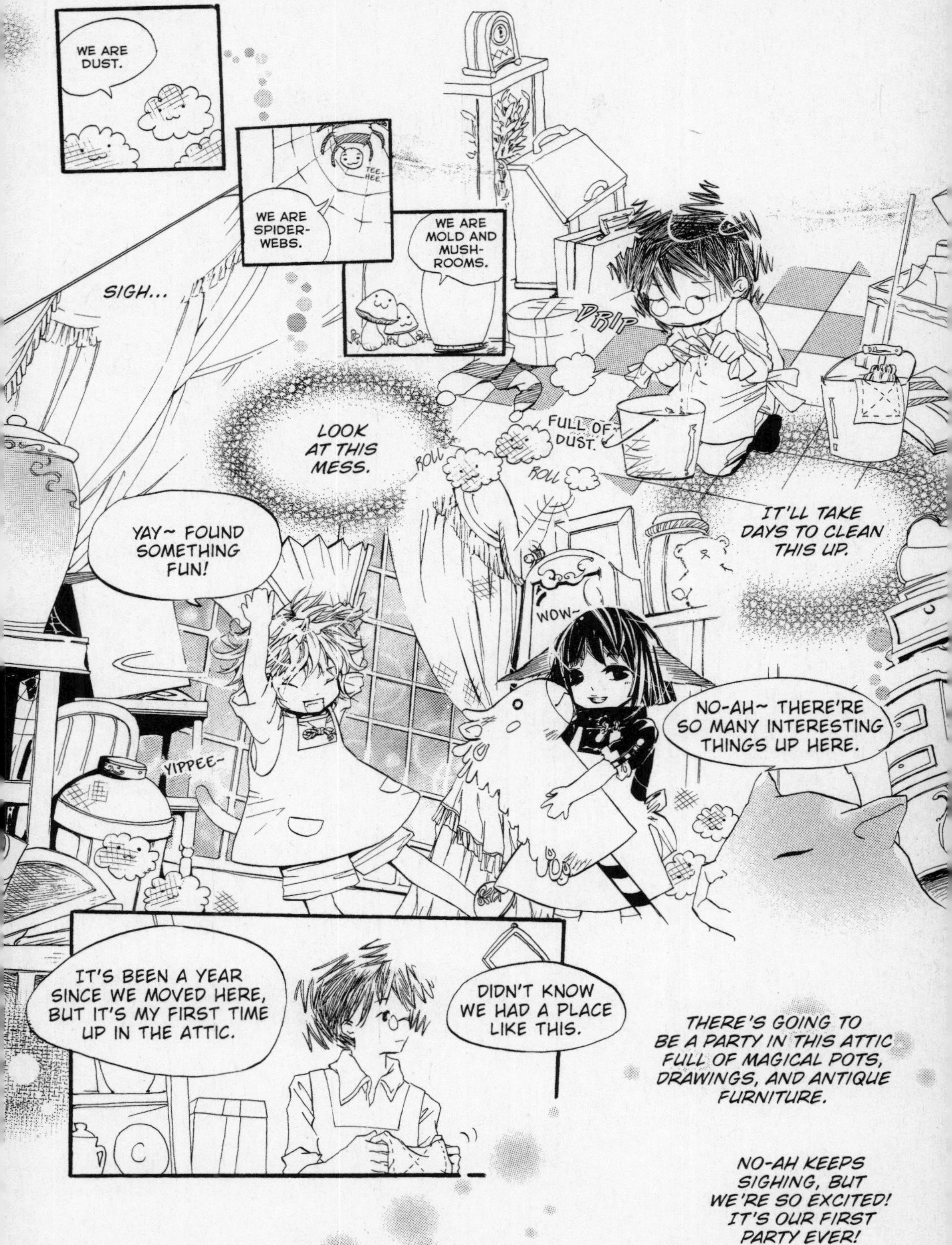

WE ARE DUST.
TEE-HEE.
WE ARE SPIDER-WEBS.
WE ARE MOLD AND MUSH-ROOMS.
SIGH...
DRIP
LOOK AT THIS MESS.
FULL OF DUST.
ROLL
ROLL
IT'LL TAKE DAYS TO CLEAN THIS UP.
YAY~ FOUND SOMETHING FUN!
WOW~
YIPPEE~
NO-AH~ THERE'RE SO MANY INTERESTING THINGS UP HERE.
IT'S BEEN A YEAR SINCE WE MOVED HERE, BUT IT'S MY FIRST TIME UP IN THE ATTIC.
DIDN'T KNOW WE HAD A PLACE LIKE THIS.
THERE'S GOING TO BE A PARTY IN THIS ATTIC FULL OF MAGICAL POTS, DRAWINGS, AND ANTIQUE FURNITURE.
NO-AH KEEPS SIGHING, BUT WE'RE SO EXCITED! IT'S OUR FIRST PARTY EVER!

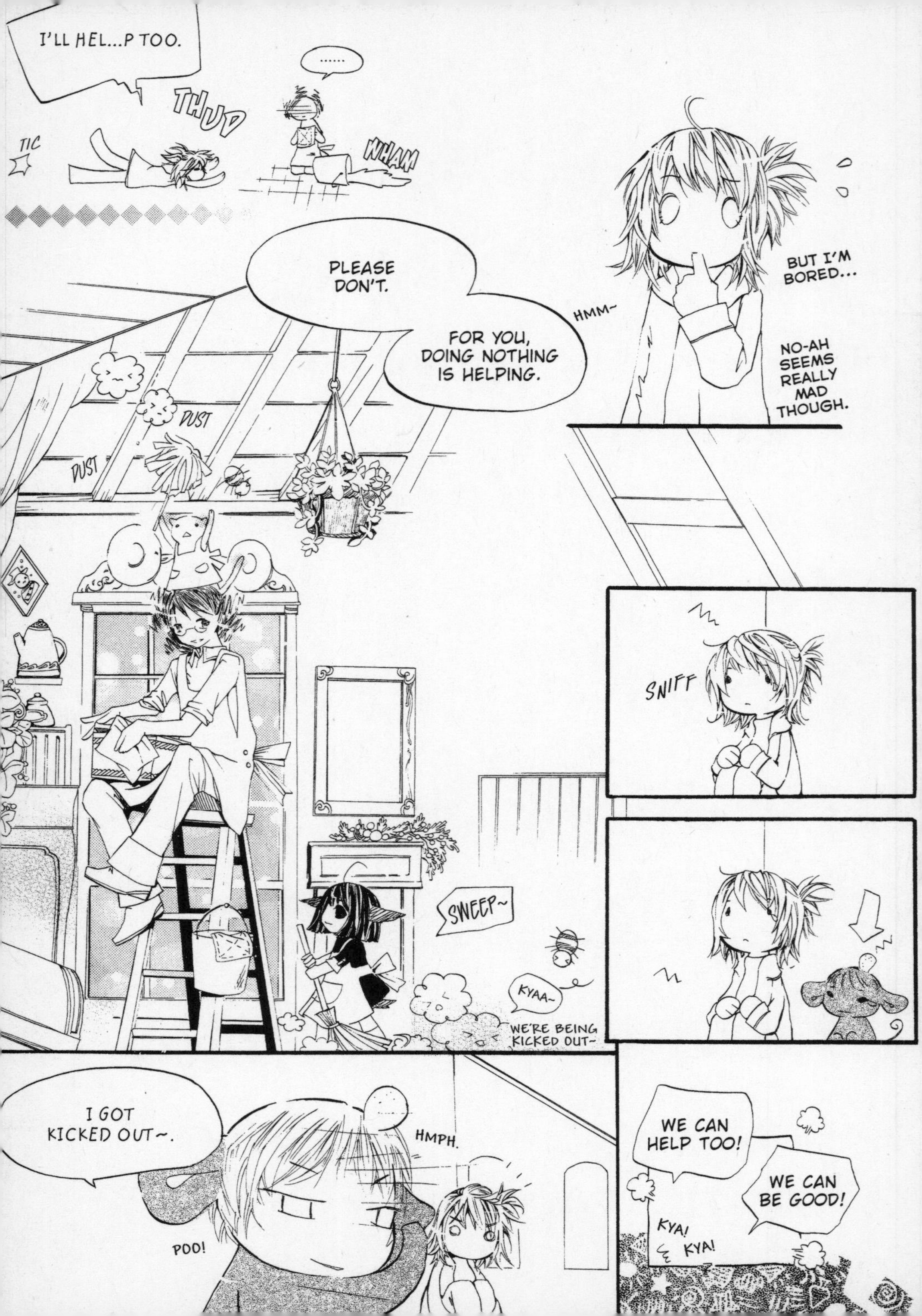
I'LL HEL...P TOO.
......
THUD
TIC
WHAM
PLEASE DON'T.
FOR YOU, DOING NOTHING IS HELPING.
DUST
DUST
SWEEP~
KYAA~
WE'RE BEING KICKED OUT~
HMM~
BUT I'M BORED...
NO-AH SEEMS REALLY MAD THOUGH.
SNIFF
I GOT KICKED OUT~.
HMPH.
POO!
WE CAN HELP TOO!
WE CAN BE GOOD!
KYA! KYA!

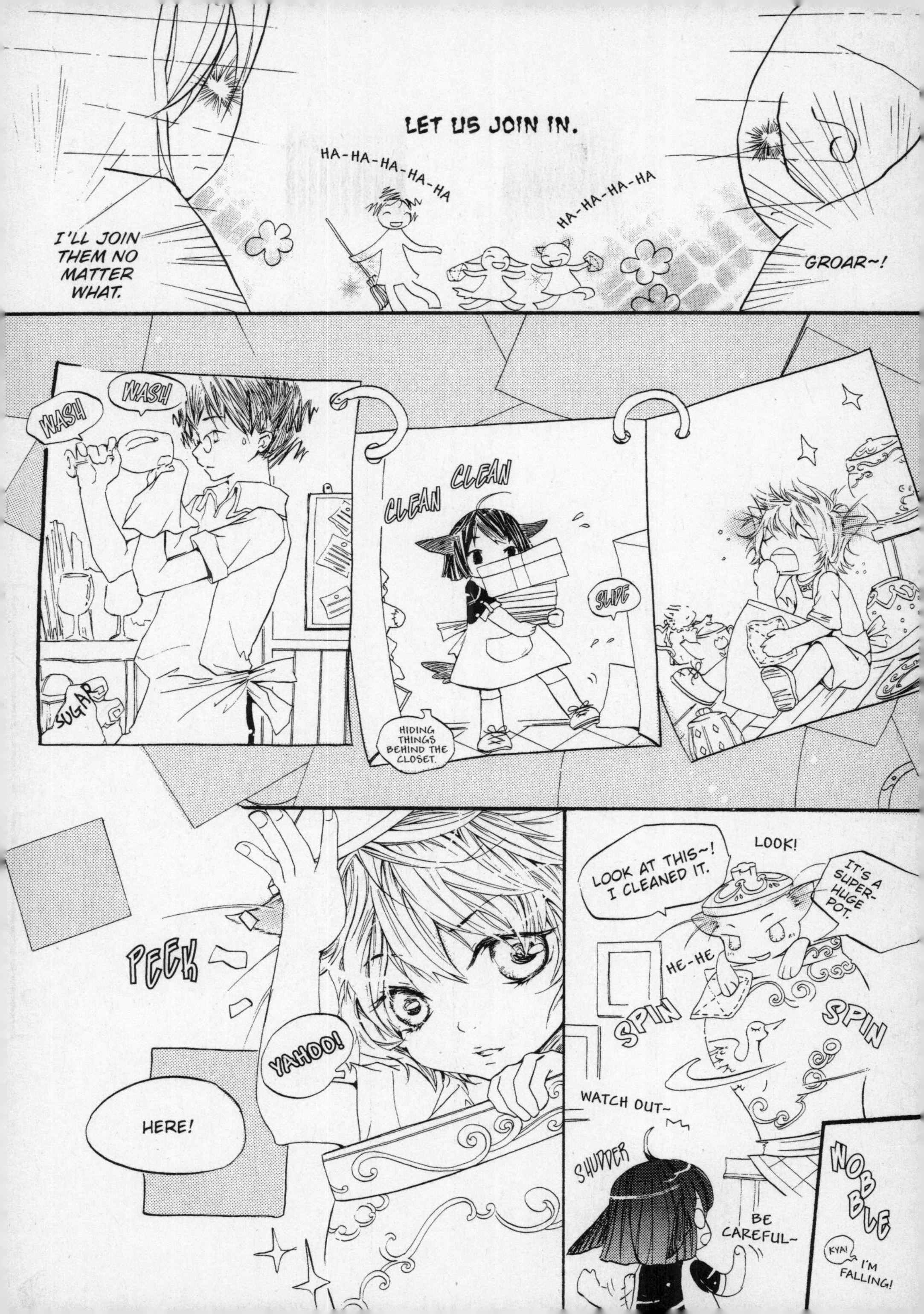

I'LL JOIN THEM NO MATTER WHAT.
LET US JOIN IN.
HA-HA-HA-HA-HA
HA-HA-HA-HA
GROAR~!
WASH
WASH
SUGAR
CLEAN
CLEAN
SLIDE
HIDING THINGS BEHIND THE CLOSET.
PEEK
YAHOO!
HERE!
LOOK AT THIS~! I CLEANED IT.
LOOK!
IT'S A SUPER-HUGE POT.
HE-HE
SPIN
SPIN
WATCH OUT~
SHUDDER
BE CAREFUL~
WOBBLE
KYA!
I'M FALLING!

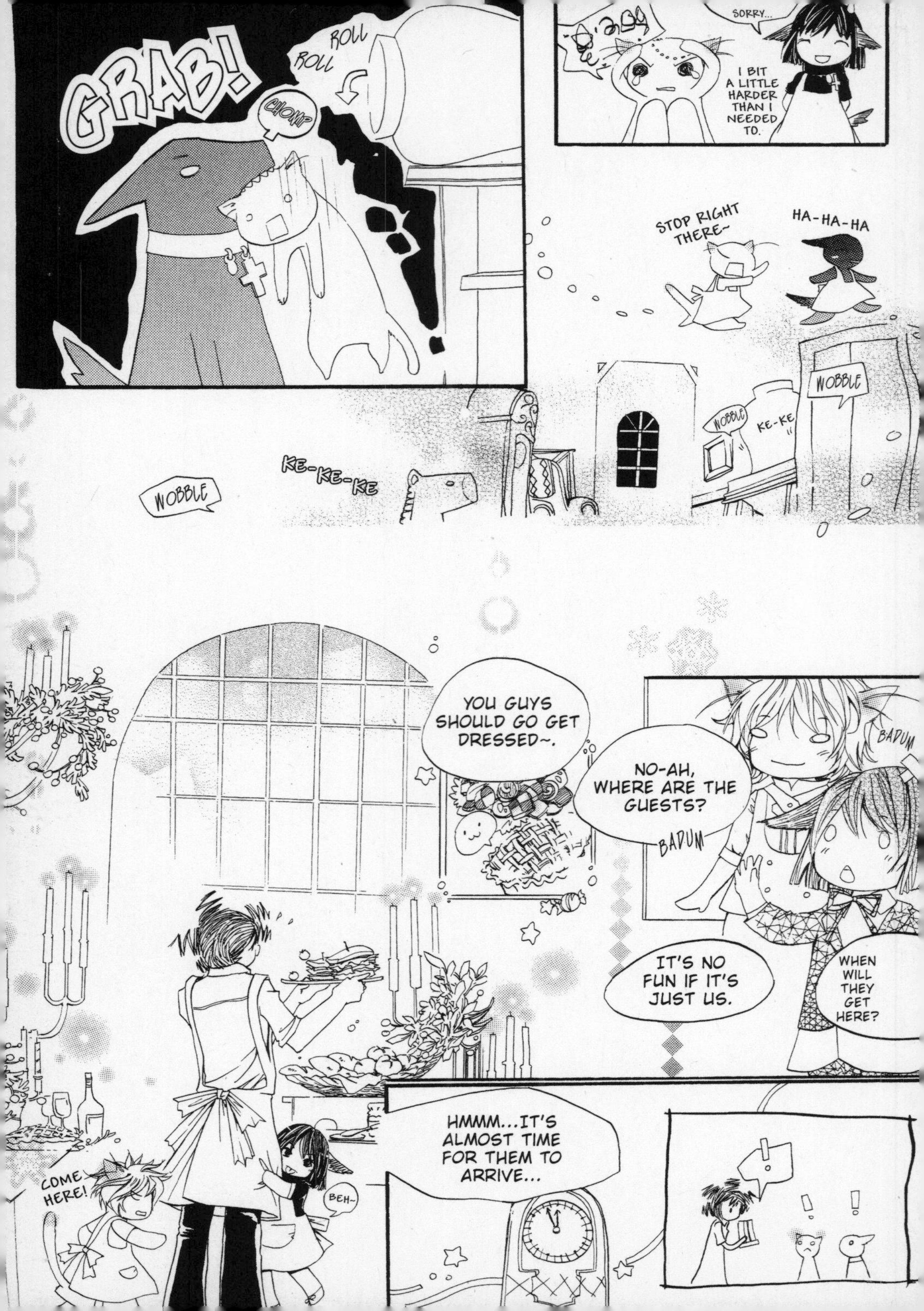
GRAB!
ROLL
ROLL
CHOMP
SORRY...
I BIT A LITTLE HARDER THAN I NEEDED TO.
STOP RIGHT THERE~
HA-HA-HA
WOBBLE
KE-KE-KE
WOBBLE
KE-KE
WOBBLE
YOU GUYS SHOULD GO GET DRESSED~.
NO-AH, WHERE ARE THE GUESTS?
BADUM
BADUM
IT'S NO FUN IF IT'S JUST US.
WHEN WILL THEY GET HERE?
COME HERE!
BEH~
HMMM...IT'S ALMOST TIME FOR THEM TO ARRIVE...
!
!

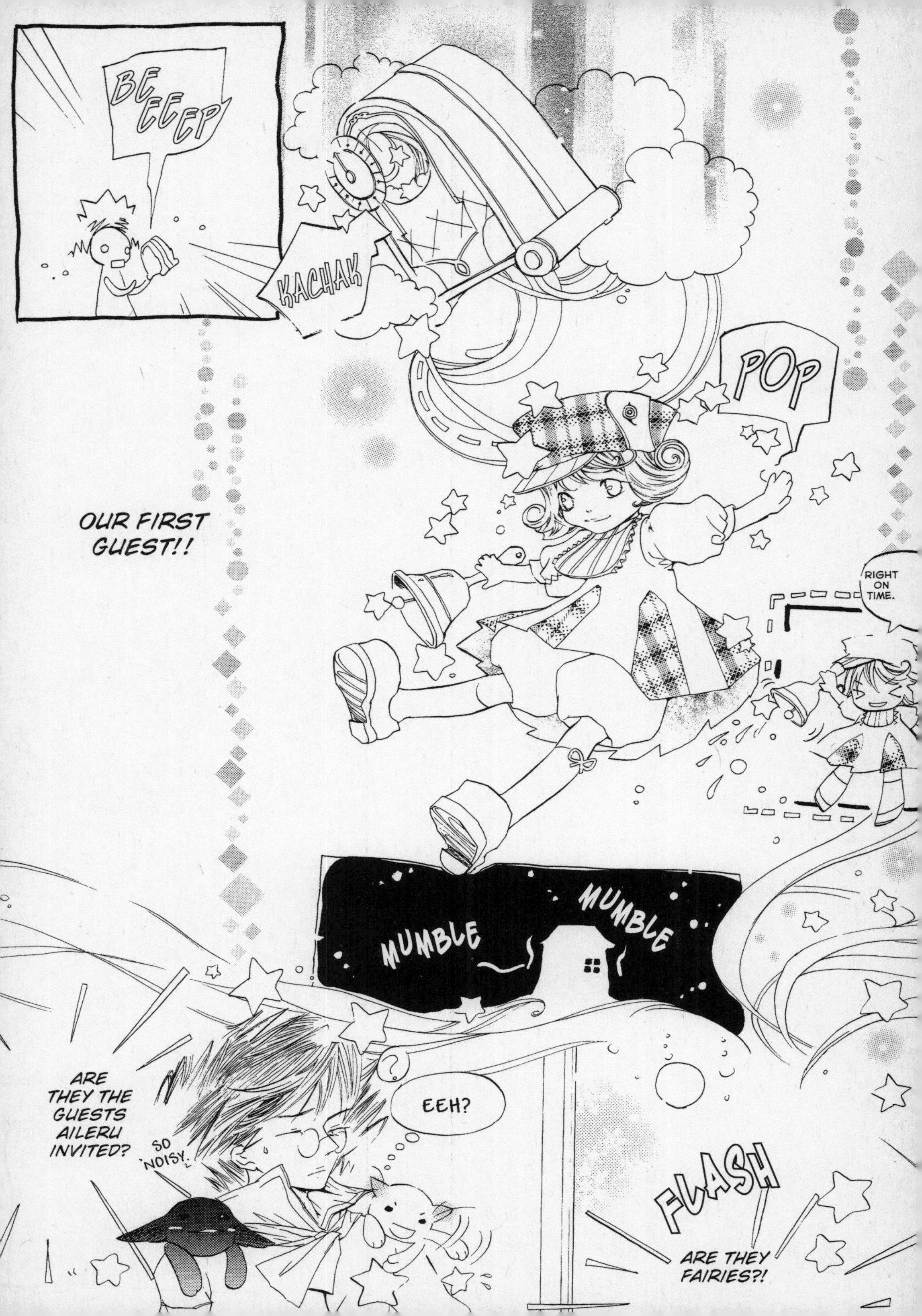
BEEEEP
KACHAK
POP
OUR FIRST GUEST!!
RIGHT ON TIME.
MUMBLE MUMBLE
ARE THEY THE GUESTS AILERU INVITED?
SO NOISY.
EEH?
FLASH
ARE THEY FAIRIES?!

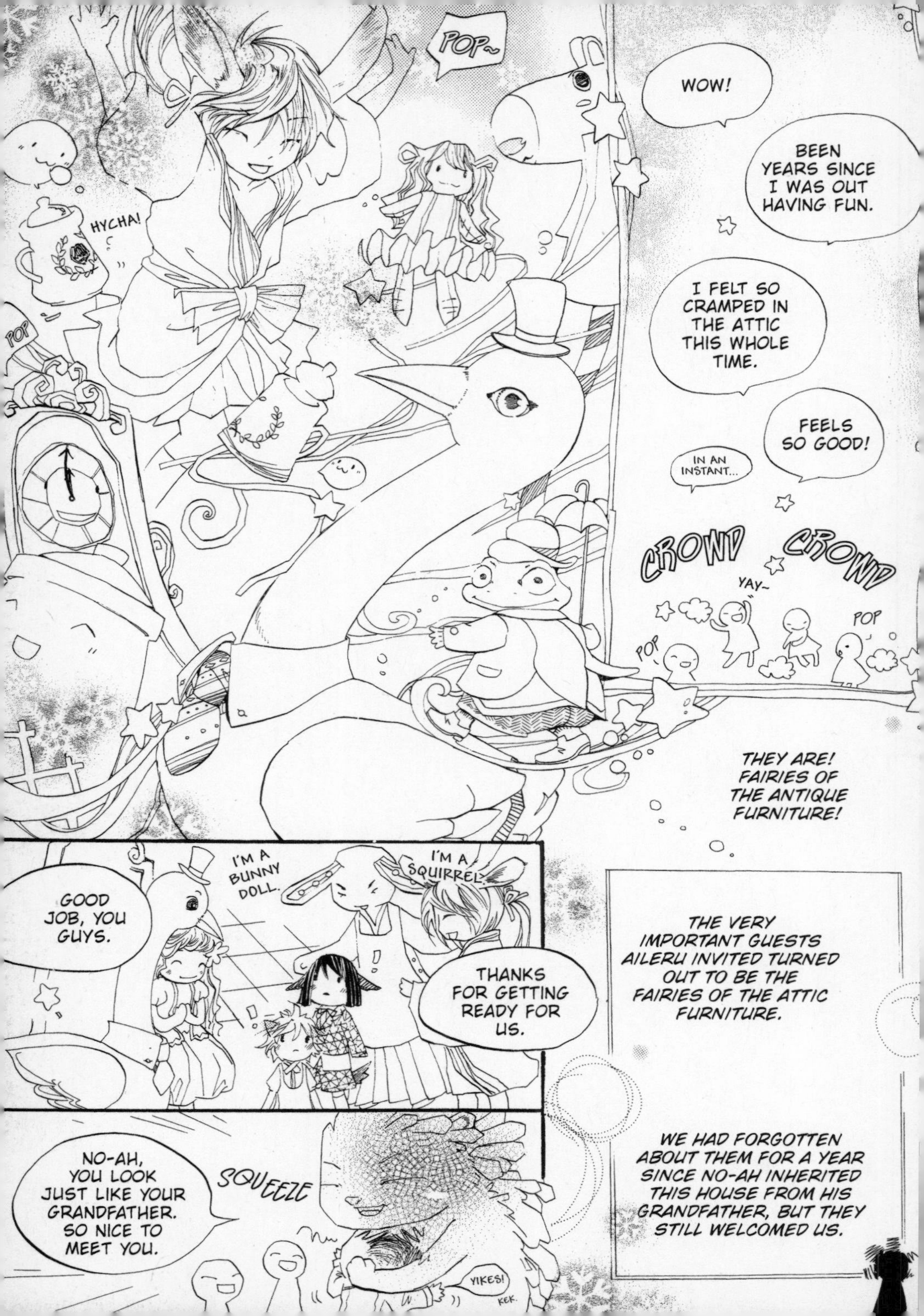
POP~
HYCHA!
POP
WOW!
BEEN YEARS SINCE I WAS OUT HAVING FUN.
I FELT SO CRAMPED IN THE ATTIC THIS WHOLE TIME.
FEELS SO GOOD!
IN AN INSTANT...
CROWD CROWD
YAY~
POP
POP
THEY ARE! FAIRIES OF THE ANTIQUE FURNITURE!
GOOD JOB, YOU GUYS.
I'M A BUNNY DOLL.
I'M A SQUIRREL.
THANKS FOR GETTING READY FOR US.
THE VERY IMPORTANT GUESTS AILERU INVITED TURNED OUT TO BE THE FAIRIES OF THE ATTIC FURNITURE.
NO-AH, YOU LOOK JUST LIKE YOUR GRANDFATHER. SO NICE TO MEET YOU.
SQUEEZE
YIKES!
KEK.
WE HAD FORGOTTEN ABOUT THEM FOR A YEAR SINCE NO-AH INHERITED THIS HOUSE FROM HIS GRANDFATHER, BUT THEY STILL WELCOMED US.

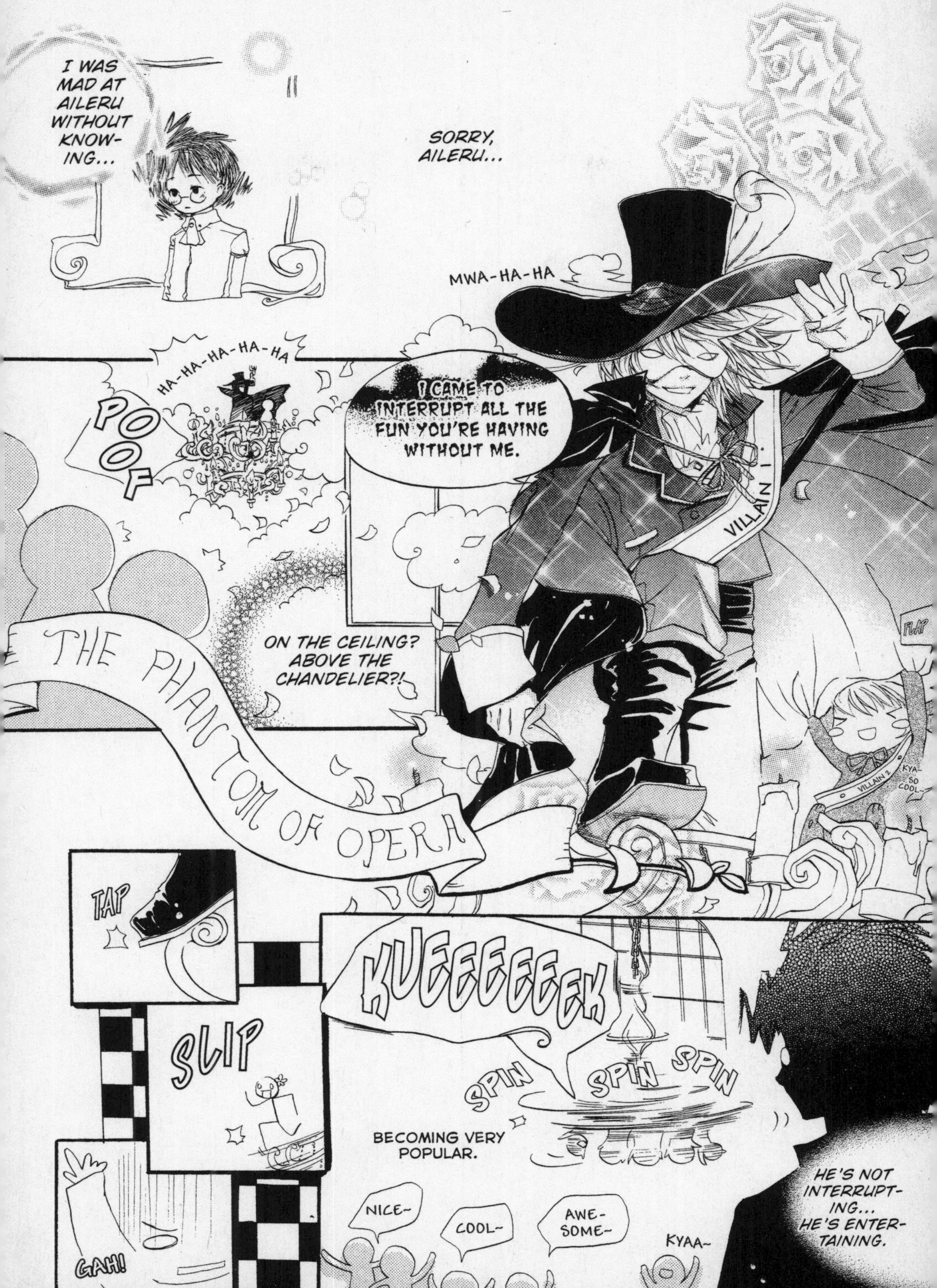
I WAS MAD AT AILERU WITHOUT KNOW-ING...
SORRY, AILERU...
MWA-HA-HA
HA-HA-HA-HA-HA
POOF
I CAME TO INTERRUPT ALL THE FUN YOU'RE HAVING WITHOUT ME.
VILLAIN 1
ON THE CEILING? ABOVE THE CHANDELIER?!
THE PHANTOM OF OPERA
FLAP
VILLAIN 2
KYA- SO COOL~
TAP
SLIP
GAH!
KUEEEEEEK
SPIN SPIN SPIN
BECOMING VERY POPULAR.
NICE~
COOL~
AWE-SOME~
KYAA~
HE'S NOT INTERRUPT-ING... HE'S ENTER-TAINING.

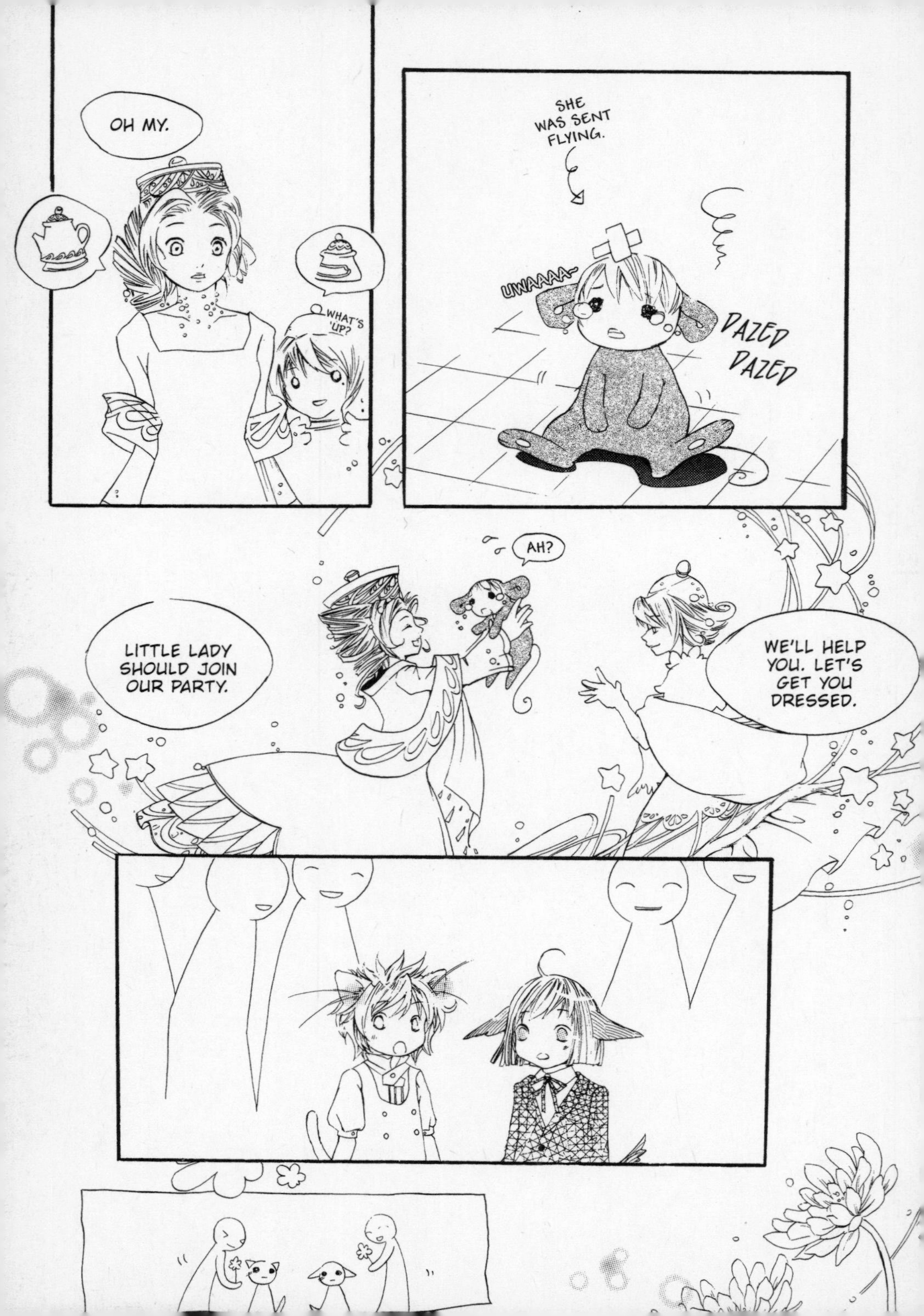

OH MY.
WHAT'S 'UP?
SHE WAS SENT FLYING.
UWAAAA-
DAZED DAZED
AH?
LITTLE LADY SHOULD JOIN OUR PARTY.
WE'LL HELP YOU. LET'S GET YOU DRESSED.

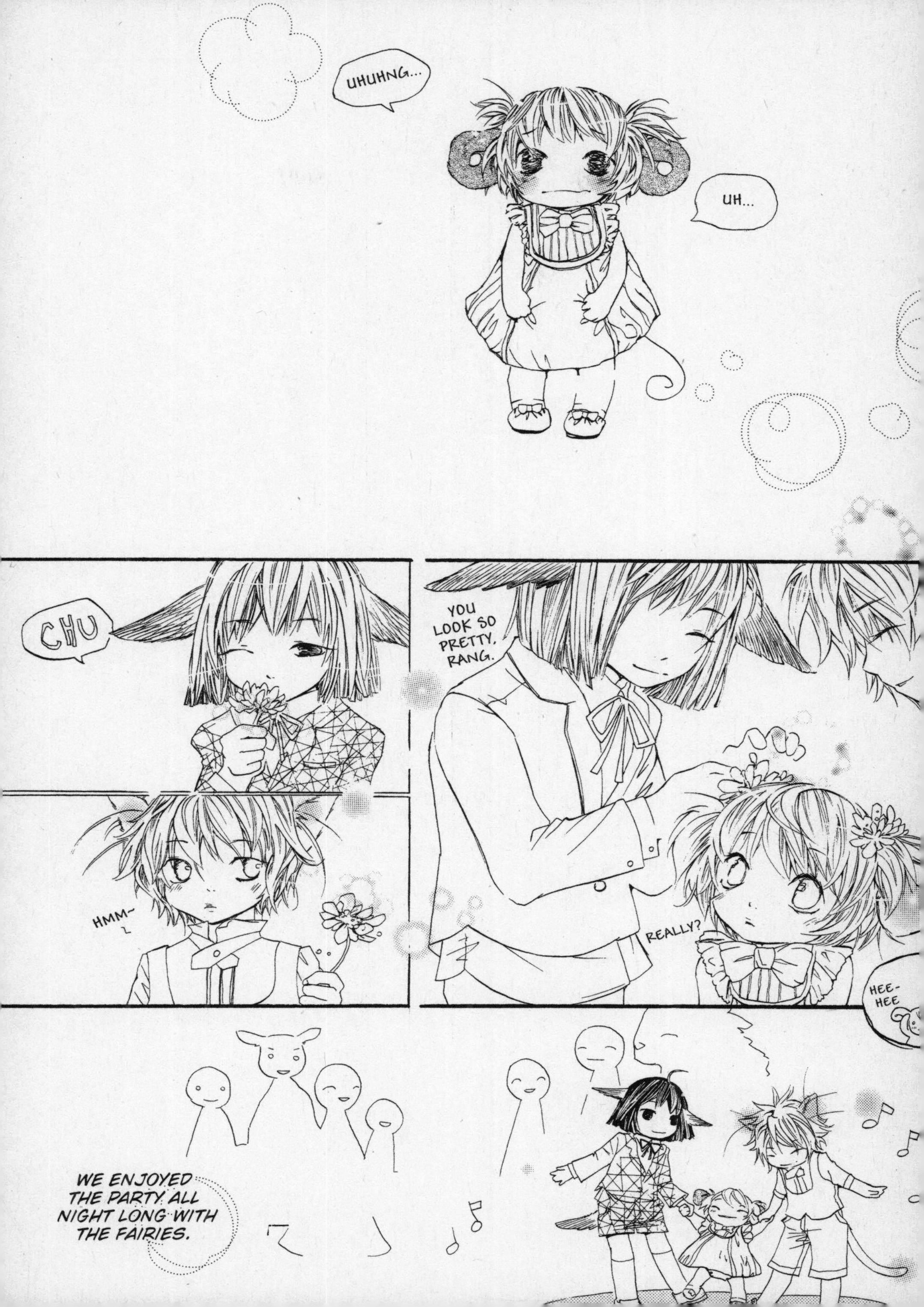
UHUHNG...
UH...
CHU
HMM-
YOU LOOK SO PRETTY, RANG.
REALLY?
HEE-HEE
WE ENJOYED THE PARTY ALL NIGHT LONG WITH THE FAIRIES.

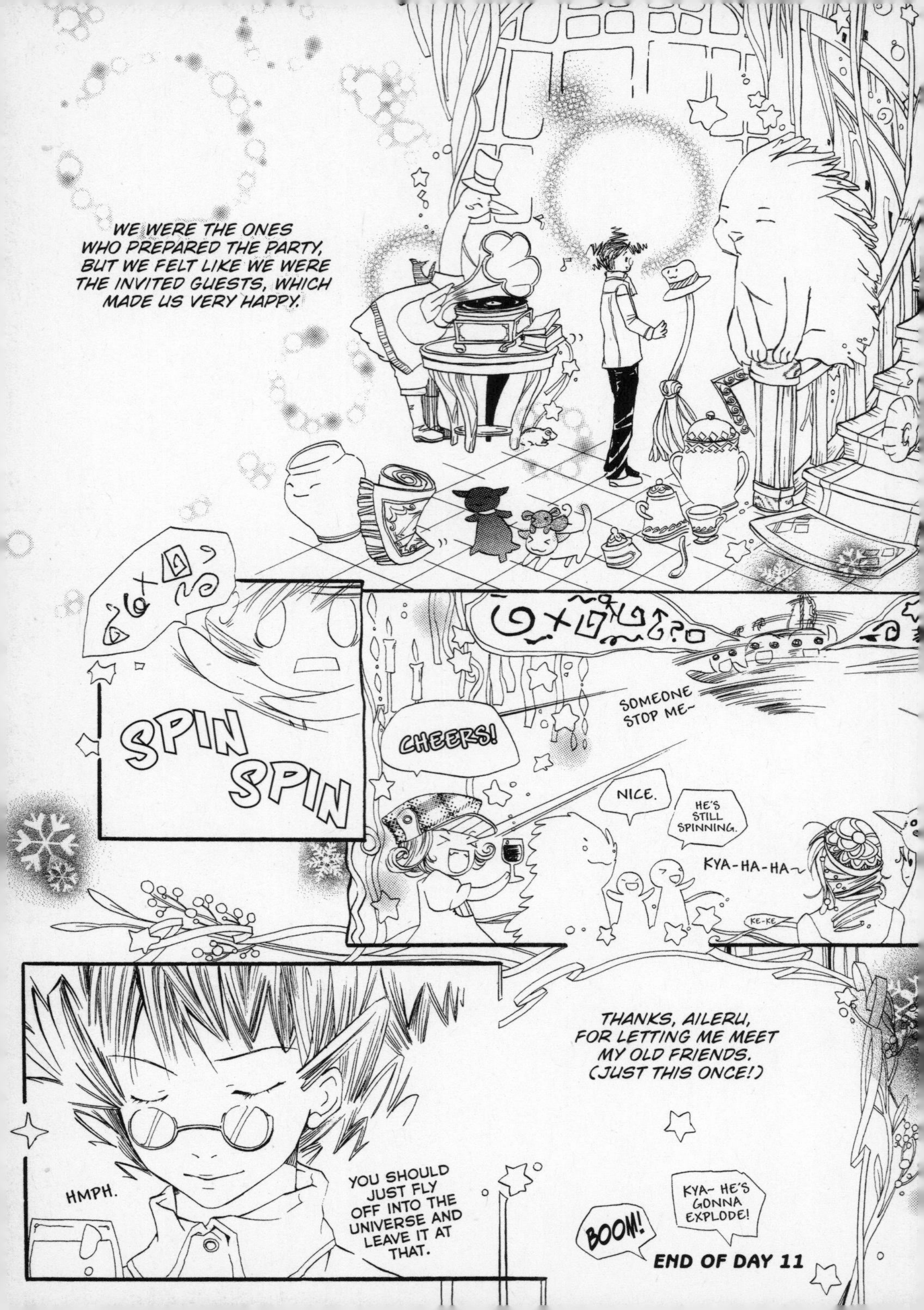
WE WERE THE ONES WHO PREPARED THE PARTY, BUT WE FELT LIKE WE WERE THE INVITED GUESTS, WHICH MADE US VERY HAPPY.
SPIN SPIN
SOMEONE STOP ME~
CHEERS!
NICE.
HE'S STILL SPINNING.
KYA-HA-HA~
KE-KE
THANKS, AILERU, FOR LETTING ME MEET MY OLD FRIENDS. (JUST THIS ONCE!)
HMPH.
YOU SHOULD JUST FLY OFF INTO THE UNIVERSE AND LEAVE IT AT THAT.
BOOM!
KYA~ HE'S GONNA EXPLODE!
END OF DAY 11

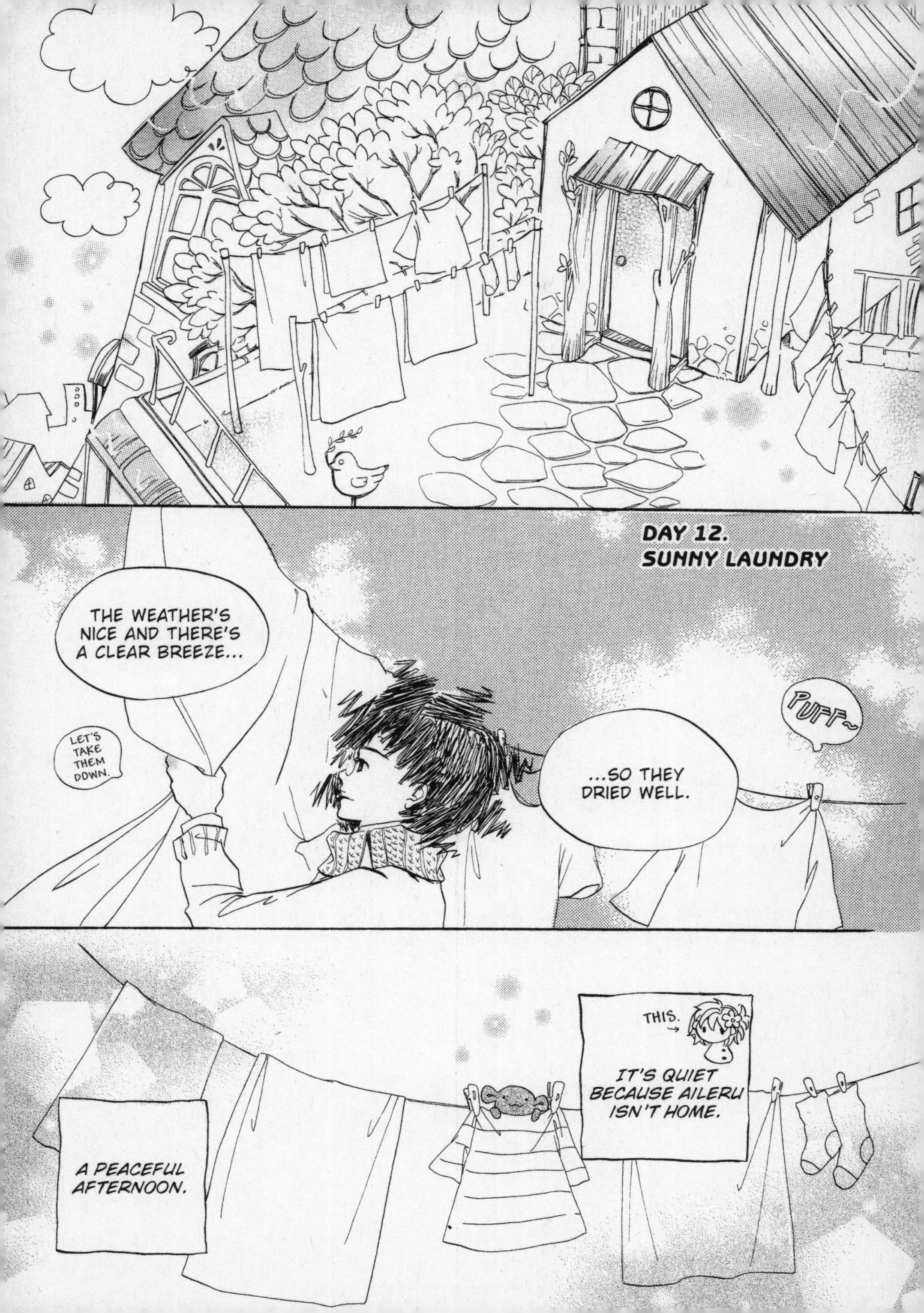
DAY 12.
SUNNY LAUNDRY
THE WEATHER'S NICE AND THERE'S A CLEAR BREEZE...
LET'S TAKE THEM DOWN.
...SO THEY DRIED WELL.
PUFF~
A PEACEFUL AFTERNOON.
THIS.
IT'S QUIET BECAUSE AILERU ISN'T HOME.

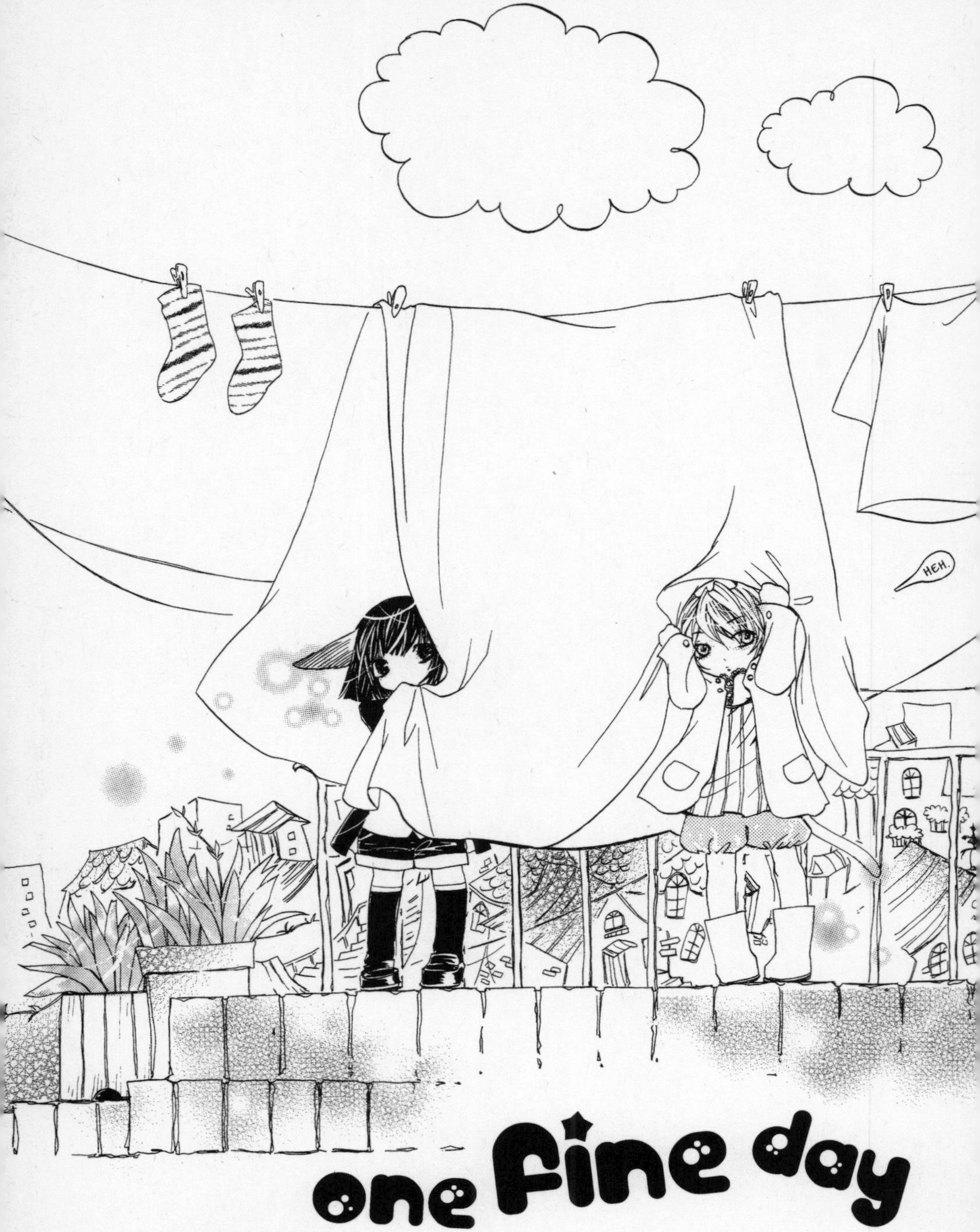
HEH.

# one fine day

**DAY 12.**
**SUNNY LAUNDRY**

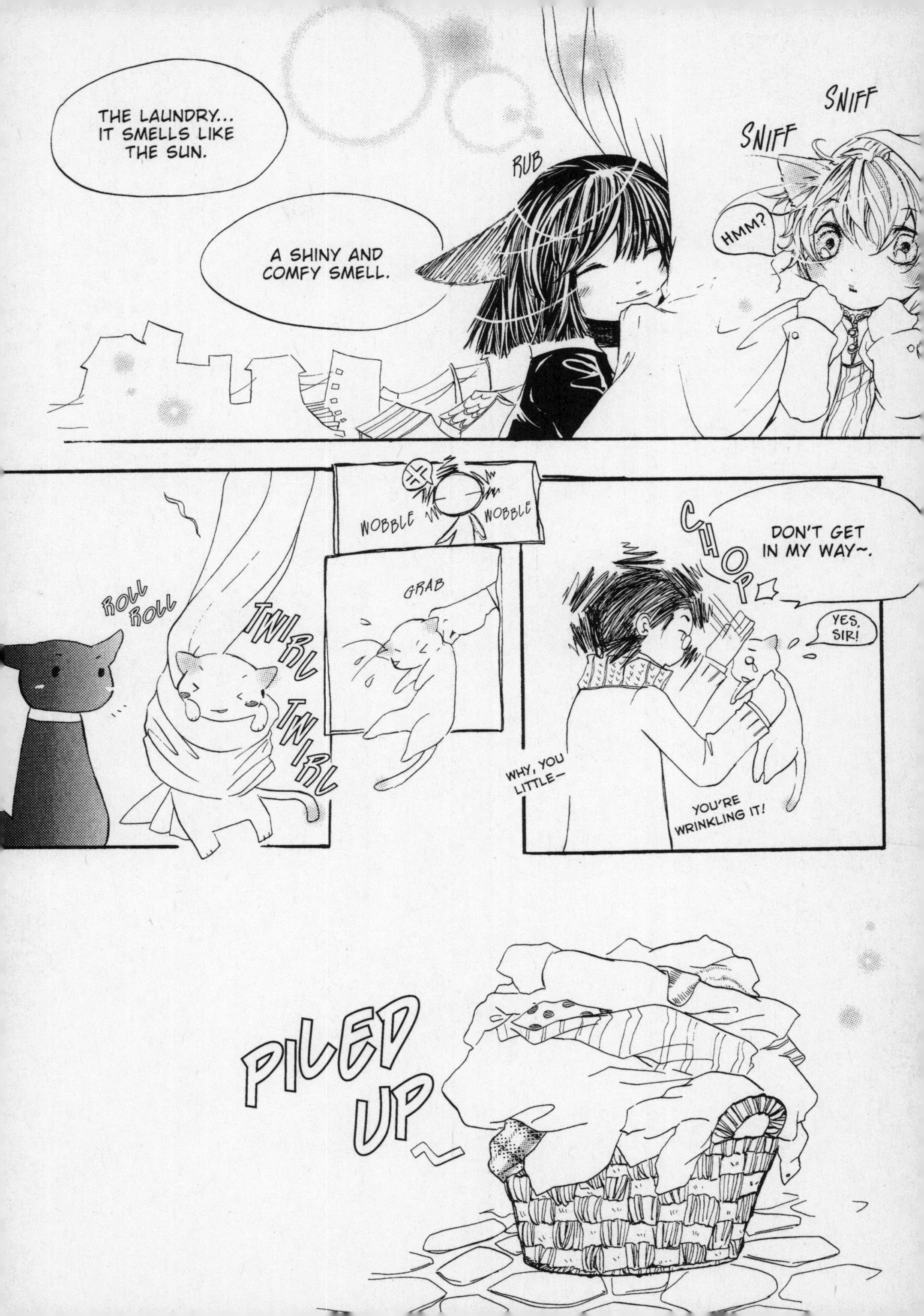
THE LAUNDRY... IT SMELLS LIKE THE SUN.
RUB
A SHINY AND COMFY SMELL.
SNIFF
SNIFF
HMM?
ROLL ROLL
TWIRL TWIRL
WOBBLE WOBBLE
GRAB
CHOP
DON'T GET IN MY WAY~.
YES, SIR!
WHY, YOU LITTLE—
YOU'RE WRINKLING IT!
PILED UP~

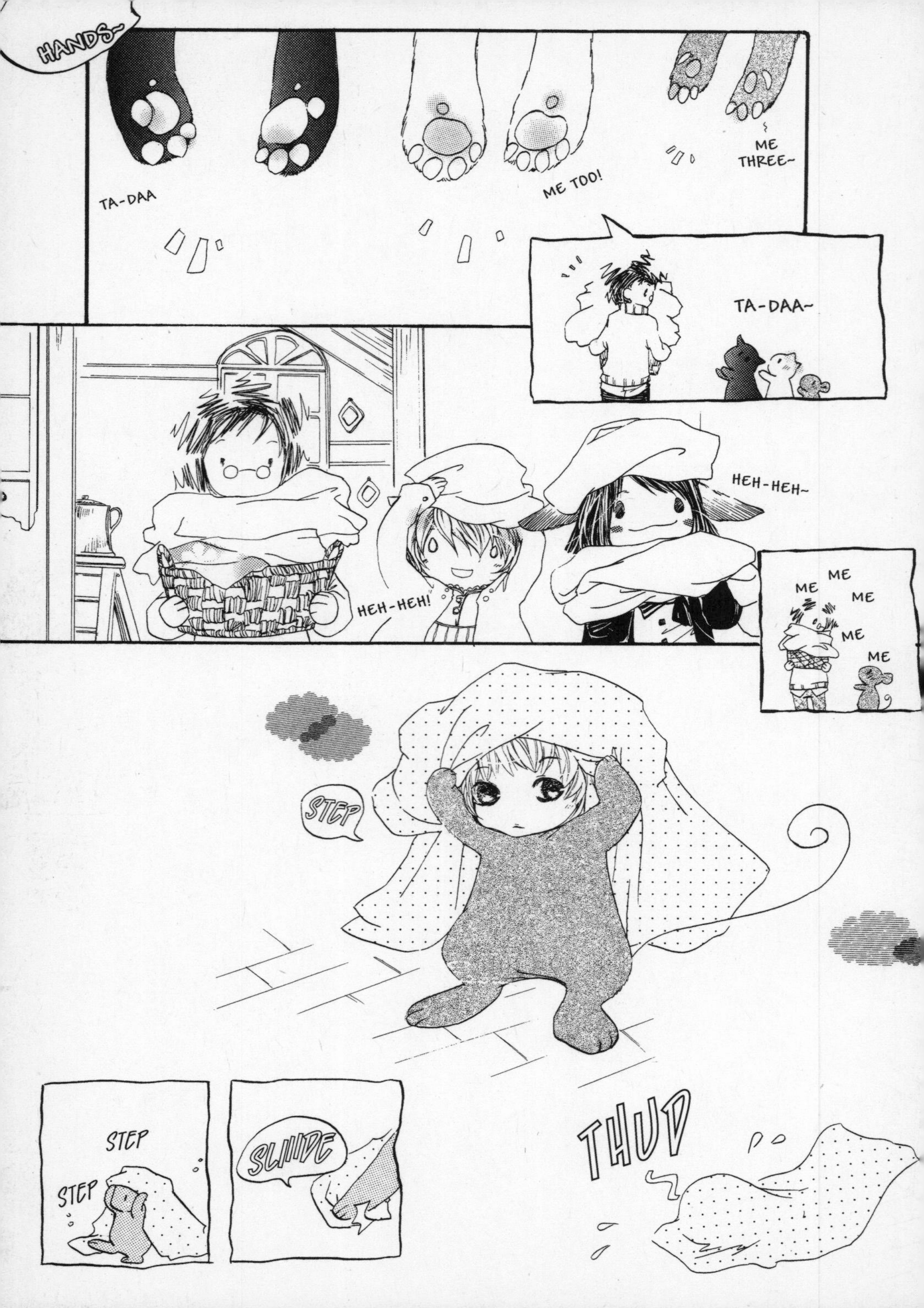
HANDS~
TA-DAA
ME TOO!
ME THREE~
TA-DAA~
HEH-HEH!
HEH-HEH~
ME
ME
ME
ME
ME
STEP
STEP
STEP
SLIIIDE
THUD

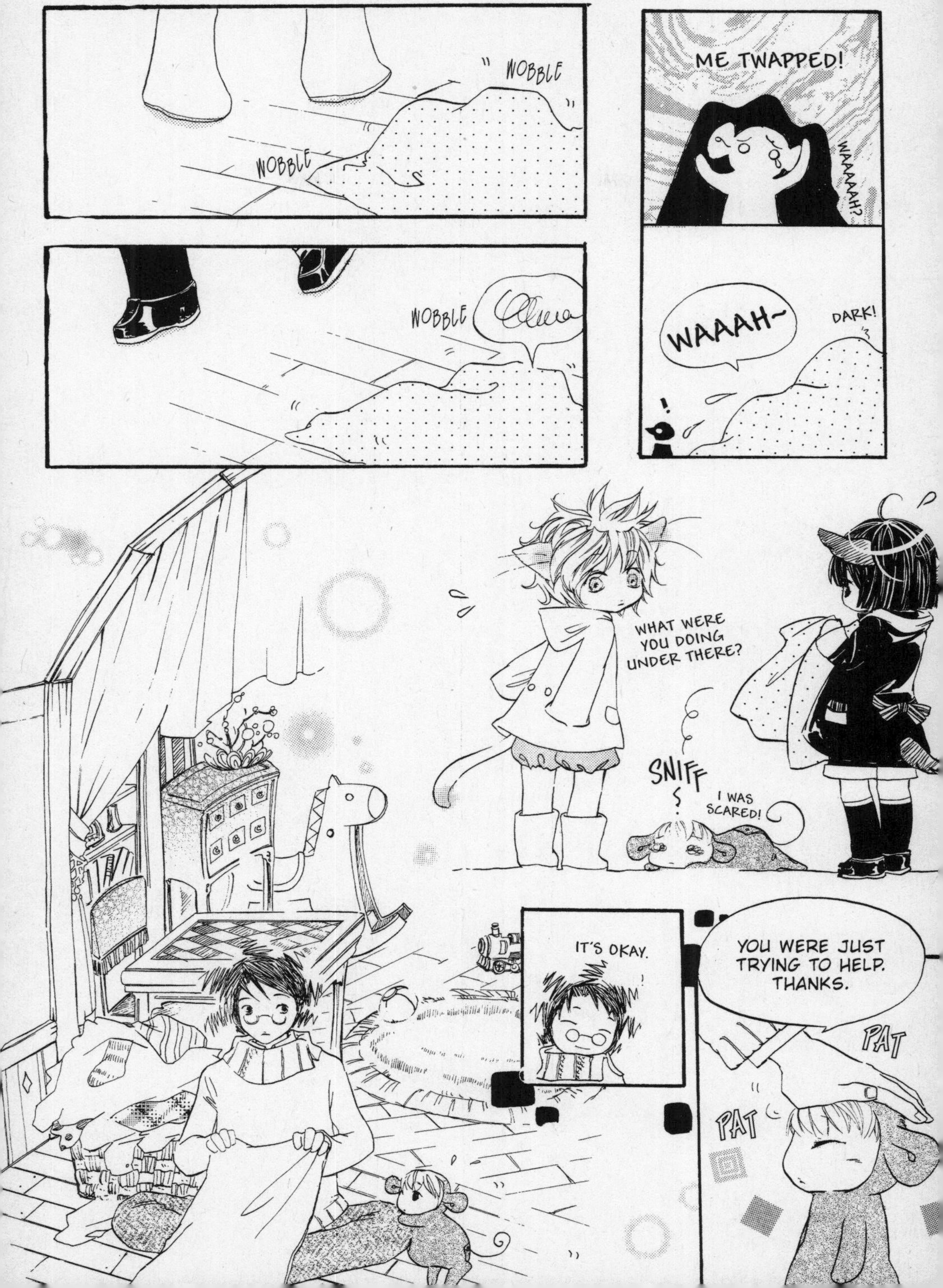
WOBBLE
WOBBLE
ME TWAPPED!
WAAAAAH?
WOBBLE
WAAAH~
DARK!
WHAT WERE YOU DOING UNDER THERE?
SNIFF
I WAS SCARED!
IT'S OKAY.
YOU WERE JUST TRYING TO HELP. THANKS.
PAT
PAT

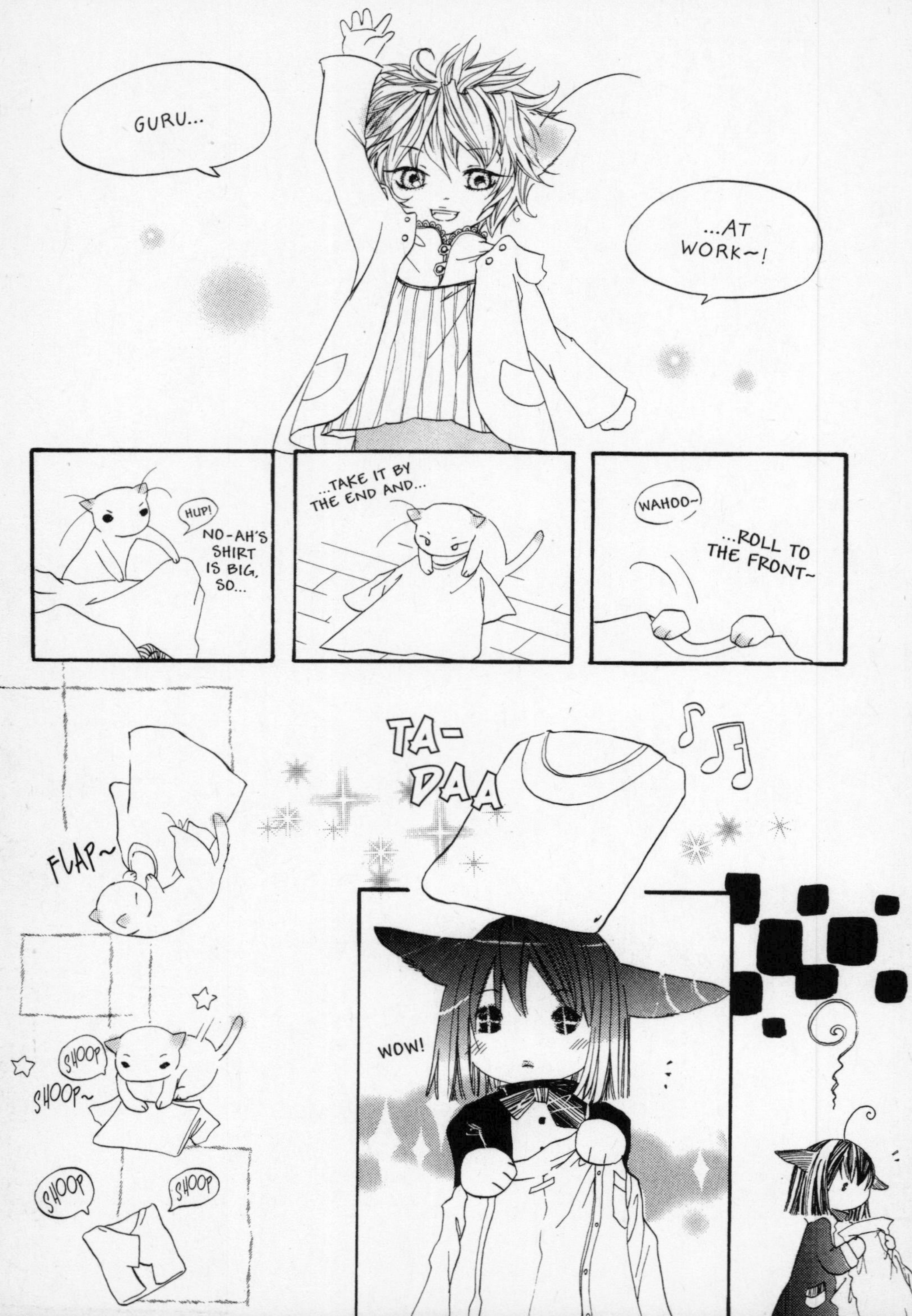
GURU...
...AT WORK~!
HUP!
NO-AH'S SHIRT IS BIG, SO...
...TAKE IT BY THE END AND...
WAHOO~
...ROLL TO THE FRONT~
FLAP~
SHOOP
SHOOP~
SHOOP
SHOOP
TA-DAA
WOW!

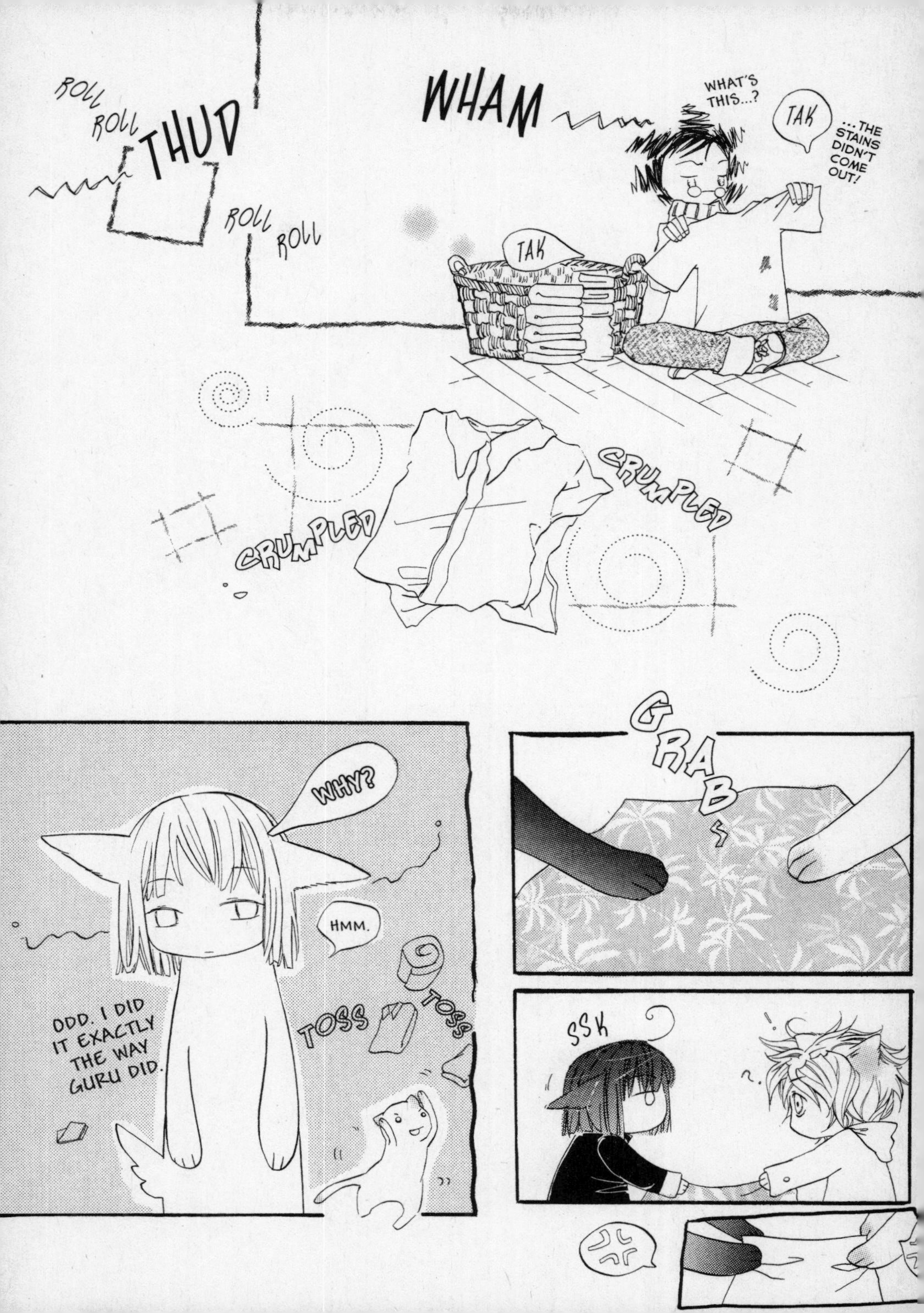
ROLL ROLL
THUD
ROLL ROLL
WHAM
WHAT'S THIS...?
TAK
...THE STAINS DIDN'T COME OUT!
TAK
CRUMPLED
CRUMPLED
WHY?
HMM.
ODD. I DID IT EXACTLY THE WAY GURU DID.
TOSS
TOSS
GRAB
SSK

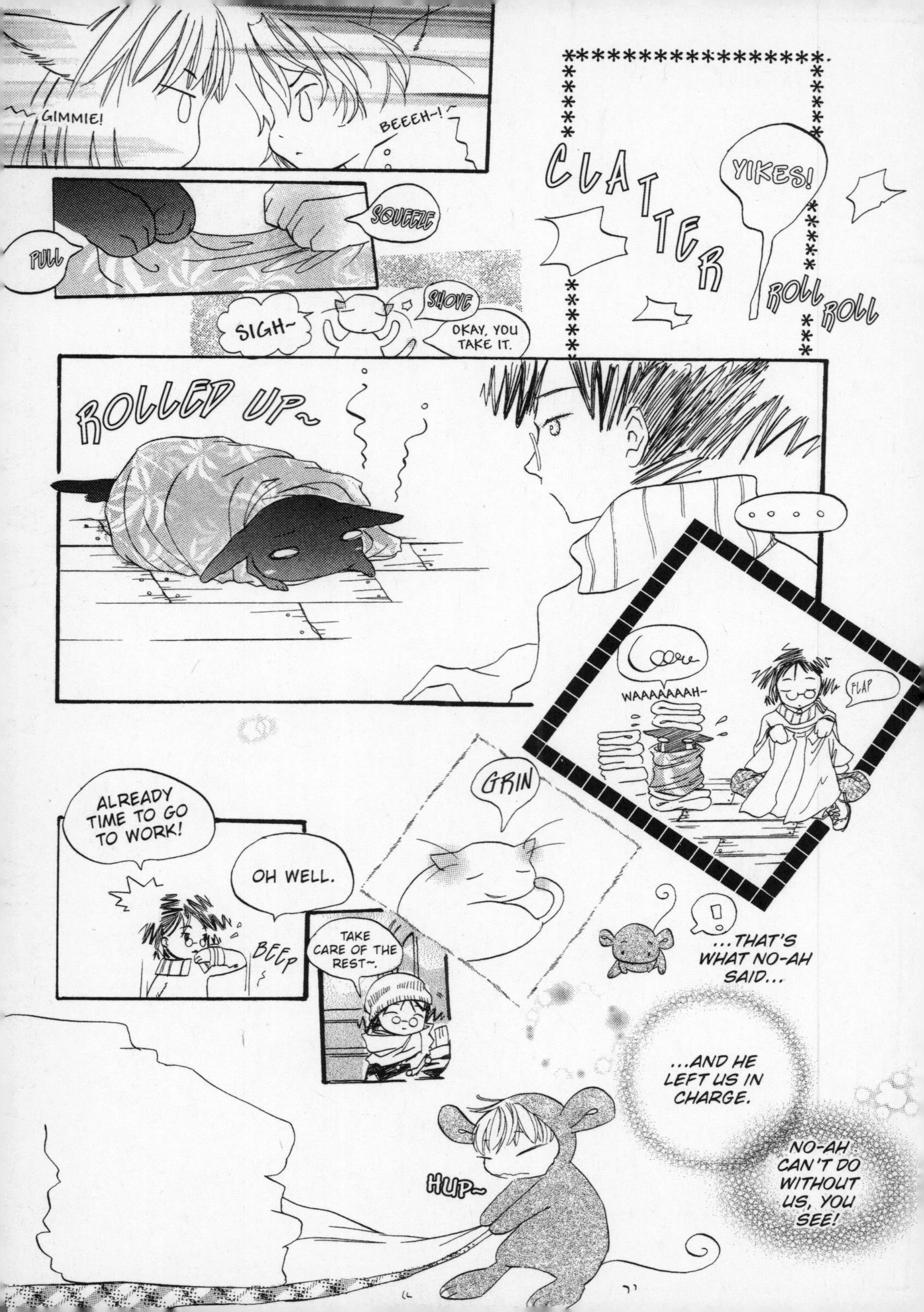
GIMMIE!
BEEEH-!
CLATTER
YIKES!
ROLL ROLL
PULL
SQUEEZE
SIGH~
SHOVE
OKAY, YOU TAKE IT.
ROLLED UP~
....
WAAAAAAAH~
FLAP
ALREADY TIME TO GO TO WORK!
OH WELL.
BEEP
GRIN
TAKE CARE OF THE REST~.
!
...THAT'S WHAT NO-AH SAID...
...AND HE LEFT US IN CHARGE.
HUP~
NO-AH CAN'T DO WITHOUT US, YOU SEE!

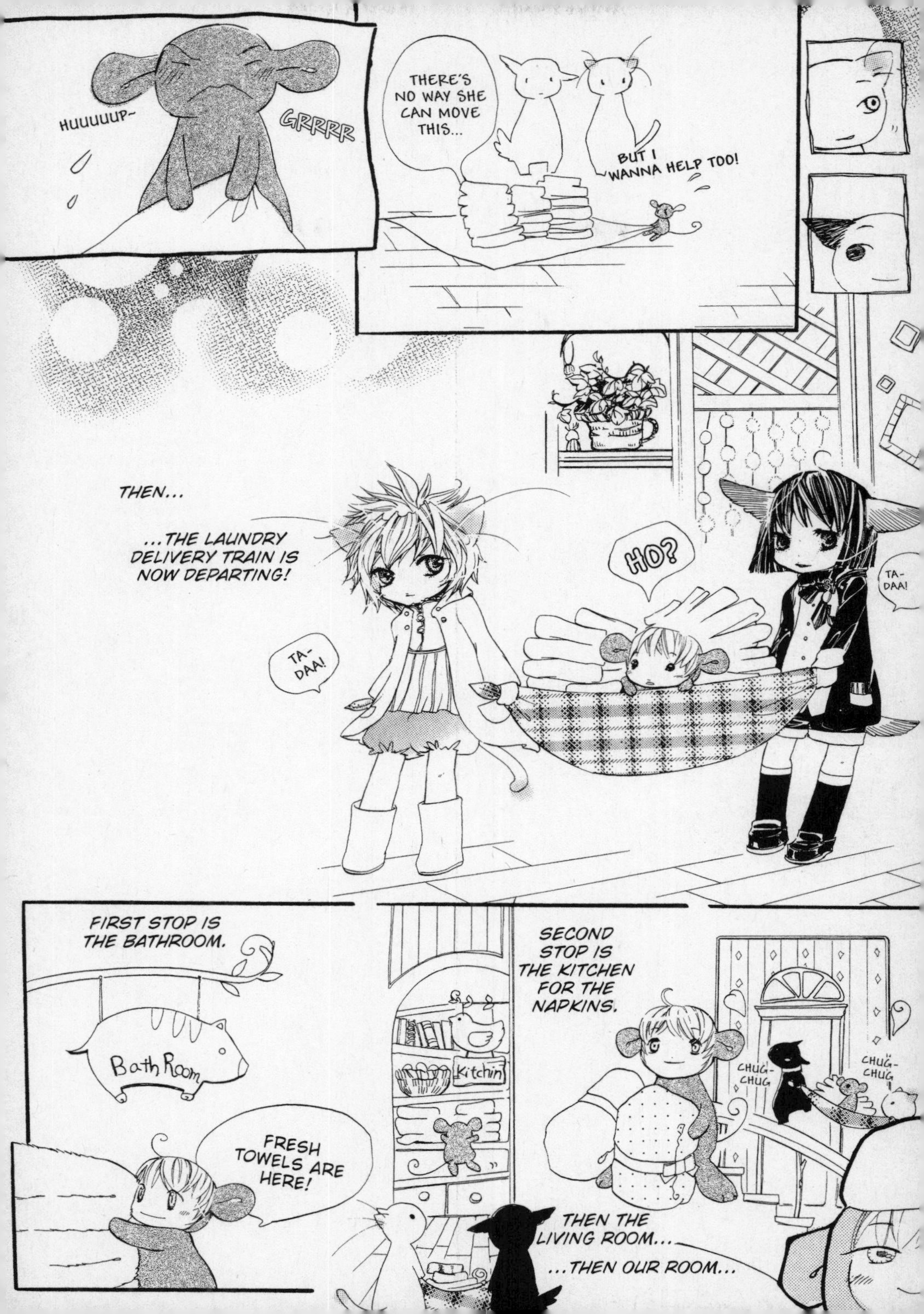
HUUUUUP-
GRRRR
THERE'S NO WAY SHE CAN MOVE THIS...
BUT I WANNA HELP TOO!
THEN...
...THE LAUNDRY DELIVERY TRAIN IS NOW DEPARTING!
HO?
TA-DAA!
TA-DAA!
FIRST STOP IS THE BATHROOM.
Bath Room
FRESH TOWELS ARE HERE!
Kitchin
SECOND STOP IS THE KITCHEN FOR THE NAPKINS.
CHUG-CHUG
CHUG-CHUG
THEN THE LIVING ROOM...
...THEN OUR ROOM...

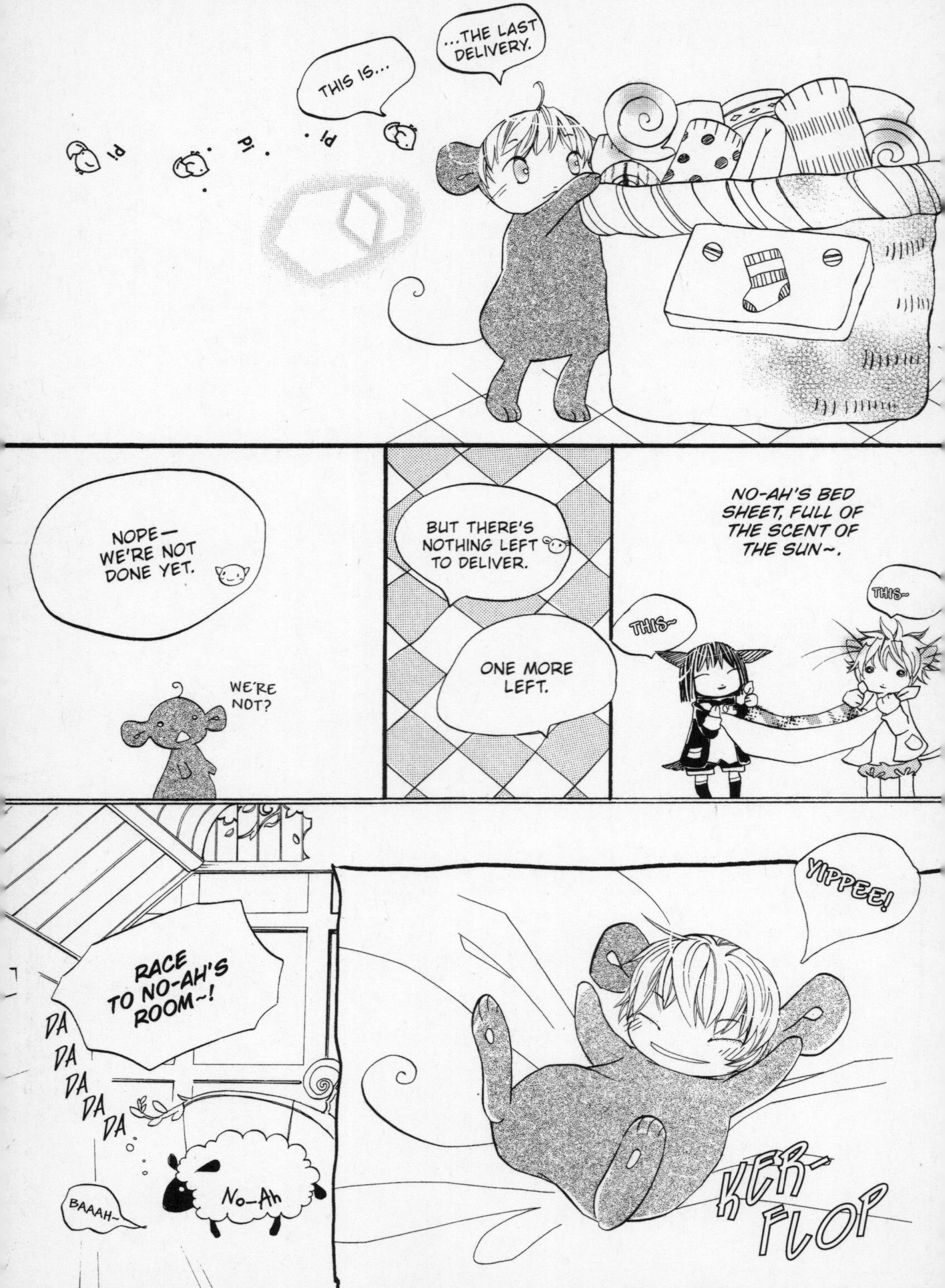
Pi
Pi
Pi
THIS IS...
...THE LAST DELIVERY.
NOPE— WE'RE NOT DONE YET.
WE'RE NOT?
BUT THERE'S NOTHING LEFT TO DELIVER.
ONE MORE LEFT.
NO-AH'S BED SHEET, FULL OF THE SCENT OF THE SUN~.
THIS~
THIS~
RACE TO NO-AH'S ROOM~!
DA DA DA DA DA
BAAAH~
No-Ah
YIPPEE!
KER-FLOP

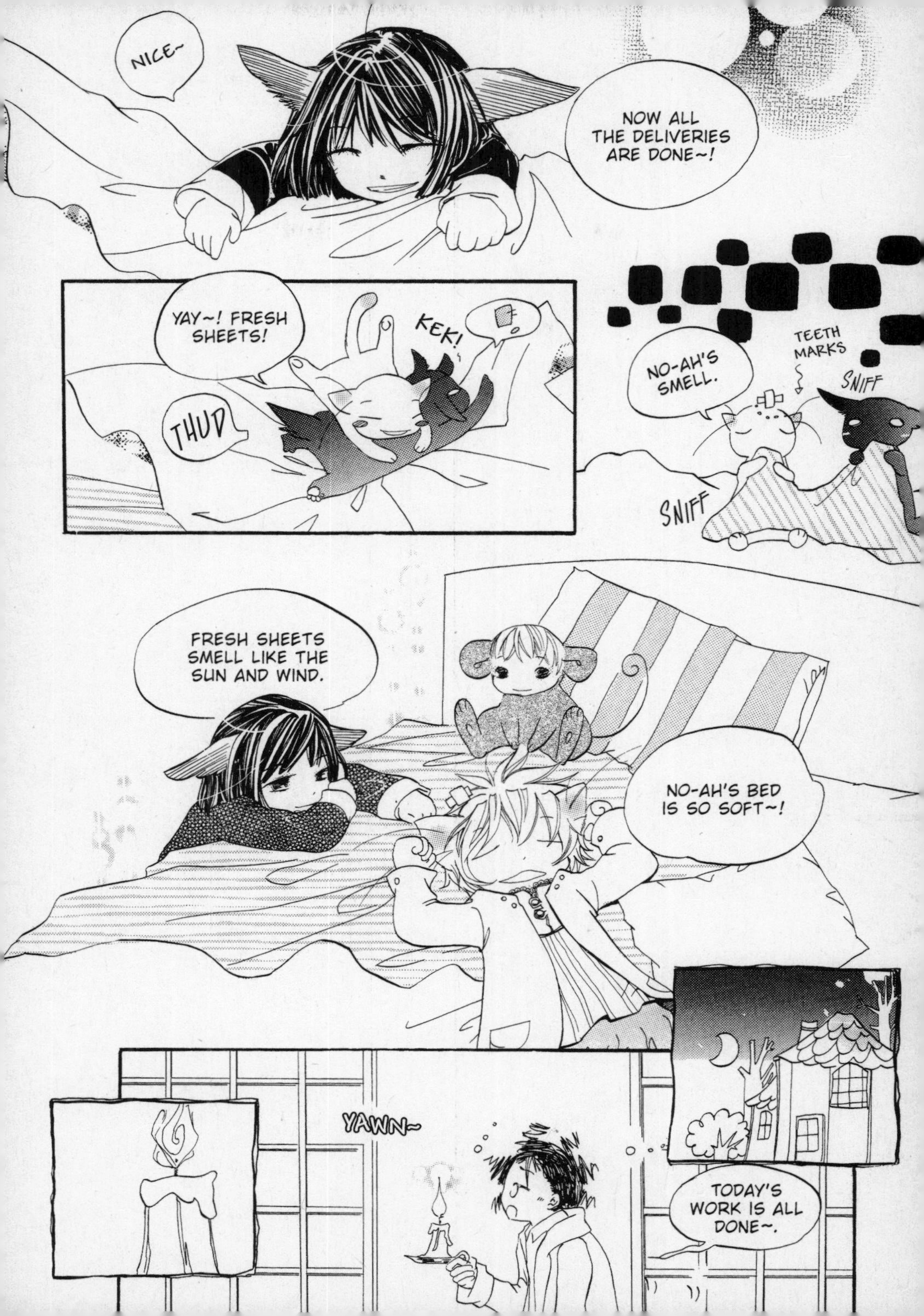
NICE~
NOW ALL THE DELIVERIES ARE DONE~!
YAY~! FRESH SHEETS!
KEK!
THUD
NO-AH'S SMELL.
TEETH MARKS
SNIFF
SNIFF
FRESH SHEETS SMELL LIKE THE SUN AND WIND.
NO-AH'S BED IS SO SOFT~!
YAWN~
TODAY'S WORK IS ALL DONE~.

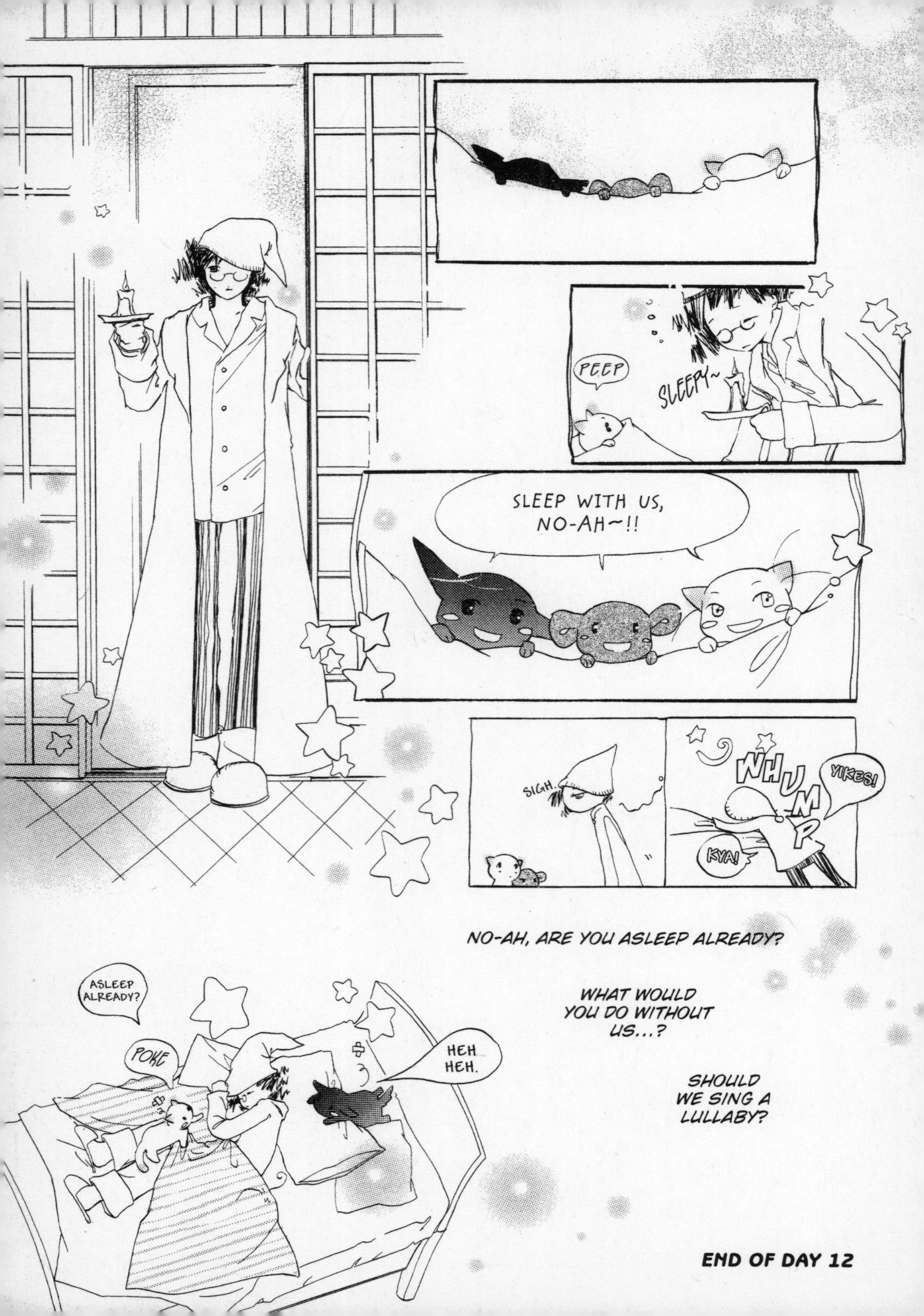
PEEP
SLEEPY~
SLEEP WITH US, NO-AH~!!
SIGH.
WHUMP
YIKES!
KYA!
NO-AH, ARE YOU ASLEEP ALREADY?
ASLEEP ALREADY?
POKE
HEH HEH.
WHAT WOULD YOU DO WITHOUT US...?
SHOULD WE SING A LULLABY?
END OF DAY 12

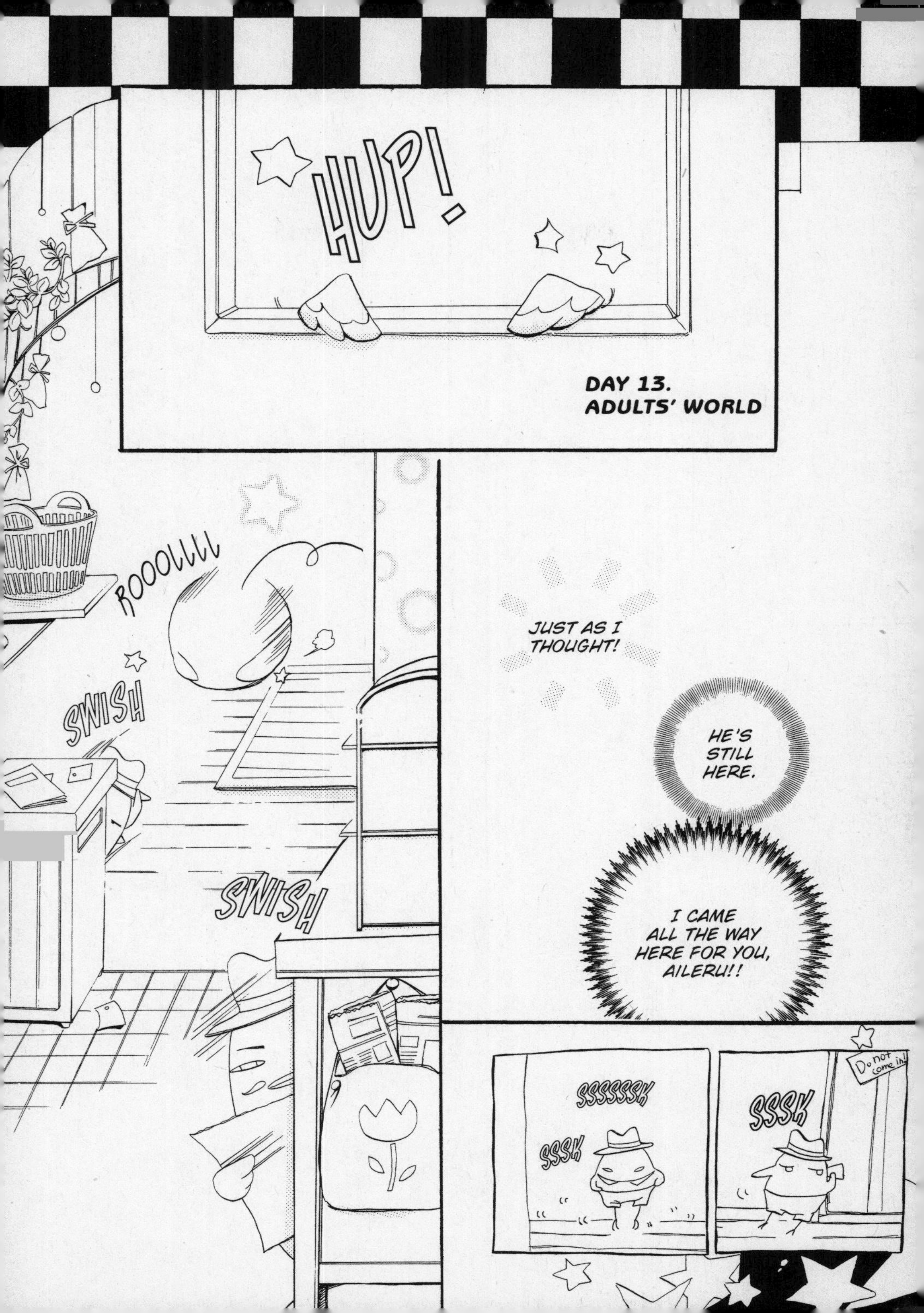
HUP!
DAY 13.
ADULTS' WORLD
ROOOLLLL
SWISH
SWISH
JUST AS I THOUGHT!
HE'S STILL HERE.
I CAME ALL THE WAY HERE FOR YOU, AILERU!!
SSSSSSK
SSSK
Do not come in!
SSSK

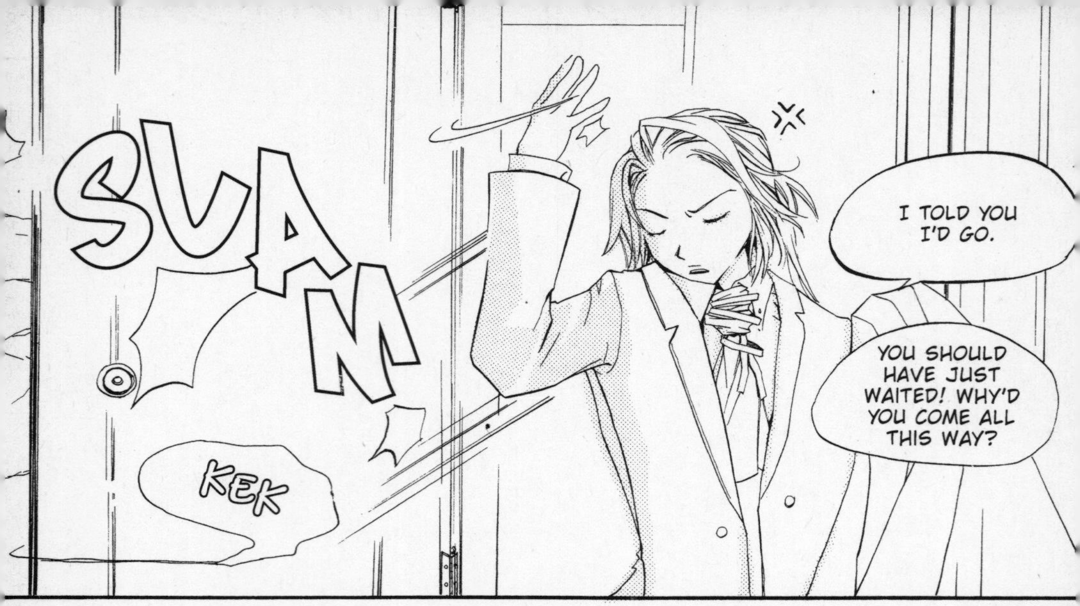
SLAM
KEK
I TOLD YOU I'D GO.
YOU SHOULD HAVE JUST WAITED! WHY'D YOU COME ALL THIS WAY?

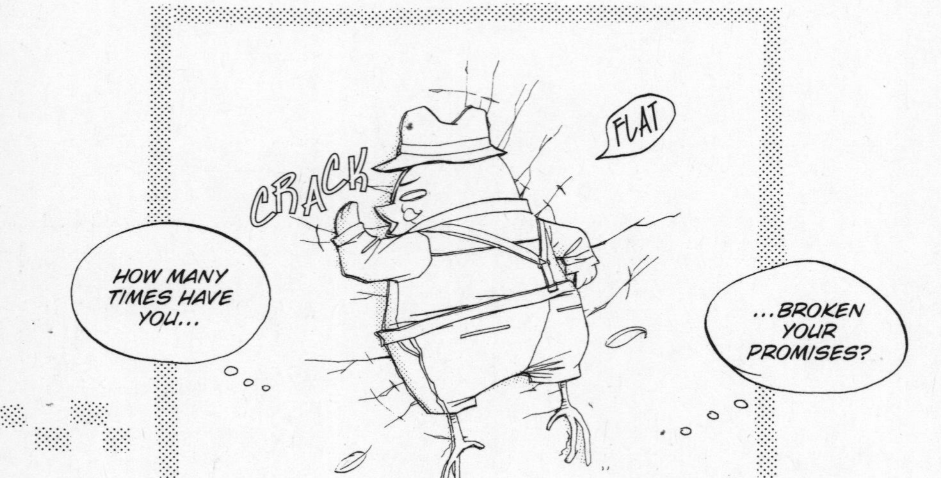
CRACK
FLAT
HOW MANY TIMES HAVE YOU...
...BROKEN YOUR PROMISES?

# one fine day

**DAY 13.**
**ADULTS' WORLD**

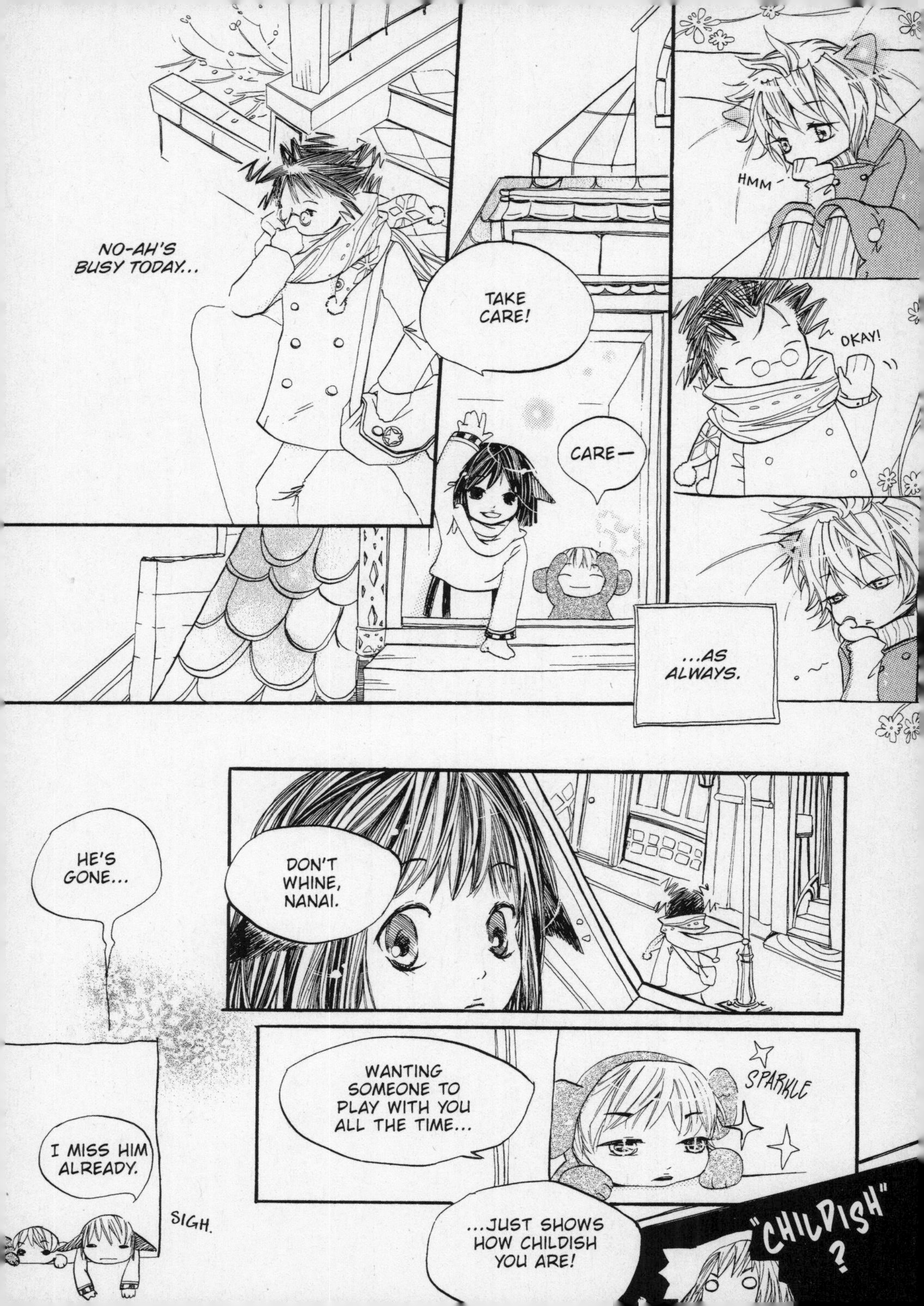
NO-AH'S BUSY TODAY...
TAKE CARE!
CARE—
HMM
OKAY!
...AS ALWAYS.
HE'S GONE...
DON'T WHINE, NANAI.
I MISS HIM ALREADY.
SIGH.
WANTING SOMEONE TO PLAY WITH YOU ALL THE TIME...
SPARKLE
...JUST SHOWS HOW CHILDISH YOU ARE!
"CHILDISH"?

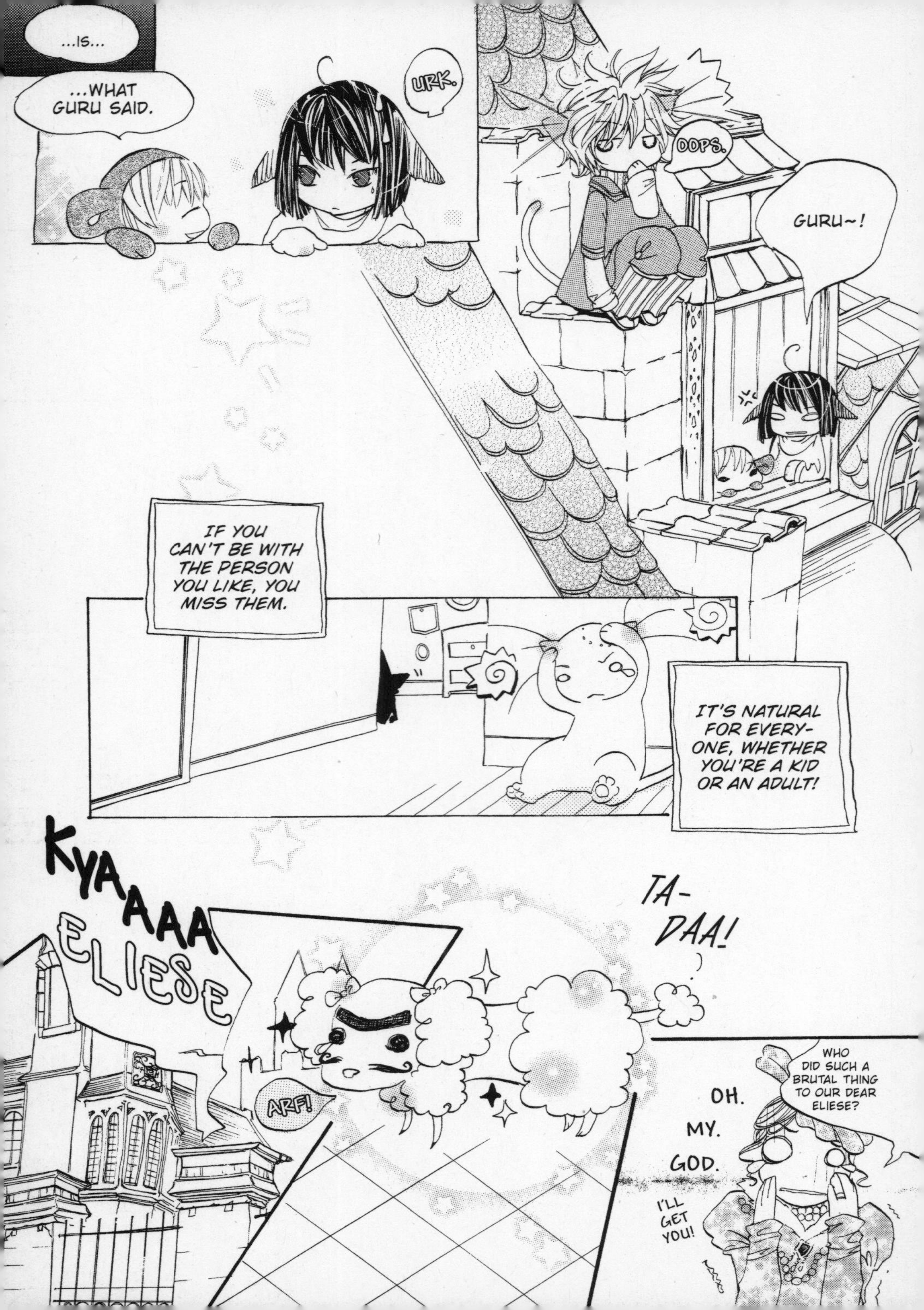

...IS...
...WHAT GURU SAID.
URK.
OOPS.
GURU~!
IF YOU CAN'T BE WITH THE PERSON YOU LIKE, YOU MISS THEM.
IT'S NATURAL FOR EVERY-ONE, WHETHER YOU'RE A KID OR AN ADULT!
KYAAAA
ELIESE
TA-DAA!
ARF!
WHO DID SUCH A BRUTAL THING TO OUR DEAR ELIESE?
OH. MY. GOD.
I'LL GET YOU!

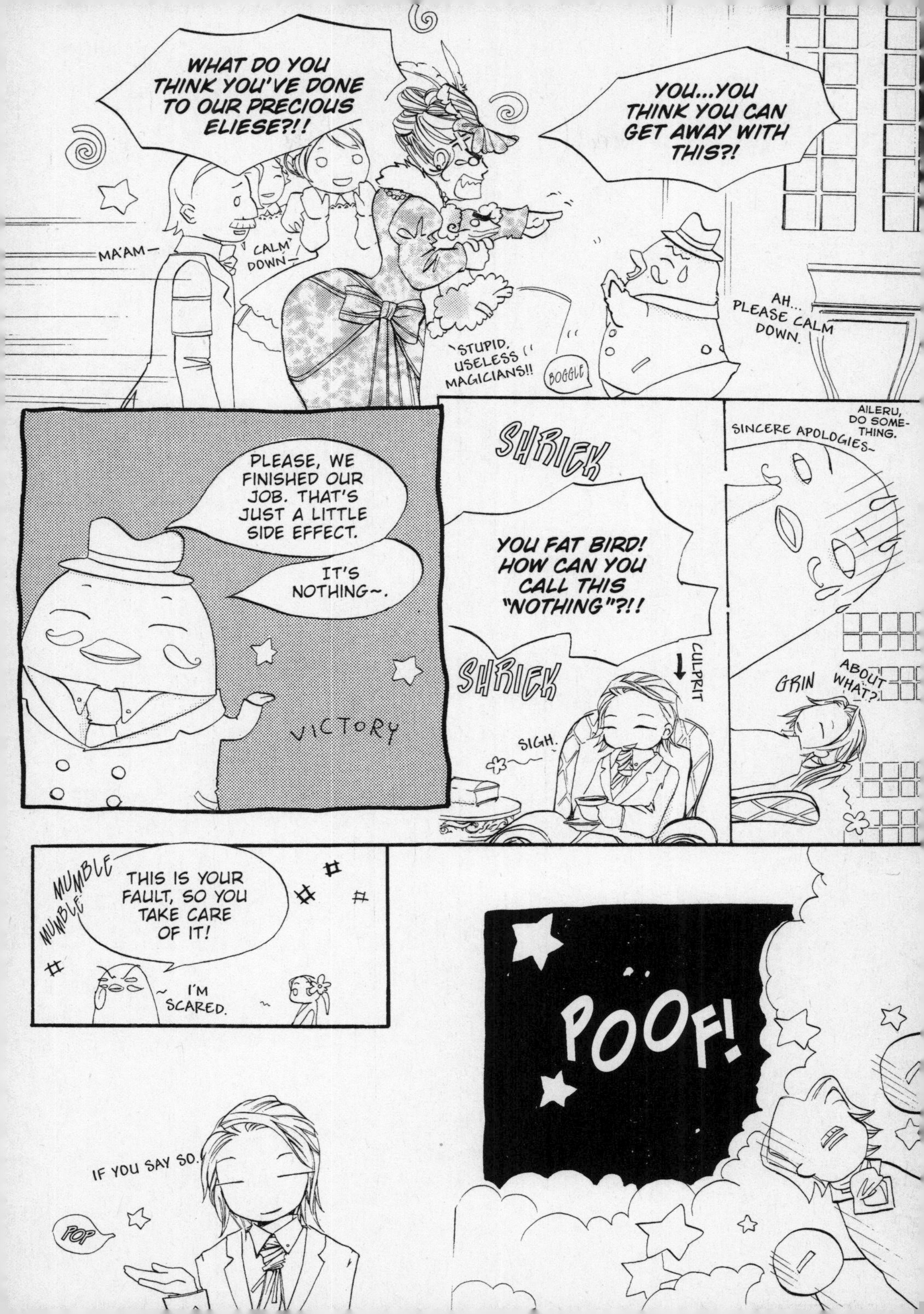
WHAT DO YOU THINK YOU'VE DONE TO OUR PRECIOUS ELIESE?!!
YOU...YOU THINK YOU CAN GET AWAY WITH THIS?!
MA'AM—
CALM DOWN—
STUPID, USELESS MAGICIANS!!
BOGGLE
AH... PLEASE CALM DOWN.
PLEASE, WE FINISHED OUR JOB. THAT'S JUST A LITTLE SIDE EFFECT.
IT'S NOTHING~.
VICTORY
SHRIEK
YOU FAT BIRD! HOW CAN YOU CALL THIS "NOTHING"?!!
SHRIEK
CULPRIT
SIGH.
SINCERE APOLOGIES~
AILERU, DO SOMETHING.
GRIN
ABOUT WHAT?
MUMBLE MUMBLE
THIS IS YOUR FAULT, SO YOU TAKE CARE OF IT!
I'M SCARED.
POOF!
IF YOU SAY SO.
POP

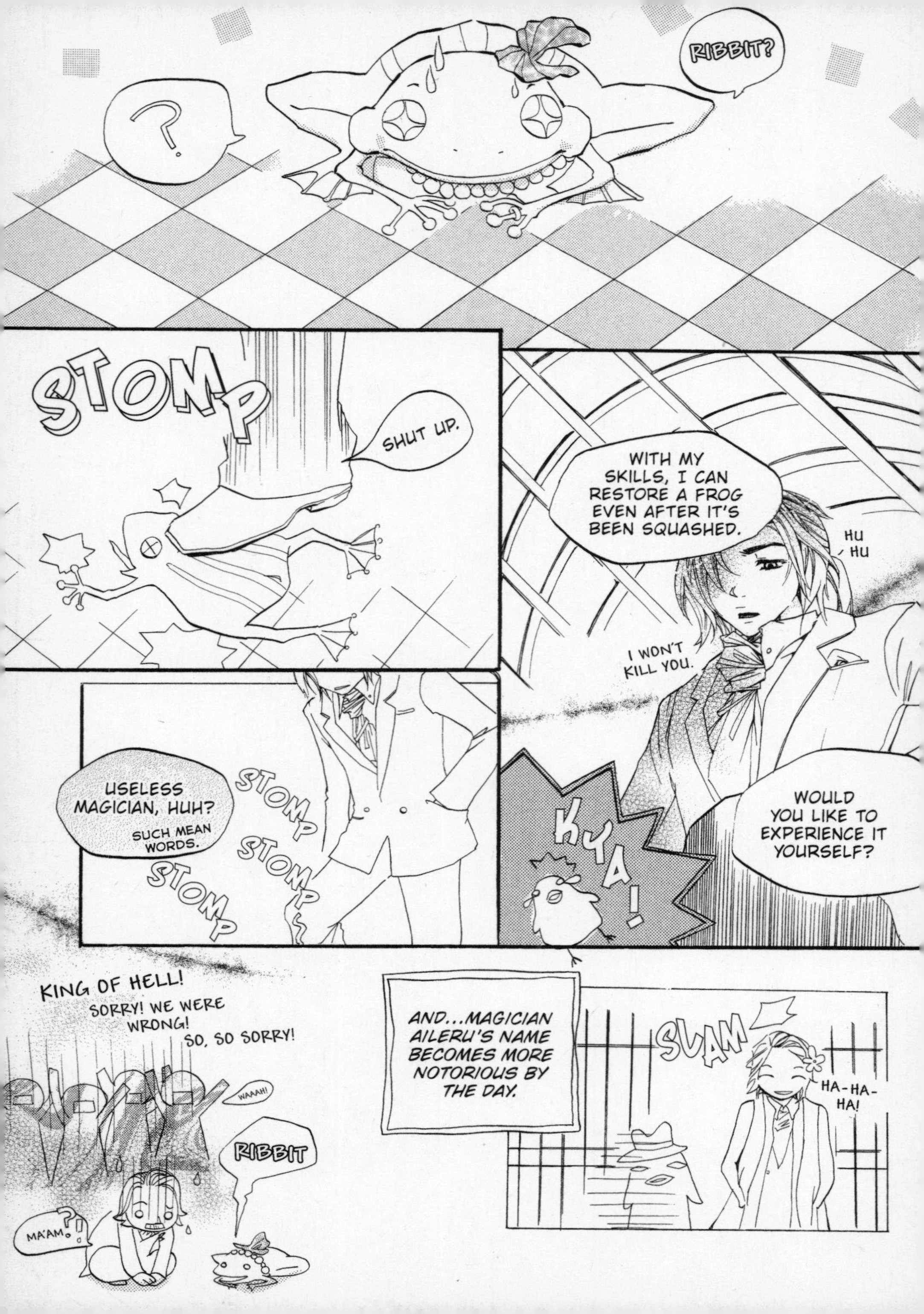
?
RIBBIT?
STOMP
SHUT UP.
WITH MY SKILLS, I CAN RESTORE A FROG EVEN AFTER IT'S BEEN SQUASHED.
HU HU
I WON'T KILL YOU.
USELESS MAGICIAN, HUH?
SUCH MEAN WORDS.
STOMP STOMP STOMP
KYA!
WOULD YOU LIKE TO EXPERIENCE IT YOURSELF?
KING OF HELL!
SORRY! WE WERE WRONG!
SO, SO SORRY!
WAAAH!
RIBBIT
MA'AM?!
AND...MAGICIAN AILERU'S NAME BECOMES MORE NOTORIOUS BY THE DAY.
SLAM
HA-HA-HA!

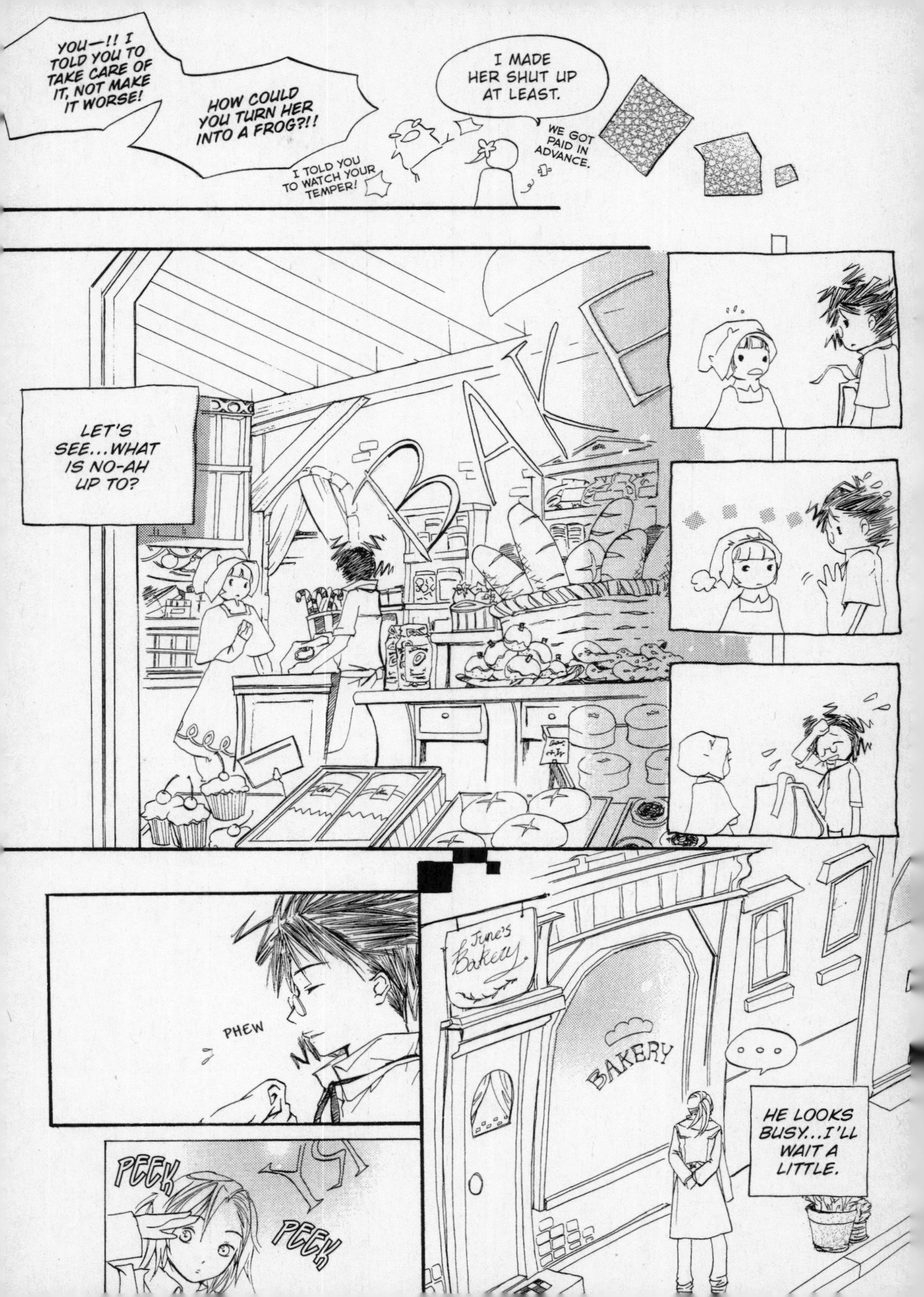

YOU—!! I TOLD YOU TO TAKE CARE OF IT, NOT MAKE IT WORSE!
HOW COULD YOU TURN HER INTO A FROG?!!
I TOLD YOU TO WATCH YOUR TEMPER!
I MADE HER SHUT UP AT LEAST.
WE GOT PAID IN ADVANCE.
LET'S SEE...WHAT IS NO-AH UP TO?
PHEW
June's Bakery
BAKERY
...
HE LOOKS BUSY...I'LL WAIT A LITTLE.
PEEK
PEEK

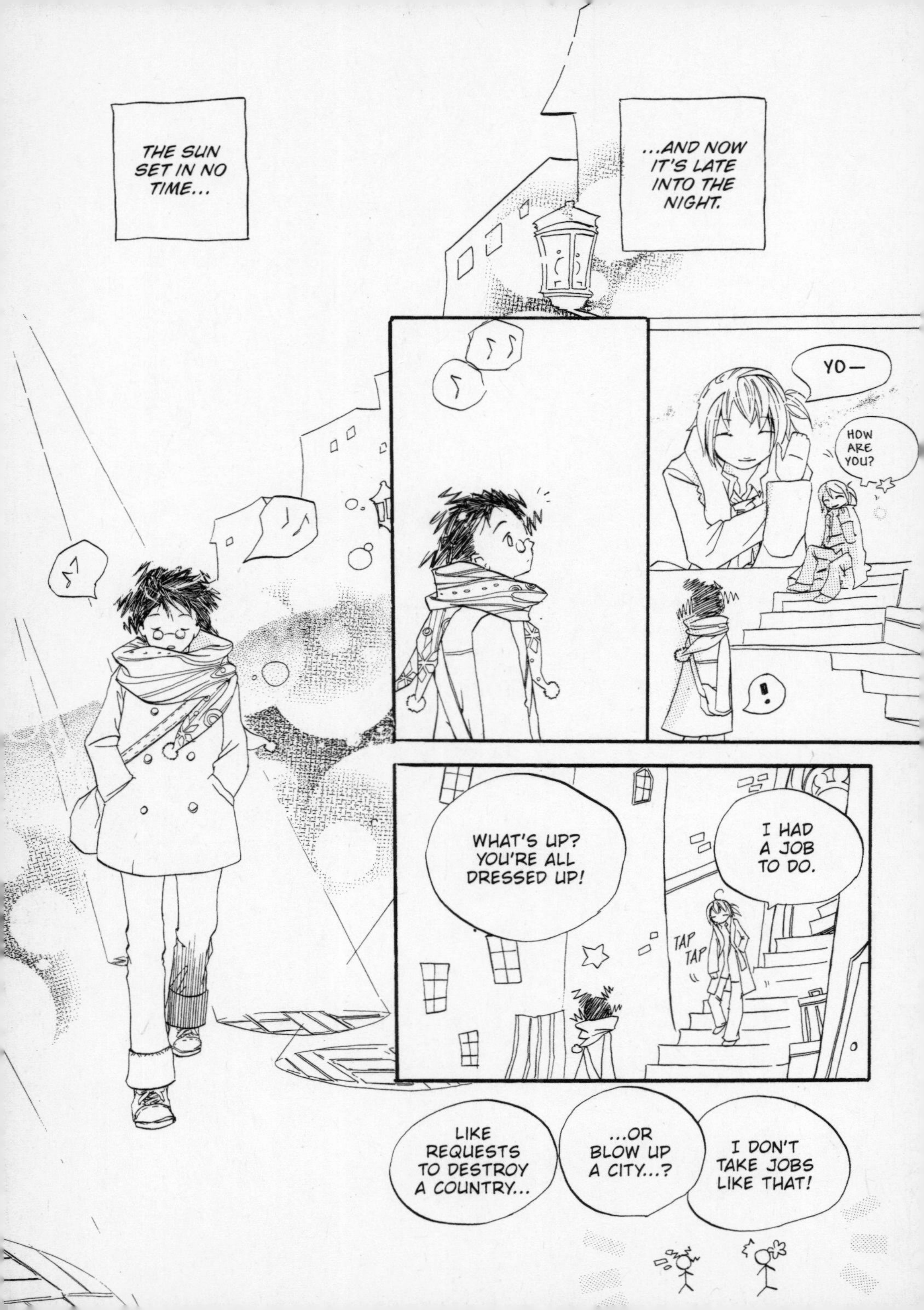

THE SUN SET IN NO TIME...
...AND NOW IT'S LATE INTO THE NIGHT.
YO—
HOW ARE YOU?
WHAT'S UP? YOU'RE ALL DRESSED UP!
I HAD A JOB TO DO.
TAP TAP
LIKE REQUESTS TO DESTROY A COUNTRY...
...OR BLOW UP A CITY...?
I DON'T TAKE JOBS LIKE THAT!

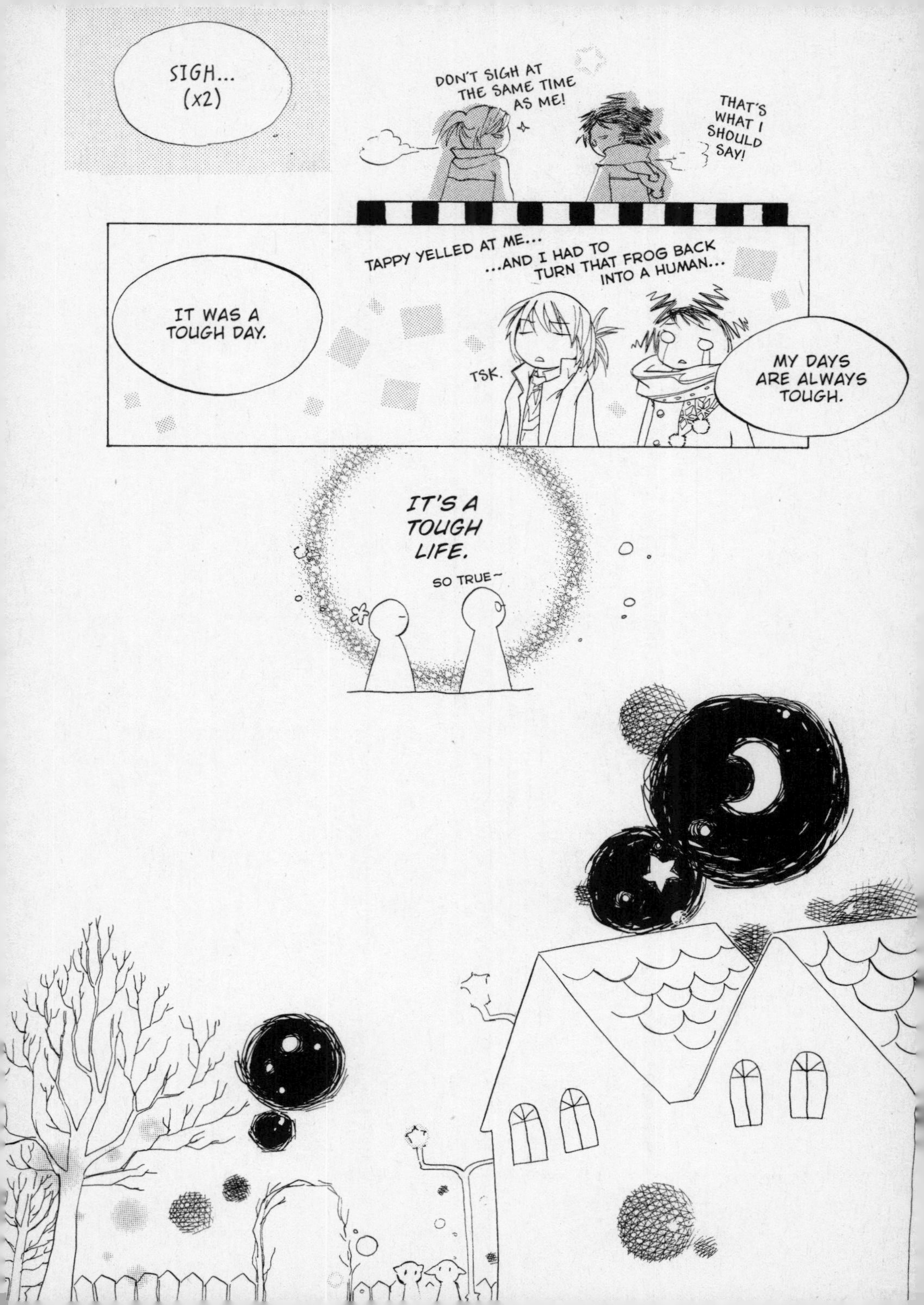
SIGH... (x2)
DON'T SIGH AT THE SAME TIME AS ME!
THAT'S WHAT I SHOULD SAY!
IT WAS A TOUGH DAY.
TAPPY YELLED AT ME...
...AND I HAD TO TURN THAT FROG BACK INTO A HUMAN...
TSK.
MY DAYS ARE ALWAYS TOUGH.
IT'S A TOUGH LIFE.
SO TRUE~

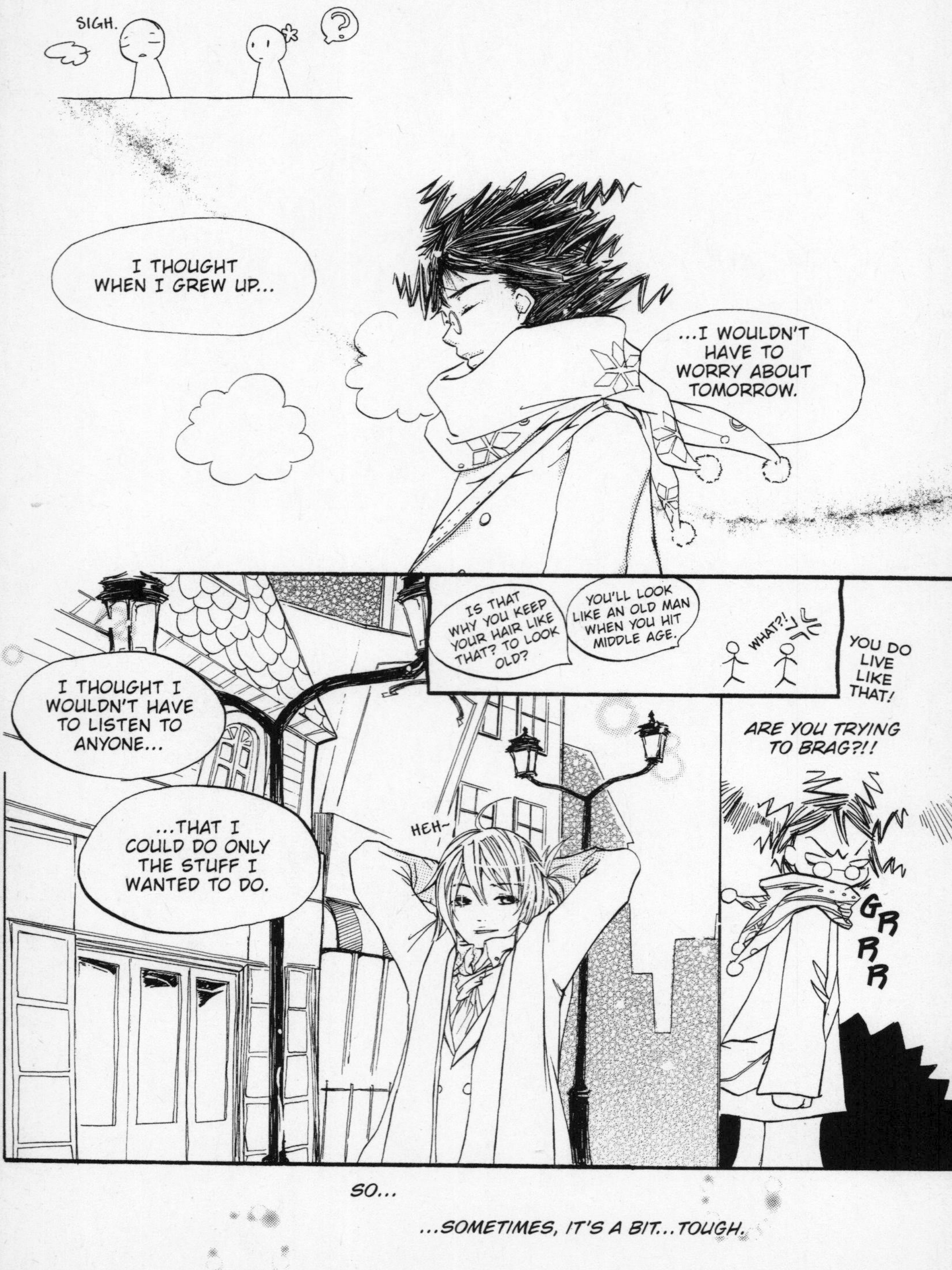
SIGH.
?
I THOUGHT WHEN I GREW UP...
...I WOULDN'T HAVE TO WORRY ABOUT TOMORROW.
I THOUGHT I WOULDN'T HAVE TO LISTEN TO ANYONE...
...THAT I COULD DO ONLY THE STUFF I WANTED TO DO.
HEH~
IS THAT WHY YOU KEEP YOUR HAIR LIKE THAT? TO LOOK OLD?
YOU'LL LOOK LIKE AN OLD MAN WHEN YOU HIT MIDDLE AGE.
WHAT?!
YOU DO LIVE LIKE THAT!
ARE YOU TRYING TO BRAG?!!
GRRR
SO...
...SOMETIMES, IT'S A BIT...TOUGH.

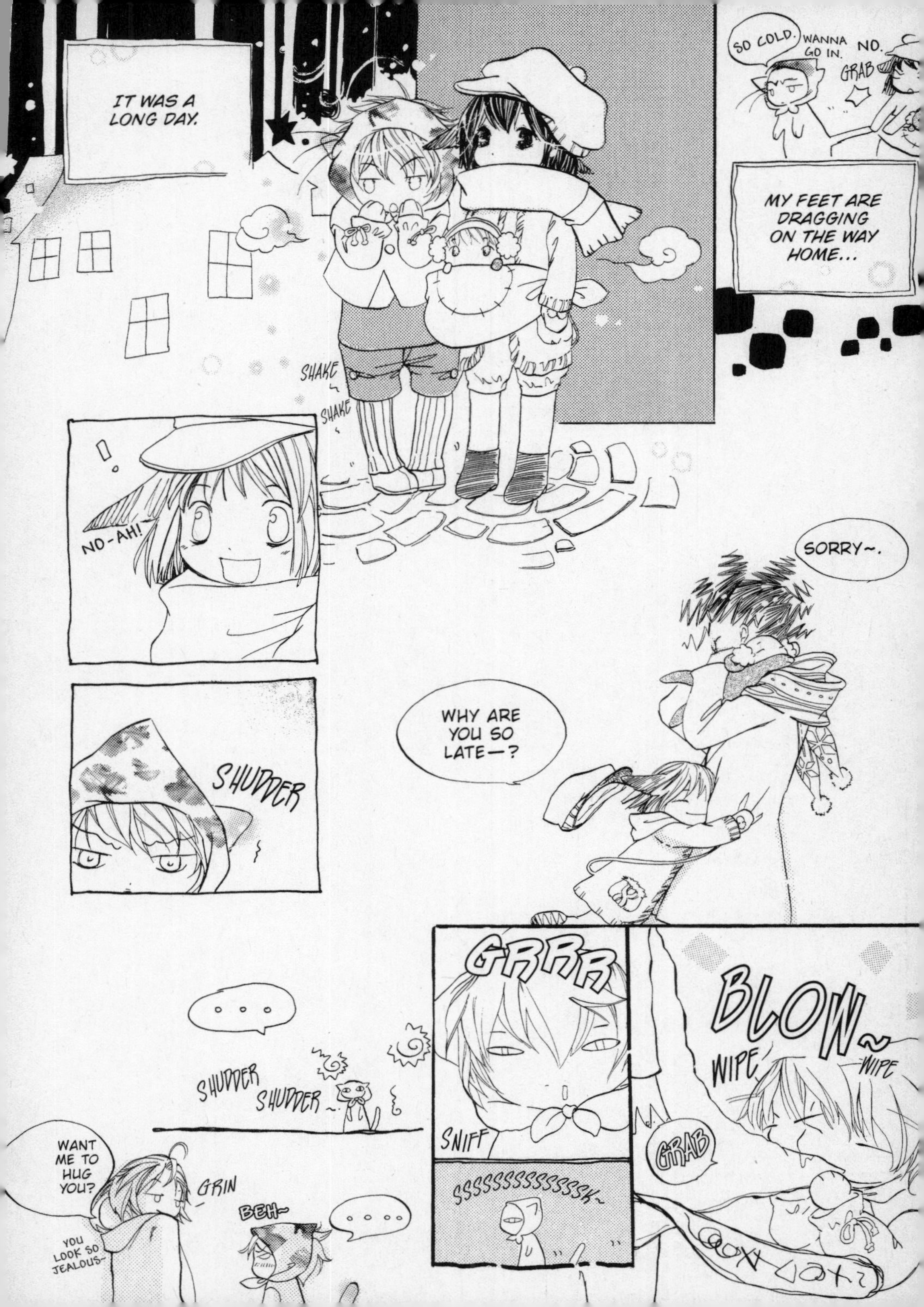
IT WAS A LONG DAY.
SO COLD.
WANNA GO IN.
NO.
GRAB
MY FEET ARE DRAGGING ON THE WAY HOME...
SHAKE SHAKE
NO-AH!
SHUDDER
SORRY~.
WHY ARE YOU SO LATE—?
. . .
SHUDDER SHUDDER~
GRRR
SNIFF
SSSSSSSSSSSSSK~
BLOW~
WIPE WIPE
GRAB
WANT ME TO HUG YOU?
GRIN
BEH~
YOU LOOK SO JEALOUS~
. . .

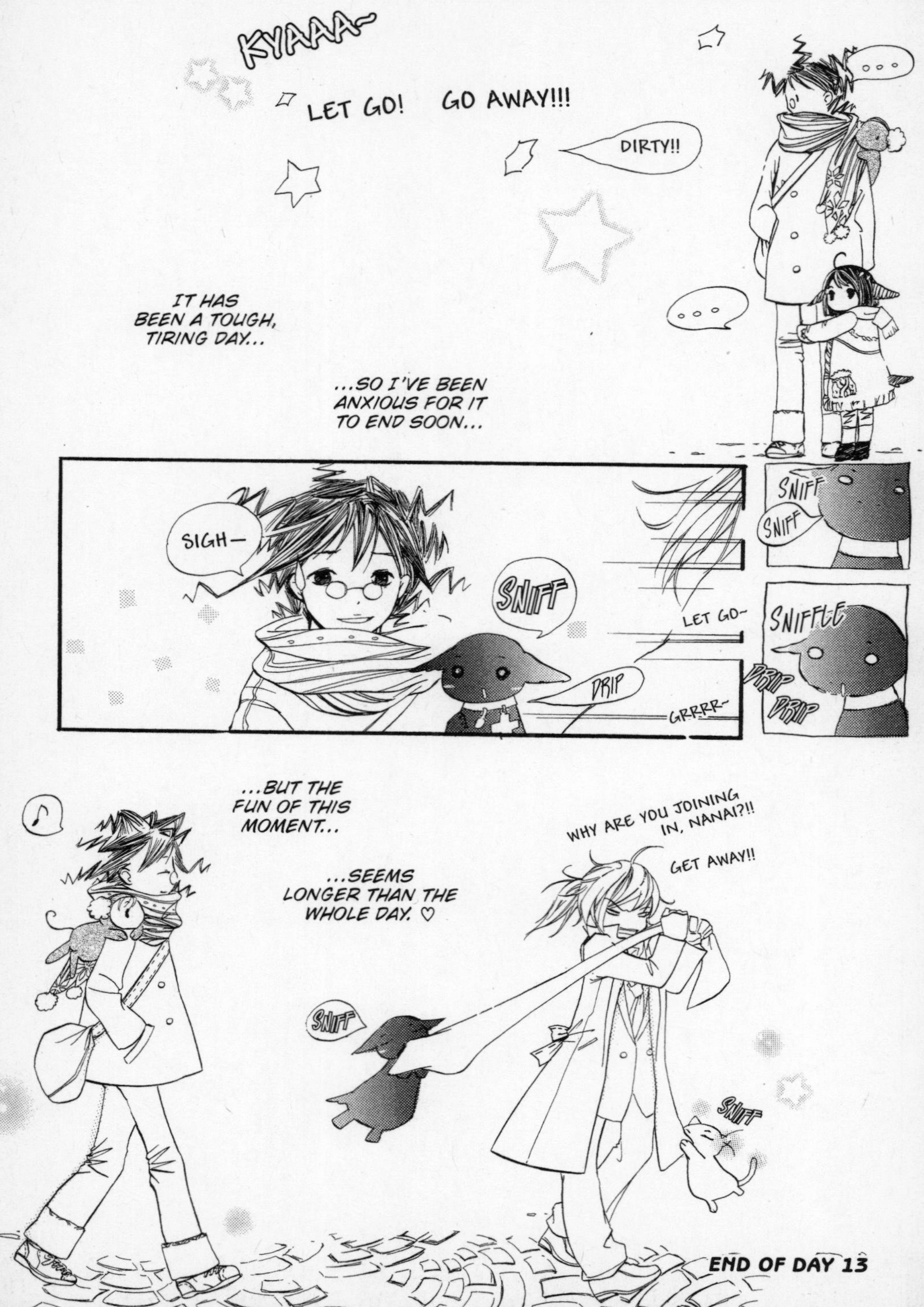
KYAAA~
LET GO!
GO AWAY!!!
DIRTY!!
...
...
IT HAS BEEN A TOUGH, TIRING DAY...
...SO I'VE BEEN ANXIOUS FOR IT TO END SOON...
SIGH—
SNIFF
LET GO~
DRIP
GRRRR~
SNIFF
SNIFF
SNIFFLE
DRIP
DRIP
...BUT THE FUN OF THIS MOMENT...
...SEEMS LONGER THAN THE WHOLE DAY. ♡
♪
WHY ARE YOU JOINING IN, NANAI?!!
GET AWAY!!
SNIFF
SNIFF
END OF DAY 13

## ANOTHER DAY #4
## FALLEN LEAVES

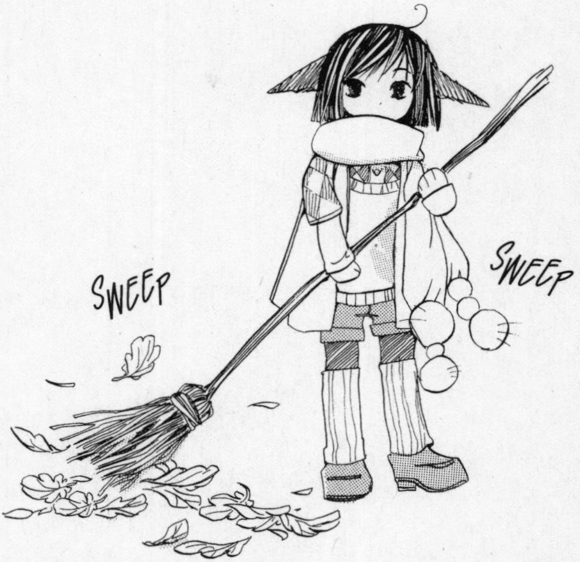
SWEEP
SWEEP

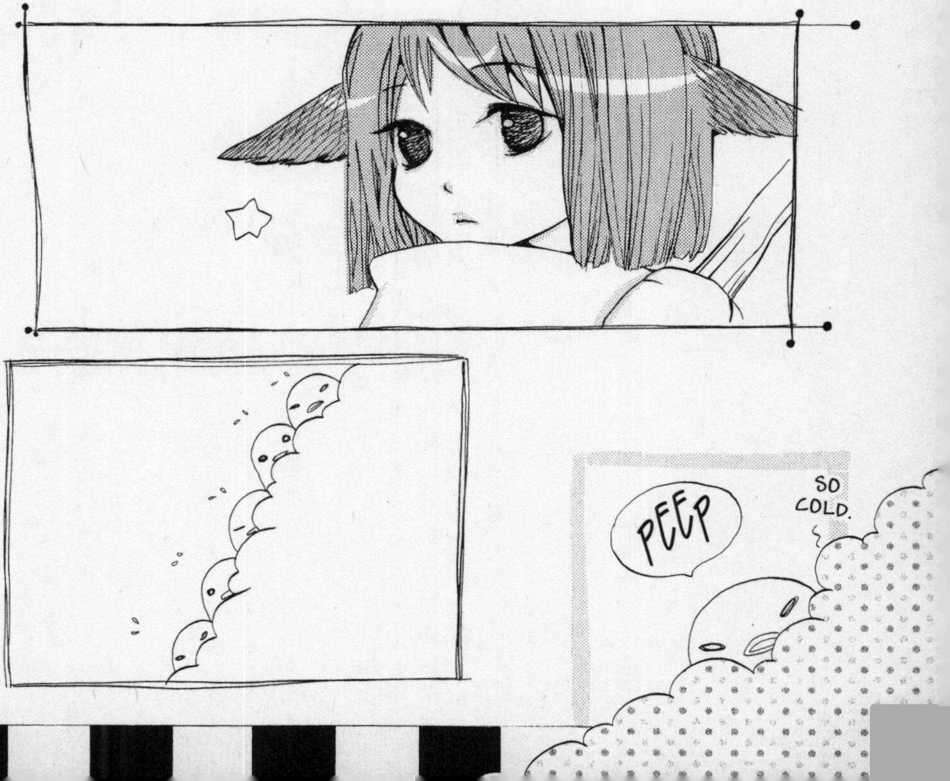
PEEP
SO COLD.

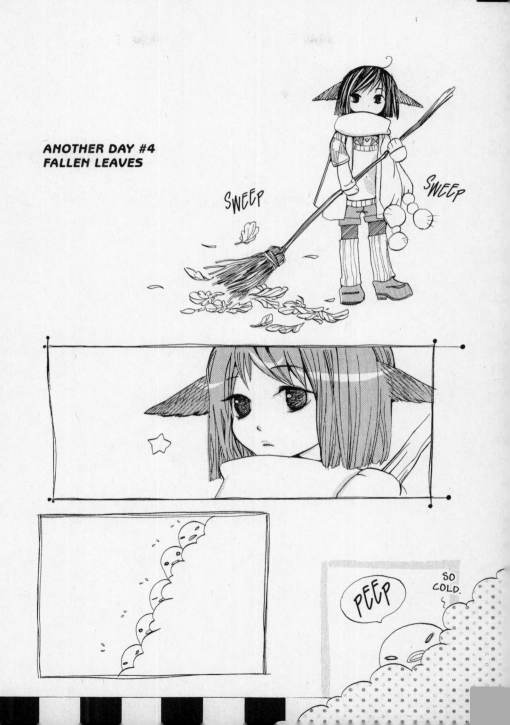

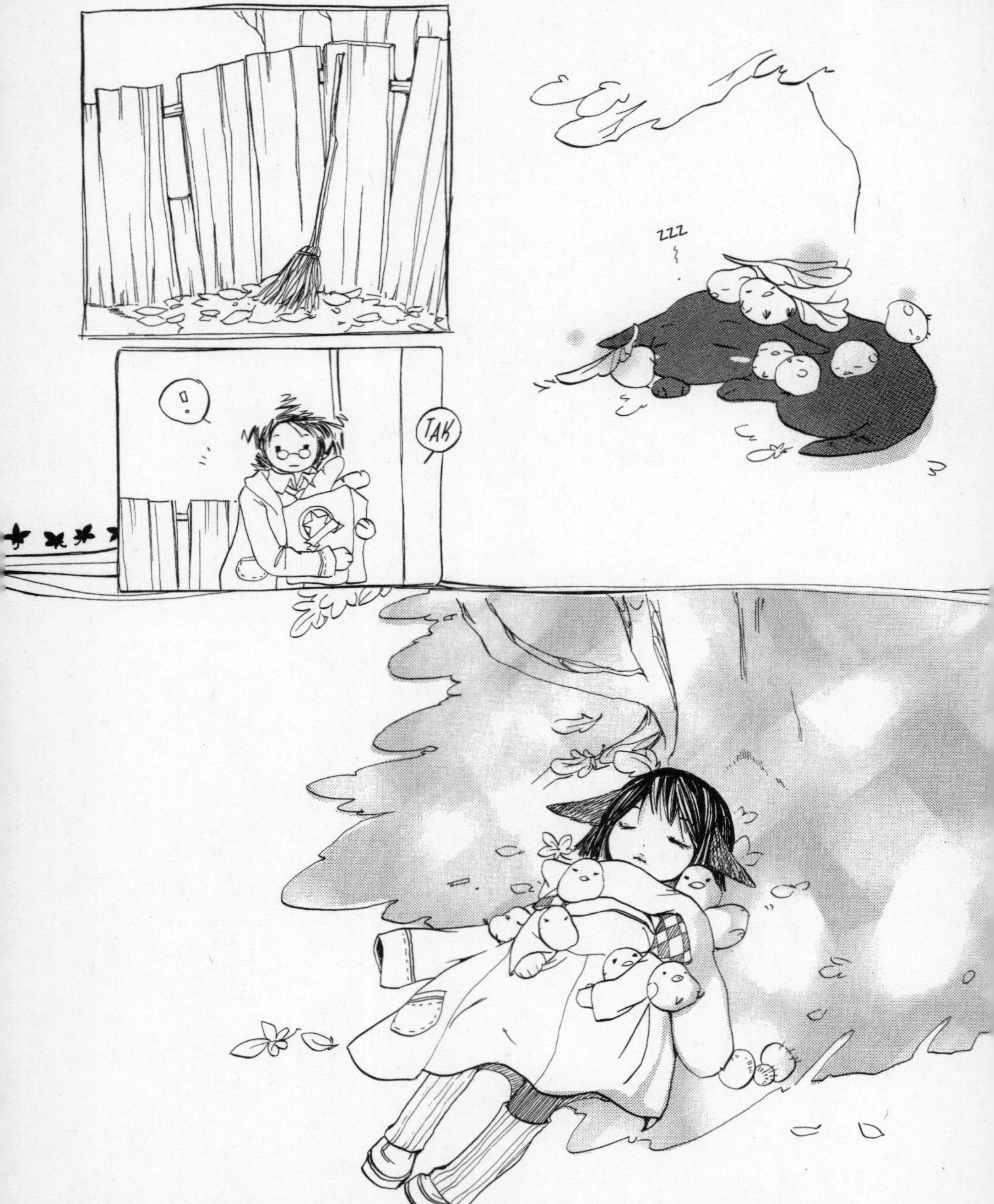
!
TAK
zzz

More adventures await in one fine day Volume 2!

Enjoy another fine day
in YEN PLUS, a monthly manga
anthology from Yen Press!

# Hello! This is YOTSUBA!

Guess what? Guess what?
Yotsuba and Daddy just moved here
from waaaay over there!

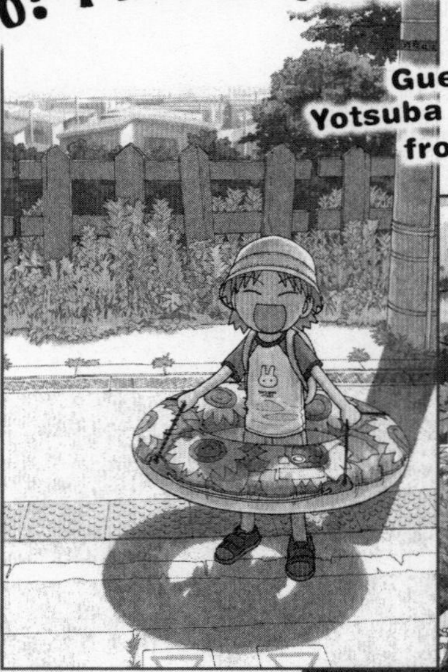

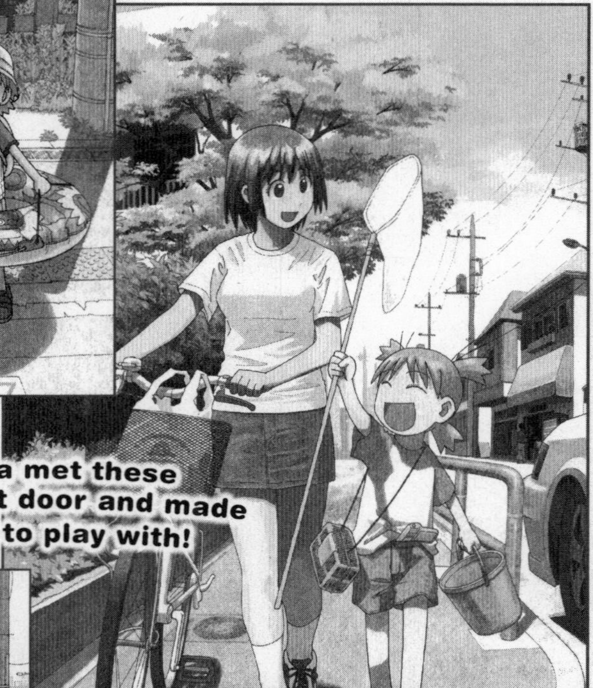

And Yotsuba met these
nice people next door and made
new friends to play with!

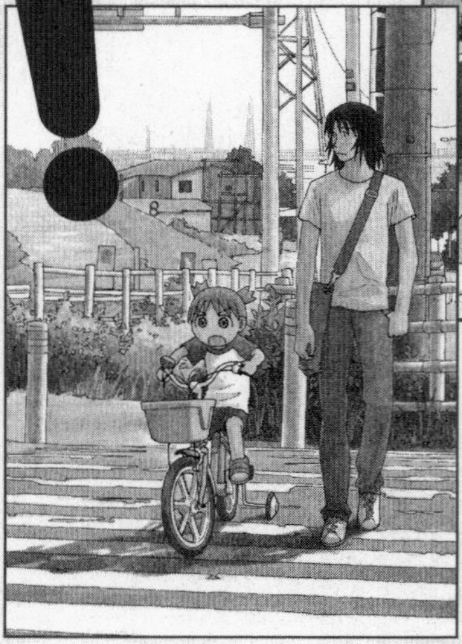

The pretty one took
Yotsuba on a bike ride!
(Whoooa! There was a big hill!)

And Ena's a good drawer!
(Almost as good as Yotsuba!)

And their mom always
gives Yotsuba ice cream!
(Yummy!)

And...
And...
OHHHH!

# ENJOY EVERYTHING.

## YOU SHOULD COME PLAY WITH YOTSUBA TOO!

Join Yotsuba as she delights in the
things many of us take for granted in
this Eisner-nominated series.

# VOLUMES 1-7
# AVAILABLE NOW!

Yen
Press

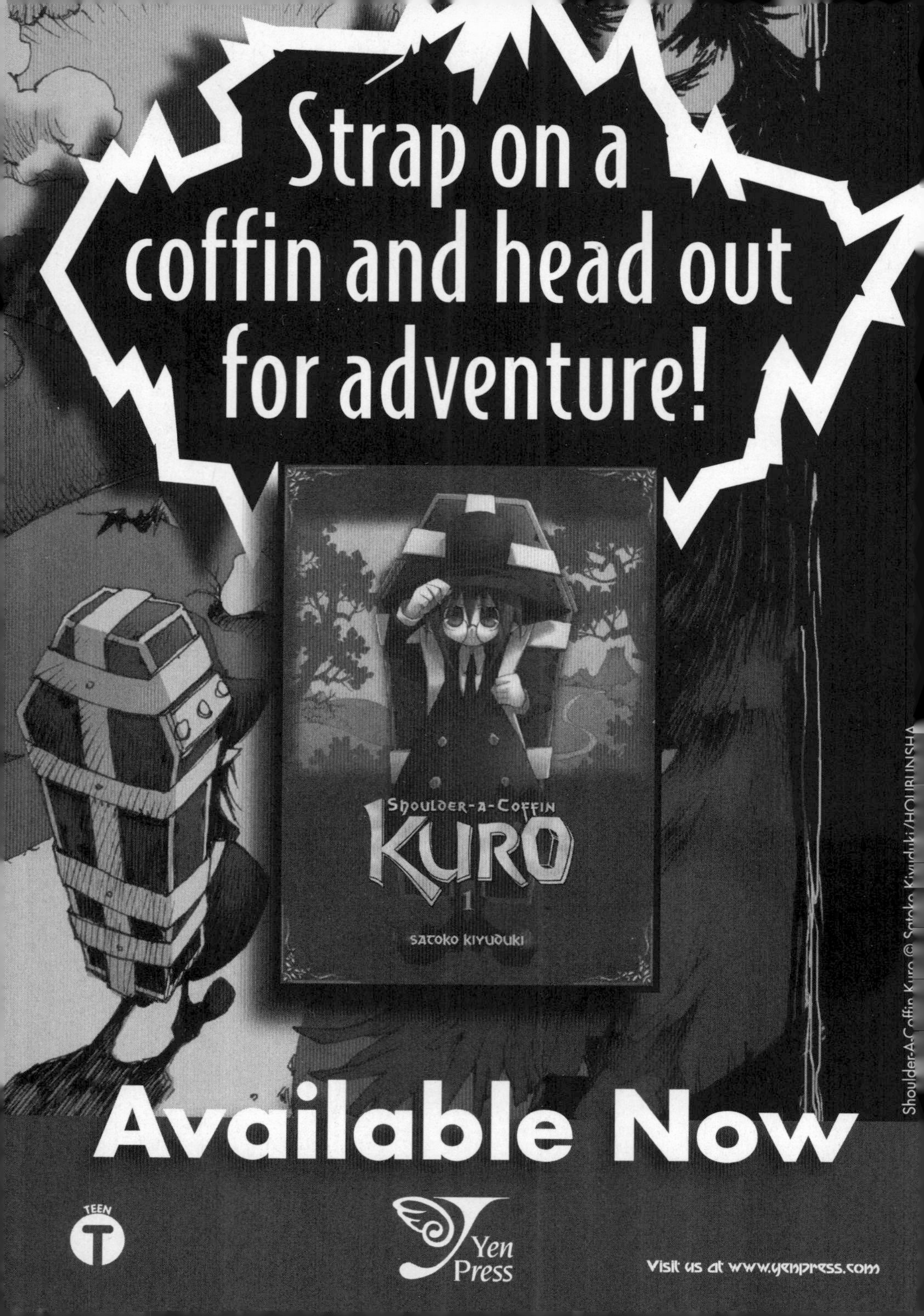

Strap on a coffin and head out for adventure!
SHOULDER-A-COFFIN
KURO
1
SATOKO KIYUDUKI
Shoulder-A-Coffin Kuro © Satoko Kiyuduki/HOUBUNSHA
Available Now
TEEN
T
Yen Press
Visit us at www.yenpress.com

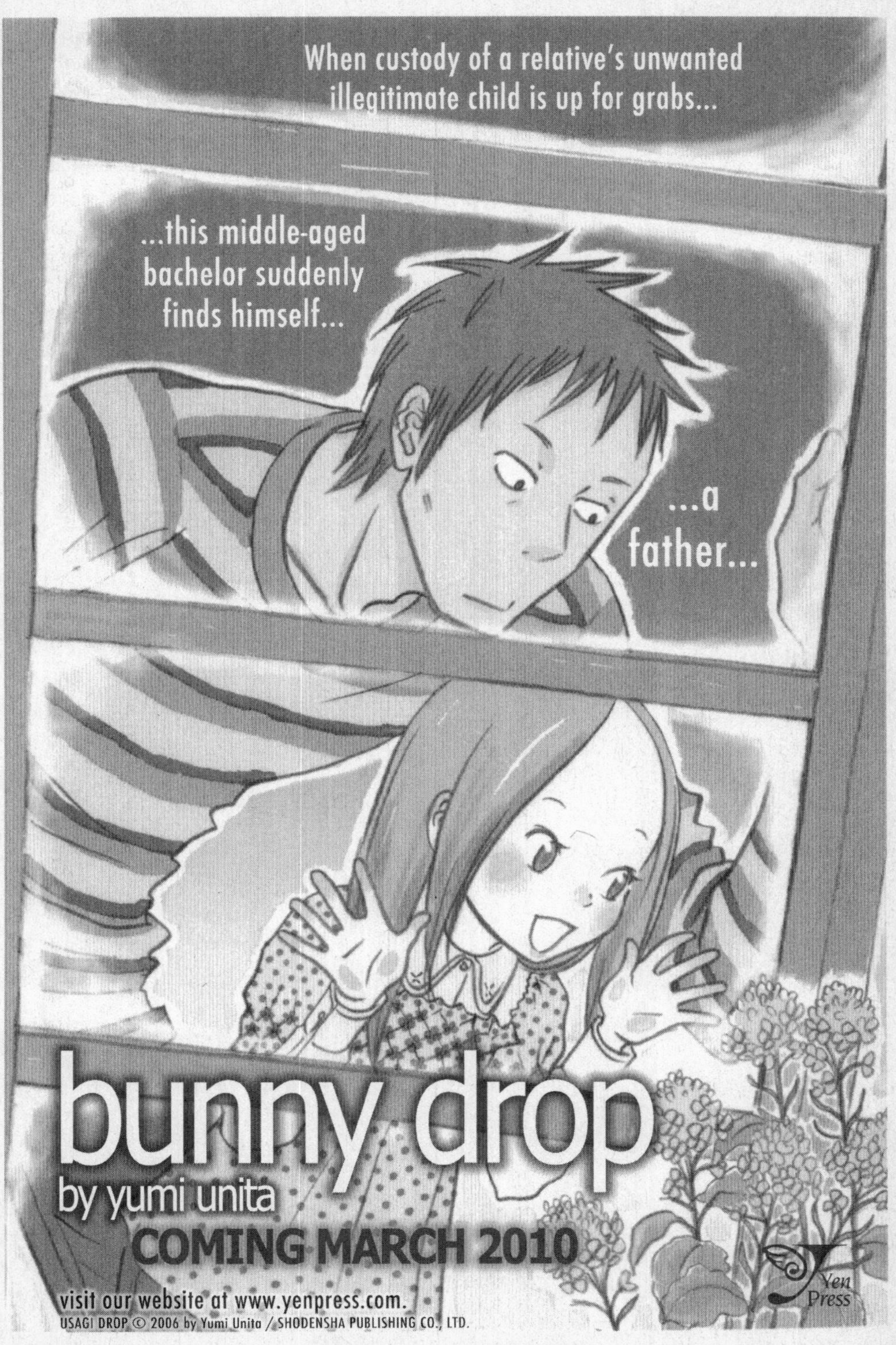

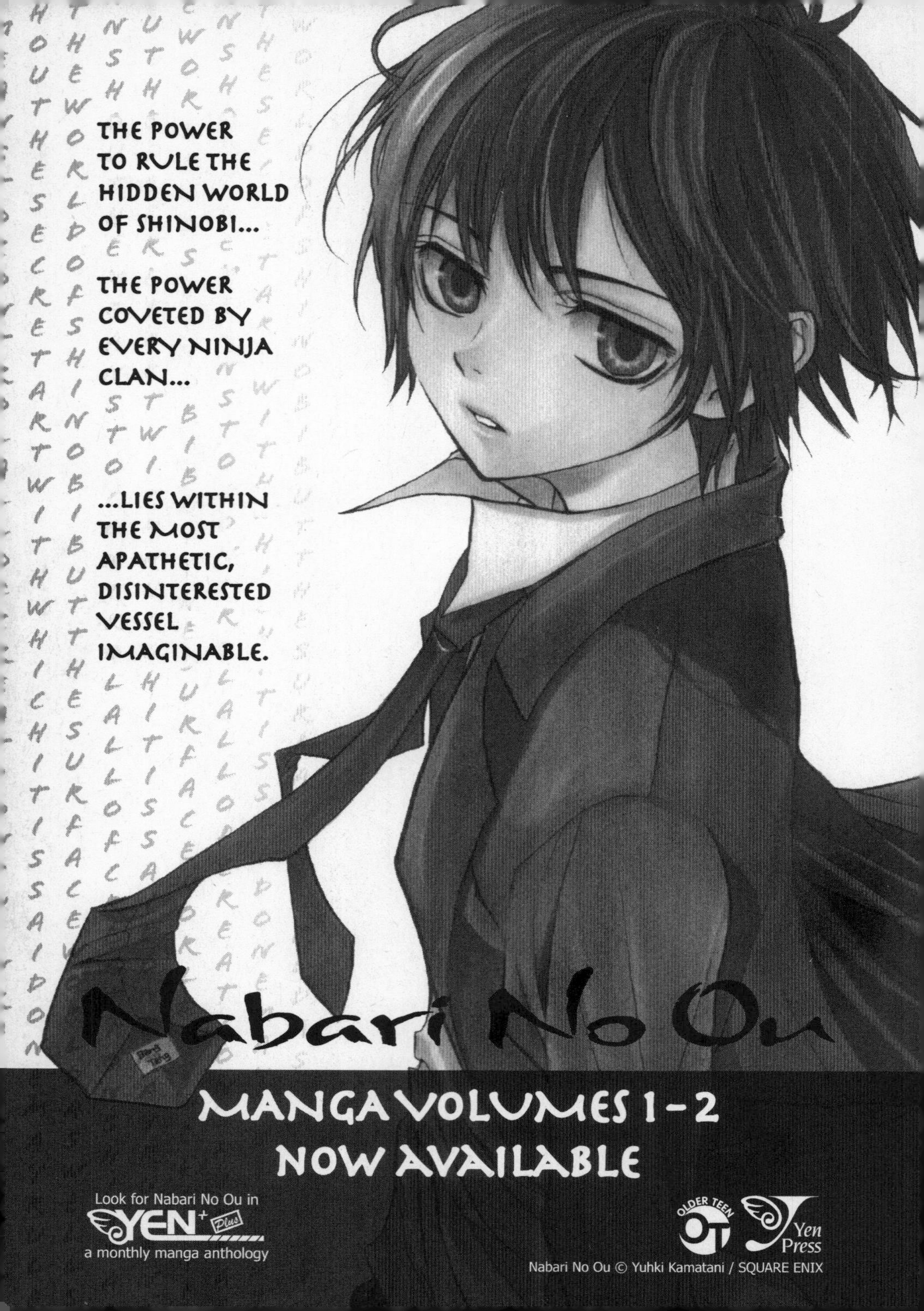
THE POWER TO RULE THE HIDDEN WORLD OF SHINOBI...
THE POWER COVETED BY EVERY NINJA CLAN...
...LIES WITHIN THE MOST APATHETIC, DISINTERESTED VESSEL IMAGINABLE.
Nabari No Ou
MANGA VOLUMES 1-2
NOW AVAILABLE
Look for Nabari No Ou in
YEN+ Plus
a monthly manga anthology
OLDER TEEN OT
Yen Press
Nabari No Ou © Yuhki Kamatani / SQUARE ENIX

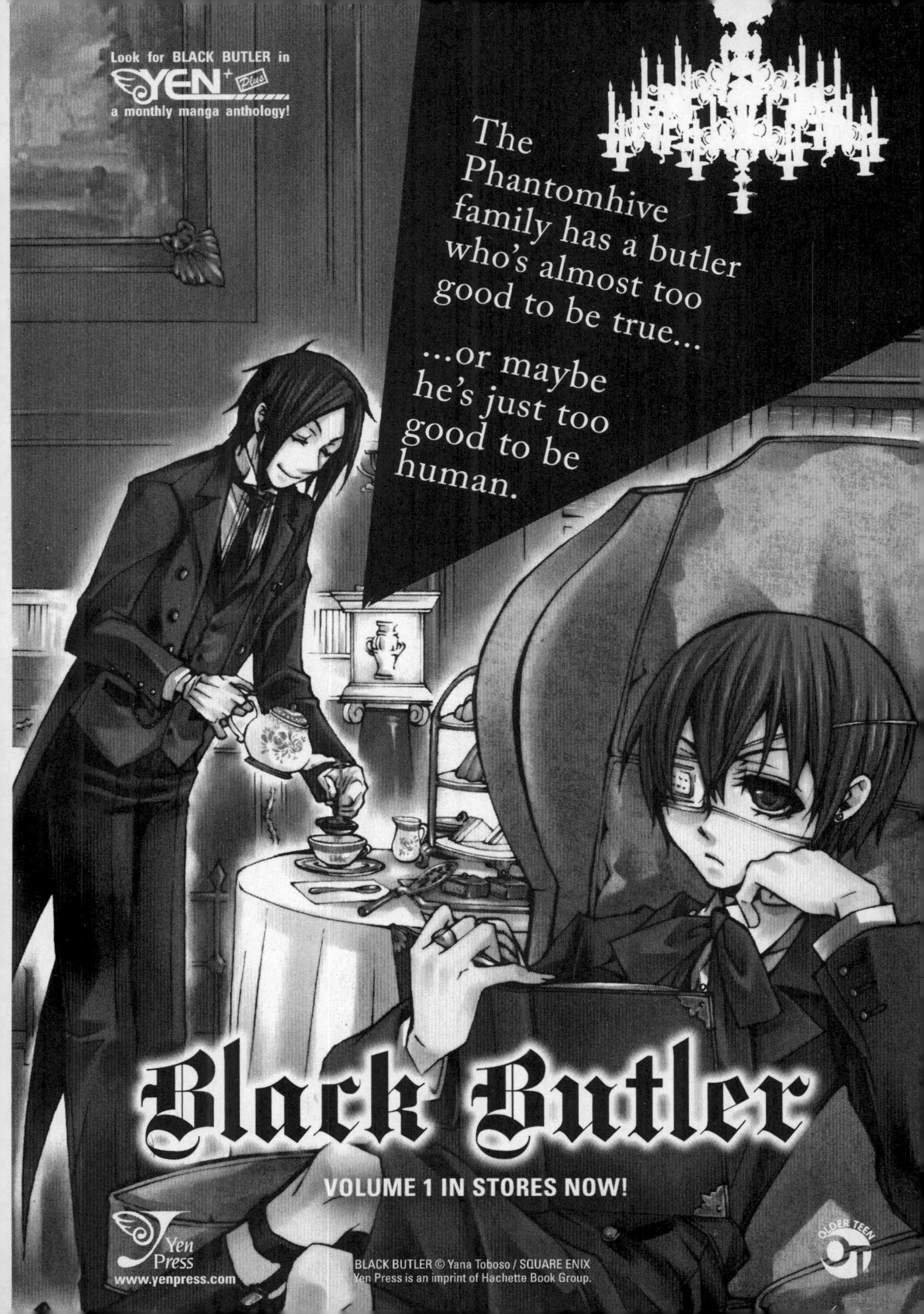
Look for BLACK BUTLER in
YEN+ Plus
a monthly manga anthology!
The Phantomhive family has a butler who's almost too good to be true...
...or maybe he's just too good to be human.
Black Butler
VOLUME 1 IN STORES NOW!
Yen Press
www.yenpress.com
BLACK BUTLER © Yana Toboso / SQUARE ENIX
Yen Press is an imprint of Hachette Book Group.
OLDER TEEN
OT

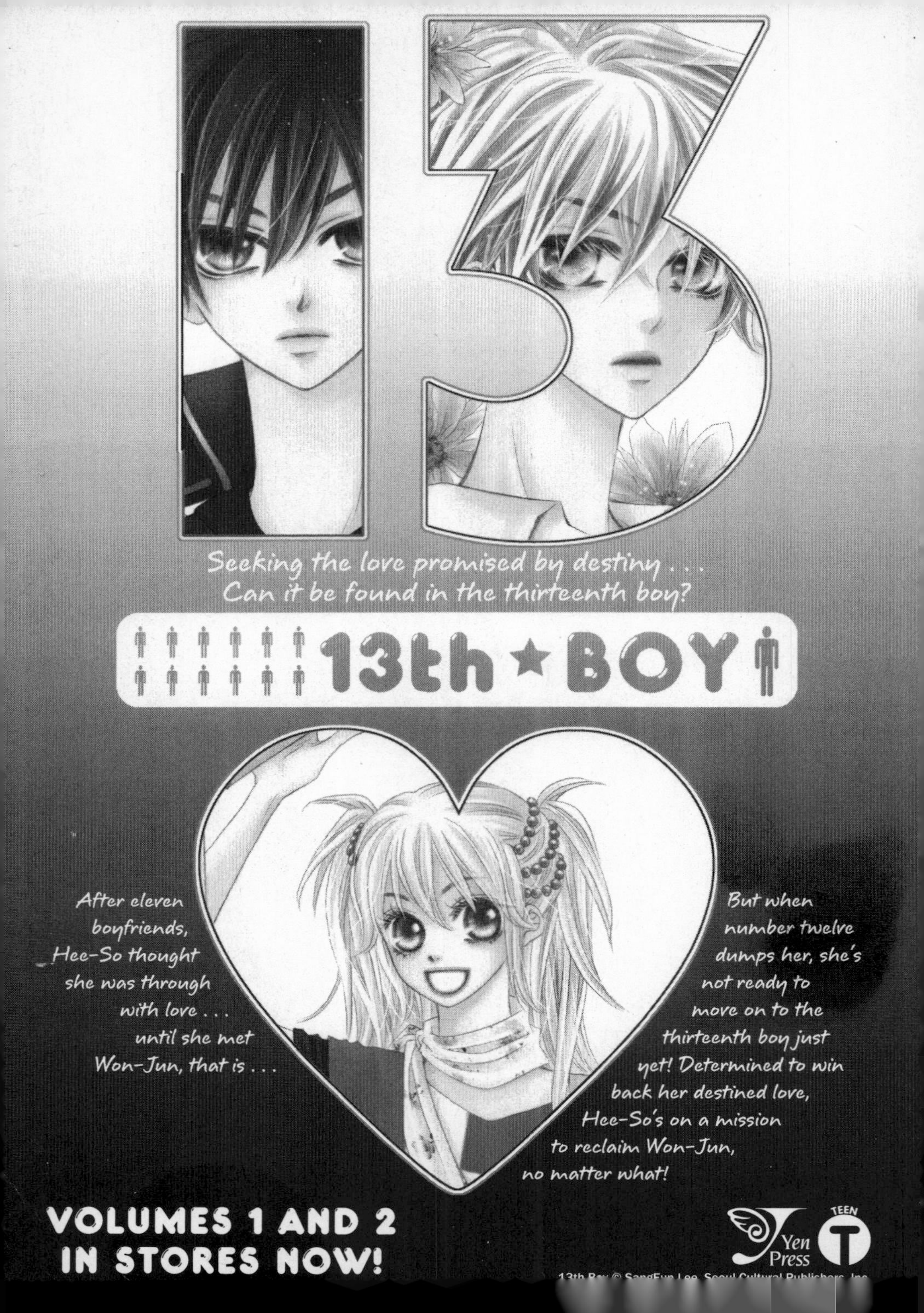
Seeking the love promised by destiny . . .
Can it be found in the thirteenth boy?
13th ★ BOY
After eleven boyfriends, Hee-So thought she was through with love . . . until she met Won-Jun, that is . . .
But when number twelve dumps her, she's not ready to move on to the thirteenth boy just yet! Determined to win back her destined love, Hee-So's on a mission to reclaim Won-Jun, no matter what!
VOLUMES 1 AND 2
IN STORES NOW!
Yen Press
TEEN
T
13th Boy © SangEun Lee, Seoul Cultural Publishers, Inc.